PRIMARY MATHEMATICS AND THE DEVELOPING PROFESSIONAL

With love & Ma[illegible]

[illegible]ther – it wouldn't have

happened without you!

[illegible]

Multiple Perspectives on Attainment in Numeracy

Volume 1 of 4

Primary Mathematics and the Developing Professional

Edited by

Alison Millett
Department of Education and Professional Studies, King's College London, U.K.

Margaret Brown
Department of Education and Professional Studies, King's College London, U.K.

and

Mike Askew
Department of Education and Professional Studies, King's College London, U.K.

Springer

A C.I.P. Catalogue record for this book is available from the Library of Congress.

ISBN-10 1-4020-5705-9 (PB)
ISBN-13 978-1-4020-5705-2 (PB)
ISBN-10 1-4020-1914-9 (HB)
ISBN-13 978-1-4020-1914-2 (HB)
ISBN-10 1-4020-1915-7 (e-book)
ISBN-13 978-1-4020-1915-9 (e-book)

Published by Springer,
P.O. Box 17, 3300 AA Dordrecht, The Netherlands.

www.springer.com

Printed on acid-free paper

TABLE OF CONTENTS

LIST OF TABLES xiii

LIST OF FIGURES xv

ACKNOWLEDGMENTS xvii

INTRODUCTION xix

Margaret Brown
1. The international context xix
2. The meaning of numeracy xxii
3. The National Numeracy Strategy xxiii
4. The Leverhulme Numeracy Research Programme xxvi
4.1. The Core Project: Tracking Numeracy xxvi
4.2. Focus Project: Case Studies of Pupil Progress xxvii
4.3. Focus Project: Teachers' Knowledge, Conceptions and Practices and Pupils' Learning xxviii
4.4. Focus Project: Whole School Action on Numeracy xxviii
4.5. Focus Project: School and Community Numeracies xxix
4.6. Focus Project: Primary CAME (Cognitive Acceleration in Mathematics Education) xxix
4.7. Relation to the National Numeracy Strategy xxx
4.8. Coherence of themes xxx
5. References xxxi

CHAPTER 1. THE CONTEXT FOR CHANGE: A MODEL FOR DISCUSSION 1
Alison Millett and Tamara Bibby
1. Introduction 1
2. A model for discussing change 2
2.1. The zone of enactment 3
2.2. The person 5
2.3. The situation – the professional community and the pupils 6
2.4. External factors – professionals, policy, the public, the private sector 8
2.5. The use of the model 12
3. Questions posed in this book 12
4. Affiliations 14
5. References 14

CHAPTER 2. THE ROLE OF THE MATHEMATICS CO-ORDINATOR: A SOURCE OF IN-SCHOOL SUPPORT 19
Alison Millett and David C. Johnson
1. Introduction 19
1.1. The Research 21
1.2. Questions posed about the role of the mathematics co-ordinator 21
2. Influencing zones of enactment 22
2.1. Creating opportunities for 'rich deliberations' with individuals and groups 23
2.2. Grounding reform ideas in classroom practice 27
2.3. Providing new materials and artefacts 29
2.4. Summary 29
3. Effectiveness in bringing about change 30
3.1. Change as perceived by headteachers and co-ordinators 31
3.2. Change as perceived by classroom teachers 33
3.3. Change attributable to the actions of the co-ordinator 35
3.4. Challenges to the co-ordinator 37
3.5. Change as perceived by the researches from lesson observations 38
3.6. Change as measured by national test results at age 11 40
3.7. Summary 40
4. Factors influencing effectiveness 41
4.1. Characteristics of the people in the role 41
4.2. Influence of the professional community – the role of the headteacher 44
4.3. Influence of the professional community – support from colleagues 45
4.4. Influence of external professionals and policy 45
4.5. Six linked constructs 48
5. Discussion 50
5.1. The influence of the mathematics co-ordinators on teachers' zones of enactment 50
5.2. The role of the co-ordinator as a source of in-service training 52
5.3. Change to the core of teaching 53
6. Affiliations 53
7. Notes 53
8. References 54

CHAPTER 3. THE ROLE OF THE SCHOOL IN DEVELOPING MATHEMATICS 57
Alison Millett and David C. Johnson
1. Introduction 57
1.1. The Research 58
1.2. Selected findings from Whole School Action on Numeracy 59
1.3. Summary of developments in the six case-study schools 60
2. The six linked constructs in Wolverton School 62
2.1. Wolverton School 62
2.2. Balance 63
2.3. High priority given to resourcing the role 68
2.4. Coherence and Consistency 70
2.5. Sustaining change at Wolverton 72
3. Alternative perceptions 73
4. Conclusions from the case studies 75
5. Whole school factors – the wider picture 75
5.1. Levels of attainment at the beginning of the research 77
5.2. Socio-economic factors 78
5.3. External pressure and support 79
5.4. Provision for Continuing Professional Development 82
5.5. Attitudes towards reform and the National Numeracy Strategy 85
5.6. Movement of staff 85
5.7. In conclusion – large-scale data from Tracking Numeracy 86
6. Discussion 87
6.1. A rich situation – a learning culture 88
6.2. A learning community 90
6.3. Sustaining change 90
6.4. How the school can make a difference 92
7. Affiliations 93
8. Notes 93
9. References 94

CHAPTER 4. THE MEDIATING ROLE OF TEXTUAL MATERIALS IN TEACHERS' RESPONSE TO CALLS FOR CLASSROOM REFORM 97
Valerie Rhodes and Alison Millett
1. Introduction 97
2. The national and international context for the use of published materials 98
3. Mathematics materials in the context of this research 101
4. The research 102
4.1. Reviewing our analytical criteria 103

5. The impact of the National Numeracy Strategy on the use of published materials 104
5.1. Scheme-driven ---> Scheme-assisted (five schools) 106
5.2. Scheme-assisted ---> Scheme-dependent (nine schools) 106
5.3. Scheme-assisted ---> Scheme-assisted (21 schools) 107
5.4. Scheme-driven ---> Scheme-dependent (six schools) 109
5.5. Summary 110
6. Making decisions about the use of published materials 112
6.1. How decisions were made 112
6.2. Reasons for reaching the decisions made 115
7. Examples of professional development through the use of materials 115
7.1. Teachers working individually 115
7.2. Teachers working collaboratively 116
7.3. Summary 121
8. Discussion 122
9. Affiliations 124
10. References 124

CHAPTER 5. RESPONSES OF TEACHERS TO A COURSE OF INTENSIVE TRAINING 127
Alison Millett, Mike Askew and Shirley Simon
1. Introduction – external influences 127
1.1. The National Numeracy Strategy 128
1.2. The Five-day course 128
1.3. Unique features of this example of professional development 129
2. The research 130
3. Individual factors – the person 132
3.1. Starting points and expectations 132
3.2. Initial responses following the course 135
3.3. Translating to the classroom 137
3.4. Responses after nine months 139
3.5. Responses after 18 months 140
4. School factors – the professional community 144
5. Peer group factors – the zone of enactment 145
6. Summary of selected findings 148
6.1. Initial responses to the Five-day course 148
6.2. Responses some time after the course 148
6.3. Changes observed by researchers 149
6.4. Changes in pupil attainment 149
7. Discussion 150
8. Affiliations 153
9. References 153

CHAPTER 6. THE DYNAMICS OF TEACHER DECISION-MAKING: CASE STUDIES OF TEACHERS RESPONDING TO THE NATIONAL NUMERACY STRATEGY 155
Shirley Simon, Alison Millett and Mike Askew
1. Introduction
2. Teachers' orientations towards teaching and theories of learning 155
3. Teachers' responding to systemic reform 157
3.1. The National Numeracy Strategy Five-day course 158
4. Case studies 158
4.1. Andy 159
4.2. Frankie 159
5. Summary 169
5.1. Context 179
5.2. Case Study – Andy 179
5.3. Case study – Frankie 180
6. Discussion 181
7. Affiliations 182
8. References 183
183

CHAPTER 7. PROFESSIONAL DEVELOPMENT FROM A COGNITIVE AND SOCIAL STANDPOINT 185
David C. Johnson, Jeremy Hodgen and Mundher Adhami
1. Introduction
2. P-CAME – Description and Methodology 185
3. Research and theory 186
4. Formulating the agenda of a lesson – the professional development 188
of the team 190
4.1. Seeing the curriculum potential of the cognitive approach
4.2. Seeing the cognitive potential of the curriculum focus 192
4.3. Charting the appropriate range of cognitive challenges 193
4.4. Communicating the agenda to generalist teachers (preparing for 194
phase two) 200
5. The research team – a community of practice
6. The professional development programme – cognitive and social 201
perspectives 201
7. Communicating the agenda of a P-CAME lesson in the professional development programme 203
7.1. A lesson simulation in the professional development programme – Pegboard Symmetry 203
7.2. Teachers discussing their experiences in teaching – the social and mathematical agendas 209

8. General features of reflection sessions in the CAME professional development programme 209
 8.1. The cognitive dimension 210
 8.2. The social-interactions dimension 211
 8.3. The culture-of-learning dimension 212
9. Discussion 212
10. Affiliations 215
11. Notes 215
12. References 216

CHAPTER 8. TEACHER REFLECTION, IDENTITY AND BELIEF CHANGE IN THE CONTEXT OF PRIMARY CAME 219
Jeremy Hodgen and David C. Johnson
1. Introduction 219
2. The research 220
 2.1. The two teachers: Alexandra and Ursula 221
 2.2. CAME professional development 221
 2.3. The fractions lessons 222
3. Reflection in mathematics teacher education 223
4. Teacher beliefs about mathematics 225
 4.1. Authority in mathematics 225
 4.2. Connections in mathematics 225
 4.3. Mathematics without closure 226
5. Identity, the zone of enactment and professional change 226
6. The case study: reflection and professional change 228
 6.1. Lesson development: reflection as part of practice 229
 6.2. Team-teaching: imagination, engagement and the other teachers 229
 6.3. An audience: the imperative to reflect 231
 6.4. Tutoring: reminders of oneself as a learner 234
 6.5. The case study: a summary 239
7. Discussion 240
8. Affiliations 242
9. Notes 242
10. References 243

CHAPTER 9. DRAWING CONCLUSIONS 245
Alison Millett, Margaret Brown and Mike Askew
1. Introduction 245
2. Identifying deep change 246
 2.1. Change to the core of teachers' practice 247
 2.2. Change to beliefs about mathematics and its teaching 248
 2.3. Examples of deep change 249
3. Realising rich zones of enactment 250
 3.1. Time 250

3.2. Talk 251
3.3. Expertise 252
3.4. Motivation 252
3.5. The zone of enactment – fresh insights 253
4. A model for professional development 254
5. References 255

ANNEX 1. Core Project: TRACKING NUMERACY 257

ANNEX 2. Focus Project: TEACHERS' KNOWLEDGE, CONCEPTIONS AND PRACTICES 265

ANNEX 3. Focus Project: WHOLE SCHOOL ACTION ON NUMERACY 271

ANNEX 4. Focus Project: Cognitive Acceleration in Mathematics Education in the Primary School (P-Came) 275

INDEX 279

LIST OF TABLES

Table 2.1. Percentages of pupils attaining Level 4 or above in national tests at age 11 — 40
Table 3.1. Percentages of pupils attaining Level 4 or above in national tests at age 11 in comparison with national averages — 60
Table 3.2. Percentages of pupils at Wolverton School attaining Level 4 or above in national tests at age 11 — 63
Table 3.3. Mean percentage scores in October 1997 and October 1999, together with a ranking on mean % gains 1997-2002 for 16 schools from the Core sample — 77
Table 3.4. Levels of deprivation for the 16 selected schools, together with pupil eligibility for free school meals — 78
Table 3.5. Results of Office for Standards in Education (Ofsted) inspections for the eight more successful schools during the span of the research project — 80
Table 3.6. Results of Office for Standards in Education (Ofsted) inspections for the eight less successful schools during the span of the research project — 81
Table 3.7. Involvement in Continuing Professional Development of the eight more successful schools — 83
Table 3.8. Involvement in Continuing Professional Development of the eight less successful schools — 84
Table 3.9. Major staff movement affecting mathematics co-ordinator or Headteacher — 86
Table 4.1. Method of planning reported in the spring Terms of 1998 and 2000/02 in primary and junior schools (n=34) and in the Spring Terms of 1998 and 2000 in infant schools (n=7) — 105
Table 4.2. Methods of planning adopted by teachers of parallel classes in Key Stage 1 and Key Stage 2 in 1999-2000 — 118
Table 5.1. Details of the teachers attending the course 2000-2001 — 133
Table 8.1. The fractions lesson development timetable — 223
Table 9.1. Mean student score on identical Year 4 tests before and after the National Numeracy Strategy (Data from the same 35 schools with n>1290 on each occasion) — 247

Table A.1.1. The two cohorts 258
Table A.2.1. Details of the schools involved in the research 1999-2002 266
Table A.2.2. Details of the teachers involved in the research 1999-2002 266
Table A.2.3. Details of the data sources 267
Table A.3.1. Details of the six schools involved in the research 1997-2001 271
Table A.3.2. The data set 1997-2001 272
Table A.4.1. P-CAME research implementation 276

LIST OF FIGURES

Figure 1.1. Model for discussing change	3
Figure 2.1. Six linked constructs	49
Figure 3.1. Six linked constructs	59
Figure 7.1. Pegboard and co-ordinates	192
Figure 7.2. Pegboard Symmetry abstract (textual)	196
Figure 7.3. Pegboard Symmetry abstract (visual)	197
Figure 7.4. Pegboard Symmetry two-page teaching sketch (1)	198
Figure 7.5. Pegboard Symmetry two-page teaching sketch (2)	199
Figure 8.1. A diagrammatic solution of the Whisky & Water problem similar to Alexandra's approach	235

ACKNOWLEDGMENTS

We would like to thank the Leverhulme Trust for the funding that enabled us to undertake the Leverhulme Numeracy Research Programme.

We would also like to thank the Local Education Authorities, the schools, the teachers and the pupils who participated in this research programme.

AFFILIATIONS

Dr Alison Millett is a Senior Research Fellow in the Department of Education and Professional Studies, King's College London
Professor Margaret Brown in Professor of Mathematics Education, Department of Education and Professional Studies, King's College London
Dr Mike Askew is Reader in Mathematics Education, Department of Education and Professional Studies, King's College London

MARGARET BROWN

INTRODUCTION

Abstract. This introduction sets the scene for the remainder of the book by considering first the international context of widespread concern about the improvement of numeracy skills. This is related to reform movements in the United Kingdom, the United States and other countries aimed at modernising primary (elementary) school mathematics curricula. A detailed account is given of the National Numeracy Strategy in England, a systemic government-imposed response to concern about standards implemented in 1999/2000. This includes a discussion of the alternative meanings of numeracy. An earlier initiative sponsored by a United Kingdom charitable trust reacting to concern about primary numeracy was the Leverhulme Numeracy Research Programme. This large-scale longitudinal study and linked set of case-study projects, focusing on reasons for low attainment, took place during 1997-2002. This book, and each other in the same series, is based on results of that research. The timescale fortuitously enabled the research team to also report on some effects of the systemic reform in the National Numeracy Strategy.

1. THE INTERNATIONAL CONTEXT

In many countries, there are recurring periods of national concern about the low standards of calculation skills shown by children in primary (elementary) schools. Recently, these concerns have become more urgent and more political with the publication of international comparisons of mathematical achievement, first at secondary and more recently at primary level (e.g. Lapointe, Mead, & Askew 1992; Mullis et al., 1997). Dismay at a low position in the international league tables has in some cases triggered a programme of systemic reform (National Commission for Excellence in Education, 1983; Brown, 1996).

A further reason for government concern over mathematical standards is the realisation that countries in the developed world will require a highly skilled numerate workforce to maintain their economic competitiveness, while developing nations will need to improve the mathematical skills of their population as a basis for building technical and financial capacity. South Korea, a country which is close to the top of every mathematical league table, provides an example to demonstrate that high attainment is possible, even for countries with relatively low Gross National Product.

In many English-speaking countries, and some others, the concern over low attainment in number skills has led to a desire by governments for increasing control of the content, teaching and assessment of primary mathematics. In some countries such increasing government control has come after, and to some extent as a response to, curriculum changes aimed at modernising the primary curriculum and emanating from mathematics educationists and teachers.

For example, in the United States the National Council of Teachers of Mathematics Standards (1989; 2000). authorised a primary curriculum which was broad, going well beyond number to statistics and geometry, and emphasised problem-solving, reasoning and mathematical communication. Understanding and appreciation of numbers and number operations, mental strategies and the ability to estimate, i.e. 'number sense' (Reys, Reys, & Hope, 1993) were seen as more important than proficiency in pencil-and-paper algorithms in a society which had ready access to calculators and computers. Informed by constructivist (e.g. Carpenter & Peterson, 1988; Davis, 1984; Maher & Davis, 1990; Steffe & Gale, 1995) and social constructivist (e.g. Cobb & Bauersfeld, 1995) results and beliefs about learning, 'reform' initiatives incorporating the Standards have aimed at making learning more participatory and discussion-based, and teachers more knowledgeable about, welcoming of, and responsive to, pupils' own methods and ideas. Such reform initiatives in fact built on a variety of earlier projects since the 1950s, aimed at active and investigatory learning, including problem-solving. Although evaluation of children's learning in the various reform projects has been overwhelmingly positive, there has been some vocal opposition among religious fundamentalists, conservative mathematicians and other right-wing groups which has given rise to the 'math wars'. Such groups, who saw the changes as undermining social control and traditional computational standards, have won control in some states, and have persuaded the federal government to impose a comprehensive programme of statewide recurrent testing of mathematical standards.

A very similar pattern has taken place in the United Kingdom. A series of initiatives from the 1950s onwards, led by people such as Edith Biggs, Geoffrey Matthews with the Nuffield Project, Elizabeth Williams and Hilary Shuard, were aimed at broadening the primary curriculum and making it more child-centred and investigatory. Changes had been at least partially implemented in most schools by the mid-1980s, encouraged by the relatively progressive report of the national Cockcroft Committee (Department of Education and Science/Welsh Office, 1982). Hilary Shuard's work in the 1980s on the Calculator Aware Number (CAN) curriculum, which emphasised investigation, mental strategies and calculator methods and avoided pencil-and-paper algorithms, received international recognition. However, after further panic about the role of mathematical standards in industrial decline in the 1980s, and concern that the Cockcroft Committee, set up originally to investigate this, had been subverted by educationist agendas, further moves were made towards government control. These included the imposition of a national curriculum in 1989 followed by a programme of national testing (Department of Education and Science/Welsh Office, 1988). In spite of government pressure, educationists responsible for the detail maintained a broad and modern curriculum and testing programme with only minor concessions in the direction of pencil-and-paper calculation.

However, in the 1990s government control tightened once again through publication of test results in league tables, a programme of frequent inspections by the Office for Standards in Education (Ofsted) which put pressure on all schools, but especially those with poor test results. As in the United States, such schools were initially entitled to additional support but could in the long term be closed. A desire to focus on number skills and revert to traditional teaching methods culminated in the National Numeracy Strategy which, because it forms an important part of the context of the research reported in this book, is described in detail later in this chapter.

As in the United States, these moves towards greater government control have been followed by teacher shortages, especially in London and the prosperous South East of England. Vacant posts are sometimes filled by teachers on temporary contracts from private employment agencies, who are often recruited from other countries.

In Australia and New Zealand similar moves were made by governments, first imposing a national curriculum which was relatively vague and progressive (Ministerial Council on Education, Employment, Training and Youth Affairs, 1989; Ministry of Education, 1991), and then with a further tightening and re-focusing on number (Ministry of Education, 1997, 2001a, 2001b; Department of Education, Training and Youth Affairs, 2000). Nevertheless the moves have stopped well short of the degree of government control that has occurred in the United States and United Kingdom, and have involved much greater co-operation with educationists in developing new programmes which are research-based and properly evaluated.

It is interesting to compare these changes with national reform of the primary mathematics curriculum and assessment in Holland. Here, the 'Realistic Maths' programme, developed largely out of research in collaboration with the Freudenthal Institute (Streefland, 1991; Treffers, 1991; Gravemeijer, 1997) has many features in common with reform programmes in other countries but with a greater emphasis on the development of mathematics out of models of real world situations. Perhaps because of good performances in national tests, the programme seems to have been allowed to go ahead with minimal political interference, and has achieved a coherence of vision that is probably unique. It has also influenced developments in several other countries, such as the United States and United Kingdom, and South Africa.

It should be noted that some other countries which have had a tradition of a much greater degree of government control are moving in the opposite direction. Countries such as Singapore, Japan and China, where there has been great emphasis on number skills are trying to shift the focus to individual creativity and problem-solving skills.

Thus it is clear that all over the world governments and educationists are examining their curricula and teaching methods in primary mathematics and comparing them with those in other countries to see if higher standards in a range of objectives can be achieved.

This means that although this series of books deals with research from the United Kingdom, the results are likely to be of interest and use in many other countries, whether they are like other Anglophone countries already moving in similar directions or whether they are simply considering a range of alternative models.

2. THE MEANING OF NUMERACY

In some countries numeracy is a synonym for mathematical literacy, and hence includes areas of mathematics beyond number, for example, geometrical properties, algebra and logical reasoning. In this book however we will restrict numeracy to dealing only with numbers and operations on numbers, recognising that this to some extent includes application of number in work on measures, statistics and metric geometry.

Numeracy is now generally understood as a competence in interpreting and using numbers in daily life, within the home, employment and society. Thus the meaning of numeracy must relate to the social context of its use and the social practices that are adopted in that context (Baker, 1999). The definition of numeracy therefore must be relative and differ not only between different national cultures, but between different subcultures and local circumstances within the same national culture. For example, within one household numeracy might be judged by the ability to purchase appropriate quantities of materials and successfully complete household decorations and repairs, such as constructing and putting up a set of book shelves, whereas in the next door household numeracy might be conceptualised in relation to ability to participate intelligently in a family discussion of changes in government economic policy. It is even clearer that different forms of employment involve different practices. Moreover the mathematics underlying employment practices such as those used by nurses can be subtle and difficult to ascertain (Noss, 1997). And even participation as an active citizen in a democratic society might be thought to range from the ability to interpret bar graphs of mean income by region presented in the popular media, to the ability to critique government scientific policy, for example on genetic modification of crops, with reference to papers in scientific journals.

Thus it is not easy for those with the power to make to decisions over mathematics curricula and assessment, whether in schools, local areas, states or countries, to agree what constitutes a minimal competence in numeracy required for social survival, what should be expected of most citizens and what additional aspects of numeracy over and above this level should be aimed for.

It was accepted by educational policymakers in the United Kingdom that numeracy was to be defined broadly as the competence and inclination to use number concepts and skills to solve problems in everyday life and employment. Nevertheless it was felt necessary, for political and educational reasons, that the aspect of numeracy to be newly emphasised at primary level should be proficiency in a culturally neutral context-free set of number skills, underpinned by abstract visual models, such as the number line (Department for Education and Employment, 1998). In contrast to 1980s developments, there is now little reference in the primary numeracy guidance to applications or problem-solving, and those which occur are mainly traditional 'word-problems', with artificial contexts.

Because this series of books concerns numeracy in English primary schools in the period 1997-2002, we will generally use numeracy in this narrow and traditional sense. However this usage is narrower than the authors would prefer.

3. THE NATIONAL NUMERACY STRATEGY

The Conservative United Kingdom Government of 1992-97 had taken 'back to basics' as one of its slogans in education as in other policy areas. As part of this theme high profile National Literacy and National Numeracy Projects were launched in 1996, each in a group of local education authorities which mainly had poor results in national tests. The Labour Party under the leadership of Tony Blair fought the 1997 election with an education policy which differed little from that of the Conservatives, and again emphasised the need to raise standards of basic skills in primary schools, with specific targets for national test results in 2002, with 75% of pupils targeted to reach the expected level for their age-group (Level 4) in mathematics at age 11.

The Labour Party when elected already had plans to extend the National Literacy Project into a National Literacy Strategy to be implemented in all schools in England during the school year 1998/99. They had also set up a Task Force to plan during 1997/98 the details of a National Numeracy Strategy, probably to be based on the National Numeracy Project, to be introduced in all primary schools in England during 1999/2000. This decision was made before any formal evaluation of the National Numeracy Project was available, although informally it was known to be welcomed by teachers and headteachers.

The key features of the National Numeracy Strategy were:

- *an increased emphasis on number and on calculation*, especially mental calculation, including estimation, with pupils being encouraged to select from a repertoire of mental strategies. Written calculation was postponed but informal and later standard written procedures were to be introduced. Calculators were discouraged, although use of them was to be taught in specific lessons starting from Year 5 (pupils aged 9-10 years)
- *a three-part template for daily mathematics lessons*, starting with 5-10 minutes of oral/mental skills practice, then direct interactive teaching of the whole class and groups, and finally 10-15 minutes of plenary review
- *detailed planning using a suggested week-by-week set of objectives*, specified for each year group. The objectives were listed, with detailed examples to explain them in a key document 'The Framework for Teaching Mathematics from Reception to Year 6' (Department for Education and Employment, 1999). This covered areas of mathematics other than number, but introduced many mental strategies earlier than previously. Teachers were expected to reduce their dependency on textbooks, using the Framework document as a day-to-day reference point and referring to published textbook schemes only as a source of examples
- *a systematic national training programme* based on standard packages of training materials, providing timetables, overhead transparencies to illustrate key points, and videos to demonstrate 'best practice'. Training in each Local Education Authority was organised for teachers from each school by newly appointed trainers acting as consultants and working to regional directors, under a national director. In all schools the training was run by school mathematics co-ordinators, with additional support from consultants for low-performing schools, both in-school and via local courses.

Although not legally imposed, the Numeracy Strategy has been almost universally implemented, and is being extended in a slightly modified form to secondary schools. Most teachers and headteachers have welcomed the Strategy, although teachers found it very hard work to implement, since it required them to plan new introductions to many topics and to prepare new teaching material for each lesson. Previous to this many had been following either commercially produced textbook schemes directly or schemes-of-work written in the school which made reference to published schemes. Many publishers worked hard to issue new textbook schemes to match the Framework but few were ready in time for the first year of the implementation.

Ministers expressed disappointment that national test results for children at age 11 in 2000 and 2001 failed to improve as much as expected after the introduction of the Strategy in the school year 1999/2000. (The proportion gaining the expected result for this age-group, Level 4, had gone from 69% in 1999 to 72% in 2000 and dropped back to 71% in 2001, against a national target of 75% in 2002.) Hence during 2001/2 detailed lesson plans were developed by the central team for all lessons in Years 4 and 6 (pupils aged 8-9 and 10-11 years) and were circulated to all teachers. These were later extended to include Year 5 (pupils aged 9-10 years) and piloted for Years 1 to 3 (pupils aged 5-8 years). While again there was no requirement to implement these, it was known that inspectors would expect teachers to be teaching from these plans and that they would need to provide a sound explanation if they chose alternatives. In fact, teachers welcomed the plans as they saved a lot of preparation time and were generally felt to be of good quality.

The Numeracy Strategy was highly resourced in terms of training and training materials with an initial funding of £55 million and a later supplement of £25 million for the first three years. The initial training just prior to the school year 1999/2000 was the Three-day course run out-of-school by the local consultants for mathematics co-ordinators (subject leaders), headteachers, one other teacher from each school and a school governor. The co-ordinator was required to 'cascade' this training for other teachers and assistants in the school during three training days during 1999/2000. Additional training and support, in the form of both school visits by the consultant and the external Five-day course for two teachers, was given to schools identified as in need of 'intensive' support. This support was extended in subsequent years to a wider range of schools.

Some local teachers were designated as 'leading mathematics teachers' and given additional training and release time; teachers from their own and other schools were invited to observe them teach and discuss the lesson and other points with them afterwards.

Schools were provided with some additional money for resources but expected to spend it on equipment which was promulgated by the Strategy and shown in videos e.g. small whiteboards, number fans and digit cards for each pupil, 100-squares, counting sticks, number lines and place-value cards. They were also expected to provide release time for their mathematics co-ordinators to work with colleagues.

More details about the Strategy are available from its central offices (e-mail: nnswebeditor@cfbt-hq.org.uk) and from reports by the official evaluators (Earl et al., 2000; Earl, Levin, Leithwood, Fullan, & Watson, 2001; Earl et al., 2003) and from the inspectorate (Office for Standards in Education, 2000a; 2000b; 2001)

4. THE LEVERHULME NUMERACY RESEARCH PROGRAMME

The national concern about standards of numeracy in England in the late 1990s also led the Trustees of the Leverhulme Trust, a charitable foundation, to offer to fund a £1 million five-year study on low attainment in basic skills at primary level. The competition for the funding was won by a team based at the Department of Education and Professional Studies, King's College London, for research focused on numeracy. The resulting programme, known as the Leverhulme Numeracy Research Programme, ran from 1997 to 2002 with the aim:

- to take forward understanding of the nature and causes of low achievement in numeracy and provide insight into effective strategies for remedying the situation.

We wanted to examine the contribution of many different factors to low attainment, in individual children, classes, schools or population groups, by studying, on both a large and small scale, cases in which these factors varied. Two intervention studies were also planned as part of the Programme.

The research design, which included a large-scale longitudinal study (the Core Project) and five focus projects, is outlined below. (Further detail of data collection and analysis procedures on individual projects which contribute to the research reported in each book in the series is provided in the Annexes at the end of each volume. Findings are reported elsewhere and will be referenced throughout this book.)

4.1. The Core Project: Tracking Numeracy (Margaret Brown, Mike Askew, Valerie Rhodes, Hazel Denvir, Esther Ranson, Dylan Wiliam, Helen Lucey and Tamara Bibby, 1997-2002)

Aim: To obtain large-scale longitudinal value-added data on numeracy to:

- inform knowledge about the progression in pupils' learning of numeracy throughout the primary years, and

- to assess relative contributions to gains in numeracy of the different factors to be investigated in the Programme.

Methods: Data on pupil attainment was gathered twice a year for four years, on two longitudinal cohorts each of about 1600 pupils, one moving from Year 1 (pupils aged 5-6 years) to Year 4 (pupils aged 8-9 years) and the other from Year 4 to Year 7 (pupils aged 11-12 years). Each cohort included all children of the appropriate age in 10 primary schools in each of four varied local education authorities (two groups of over 70 classes). Only a small subset of 180 pupils in seven secondary schools, including at least one in each of the four local education authorities, were followed into Year 7 and were tested only at the end of the year, because of the logistical problems of observing lessons and testing specific children in large numbers of secondary schools. Detailed data was collected annually on pupils, teachers and schools, including lesson observations, teacher questionnaires and interviews with teachers, mathematics co-ordinators and headteachers. (This data relates also to the younger cohort in the Reception year (pupils aged 4-5 years) although it was not practicable to test the pupils at that age.) Many instruments were modifications of those designed for our 'Effective Teachers of Numeracy' project (Askew, Brown, Rhodes, Johnson, & Wiliam, 1997). This data formed the basis for both statistical and qualitative analysis to investigate the relative contributions of different factors.

The Core Project provided a base for the case-study investigations in the focus projects, and both generated hypotheses to be explored in the focus projects and allowed hypotheses arising from those to be checked on a larger sample.

4.2. Focus Project: Case studies of Pupil Progress (Mike Askew, Hazel Denvir, Valerie Rhodes and Margaret Brown, 1997-2002)

Aim: To obtain a clear and detailed longitudinal picture of the numeracy development of a range of pupils taught in a varied set of schools and to examine this in the light of their classroom experiences, to ascertain what works, what goes wrong, and why.

Methods: This project explored the classroom practice factors influencing pupil attainment, including school, teacher, teaching, curriculum and individual pupil factors. From the longitudinal core sample we selected five schools which presented interesting contrasts. In each of these schools we selected children of varied attainment, six from a Reception (pupils aged 4-5 years) and six from a Year 4 class (pupils aged 8-9 years) to provide longitudinal case-study data, plotting progression in learning over four or five years. Children were observed and informally interviewed in two blocks of five lessons each year, and their written work collected.

Longer interviews concerning perceptions of progress, attitudes and home support, and involving assessment questions, occurred at the end of Years 3 (pupils aged 7-8 years) and 6 (pupils aged 10-11 years).

4.3. Focus Project: Teachers' Knowledge, Conceptions and Practices and Pupils' Learning (Mike Askew, Alison Millett and Shirley Simon, 1999-2002)

Aim: To investigate the relationships between teachers' beliefs about, knowledge of and practices in teaching numeracy and whether changes in beliefs, knowledge and/or practices raise standards.
Methods: The project followed 12 teachers before, during and after their experience of a short course of professional development as part of the National Numeracy Strategy. We adapted the methods of eliciting teachers' subject knowledge and beliefs in a series of interviews from our earlier work (Askew et al., 1997) in order to construct teacher profiles. Changes in teachers' practices were monitored using video recording of lessons, and changes in pupils' attainment by using the tests developed for the Core Project. The teachers' profiles, their classroom practices and their pupils' attainment were monitored over three years.

4.4. Focus Project: Whole School Action on Numeracy (Alison Millett and David Johnson, 1997-2001)

Aim: To identify whole-school and teacher factors which appear to facilitate or inhibit the development of strategies for raising attainment in numeracy.
Methods: This research focused on six schools as they each experienced an inspection and then implemented the National Numeracy Strategy. Each school had identified the need for improvements in their teaching of numeracy and we have collected data both on the strategies schools used to develop the teaching of numeracy and the effect of these strategies on pupils' attainment. The research investigated the complex interplay of school factors, such as school policies and leadership, and teacher factors involved in the implementation of change over four years. The research used documentary analysis, observation in classrooms and at meetings, and interviews with a range of informants (headteachers, mathematics co-ordinators, classroom teachers, governors and parents).

4.5. Focus Project: School and Community Numeracies (Brian Street, Alison Tomlin, Dave Bake and Helen Lucey, 1998-2002)

Aim: To refine and establish the meanings and uses of numeracy in home and school contexts; to establish differences between practices in the two environments and to draw inferences for pedagogy.

Methods: This project investigated the influence of social factors on attainment, in particular differences between numeracy practices, and the linguistic practices associated with them, in the pupils' home and school contexts. Three schools were selected to provide a range of home cultures. Case-study pupils were then chosen from Reception classes (pupils aged 4-5 years) and followed through Year 1 (pupils aged 5-6 years) and into Year 2 (pupils aged 6-7 years). We used ethnographic methods including participant observation of classrooms and of informal situations in and out of school, and interviews with teachers, parents and pupils. The study extended previous work on literacy practices (Street, 1999) into numeracy, but retained a comparative element between the two.

4.6. Focus Project: Primary CAME (Cognitive Acceleration in Mathematics Education) (David Johnson, Mundher Adhami, Michael Shayer, Rosemary Hafeez, Sally Dubben, Ann Longfield and Jeremy Hodgen, 1997-2000)

Aim: To investigate the effect on the development of numeracy of managed cognitive challenge/conflict designed to encourage verbal interactions and metacognitive activity in whole-class and various small-group arrangements of children in Year 5 (pupils aged 9-10 years) and Year 6 (pupils aged 10-11 years).

Methods: An experimental design was used to investigate whether intervention in classroom practices aimed at promoting intellectual development could be effective. It extended our earlier work on CAME (Cognitive Acceleration in Mathematics Education) in secondary schools (Adhami, Johnson, & Shayer, 1998) which used Piagetian and Vygotskian paradigms. The research team, including teacher-researchers in each of two laboratory schools, first devised and trialled a sequence of mathematical problem situations designed to challenge children, and to promote teacher-child and child-child discussion in co-operative small-group work and whole-class discussion. This led to the main fieldwork involving research with teachers in a further eight schools, with the teacher-researchers as tutors. We used systematic observation of lessons and professional development sessions, and pre- and post- intervention pupil assessments of cognitive development and mathematical attainment. A linked study has demonstrated how this intervention acted as a basis for teachers' continuous professional development.

4.7. Relation to the National Numeracy Strategy

When the Leverhulme proposal was written it could not have been anticipated that a new government would quickly implement the National Numeracy Strategy. Clearly this affected the Leverhulme Programme as the implementation of the Strategy in schools occurred in the middle year (1999/2000) of the five-year research programme. For example, it meant that curriculum objectives, teaching sequence and aspects of teaching methods no longer varied between classes, and thus the effects of differences in these could only be perceived in data from the early years of the project. The original plan for an intervention project concerning teacher professional development (*Teachers' Knowledge, Conceptions and Practices*) also had to be modified to fit with the Strategy training courses, since schools would not have been able to support additional training in the year of implementation of the Strategy.

The Leverhulme work addressed fundamental issues in primary numeracy and was by no means merely an evaluation of the implementation of the Numeracy Strategy. Indeed there was a government authorised evaluation which was carried out, with the parallel Literacy Strategy, by a Canadian team (Earl et al., 2000; 2001; 2003). But our data was used to inform this evaluation and, as well as tackling its own wider brief, was able to illuminate some effects of a particular attempt at systemic reform.

4.8. Coherence of themes

Although the structure of the Leverhulme Programme has been described as six projects, there has been great added benefit in the projects being part of the larger Programme. The results of the Programme were first analysed separately for each project and then integrated into a sequence of four common linked themes, to each of which several projects contribute.

- children's learning and progression
- teachers and teaching
- home, culture and school
- professional development of teachers.

These four themes are the topics of the four books in this current series. The first two themes are combined into two books, the first addressing generic features of teaching and learning numeracy and the second examining teaching and learning in different numeracy topics. The third and fourth themes form a book each. Thus the four titles in the series are:

- Teaching and learning about number: interactions in primary lessons and pupil progression
- Teaching, learning and progression in key numeracy topics
- Numeracy practices at home and at school
- Primary mathematics and the developing professional.

5. REFERENCES

Adhami, M., Johnson, D., & Shayer, M. (1998). *Thinking Maths: The Programme for Accelerated Learning in Mathematics*. Oxford: Heinemann Educational Books.

Askew, M., Brown, M., Rhodes, V., Johnson, D., & Wiliam, D. (1997). *Effective teachers of numeracy: Final report*. London: King's College.

Baker, D. (1999). *What does it mean to understand maths as social*? Paper presented at the British Congress of Mathematics Education, 15-17 July 1999. University College, Northampton.

Brown, M. (1996). The context of the research – the evolution of the National Curriculum for mathematics. In D. C. Johnson & A. Millett (Eds.), *Implementing the mathematics National Curriculum: policy, politics and practice* (pp. 1-28). London: Paul Chapman.

Carpenter, T. P., & Peterson, P. L. (1988). Learning through instruction: The study of students' thinking during instruction in mathematics. *Educational Psychologist, 23*(2), 79-85.

Cobb, P., & Bauersfeld, H. (Eds.). (1995). *The emergence of mathematical meaning: interaction in classroom cultures*. Hillsdale, NJ: Lawrence Erlbaum Associates.

Davis, R. B. (1984). *Learning Mathematics: The Cognitive Science Approach to Mathematics Education*. London: Croom Helm.

Department for Education and Employment (DfEE). (1998). *The implementation of the National Numeracy Strategy: The final report of the Numeracy Task Force*. London: Department for Education and Employment

Department for Education and Employment (DfEE). (1999). *The National Numeracy Strategy: Framework for teaching mathematics from Reception to Year 6*. London: Department for Education and Employment.

Department of Education and Science/Welsh Office. (1982). *Mathematics Counts: report of the Committee of Inquiry into the Teaching of Mathematics in Schools*. London: Her Majesty's Stationery Office.

Department of Education and Science/Welsh Office. (1988). *Mathematics for ages 5-16*. London: Department of Education and Science.

Department of Education, Training and Youth Affairs. (2000). *Numeracy, a priority for all: challenges for Australian schools*. Canberra: Department of Education and Youth Affairs.

Earl, L., Fullan, M., Leithwood, K., Watson, N., with Jantzi, D., Levin, B., & Torrance, N. (2000). *Watching & Learning. OISE/UT Evaluation of the implementation of the National Literacy and Numeracy Strategies. First annual report*. Toronto: Ontario Institute for Studies in Education, University of Toronto.

Earl, L., Levin, B., Leithwood, K., Fullan, M., & Watson, N. (2001). *Watching & Learning 2: OISE/UT Evaluation of the Implementation of the National Literacy and Numeracy Strategies. Second Annual Report.* Toronto: Ontario Institute for Studies in Education, University of Toronto.

Earl, L., Watson, N., Levin, B., Leithwood, K., Fullan, M., Torrance, N., with Jantzi, D., Mascall, B., & Volante, L. (2003). *Watching & Learning 3: Final Report of the External Evaluation of England's National Literacy and Numeracy Strategies.* Toronto: Ontario Institute for Studies in Education, University of Toronto.

Gravemeijer, K. (1997). Instructional design for reform in mathematics education. In M. Beishuizen, K. Gravemeijer, & E. C. D. M. Van Leishout (Eds.), *The Role of Contexts and Models in the Development of Mathematical Strategies and Procedures.* Utrecht: Freudenthal Institute.

Lapointe, A. E., Mead, N. A., & Askew, J. M. (1992). *Learning Mathematics (Report of the IAEP 1990/1 survey).* Princetown, NJ: Educational Testing Service.

Maher, C., & Davis, R. B. (1990). Teachers' learning: building representations of children's meanings. In R. B. Davis, C. Maher, & N. Noddings (Eds.), *Constructivist views on the teaching and learning of mathematics.* Reston, VA: National Council of Teachers of Mathematics.

Ministerial Council on Education, Employment, Training and Youth Affairs. (1989). *Hobart Declaration – National Goals for Schooling.* Victoria, AUS: Ministerial Council on Education, Employment, Training and Youth Affairs.

Ministry of Education. (1991). *The New Zealand Curriculum Framework.* Wellington, NZ: Ministry of Education.

Ministry of Education. (1997). *Report of the Mathematics and Science Taskforce.* Wellington, NZ: Ministry of Education.

Ministry of Education. (2001a). *Curriculum Update 45: The Numeracy Story.* Wellington, NZ: Learning Media.

Ministry of Education. (2001b). *Early Numeracy Project.* Wellington, NZ: Learning Media.

Mullis, I. V. S., Martin, M. O., Beaton, A. E., Gonzalez, E. J., Kelly, D. L., & Smith, T. A. (1997). *Mathematics Achievement in the Primary School Years: IES's Third Mathematics and Science Study.* Massachusetts: Boston College.

National Commission for Excellence in Education. (1983). *A Nation at Risk: the imperative for educational reform.* Washington, DC: US Government Printing

National Council of Teachers of Mathematics. (1989). *Curriculum and evaluation standards for school mathematics.* Reston, VA: National Council of Teachers of Mathematics.

National Council of Teachers of Mathematics. (2000). *Principles and Standards for School Mathematics.* Reston, VA: National Council of Teachers of Mathematics.

Noss, R. (1997). *New cultures, new literacies.* London: Institute of Education.

Office for Standards in Education. (2000a). *The National Numeracy Strategy: an interim evaluation by HMI.* London: Office for Standards in Education.

Office for Standards in Education. (2000b). *The National Numeracy Strategy: the first year.* London: Office for Standards in Education.

Office for Standards in Education. (2001). *The National Numeracy Strategy: the second year.* London: Office for Standards in Education.

Reys, B., Reys, R. E., & Hope, J. A. (1993). Mental computation: A snapshot of second, fifth and seventh grade student performance, *Journal for Research in Mathematics Education*, 93(6), 306-315.

Steffe, L. P., & Gale, J. (Eds.). (1995). *Constructivism in education.* Hillsdale, NJ: Lawrence Erlbaum Associates.

Streefland, L., Ed. (1991). *Realistic mathematics education in primary schools.* Utrecht: Freudenthal Institute, Utrecht University.

Street, B. (1999). Literacy 'events' and literacy 'practices: theory and practice in the 'New Literacy Studies'. In K. Jones & M. Martin-Jones (Eds.), *Multilingual literacies: comparative perspectives on research and practice*. Amsterdam: John Benjamin.

Treffers, A. (1991). Didactical background of a mathematics program for primary education. In L. Streefland (Ed.), *Realistic mathematics education in primary schools*. Utrecht: Freudenthal Institute, Utrecht University.

ALISON MILLETT AND TAMARA BIBBY

CHAPTER 1

THE CONTEXT FOR CHANGE: A MODEL FOR DISCUSSION

Abstract. In this chapter we present a model for discussing the implementation of change upon which subsequent chapters will draw. Taking insights particularly from the work of Spillane (1999) and Leithwood, Jantzi and Mascall (1999), we have developed a model where context is taken as that which surrounds and influences an individual making decisions about teaching mathematics in the primary school. The *situation*, normally the immediate school environment, contains both the *pupils* and the *professional community* of colleagues with whom the individual works closely. More distant, but still exerting influence, are the *external professionals*, *policy makers*, the *public* and aspects of *private sector* enterprise. Critical to our model is the notion of a *zone of enactment* – an area of potential for professional development, the space in which the individual makes sense of reform or change initiatives in an essentially social process. We outline how work from the Leverhulme Numeracy Research Programme has given rise to a set of questions about what makes a difference in influencing the way in which change is taken on board, and indicate how these questions will be addressed in the chapters that follow.

1. INTRODUCTION

For over a decade, those researching and writing on teachers' professional development have found conventional models ill-suited to the task of studying teacher development. Most models focus on individual teachers and how individual knowledge and beliefs affect instruction (Stein, Silver, & Smith, 1998) and pay little attention to the social setting of teaching. Models that featured social interaction with colleagues and also addressed teacher learning (e.g. Lave & Wenger, 1991; Tharp & Gallimore, 1988) were felt to more appropriately reflect the conditions in which teacher learning took place (Stein & Brown, 1997). The importance of the social setting, of which the individual teacher is a member, is reflected in the use of terms such as 'professional communities' (Louis & Kruse, 1995; Secada & Adajian, 1997), 'learning communities' (Collins, 1998), 'learning cultures' (King &

Alison Millett, Margaret Brown and Mike Askew (eds.), Primary Mathematics and the Developing Professional.

Newmann, 2000) to characterise both collective and individual actions and interactions. Recent writing from those researching the long-term effects of Cognitively Guided Instruction, essentially a programme involving individual teachers and their knowledge of children's learning (Franke, Carpenter, Levi, & Fennema, 2001), has stressed the role of colleagues in establishing generative or continuing change.

This book contains contributions from several of the focus projects of the Leverhulme Numeracy Research Programme (see Introduction). These varied projects were supported by different literature bases and theoretical positions. They engaged with different aspects of professional development involving, for example:

- individual teachers' knowledge and beliefs (e.g. Thompson, 1992; Ball, Lubienski, & Mewborn, 2001)
- in-service training courses or interventions (e.g. Eraut, 1994; Guskey & Huberman, 1995; Joyce & Showers, 1995)
- development embedded in the social community of the school (e.g. Joyce, Calhoun, & Hopkins, 1999; Fullan, 2001).

In presenting our work we have felt the need for a common vocabulary, a set of constructs recognisable in each area addressed by the different foci to give coherence to the whole theme of teacher professional development.

2. A MODEL FOR DISCUSSING CHANGE

We were anxious to develop a model for discussion which placed the individual making decisions firmly at the centre, but which also embraced the context and culture within which the individual works and the external factors that exert influence, either directly or indirectly (See Figure 1.1), thus crossing boundaries between the individual and the organisational literatures (Richardson & Placier, 2001). Several sources in the literature, particularly a paper by Spillane (1999) in which he outlines a model for explaining why some teachers seem able to take change on board and others do not, have helped us in this. We have thus taken initial ideas from the work of Spillane (1999) which we feel are of particular relevance to the creation of our own model.

Spillane (1999) presents a model with the individual at the centre, upon whom are operating five external influences or constraints of various types (Professional, Policy, Pupil, Public, Private). Our model differs in a major way from Spillane's in that we make use of Leithwood, Jantzi and Mascall's (1999) notion of *situation* to provide what we regard as a more appropriate reflection of the intimate and day-to-day influences upon teachers of the colleagues and school structures and cultures that surround them in their working environment. These influences mediate the constraints and effect of the less immediate *external factors* suggested by Spillane. Within the *situation*, we include both the *pupils* and the *professional community* of colleagues. It could be argued that the external influences should be regarded as part of the *situation* as they are part of the working environment of the teacher, although not necessarily encountered on a day-to-day basis. We prefer, however, to retain the definition of *situation* specifically for the whole-school context as we believe that whole-school characteristics play a major role in distinguishing between success and failure in initiating, implementing and sustaining change. The responses of schools can be entirely different even though external factors are virtually the same.

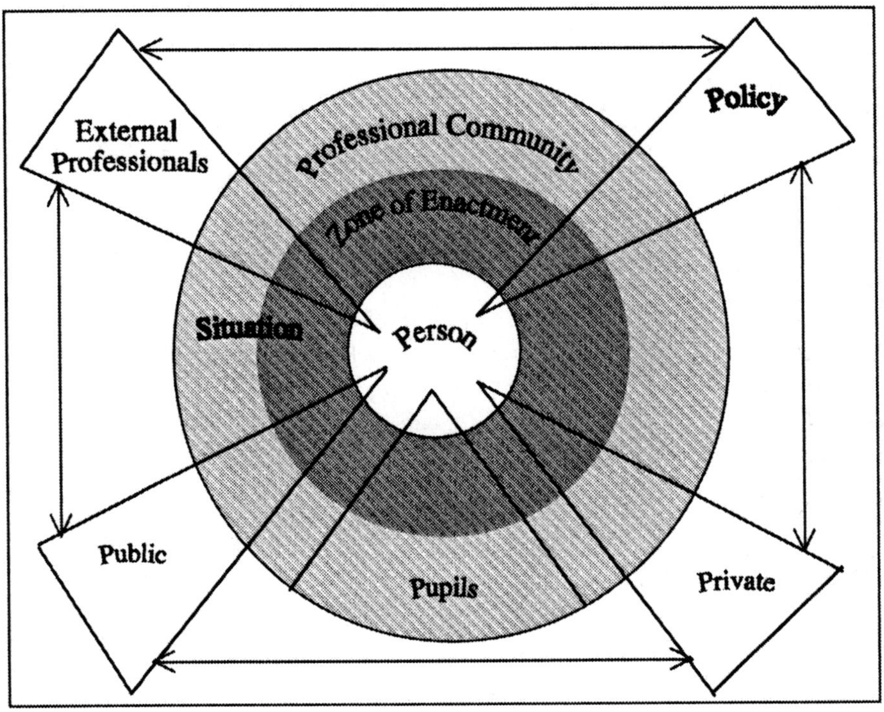

Figure 1.1. Model for discussing change

2.1. The zone of enactment

Richardson and Placier (2001) draw on Zeichner and Gore (1990) to suggest that the interface between individual teachers and their schools reveals a "critical gap in our understanding of change" (p. 939). In addressing this gap, we regard the *zone of enactment* as the key element in our model. Spillane (1999) draws attention to the nature of the interactions between individuals and those exerting influence upon them as being of vital importance to professional change, and he calls this interface the *zone of enactment* (p. 144). Although possessed by all individuals, it is the nature of this *zone of enactment* and how it can be utilised that is important. As an essentially social construct, it is not solely determined by an individual's personal and professional characteristics. Spillane identified three key characteristics that differentiated the *zones of enactment* of teachers in his research who changed the core of their practice from those who did not, whose *zones of enactment* remained essentially individualistic. He described situations where:

> Ongoing deliberations with colleagues as well as experts, from inside and outside the district, about mathematics instruction were central in these teachers' reform efforts. [...] Their conversations were grounded in their day-to-day attempts to enact the reform ideas in their classrooms. [...] ... their deliberations about practice and its reform were enabled not only by human resources, including local expert teachers and university academics, but also by material resources or artefacts that were consistent with the reform ideas. (Spillane, 1999, p. 160)

These three factors - rich deliberations, grounded in practice and supported by resources - are essential constituents for Spillane of the *zone of enactment*, if teachers are to "notice, construe, construct and operationalise the ideas advanced by reformers" (p. 144). He saw *zones of enactment* as potentially serving a "powerful mediating function" (Spillane, 1999, p. 170) between reform initiatives and practice and drew on Vygotsky's notion of 'zones of proximal development' with their emphasis on the social dimensions of learning (Vygotsky, 1978) to support his perspective. In order to develop their beliefs and practices, teachers may have to question, unlearn and discard some of their current, deeply rooted understandings of teaching, learning and subject matter. They may need to be asked questions about existing practices to encourage the construction of alternative practices. Spillane (1999) focuses on the importance of language through which new ideas and practices are represented.

In the context of mathematics teaching, teachers face many dilemmas about the nature of the mathematics they are teaching. These include: what is the optimum balance between efficient performance and mathematical thinking? If there are state or national tests, is covering the curriculum more important than spending long enough on topics for most children to have grasped them? The ways that reforms or policies interact with such dilemmas and their effects on teachers' emotions, attitudes and beliefs are of central importance to the realisation of *zones of enactment*.

We find this notion of *zones of enactment*, as areas of potential and possibility, a powerful one. From the viewpoints of the individual focus projects within the overall Leverhulme Numeracy Research Programme, we would want to expand on and extend this notion of *zone of enactment* as being of critical importance in how the individual takes change on board and develops his/her practice. A contributing stimulus for development might be a state of disequilibrium (Leithwood et al., 1999) where the potential need for change worth making is identified. The views of individuals and professional colleagues on the "merit" and "worth" of new reform ideas (Guba & Lincoln, 1985, pp. 39/40) will also play a role in whether and how *zones of enactment* that foster development can be realised. Different models of professional development, for example peer coaching, might succeed or fail to produce the 'rich deliberations' that can characterise this zone.

2.2. *The person*

The individual teacher making decisions is at the centre of our model. Within the *person* we would want to include that store of stories that teachers draw on as a kind of professional case law (Shulman, 1986); their experiences within school, current and past, of children and colleagues; their own more personal professional experiences; their knowledge of subject matter and pedagogy and the source of their professional strength (convictions/beliefs and warrants for these).

To develop the personal aspect of the model more fully, we draw upon the work of Leithwood, Jantzi and Mascall (1999), who discuss the individual working within her immediate *situation*. Leithwood et al. use the terms 'will' and 'capacity' to describe two factors which affect how the individual takes change on board. (We use the female gender in future writing as it reflects the fact that the overwhelming majority of primary teachers are female.) Preferring the term 'motivation', rather than 'will', we agree with their perception of motivational processes as a function of personal goals – the wants, needs and aspirations of the individual. Leithwood et al. describe two sets of personal agency beliefs interacting with personal goals. The first of these they call capacity beliefs and include here beliefs about self-efficacy, self-confidence and academic self-esteem (p. 10); the second they call context beliefs and include here beliefs about the *situation* as a context for reform.

As the context here is primary mathematics, we would expect both cognitive and affective issues relating to a teacher's experience of mathematics to be involved – her feelings about herself as a learner of mathematics (Bibby, 2002), her beliefs about the nature of the subject, her conceptions about the teaching and learning of mathematics for her pupils (Askew et al., 1997). This is a wide area and would need to include recognition of the ways policy reforms interact with personal and professional ideologies and beliefs, and therefore some notion of personal histories and how and why such beliefs are held – how deeply rooted and fundamental they are.

> Practitioners do not confront policy texts as naïve readers, they come with histories, with experience, with values and purposes of their own, they have vested interests in the meaning of policy. (Bowe, Ball, & Gold, 1992)

For example, if a core aspect of a teacher's professional identity is that children need to be nurtured and their interests fostered, then conflict is likely to be experienced if reform is perceived as asking her to act against this fundamental belief about herself as a teacher.

In terms of her broader professional role, we need to know how the teacher sees herself as a professional, her views about more general pedagogical issues and how these have developed over time (her career and experience). Factors in her personal life may also affect how she can take change on board, as will factors to do with the nature of the innovation itself, or implications related to career development (see for example Joyce & Showers, 1995; Sikes, Measor, & Woods, 1995; Goodson & Hargreaves, 1996). The personal aspect of the model will be taken up again in Chapters 2, 5, 6 and 8.

2.3. The situation – the professional community and the pupils

We have chosen to define the *situation* as including all the everyday influences of professional colleagues and pupils that impinge upon the teacher as she carries out her role, be it as class teacher, mathematics co-ordinator or subject leader, or in a role of more general leadership and management in the school. The role of the subject leader or co-ordinator in primary schools in the United Kingdom has become increasingly important in recent years, moving "from a position of marginality in the curriculum, to one of centrality" (Campbell, 1987, p. 54). Pressure and support from colleagues and headteacher, resourcing of professional development, emotional support and friendship, coherence and consistency of views are all part of the influence of the *professional community*. Nias, Southworth and Campbell (1992) described different cultures existing in primary schools, with a culture of collaboration being characterised by factors such as the valuing of individuals and their contribution to others; valuing interdependence and working as a team; valuing security and openness. The quality of leadership shown by headteachers

(Southworth, 1998; Day, Harris, Hadfield, Tolley, & Beresford, 2000) and by subject leaders, in this case of mathematics, (Campbell, 1987; Millett, 1998; Millett & Johnson, 2000) and their chosen ways of working form another aspect of the *situation*.

Within varied contexts and cultures, the individual teacher works with colleagues at different levels of intensity and in different power relationships. A new teacher may be mentored by a more senior member of staff, but may find greater help from working collaboratively with the teacher in the nextdoor classroom. A teacher may have skills that are in demand by other teachers in the school, or she may be regarded as a novice with little to offer until she becomes more experienced. The management structure of the school may reflect these differences in ethos and ways of working and may or may not lead to situations where dialogue on pedagogical and curriculum issues is encouraged and valued. This is all part of the *situation* in which the teacher is centred. The individual teacher, in turn, has an effect on how her *situation* develops.

Leithwood et al. (1999) talk about the "collective capacity and infrastructure for reform" (p. 16) existing in some schools with certain conditions being likely to support change including the supporting of dialogue and discussion, opportunities for teachers to learn both inside and outside school, structures that minimise isolation and expectations that teachers will be responsible for school-wide as well as classroom decisions (p. 17). Alternative styles of management affect the development of such collective capacity. Gray (2001) and Maden (2001) also discuss the importance of a school's capacity for reform. When flexibility is an element in this capacity, schools are more likely to be able to sustain change once initiated.

In many cases, decision-making about the planning of mathematics activities is likely to be part of a whole-school strategy, or may even be part of a national strategy; it may be carried out mainly alone or as a collaborative activity. The teacher's choice of materials (see Section 2.4.4.) plays an important part in this planning process, with the *situation* affecting the range of materials available for use.

Whilst not exerting a direct influence on the teacher's professional development in the sense of any intentional provision of learning opportunities, the *pupils* still play an important role. The arena of the classroom is where attempts at reform are trialled and reflected upon – the intimate detail of decision-making about the sorts of experiences to provide for pupils, and responses to the effect these experiences have. We have therefore included the *pupils* as part of the *situation*. The *situation* provides an important focus for discussion in Chapters 2, 3 and 5.

2.4. External factors – professionals, policy, the public, the private sector

At the periphery of our model (See Figure 1.1) we have drawn attention to four external factors that we regard as important influences on teachers' professional development:

- external professionals
- policy
- the public
- the private sector.

In describing the model portrayed in Figure 1.1, we have of necessity paid attention to each of its elements separately. It will be noted that links are indicated between the external factors. In order not to complicate the diagram we have not used arrows to indicate links between all the external factors. However, these external factors are not mutually exclusive and interact with one another in a variety of ways: for example, policy implementation is likely to involve external professionals; the private sector is peopled by the public (see also Section 2.4.5.).

The teacher's *situation* acts as a filter through which external influences and constraints find their way. Our model differs from Spillane's in that we show these external influences impinging directly on the individual as well as being mediated through the *situation* (as indicated in Figure 1.1). Sometimes both of these may be happening concurrently. For example, an inexperienced teacher may be regarded as a novice in her school *situation*, viewed as being on the receiving end of advice and encouragement from more senior colleagues who are in close contact with local authority advisers, consultants or superintendents. This teacher may also belong to a working group outside school developing curriculum materials through an interest developed at college and encouraged by her tutor. She is therefore subject to both mediated and direct influences from external professionals simultaneously. Whether mediated or direct, all these influences affect her view of herself as a professional, a teacher of mathematics and a *person*.

2.4.1. External professionals

The *external professional* refers to all those professionals outside the school with whom the individual teacher or the school as a whole has contact. Included here would be support and pressure from officers (superintendents), advisers and inspectors from the Local Education Authority (generally equivalent to several school districts), and any local provision of a developmental nature in the form of in-service training or regular support mechanisms that provide a forum for discussion. With the introduction of the National Numeracy Strategy in England in

1999 (see Introduction), additional tiers of professionals including numeracy consultants, regional directors and leading mathematics teachers have begun to exert a significant influence on schools. The influence of the school district in supporting development in schools has been noted recently by Fullan (2001) and Louis and Kruse (1995).

Also included here would be inspectors. In England, Office for Standards in Education (referred to throughout this volume as 'Ofsted') inspectors conduct inspections of schools; Local Education Authority staff and members of Her Majesty's Inspectorate also visit schools and report on progress (see particularly Chapters 2 and 3).

2.4.2. Policy

In the United Kingdom, the late 1980s and the 1990s saw an "avalanche" of policy initiatives (Pollard, 2001, p. 17). The National Curriculum was introduced in 1989 and was in its second version by 1991. Slotted in between this and the third version in 1995 came the introduction of a new system of external evaluation in the form of Ofsted inspections. This external evaluation, conducted for every school on average every four years, identifies priorities for action and spells these out as key issues in an inspection report. The publication of inspection reports puts schools' strengths and weaknesses, as identified by the team of inspectors, firmly in the public domain. Primary schools have also been under pressure to undertake self-review or internal evaluation and develop their own plans for future improvement.

Alongside these major curriculum and inspection initiatives came a new system of national testing that not only required primary schools to administer tests to all children aged 5, 7 and 11, but also to face comparison with other schools with the results of these tests at age 11 being published in local and national newspapers in the form of league tables.

Heated public debate from 1995 about poor attainment in literacy and numeracy led to the imposition of a different sort of reform on primary schools in England – different in that the Government had decided to intervene in the 'how' as well as the 'what' of teaching. Starting in September 1998, the introduction of a national focus on literacy was to be closely followed by its numeracy sibling (Brown, Millett, Bibby, & Johnson, 2000). This National Numeracy Strategy (Department for Education and Employment, 1999) required a daily mathematics lesson from September 1999 (see Introduction).

The United Kingdom has not been alone in initiating reform efforts (see Introduction). In the area of mathematics education, teachers in the United States have faced both pressure to implement, and state reluctance to support, the

Curriculum and Evaluation Standards for School Mathematics introduced in 1989 and recently revised and updated (National Council of Teachers of Mathematics, 1989; 2000). New Zealand (Ministry of Education, 1997; 2001a; 2001b) and Australia (Department of Education, Training and Youth Affairs, 2000) have also introduced numeracy initiatives. The mathematics curriculum is undergoing re-structuring in Japan (Hashimoto, 1999) and reform in China (Er-Sheng, 1999) and South Africa (Volmink, 1999) is also ongoing. It is thus a common experience for schools and teachers world-wide to be in a position of responding to reform initiatives.

2.4.3. The public

Non-government sources, such as the media, 'public opinion' and parents – those beyond the school gates but with a keen interest in education – may also influence schools and the teachers working within them. The accountability of schools in England for the performance of their pupils has grown over recent years (Hopkins, 2001) with, as noted above, the development of systems for publishing the results of Ofsted inspections and of national test results in league tables. Schools are thus placed in competition one with another, and the media has encouraged the public to attend to this. Government policies such as the introduction of Beacon status for schools with acknowledged excellence, based on Ofsted reports and national test data, has raised the stakes still further (www.standards.dfee.gov.uk/beaconschools) The influence of the media can be direct, for example by teachers listening to television news bulletins or reading newspapers, or indirect, through parents' comments informed through these channels. The ownership of media outlets affects the views and opinions expressed, and leads us to the *private sector.*

2.4.4. The private sector

The link with the *private sector* includes influences on teachers' practice from commercial sources outside central or local government. The use of paid private consultants (who might also have a role as external professionals) by schools would be included here, as would the much more common influence of commercially produced mathematics materials for teachers and pupils.

The use of textbooks or commercial mathematics schemes as a main resource for the teaching of mathematics in both primary and secondary schools has long been common world-wide (Robitaille & Garden, 1989; Miwa, 1991; Zhang, 1991). However, this practice has also been viewed with concern in the United Kingdom. The Cockcroft Report (Department of Education and Science and the Welsh Office,

1982), in discussing primary mathematics, warned that any textbook should be used with discrimination and should not be expected to provide a complete course to meet the needs of all children.

With the implementation of the National Curriculum in England and Wales in 1989, concern about over-reliance on commercial schemes continued (Her Majesty's Inspectorate, 1992). The introduction of another major national intervention in primary mathematics in England in 1999, the National Numeracy Strategy (see Introduction) has foregrounded once more schools' decisions about resources and materials for classroom use. The *private sector* is responding to this recent innovation by providing new or adapted equipment and commercial schemes that fit its structure and requirements. For some schools, these schemes are becoming powerful mediators of the National Numeracy Strategy (Rhodes & Millett, 2001). (See also Chapter 4.)

More recent involvement of the private sector in state education in England is the involvement of commercial companies in the funding of such initiatives as Education Action Zones, although profit-making was not intended by government. Contributions might include cash, equipment and materials or human resources providing curriculum enrichment, managerial services or mentoring (Dickson, Gewirtz, Halpin, Power & Whitty, 2003).

2.4.5. Links between the external factors

The external influences or constraints described in Section 2.4. will move in and out of the spotlight for individual teachers or schools at different times. The influence of the professionals from the Local Education Authority in which the school is situated will always be close and compelling. The influence of the *policy*-maker and the *private sector* is likely to follow the fluctuating imperatives of reform initiatives; the influence of the public may be a focus at the time of an inspection and then recede again. Examples of links between these external factors are given below:

- *policy* and the *private sector* – in the response of commercial organisations or individuals to policy initiatives in the form of curriculum materials or consultancy, and, for example, in the provision of research reports commissioned by government from independent consultants
- the *private sector* and the *public* – in the purchase by parents of educational workbooks and reference materials for their children or the provision of private tutoring outside school
- the *public* and *policy* – in the response of the public to policy initiatives, whether directly through experience as parents of school-age children, or indirectly through the media, or in policy reacting to public outcry

- the *external professional* and *policy* – in the interpretation and implementation of *policy* and in the provision of training and support for schools related to policy initiatives
- the *external professional* and the *public* – in the publication of inspection reports and the consultation with parents during an inspection. Also in decisions made by Local Education Authority inspectors that can affect the future of schools in an area
- the *external professional* and the *private sector* – in the involvement of *external professionals* with *private sector* enterprises such as the provision of consultancy and training, or the writing of curriculum materials.

2.5. The use of the model

We are intending that this should be a flexible model, but with a central core of common constructs, with different aspects of it being highlighted by contributors to this book who have worked on different Leverhulme projects. The attraction of this model for us is that it portrays the complexity of change – simultaneously intrapersonal (with its focus on the characteristics of the individual), interpersonal (with its focus on interaction with pupils and colleagues in the immediate situation) and external (with its focus on rather more distant, but nevertheless important influences). Whilst having individual characteristics, the elements of the model – the *person*, the *situation*, the *zone of enactment*, the *external factors* – are deeply interconnected in the ways outlined in Section 2 of this chapter.

3. QUESTIONS POSED IN THIS BOOK

The decision to undertake some form of professional development in mathematics may be self-initiated by individual teachers or schools, or made in response to external reform initiatives. Change may or may not ensue from this development in terms of teachers' knowledge, understanding and beliefs, mathematics classroom practice and pupils' learning of mathematics. The context for our work has included a national intervention in primary mathematics in England, which, although not in place at the beginning of our work, has meant that response to reform necessarily played a large part in the reporting of our findings.

Having established the context in which this research was situated, and our model for discussing the contribution of the Leverhulme Numeracy Research Programme to the literature on the professional development of those teaching mathematics in primary schools, we turn now to a consideration of the questions we are hoping to answer. From the varied foci of our individual projects within the Leverhulme Programme, we ask:

What factors can make a significant difference in the realisation of rich *zones of enactment* that enable teachers to take change on board:

- the source of in-school support provided by the mathematics co-ordinator
- whole-school factors
- the use of published curriculum materials
- intervention in the form of externally provided in-service training
- intervention in the form of ongoing involvement in the design, development and teaching of mathematics lessons?

We look first to the source of in-service support common to primary schools in England and some other countries, for example Australia – the subject co-ordinator or leader. In Chapter 2 we report on what we have learnt about the efficacy of this source of support to the implementation of change. How can the co-ordinator as part of the *professional community* contribute towards the development of rich *zones of enactment*? We then look more broadly at the *professional community*, to consider the effect of whole-school factors on the ability of classroom teachers to implement change (Chapter 3).

Moving on to *external factors*, in Chapter 4 we focus on the materials produced by makers of *policy*, *external professionals*, and by commercial publishers in the *private sector*, and ask how the use of these materials mediates the implementation of change. The four chapters that follow, Chapters 5 to 8, all consider the impact of external intervention. Chapters 5 and 6 consider the effect of a nationally-provided course of in-service training experienced by a small group of teachers. Chapters 7 and 8 document the role of professional development in the Primary Cognitive Acceleration in Mathematics Education project (P-CAME), and ask how this form of professional development has affected the beliefs and practice of those acting as teacher-researchers.

In Chapter 9 we return to debate what constitutes change. Can what we have identified as change be described as "deep" change (Earl et al., 2000, p. 39)? What level of change can be considered as sustainable and what does this change look like in the context of primary mathematics? We summarise the contribution of this book at a descriptive, theoretical and predictive level to the body of knowledge on professional development in primary mathematics.

4. AFFILIATIONS

Dr Tamara Bibby is a Lecturer in Mathematics Education in the Department of Education and Professional Studies, King's College London.

5. REFERENCES

Askew, M., Brown, M., Rhodes, V., Johnson, D., & Wiliam, D. (1997). *Effective teachers of numeracy: Final report*. London: King's College.

Ball, D. L., Lubienski, S. T., & Mewborn, D. S. (2001). Research on Teaching Mathematics: the unsolved problem of teachers' mathematical knowledge. In V. Richardson (Ed.), *Handbook of Research on Teaching. Fourth Edition* (pp. 433-456). Washington DC: American Educational Research Association.

Bibby, T. (2002). Shame: an emotional response to doing mathematics as an adult and as a teacher. *British Educational Research Journal, 28*(5), 706-721.

Bowe, R., Ball, S., & Gold, A. (1992). *Reforming education and changing schools: case studies in policy sociology*. London: Routledge.

Brown, M., Millett, A., Bibby, T., & Johnson, D. C. (2000). Turning Our Attention from the What to the How: the National Numeracy Strategy. *British Educational Research Journal, 26*(4), 457-471.

Campbell, J. (1987). The role of the curriculum postholder. In G. Southworth (Ed.), *Readings in primary school management* (pp. 54-60). London: Falmer Press.

Collins, A. (1998). Learning Communities: A Commentary on Chapters by Brown, Ellery and Campione, and by Riel. In J. G. Greeno & S. V. Goldman (Eds.), *Thinking Practices in Mathematics and Science Learning* (pp. 399-405). Mahwah, NJ: Lawrence Erlbaum Associates, Inc.

Day, C., Harris, A., Hadfield, M., Tolley, H., & Beresford, J. (2000). *Leading schools in times of change*. Buckingham: Open University Press.

Department for Education and Employment. (1999). *The National Numeracy Strategy: Framework for Teaching Mathematics from Reception to Year 6*. London: Department for Education and Employment.

Department of Education and Science/Welsh Office. (1982). *Mathematics Counts: report of the Committee of Inquiry into the Teaching of Mathematics in Schools*. London: Her Majesty's Stationery Office.

Department of Education, Training and Youth Affairs. (2000). *Numeracy, a priority for all: challenges for Australian schools*. Canberra: Department of Education and Youth Affairs.

Dickson, M., Gewirtz, S., Halpin, D., Power, S., & Whitty, G. (2003). Education Action Zones: model partnerships? In B. Franklin, M. Bloch, & T. S. Popkewitz (Eds.), *Educational Partnerships: Democracy, Citizenship, and Salvation in a Globalized World*. New York: Palgrave Macmillan.

Earl, L., Fullan, M., Leithwood, K., Watson, N., with Jantzi, D., Levin, B., & Torrance, N. (2000). *Watching and Learning. OISE/UT Evaluation of the implementation of the National Literacy and Numeracy Strategies. First annual report*. Toronto: Ontario Institute for Studies in Education, University of Toronto.

Er-sheng, D. (1999). Mathematics Curriculum Reform Facing the New Century in China. In Z. Usiskin (Ed.), *Developments in School Mathematics Education Around the World. Proceedings of the Fourth UCSMP International Conference on Mathematics Education* (Vol. 4, pp. 58-70). Reston, VA: National Council of Teachers of Mathematics.

Eraut, M. (1994). *Developing professional knowledge and competence*. London: Falmer Press.

Franke, M. L., Carpenter, T. P., Levi, L., & Fennema, E. (2001). Capturing Teachers' Generative Change: A Follow-up Study of Professional Development in Mathematics. *American Educational Research Journal, 38*(3), 653-689.

Fullan, M. (2001). *The new meaning of educational change. Third Edition*. New York: Teachers College Press.

Goodson, I. F., & Hargreaves, A. (Eds.). (1996). *Teachers' Professional Lives*. London: Falmer Press.

Gray, J. (2001). Introduction: building for improvement and sustaining change in schools serving disadvantaged communities. In M. Maden (Ed.), *Success against the odds – five years on* (pp. 1-39). London: RoutledgeFalmer.

Guba, E. G., & Lincoln, Y. S. (1985). *Effective evaluation*. San Francisco, CA: Jossey-Bass.

Guskey, T. R. (1995). Professional development in education: in search of the optimal mix. In T. R. Guskey & M. Huberman (Eds.), *Professional development in education: new paradigms and practices* (pp. 114-131). NY: Teachers College Press.

Guskey, T. R., & Huberman, M. (1995). *Professional development in education: new paradigms and practices*. New York: Teachers College Press.

Hashimoto, Y. (1999). The Latest Thinking in Japanese Mathematics Education: Creating Mathematics Curricula For All Students. In Z. Usiskin (Ed.), *Developments in School Mathematics Education Around the World. Proceedings of the Fourth UCSMP International Conference on Mathematics Education* (Vol. 4, pp. 50-57). Reston, VA: National Council of Teachers of Mathematics.

Her Majesty's Inspectorate. (1992). *Mathematics key stages 1, 2 and 3: a report by HM Inspectorate on the second year 1990-1991*. London: Her Majesty's Stationery Office.

Hopkins, D. (2001). *School improvement for real*. London: Routledge.

Joyce, B., Calhoon, E., & Hopkins, D. (1999). *The new structure of school improvement: inquiring schools and achieving students*. Buckingham: Oxford University Press.

Joyce, B., & Showers, B. (1995). *Student achievement through staff development*. NY: Longmans.

King, B., & Newmann, F. (2000). Will teacher learning advance school goals? *Phi Delta Kappen, 8*(8), 576-580.

Lave, J., & Wenger, E. (1991). *Situated Learning: legitimate peripheral participation*. Cambridge, England: Cambridge University Press.

Leithwood, K., Jantzi, D., & Mascall, B. (1999). *Large-Scale Reform: What Works? Submitted as part of the first annual report: External Evaluation of the UK National Literacy and National Numeracy Strategy*. Ontario: Ontario Institute for Studies in Education, University of Toronto.

Louis, K. S., & Kruse, S. (1995). *Professionalism and community in schools*. Newbury Park, CA: Corwin.

Maden, M. (Ed.). (2001). *Success against the odds – five years on*. London: RoutledgeFalmer.

Millett, A. (1998). Expectations of the primary maths co-ordinator: demands and tensions within the role. *Teacher Development, 2*(2), 235-249.

Millett, A., & Johnson, D. C. (2000). The role of the maths co-ordinator and the National Numeracy Strategy in England. *Teacher Development, 4*(3), 393-410.

Ministry of Education. (1997). *Report of the Mathematics and Science Taskforce*. Wellington, NZ: Ministry of Education.

Ministry of Education. (2001a). *Curriculum Update 45: The Numeracy Story*. Wellington, NZ: Learning Media.

Ministry of Education. (2001b). *Early Numeracy Project*. Wellington, NZ: Learning Media.

Miwa, T. (1991). School mathematics in Japan and the US: focusing on recent trends in elementary and lower secondary school. In I. Wirszup & R. Streit (Eds.), *Developments in School Mathematics*

Education Around the World, Volume Three. Reston, VA: National Council of Teachers of Mathematics.

National Council of Teachers of Mathematics. (1989). *Curriculum and evaluation standards for school mathematics*. Reston, VA: National Council of Teachers of Mathematics.

National Council of Teachers of Mathematics. (2000). *Principles and Standards for School Mathematics*. Reston, VA: National Council of Teachers of Mathematics.

Nias, J., Southworth, G., & Campbell, P. (1992). *Whole school curriculum development in the primary school*. London, UK: Falmer Press.

Pollard, A. (2001). *Possible consequences of strong constraints on teachers and pupils: some fuzzy generalisations from the PACE project*. Paper presented at the American Educational Research Association, Seattle.

Rhodes, V., & Millett, A. (2001, September). *'Scheme-driven' or 'scheme-assisted'? How has the National Numeracy Strategy affected the use of commercial mathematics schemes in the primary school?* Paper presented at the British Educational Research Association Conference, 13-15 September, University of Leeds.

Richardson, V., & Placier, P. (2001). Teacher Change. In V. Richardson (Ed.), *Handbook of Research on Teaching. Fourth Edition* (pp. 905-947). Washington DC: American Educational Research Association.

Robitaille, D. F., & Garden, R. A. (Eds.). (1989). *The IEA Study of Mathematics II: Contexts and Outcomes of School Mathematics*. Oxford: Pergamon Press.

Secada, W. G., & Adajian, L. B. (1997). Mathematics Teachers' Change in the Context of their Professional Communities. In E. Fennema & B. S. Nelson (Eds.), *Mathematics Teachers in Transition* (pp. 193-219). Mahwah, NJ: Lawrence Erlbaum Associates, Inc.

Shulman, L. (1986). Those who understand: knowledge growth in teaching. *Educational Researcher, 15*(2), 4-14.

Sikes, P., J, Measor, L., & Woods, P. (1985). *Teacher careers: crises and continuities*. London: Falmer Press.

Southworth, G. (1998). *Leading improving primary schools*. London: Falmer Press.

Spillane, J. P. (1999). External reform initiatives and teachers' efforts to reconstruct their practice: the mediating role of teachers' zones of enactment. *Journal of Curriculum Studies, 31*(2), 143-175.

Stein, M. K., & Brown, C. (1997). Teacher Learning in a Social Context: Integrating Collaborative and Institutional Processes with the Study of Teacher Change. In E. Fennema & B. S. Nelson (Eds.), *Mathematics Teachers in Transition* (pp. 155-191). Mahwah, NJ: Lawrence Erlbaum Associates, Inc.

Stein, M. K., Silver, E. A., & Smith, M. S. (1998). Mathematics Reform and Teacher Development: a Community of Practice Perspective. In J. G. Greeno & S. V. Goldman (Eds.), *Thinking Practices in Mathematics and Science Learning* (pp. 17-52). Mahwah, NJ: Lawrence Erlbaum Associates, Inc.

Tharp, R., & Gallimore, R. (1988). *Rousing minds to life: Teaching, learning and schooling in social context*. Cambridge: Cambridge University Press.

Thompson, A. G. (1992). Teachers' beliefs and conceptions: a synthesis of the research. In D. A. Grouws (Ed.), *Handbook of research on mathematics teaching and learning: a project of the National Council of Teachers of Mathematics* (pp. 127-146). New York, NY: Macmillan.

Volmink, J. D. (1999). School Mathematics and Outcomes-Based Education: A View from South Africa. In Z. Usiskin (Ed.), *Developments in School Mathematics Education Around the World. Proceedings of the Fourth UCSMP International Conference on Mathematics Education* (Vol. 4, pp. 84-95). Reston, VA: National Council of Teachers of Mathematics.

Vygotsky, L. S. (1978). *Mind in Society: The Development of Higher Psychological Processes*. Cambridge, MA: Harvard University Press.

Zeichner, K. M., & Gore, J. (1990). Teacher socialisation. In W. R. Houston (Ed.), *Handbook of Research on Teacher Education* (pp. 329-348). New York, NY: Macmillan.

Zhang, D. (1991). Some puzzling questions arising from mathematics education in China. In I. Wirszup & R. Streit (Eds.), *Developments in School Mathematics Education Around the World, Volume Three*. Reston, VA: National Council of Teachers of Mathematics.

ALISON MILLETT AND DAVID C. JOHNSON

CHAPTER 2

THE ROLE OF THE MATHEMATICS CO-ORDINATOR: A SOURCE OF IN-SCHOOL SUPPORT

Abstract. In this chapter mathematics co-ordinators (subject leaders) in primary schools take central place, with their own personal resources, expertise and attitudes relating to mathematics development. In their attempts to initiate, implement and sustain change in the teaching of mathematics in their schools the co-ordinators make decisions about appropriate ways of working and themselves learn from interacting with others. The contribution of co-ordinators to the realisation of *zones of enactment* through which teachers can engage with change is the key element in this chapter, together with the factors that facilitate or inhibit this development. Co-ordinators are enabled or constrained by the level of support and resourcing they receive from their school *situation*, the wider network of *external professionals*, and national *policy* interventions. Also explored are the ways in which different co-ordinators in six schools carry out their roles, their effectiveness in initiating change, the characteristics which appear to affect their success as agents of change and the nature of this source of in-school support.

1. INTRODUCTION

In Chapter 1 we drew attention to the importance of the *zone of enactment*, the area of potential development where individuals "notice, construe, construct and operationalize" reform ideas (Spillane, 1999, p. 144). In this chapter we focus on the most immediate source of professional development in mathematics for the primary teacher – the primary mathematics co-ordinator or subject leader. We consider the co-ordinator's role as exemplifying a source of in-school support, developed and extended over several decades, and considered to have value in the English primary school. We ask how this particular source of support can affect teachers' *zones of enactment* and make a difference to their ability to make identifiable changes in their classroom practice.

Alison Millett, Margaret Brown and Mike Askew (eds.), Primary Mathematics and the Developing Professional.

The role of the co-ordinator or subject leader has grown over recent years in the English primary (elementary) school as a way of providing in-school support to classroom teachers. The introduction of the National Curriculum in England and Wales brought with it the need for schools to cope with increased subject content. The enlargement of some subjects which had in the past been regarded as fairly peripheral in the primary school, meant that it became common to find all teachers in a school holding responsibility for a subject. More and more teachers were required to provide subject expertise and to manage the resourcing and planning of their subject across the school.

An additional constraint, introduced in 1994, was the system of Office for Standards in Education (Ofsted) inspections. The stated purpose of this government funded inspection agency is to:

> identify strengths and weaknesses in schools so that they may improve the quality of education offered and raise the standards achieved by their pupils. (Office for Standards in Education, 1994, p. 5)

During an inspection the subject co-ordinator is required to present an overview of what had been done in the school and justify plans for future action. Thus inspections have increased the degree of accountability in the role. This has resulted in a move away from a developmental model of co-ordination concerned with the process of change (Osborn & Black, 1994) to a more supervisory role concerned with the products of nationally imposed reforms (Millett & Johnson, 2000a[1]).

Over and above this, co-ordinators responsible for mathematics during the later part of the 1990s were expected to keep abreast of policy developments such as the National Numeracy Project (which acted as a pilot for the later Strategy), and issues being debated nationally such as standards of attainment in numeracy and the need for an increased focus on mental mathematics (see Introduction). The introduction in England of the National Numeracy Strategy in September 1999 raised the demands of the role still further to include subject consultancy at a high level, with an emphasis on monitoring, evaluating and changing the practice of others.

Although the job specification of a co-ordinator might vary from school to school, the following duties, which would almost always be in addition to full-time class teaching duties, might be allocated in a school with high expectations of the role:

- organisation and facilitation of the use of mathematics materials and resources
- production of school mathematics curriculum documents

- provision of subject leadership and consultancy
- provision of in-class support
- monitoring and evaluation
- initiation of change and response to reform initiatives
- organisation and delivery of continuing professional development activities.

Co-ordinators may therefore be both colleague and expert; peer-coach and evaluator; initiator and a mediator of change for others as well as implementer of change in their own classrooms.

1.1. The research

This chapter is based on data collected for the Focus Project *Whole School Action on Numeracy* (see Introduction/Annex 3). This research project, conducted from September 1997 to August 2001, was concerned with the effect of whole-school action in the area of numeracy within the ever increasing demands of government policies – from the National Curriculum, national assessments at ages 7 and 11, to the more recent National Numeracy Strategy.

The research focused on six primary schools (see Annex 3) as they prepared for, experienced and followed up an inspection carried out during 1998 by the Office for Standards in Education (Ofsted). The research continued for a total of four years, during which the National Numeracy Strategy was introduced at the beginning of the third year, in September 1999. Data collection focused particularly on the mathematics co-ordinator and her effect on classroom teachers. The need to develop mathematics had been identified in all six schools before the start of the implementation of the National Numeracy Strategy, and the schools were attempting to meet this need in a variety of ways. The research team made judgements about the existence and effectiveness of change from analysis of:

- perceptions of those in the schools established through ongoing interviews
- observation of a selection of lessons over the course of the four years
- trends in the schools' national test results at age 11.

1.2. Questions posed about the role of the mathematics co-ordinator

For the majority of classroom teachers, a key influence on their mathematics teaching is interaction with the mathematics co-ordinator. This influence may relate to new or ongoing development activities initiated within the school, or to response to external reform initiatives. In order to assess the impact of this particular source of support on the engagement of classroom teachers with change, we looked at the actions taken by the mathematics co-ordinators studied during our research, and asked the following questions about their work with the teachers in their schools:

- how did their ways of working help to influence the *zones of enactment* of their colleagues
- were they effective in bringing about change
- what were the factors that influenced their effectiveness?

We address these three questions in the sections that follow.

2. INFLUENCING ZONES OF ENACTMENT

We look first at the contexts within which the co-ordinators in our six schools were attempting to initiate change. Competing external pressures faced the schools during the first two years of the research (1997-1999). Each school had undergone an Ofsted inspection, and was under an obligation to produce an 'action plan' to address issues raised by the inspectors. However, although all the schools had made the decision to make mathematics development a priority, the results of their inspections raised other key issues that the schools were expected to address. In only one case was the development of mathematics made a priority by inspectors. In two other cases, the schools decided to address their more general key issues (for example a requirement to develop monitoring practice) through the subject area of mathematics. By the time the other three schools were inspected, the imminent introduction of the National Numeracy Strategy was overtaking them and demanding the mathematics co-ordinators' attention (Millett & Johnson, 2000b). The schools were therefore under different constraints as they attempted to rationalise these conflicting priorities.

When the Strategy was introduced in September 1999, the mathematics co-ordinators were responsible for leading in-service training for teachers in their schools. As we have seen in the Introduction, the content and materials to support the in-service training were provided by the Numeracy Strategy, as was an initial Three-day course for co-ordinators, headteachers and school governors. The mathematics co-ordinators observed during this research working in their role as 'educationalist' (Campbell, 1985) were required to absorb what was presented to them in their own training, and then present this to colleagues.

During the four years of *Whole School Action on Numeracy*, 12 individuals occupied the role of mathematics co-ordinator across the six schools (all women except for two men who also occupied the role of deputy head, with one going on to become headteacher by the end of the research). Some occupied the role for only short periods of time or with responsibility for only one Key Stage (ages 5-7 or 7-

11). At a later stage in the research, one co-ordinator in a small school was also the headteacher. In the extracts from the data that follow, all quotations are from interviews with mathematics co-ordinators, unless otherwise indicated.

"Teachers' zones of enactment refer to the space in which they make sense of, and operationalize for their own practice, the ideas advanced by reformers" (Spillane, 1999, p. 159). We consider now the work of the co-ordinators in our research, and their taking a mediating role between classroom teachers and change initiatives. At the beginning of the research, these initiatives were based on policy decisions made within the schools, but these were quickly superseded by the introduction of the National Numeracy Strategy in 1999. To structure this section, we use Spillane's (1999) three essential characteristics of the *zone of enactment* – rich deliberations, grounded in practice and supported by resources.

2.1. Creating opportunities for 'rich deliberations' with individuals and groups

In terms of individual abilities to change practice, 'capacity' in Leithwood, Jantzi and Mascall's terms (1999), some co-ordinators were able to articulate clearly their vision for ways of working with teachers to encourage preferred courses of action. Three co-ordinators working during the first 18 months of the research described the ways of working they intended to use. These three co-ordinators showed what we have described as *clarity of vision* in decisions about how to work with colleagues. One co-ordinator described her approach as follows:

> I've tried to pace people and I've tried to be very sensitive to those people who are generally always more resistant to change and I've tried to disarm them at the very beginning. So when they have immediately said to me well, you know, 'oh I've tried that 20 years ago and that never works' or 'I've never used that strategy because this is what happens and the government are only going to do this again'. And I immediately pace them and I'll say 'yes, you are right, that did happen, that could happen again', and 'yes that's what happened, isn't it bloody awful, however ...'. So I'm actually acknowledging all of the negative stuff as well and hopefully taking them on very gently to explore other avenues without actually instructing and dictating to them saying to them 'look I know best' because that isn't the way, even with children. (Clare)

She left messages on the staffroom notice board giving times when she was available and reported that this invitation had been taken up.

> I spoke with staff at the beginning of term about being available and being given quite a substantial amount of release time this term and offered my services in various ways and a few people have come forward asking me for support with lots of different things, and I've been into two classrooms just purely for numeracy hours just to model a lesson. (Clare)

Another co-ordinator, coming new to a school, anticipated using strategies that had been successful at his previous school.

> I went through a period of monitoring in my previous school and during the monitoring process you saw the difference in particular members of staff. Because it was over a four-week session – like they'd do the first session and we'd have feedback on it – this was after doing an initial questionnaire and then I would take the second and third weeks and they'll take the fourth week – and that fourth-week session for them was a lot better than the first session I would have seen. And members of staff would come to me with feedback and say 'I'm doing such and such now and I'm doing such and such' and it was much more than they were doing before .... (Eric)

The three co-ordinators indicated their awareness of having to make fine judgements about the best ways of approaching other teachers. Different stages in career, different professional foci, different beliefs and values, different interpretations of events, might lead to a minimal overlap between teachers' *zones of enactment* in any one school and had to be taken into account. They expended a great deal of energy in determining the best ways of working, and described different approaches being successful with different teachers. This was a learning experience for them. They made mistakes and reflected on these. Two of the three co-ordinators tackled individual difficulties as school difficulties in staff meetings, and thus avoided any embarrassment for individual teachers.

During the first 18 months of the research, co-ordinators at the three other schools did not exhibit this *clarity of vision* about ways of working with other teachers. By the end of this timespan, all three had relinquished the role and had been replaced. We will return to the reasons for this later in the chapter, and in Chapter 3. After the introduction of the National Numeracy Strategy in 1999, co-ordinators in five of the six schools appeared to have clear ideas about choosing ways to work with colleagues, sometimes working with individuals, sometimes with groups. Strategies for creating opportunities for dialogue were in evidence.

Millett (1996), reporting on earlier case-study research, identified teachers who responded positively on an individual basis, but were unable to participate in larger gatherings such as in-service training (Inset) meetings. One of our co-ordinators, noticing a similar situation, realised an individual approach was called for in a particular case:

> So I spoke to her [Year 3 teacher, pupils aged 7-8 years] and said, you know, 'you find English easy to do and yes so you are struggling with the mathematics' and she actually said 'I can't do it and it's hard' and whatever and I said 'well the same enthusiasm that you have for English I have for the mathematics but if there are certain areas that you do find extremely difficult, speak to me about them'. And in fact she did come and speak to me about certain things, 'I'm doing this with my children and this is what they told me

> and this is what I told them, have I told them the right thing' and I was able to say, 'yes you have', and that sort of boosted the confidence a bit more and enabled her to come to me on another occasion. (Eric)

The Year 3 teacher referred to here described to us a situation in her own classroom where she felt able to request the expertise of the co-ordinator on the spot, illustrating her confidence in the 'educationalist' relationship (Campbell, 1985) he had built up.

> I've asked Eric to come in a couple of times in the autumn term just either to look at me to make sure I was doing the right thing or he's come in and he's done a bit of a lesson. Yesterday he happened to be in my room on the computer and I was doing patterns with them and I suddenly, actually I suddenly got lost myself so I said 'what is happening here' and he jumped up and joined in, so that was nice. (Year 3 teacher, pupils aged 7-8 years)

The chosen way of working of another co-ordinator took the form of a mathematics surgery – a regular time each week when teachers could come for help informally from the co-ordination team that had recently been established (see also Section 4.3.).

Co-ordinators also made decisions about how their Inset sessions should be presented, based on their knowledge of the teachers involved. One co-ordinator, working with a group of keen, outspoken and knowledgeable staff discounted a 'transmission' approach to dissemination and presented herself as having views to share, rather than to deliver. She told them about her perceptions.

> No, the stand we've taken at the moment is that I've been doing Inset telling people sort of how I perceive it [the National Numeracy Strategy] should be and then people at the moment, we are taking it on but we're trialling it more than anything still. (Jodie)

The teachers in this school were encouraged to debate issues and appeared happy to put forward fairly contentious views in Inset sessions.

Teachers in another school, where a new and more experienced co-ordinator had taken over the role, felt able to insist upon discussion and clarification. They questioned various aspects of things recommended by the Strategy.

> Teacher 1: There are some contradictory statements in here ... Thou shalt not move on until thou hast done this ... but it also says don't be too hard and fast ... .
>
> Teacher 2: I had problems understanding this. So I spoke to [the mathematics co-ordinator] and she said move on then you can come back and revisit it. So I did and it seemed to work. They do understand a bit more each time you revisit it. (Fieldnotes, Inset meeting)

In an Inset meeting at another school, the co-ordinator used the strategy of presenting herself as a learner alongside her colleagues:

> The morning had a good feel to it. Teachers were willing to discuss although there was not a great deal of feedback asked for, and were on task for the whole session. [The mathematics co-ordinator]'s manner was quite brisk and matter-of-fact, but she shared her predecessor's strategy of making plain her own faults, where she felt she didn't do things particularly well. (Fieldnotes, Inset meeting: comments of the observer)

This co-ordinator described her anxieties about getting the approach with colleagues just right.

> I hope people find that I'm quite approachable, I mean [one teacher] came to me and said, 'will you come in and watch'. The only thing I'm a bit concerned about is I'm quite – I want to do things well and I don't know whether I'm going to push people too much and say 'you should be doing this, you should be doing that'. I don't feel like I know everything about the Framework and what everyone should be doing. I mean sometimes people ask me a question and I'll say, 'I don't know, but I'll try and find out'. (Abbie)

Others were observed using the strategy of personal legitimation, described by McNamara and Corbin (2001) as an "essential element of the armoury" (p. 275), exemplifying new developments from their own classroom practice.

However, to the researcher observing these Inset sessions, some appeared quite patchy, providing richness for some teachers, some of the time. On one occasion, two teachers dominated a discussion about whole-class teaching that did not appear to involve many of the other teachers present. On another occasion when the co-ordinator adopted a transmission mode of delivery, reading through overhead transparencies provided in the training pack, interaction with the audience was restricted.

> This was a heavily 'led' day. Very much 'by the book'. It was not enlivened by the co-ordinator with examples of practice. Apart from the outbursts from [two teachers] about what education was coming to, there was little real feedback. (Fieldnotes, Inset meeting; comments of the observer)

In contrast:

> Juliet [co-ordinator] had selected the overheads and used them sparingly. Resources were displayed and were talked about enthusiastically. The end of the first half of term was a good time to have the day as the teachers had experiences to draw on, but were only just beginning to fully implement the mathematics lesson. [...] The headteacher said to me afterwards that she was very aware of the large degree of expertise needed by teachers to run this sort of Inset. (Fieldnotes, Inset meeting; comments of the observer)

One co-ordinator managed to induct others into developing their own skills in delivering Inset sessions.

> I said 'well, you know, maybe you can give me a hand there', because she knows more about Reception [pupils aged 5-6 years] than I do. She said 'but you know more about mathematics than I do' so maybe we'll do a joint one. (Abbie)

This joint session resulted in substantial learning about the needs and priorities of different age groups, according to the co-ordinator.

> We didn't get through everything that I'd planned to do but it was really valuable just to have some time and to sort of, not decide completely what we were going to do, but get a better understanding of where we were going and what we were trying to do and also to try and, I'm not very good at this, but trying to get some more practical stuff into Year 1 so that we weren't always sitting down, we were getting up and doing things. So it was useful joining with the early years people. (Abbie)

2.2. *Grounding reform ideas in classroom practice*

Although many of the individual and group discussions exemplified above were based around classroom practice, they were to some extent distant from the classroom. The National Numeracy Strategy, however, provided an entitlement for all teachers to have the opportunity to actually see a numeracy lesson being taught, either in their own school, or through visiting a 'leading mathematics teacher' in another school (these were teachers identified as successful and given extra training by the Local Education Authority as part of the National Numeracy Strategy, see Introduction). Co-ordinators working in an exemplary role in the classrooms of colleagues face judgement in terms of their skills and effectiveness. Not only must co-ordinators be seen to be successful in terms of their own class teaching and in their role as subject consultants, but they must also be able to exhibit those interpersonal skills which enable advice to be given and taken without loss of face on either side and create an atmosphere where such advice will be freely sought.

The National Numeracy Strategy also provided funding for the provision of monitoring by co-ordinators of colleagues' classroom practice. Having realised that some classroom teachers were feeling threatened and anxious about the proposed observation and monitoring of their teaching, several co-ordinators made the decision to provide demonstration lessons before starting their monitoring duties.

> That was part of the thinking really that I'd do demonstrations first so at least it showed that I don't mind people watching me. (Hannah)

For some co-ordinators, these demonstration lessons were extremely stressful. Several teachers at a time could be watching, and the co-ordinator might have to take an unfamiliar age group. One kept her own class after consultation with other teachers.

Another described her anxiety stemming from just this situation:

> ... because I've never taught infants [pupils aged 5-7 years] before. I don't mind people coming in and watching me so much, I'm quite used to that now, but it was quite hard work doing the other because you had to make sure everything was right and organised. (Hannah)

One co-ordinator displayed an awareness that demonstration lessons should be opportunities for discussion as well as observation to make them a useful learning experience.

> But we felt that discussion was really important as well. It was stupid just going to see a lesson and then going away, as much for the teacher that was teaching it to say 'I did that because ...', but I've got to point out that it's supposed to be a positive thing and we're not going in there as inspectors we're going in there to work together really. (Abbie)

The fact that many teachers observed other teachers in their own schools helped to break down the "norm of privacy" (Spillane, 1999, p. 164) that has been so prevalent in school cultures (Hargreaves, 1992), and to create a more open atmosphere about changes in practice. One co-ordinator described how her observation of a colleague's lesson led to the identification of a problem that could be worked on.

> It was interesting to see how different people taught maths and approached it ... and also where people need support. Like one member of staff, the activity that she was doing was really good, but her children were finding difficulty with her practical apparatus, because she hadn't thought that through, but all the rest of it was good but it was getting people to think 'well how can I make that easier for that particular group of children, do I have to do it in the same, do we have to do it in the same way for the whole class'. (Juliet)

Monitoring of practice could provide opportunities for in-depth discussion about practice, or it could be a source of anxiety; many teachers feel defensive about being monitored by colleagues. In one school, monitoring and lesson observation were already firmly established by the co-ordinator in the role of 'critical friend' before the National Numeracy Strategy was formulated. However, another co-ordinator was struggling with the awareness that, with the increased accountability of the Numeracy Strategy came a move from the 'critical friend' to a much more judgmental, monitoring role.

> We made sure that when everybody went into another class it wasn't going to be critical it was going to be looking for the positive and helping each other. I think I've got to make sure that my monitoring is like that as well, but you've also got to pick up on things that aren't going well. I think it's slightly different isn't it? (Abbie)

Even-handed discussions did not necessarily result from monitoring, even if the co-ordinator was teaching alongside rather than observing.

> It requires a confident staff for me to go in and team teach and, it needs a good working relationship with the other teacher for me to be able to say maybe you should do it like that or could do it like that and for them to say well actually my class does this, this, we've done it like this. But it's worked well here, with everyone I've worked with. (Jodie)

2.3. *Providing new materials and artefacts*

Spillane (1999) includes the support of resources as part of the process of ongoing deliberations within schools. Resources, or artefacts, have been given an extremely high profile in the examples of good practice promoted by the National Numeracy Strategy. Training videos, trainers' scripts, co-ordinators' presentations have recommended number lines, counting sticks, 100 squares, individual whiteboards, overhead projector calculators etc. In some in-service sessions, resources were used as a starting point for conversations about practice. However, one co-ordinator was disappointed that requests for assistance remained at the level of resources and never got beyond this, almost creating a barrier to richness, rather than promoting it, "It's more 'can I have this, can I have that?'" (Hannah). Another had responded to requests for help in using resources:

> And I've actually asked them where they want support, what they want to talk about and it's, I mean a lot of it is things like using resources with a mental and oral starter is the most problematic. [...] It's that people are still finding difficult, trying to make the mental and oral starter catching and riveting. But when you are delivering the same thing day after day, you know, to find different ways of doing it. We've found a few but that, I mean that I think that's where – not so much with the main teaching but getting, varying the oral and mental starter and using the resources to do it. (Juliet)

The National Numeracy Strategy was not so positive about the use of commercially produced texts for the teaching of mathematics, as will be discussed further in Chapter 4. However, discussion and trialling of materials to be used for planning and for classroom activities provided another avenue for dialogue, particularly when teachers were planning collaboratively across year groups.

2.4. *Summary*

In this section we have looked at some of the decisions made by co-ordinators about facilitating colleagues' change and the ways in which they have set about putting those decisions into operation. In three schools initially, and later in another two, the co-ordinator in post at the time appeared to be making clear choices about ways to initiate debate and discussion, firstly about the school's own priorities for change, and later about the implementation of the Numeracy Strategy itself. We have called this *clarity of vision*. We have noted the different ways in which they chose to run meetings, work with individuals, engage in demonstrating or monitoring classroom practice and use materials as a focus for discussion, and the heavy demands these ways of working placed upon them in some cases. We now move on to consider their effectiveness as agents of change.

In Spillane's view (1999), if teachers are to change the core of their practice, the realisation of their *zones of enactment* will involve social interaction that includes rich deliberations based around the substance of change, grounded in practice and supported by resources. Having looked in this section as the ways in which mathematics co-ordinators in our research might be contributing to such realisation, we turn now to a consideration of the change that could be said to have taken place in the six schools studied.

3. EFFECTIVENESS IN BRINGING ABOUT CHANGE

In attributing to the co-ordinator an effect on the *zones of enactment* of the classroom teachers in our study, we need to consider the extent of change and the teachers' responses to the co-ordinators' mediation of change initiatives. We now look at evidence relating to the identification of change from interviews with members of the *professional community* (headteachers, co-ordinators, classroom teachers) in the six schools; from observations carried out during the research, and from national test results at age 11.

It should be noted that the changes being promoted by the National Numeracy Strategy were focused on a daily, three-part mathematics lesson (that included an oral/mental starter, direct interactive teaching in the main part of the lesson, and a plenary session), an increased focus on number and calculation and detailed planning using a week-by-week set of objectives (see Introduction).

During the four years of the research, there were nine headteachers in the six schools (one of whom was also the mathematics co-ordinator); 12 mathematics co-ordinators, one of whom was also the headteacher and one a temporary replacement for maternity leave; 24 class teachers, 11 of whom were also mathematics co-ordinators and 20 of whom were observed in the classroom.

3.1. Change as perceived by headteachers and co-ordinators

During September 1997-July 1999, the National Numeracy Strategy was on the horizon, but in the development stage, with frequent new drafts of the Framework document (Department for Education and Employment, 1999), containing learning objectives and exemplar outcomes (see Introduction), succeeding each other. Some of these drafts were available to, and distributed within schools, and two headteachers commented on their early adoption. Other issues affecting headteachers at this time were demands in terms of resourcing, with new commercially produced scheme materials, practical equipment and artefacts being suggested to resource the new Strategy.

The main concern of co-ordinators during this time was in responding to the need, emanating from the advisory service and national pronouncements on mathematics, to initiate changes in mental mathematics and noting how teachers were putting this into practice. The use of their commercial materials to support this need and the needs of the draft Framework was also noted as an aspect of change (see Chapter 4). Instances of better questioning of pupils, higher quality mathematics display and more requests for help and advice were also being reported. One co-ordinator felt that her early attempts to initiate dialogue were bearing fruit.

> I hear more mathematics talk from staff and I hear people discussing their mathematics lessons more often. People come to me and ask me for help more, and they don't seem to be embarrassed about asking for help with things. People will more readily share their ideas than they did. (Clare)

During the first and second year of the implementation of the National Numeracy Strategy (September 1999-July 2001), headteachers' attention was focused on four main areas of change: more direct teaching; changes in the use of commercially produced mathematics materials; more detailed planning, and higher expectations of pupils. Turning to co-ordinators, the following areas of change were mentioned by co-ordinators in all six schools:

- changes in the use of commercially produced mathematics materials
- more detailed planning
- changes in mental mathematics
- changes in use of resources.

As was the case with headteachers, opinions about the use of commercially produced mathematics materials (commonly known as schemes) were varied. One co-ordinator described resisting requests for more prescriptive materials across the board. In one school they were still making use of their previous materials as and when they fitted in, together with the purchase of a range of other materials. Co-ordinators in two other schools were presiding over a major purchase of new materials (see also Chapter 4).

Co-ordinators in all six schools described the introduction of a style of planning for the numeracy lesson that was more detailed than previous practice. This planning included a focus on the learning objectives from the Framework for teaching mathematics from Reception to Year 6 (Department for Education and Employment, 1999), produced by the National Numeracy Strategy.

Co-ordinators in all six schools also talked about changes in mental mathematics. Mental mathematics at the beginning of each lesson was occurring and differentiation was being noted by those co-ordinators able to monitor practice.

> The mental mathematics now is definitely moving and you can see evidence of it through planning and through work in all classes and the way the children respond to things, much more positive. (Marjorie, headteacher/mathematics co-ordinator)

By the second year of implementation, 2000-2001, the emphasis was on making mental mathematics more varied and interesting, now that it had been established as a part of the numeracy lesson. One co-ordinator described using support from her numeracy consultant (employed through the Local Education Authority with National Numeracy Strategy funding – see Introduction).

> Yes and I was finding that we were tending to do the same types of things – tending to use the same equipment as well so we wanted to see variety of work. So I went round with her and then at the end she did a staff meeting, so we went through all the games that they'd done and gave us lots of ideas and worksheets and things to make for them, it was very good. (Hannah)

Another co-ordinator described the changes she was trying to initiate:

> I think I would just like to see the mental developed more. I'm trying to get through to people that they can cover other areas other than just quick number bonds in that time. I've suggested that they actually do two activities in that time, just very short, and I also think the emphasis is on all the class joining in rather than just one person coming up and writing things on the board, or ten questions on the board. (Imogen)

As noted earlier, a range of resources and artefacts was suggested by the National Numeracy Strategy training, and co-ordinators were following up these suggestions and overseeing their use. They reported acquiring such items as number lines, one hundred squares, counting sticks, digit cards, 'follow-me' cards (a mental mathematics game sometimes known as the 'loop' game), individual pupil whiteboards and calculator transparencies for the overhead projector.

Co-ordinators in four schools reported change in the development of the plenary or final part of the daily mathematics lesson and the difficulties involved in getting this established. The plenary session was defined in the Framework document (Department for Education and Employment, 1999) as:

> work with the whole class to sort out misconceptions and identify progress, to summarise key facts and ideas and what to remember, to make links to other work and discuss the next steps, and to set work to do at home. (p. 13)

Other changes mentioned by at least four co-ordinators were teachers requesting help and advice with mathematics more; a delay in the introduction of written methods of calculation; more direct teaching; better pace in lessons and an improvement in pupil attainment evidenced not only in test results, but also from lesson observations and children's books.

3.2. Change as perceived by classroom teachers

In order to assess the impact of the co-ordinator on the practices of individual class teachers, we have also looked at the perceptions of the sample of teachers interviewed in the six schools. Between September 1997 and June 1999, the first important change in practice reported by classroom teachers in five schools was in mental mathematics. It should be noted here that an element of mental mathematics was included for the first time in the national tests at age 11 in 1998, before the National Numeracy Strategy raised its profile still further. In one school, teachers were describing teaching mental mathematics not only more frequently, but differently, focusing on teaching strategies for calculating which they might not have done in the past.

Those teachers in schools which had adopted the Framework early had started to use it for their planning; some teachers felt they were including more practical activities and games, and some that they were making changes in the structure of lessons – adopting a three-part structure – in advance of the implementation of the Strategy (see Introduction). More detailed planning was beginning to be seen as necessary, with a different role for the teacher in the classroom being implied by the National Numeracy Strategy. Two classroom teachers were also beginning to express anxieties about the plenary session – the third part of the recommended three-part lesson; others reported asking for help and advice.

During the period September 1999-June 2001, after the official introduction of the National Numeracy Strategy, classroom teachers in all six schools reported change in the following areas (in order of those most frequently reported):

- changes in mental mathematics
- change in the use of resources
- more detailed planning

• more revisiting of mathematics topics
• changes in the use of commercially produced mathematics materials.

The biggest change for the teachers who reported changes in mental mathematics was not necessarily in the amount, although most were doing more, but in the structure of their mental mathematics session. They had objectives for the mental mathematics session as well as for the main part of the lesson; they were more likely to be teaching mental strategies than previously; they were making use of different resources.

> I think for me that's the biggest change because I had been doing the mental mathematics bit to start with but maybe not as structured with as many objectives as the Numeracy Strategy asks. (Year 4 teacher, pupils aged 8-9 years)

Although concerns were voiced about differentiation in this session, there was a generally positive attitude to this change in practice, both pupils and teachers were enjoying it, and improvements in mental agility and recall were commented upon. "I like the mental mathematics at the beginning, and I wasn't doing much of that" (Year 6 teacher, pupils aged 10-11 years). Many of the new resources described were reported as being used in this part of the lesson. Several teachers reported favourably on the increased variety and availability of resources, but admitted that they were not all being used.

> We've used the number lines quite a lot with the children. Sometimes there's a lot of things – use these cards, use these [number] fans or whatever, well that's a bit, I haven't used a lot of cards and fans and so on. (Year 3 teacher, pupils aged 7-8 years)

Four teachers reported improvements in their own mental mathematics as a result of teaching the strategies suggested in the Framework. Jodie, a mathematics co-ordinator commenting in her other role as classroom teacher, reported that the increased emphasis on teaching mental strategies had affected her personal practice:

> I've started doing much more mental maths. I've also improved personally with my mental maths because of using the strategies. I definitely feel my mental maths has improved, so that's I think maybe my biggest area of change, mental maths. [...] I use the strategies, teach the children, use them myself now which I didn't before, I didn't know them, some of them. (Jodie)

The other aspects of change talked about more frequently by class teachers were related to the planning and the organisation of the curriculum. The planning was more detailed than they had been used to, focused on learning objectives, and took up a great deal of time. They were having to change their use of commercially produced materials – sometimes abandoning old materials, sometimes beginning to use new ones quite heavily (see also Chapter 4).

> ... before I got this scheme thing from [publisher] I'd say it was taking me probably about three to four hours just to plan my mathematics lessons and to prepare things for them which is just unworkable week in, week out. It was becoming an absolute nightmare. I mean now I've got that scheme it's better. [...] It gives you, you know, your oral starter, your main teaching things and it gives you tasks for them to do as well. (Year 3 teacher, pupils aged 7-8 years)

The way in which the mathematics curriculum was organised in the Framework was another major change for class teachers. Almost without exception, they had been used to spending up to half a term on a mathematics topic such as 'time' or 'shape and space', sometimes not returning to it again before the end of the year. The Framework was perceived as requiring frequent revisiting of topics throughout the year and, once having got used to it, most teachers appeared converted to this way of working.

> Whereas the numeracy at this stage, I mean maybe later on in the year I may change my mind, but at this stage it's more manageable and also it's, you know you are going to be revisiting so you don't feel quite so sort of despondent if you know that they definitely haven't grasped something, because in a few weeks or so or however you plan it, you are going to come back to it. (Year 1 teacher, pupils aged 5-6 years)

Other changes reported related to the need to give their attention to the plenary session, something they were finding difficult to implement fully, and to what they described as a faster pace in their lessons. Greater enthusiasm and feelings of confidence about mathematics from teachers themselves as well as from their pupils were among the more frequently mentioned aspects of change.

As we have seen from the example of Jodie (above), it was also the case that co-ordinators, working in their role as classroom teachers, made mention of changes in their practice. One of these co-ordinators in particular, Abbie, referred to a wide range of aspects of changed classroom practice over the course of several interviews. Apart from the increased amount of time spent on mathematics, she reported the introduction of different ways of recording, changes in mental mathematics, changes in curriculum structure, and higher expectations of her pupils who, she felt, were showing increased confidence and enthusiasm for mathematics.

3.3. Change attributable to the actions of the co-ordinator

Almost without exception, classroom teachers in these six schools were introduced to reform ideas, both before and after the introduction of the National Numeracy Strategy, through the actions of their co-ordinators. Whole-school Inset meetings, conducted by the co-ordinator, were their main source of information, apart, as we have seen, from individual interactions. The co-ordinator was therefore the essential mediator in how these reform ideas were taken up and implemented. Our focus in this chapter has been on the mathematics co-ordinators and their ways of working to develop individual teachers' *zones of enactment*. Just as individual co-ordinators exhibited different skills and adopted different strategies for encouraging change, so individual teachers responded in different ways to their co-ordinator.

In four schools, classroom teachers interviewed described how they were putting suggestions from co-ordinators into practice in the classroom. This teacher, for example, had used an idea presented at a meeting:

> That [classroom number line] was given out at the staff meetings yes, and I've asked for ideas on how to use that [...] Yes, and that [100 square] – I thought that was useful the way she was saying about starting at zero [0-99, rather than 1-100], it's just things that you don't think about until somebody mentions it to you and then you think 'gosh that's really obvious, it would be much more helpful'. (Year 5 teacher, pupils aged 9-10 years)

Another described the results of less formal interactions:

> Juliet's brilliant. If I am doing my planning and I wander in there and she goes 'come on let's have a look then' and we sit there and I'm looking at these objectives and thinking 'what am I going to do for this' and she goes 'oh how about this' ... she's got loads of ideas and things so I sort of ask her. (Year 5 teacher, pupils aged 9-10 years)

Asked about interaction with the co-ordinator, one Year 2 teacher (pupils aged 6-7 years) said:

> Oh God yes, yes all the time. I mean Abbie's only next door anyway but even over lunch time or break times I'll sort of say 'have you got any ideas about this or that', ... subtracting eleven and take away ten and then you take away one more and all that, I was really stuck for ideas and Abbie was a great help, you know, number lines and different sort of games you can play, so yes, very, very helpful.

New resources, particularly for mental mathematics were remarked on by another teacher.

> Yesterday Jodie was doing, you know the, I call them circle games but she says they are called loop games where everyone has a question and I just made one of those yesterday so I'll be interested to see how that's gone today. (Year 6 teacher, pupils aged 10-11 years)

In four schools there were examples of classroom teachers responding positively to ideas discussed with them either at meetings or individually, with informal, ongoing relationships characterising these examples. The Year 3 teacher receiving peer coaching from Eric in introducing the Strategy (see Section 2.1.) made frequent mention of his help in interview, and described increased feelings of confidence.

> I've explained things to the children and as I've explained how to do something I've thought 'oh yes, why didn't I know this before' but I obviously did know it because I'd

> explained it to children but I'd never had it explained in a sort of clear way just, so yes, I think it's [The National Numeracy Strategy] been very helpful to me. (Year 3 teacher, pupils aged 7-8 years)

In two of these four schools, all the teachers interviewed made mention of this subject consultancy. In all these situations, co-ordinators were creating opportunities to develop teachers' *zones of enactment*.

3.4. Challenges to the co-ordinator

We have seen from the examples of in-school meetings that some teachers questioned the merit of certain aspects of the reform ideas being promoted by the co-ordinator. This appeared to be more explicit at the beginning of the project as the Numeracy Strategy was being introduced and such questioning declined as teachers became more familiar with the reforms, but it may also be the case that this questioning was not so apparent to the researchers in the final year of the project as data collection diminished.

In the early stages of implementation, questions about the suitability of whole-class teaching recommended by the National Numeracy Strategy (see Introduction) for younger children (ages 5-7) and for children with special needs were raised by some teachers. One teacher interviewed expressed anger at being expected to implement whole-class teaching when she had found it totally unsuited to the range of attainment in her Year 6 class (pupils aged 10-11 years).

> I used to do whole-class mathematics teaching, start off and then going round and visit each group and I found it, to be absolutely frank, an absolute nightmare the further you get up the school. ... by the time they get up to this stage, they are at such vastly different things that to start from the same point seems ludicrous. I could not start, I could not think of a way of starting with this group at a single point. How could I?

The required detail of planning was another issue of concern.

> Sally [class teacher] complained about the amount of written planning you had to do. Sometimes it was too inflexible to have everything written down all the time. (Fieldnotes Inset Meeting)

Teachers in one school raised anxieties about the problem of more mental work meaning less written work in books, and how to explain this to parents. They were reassured by the co-ordinator that this was expected by policy-makers initiating the reform. Other questions raised related less to the specifics of the reform, and more to the effect that such a concentration on mathematics was having on the rest of the curriculum.

It was not the case, therefore, that goals were shared for all teachers from the beginning of implementation of the reform; however, disagreement could enhance the discussion as well as making it less productive. Efforts were generally made by co-ordinators to exemplify successful strategies and thus convince their colleagues. They could not always be said to have been successful.

> But no, I haven't really had a lot of communication with other members of staff about teaching maths. The person that I talk to probably mostly about maths is my Teaching Assistant who helps me in the classroom with maths and she has been an asset. (Year 6 teacher, pupils aged 10-11 years)

3.5. Change as perceived by the researchers from lesson observations

As outlined in Annex 3, 23 lesson observations were carried out in 1997/98, 25 in 1998/99 and 10 during the period 1999-2001, when the research focus had decreased in terms of researcher time. Observation evidence is reported here under the four main aspects of change observed:

- mental mathematics
- whole-class teaching
- the development of the plenary session at the end of the lesson
- use of resources.

Three time spans are referred to in this case, 1997/98, 1998/99 and 1999-2001, to reflect differences observed between 1997 and 1999.

3.5.1. Mental mathematics

Observation evidence would support the perception of an increased focus on mental mathematics, reported by both teachers and co-ordinators. The proportion of lessons with a dedicated mental/oral session (not always at the beginning of the lesson) rose between 1997/98 and 1998/99 from 39% (of 23 lessons) to 56% (of 25 lessons), and this session was a feature of eight out of the 10 lessons observed between 1999-2001. However, the nature and content of these sessions varied. During each time span, there were several examples of the more routine revision of number facts (e.g. in the use of the game Fizz-Buzz to revise multiplication facts, or quick-fire question and answer sessions where explanations of how answers were arrived at were not requested). There were also examples of a more demanding level of interaction, with a greater proportion of these being observed during the period 1998/99 than in the other two time spans.

3.5.2. Whole-class teaching

As early as 1997-99 (before the National Numeracy Strategy was introduced), the majority of lessons observed (75%) included teaching the whole class together and generally included teachers requesting contributions from pupils. In two thirds of these cases children were also asked to explain their methods or thinking, although such contributions and explanations could be very limited. After 1999, all the 10 lessons observed included teaching the whole class together, with pupils being asked for contributions and explanations.

3.5.3. The plenary session

An increased focus on implementing the plenary session was also supported by observation evidence. A plenary session was observed in about half of lessons in 1997/98, rising through 1998/99 to nine out of 10 lessons in 1999-2001. However, many of these sessions consisted of little more than children feeding back descriptions of what they had done, rather than what they had learnt, although there were examples that drew from the work done, or addressed problems that had arisen. In each time span about half the plenary sessions observed fell into each category.

3.5.4. Use of resources

Evidence for increased use of the resources and artefacts suggested in the National Numeracy Strategy was more patchy. Although many teachers had talked in interview about the availability and use of resources that they had not used before, these artefacts could not be said to be frequently used in the lessons observed. Number lines were observed in use twice (out of 23 lessons) in 1997/98, three times (out of 25 lessons) in 1998/99, and not at all in the 10 lessons observed in 1999-2001. Digit cards were observed in two lessons in 1998/99 and once in 1999-2001; the use of 100 squares increased slightly in the third time span; whiteboards and counting sticks began to be used during this time, not having been observed before. The 'follow-me' mental mathematics game (loop game) appeared to be more popular during 1997/98 and was not observed in subsequent years. It would appear that the reservations expressed by co-ordinators about whether these resources were continuing to be used were well founded and a continuing emphasis would be needed if their use was to be sustained over time and become part of routine practice.

3.6. *Change as measured by national test results at age 11*

Table 2.1. Percentages of pupils attaining Level 4 or above in national tests at age 11.

School	*1997*	*1998*	*1999*	*2000*	*2001*
Woodbury	46	47	62	84	79
The Grove	43	88	50	81	78
Maple	78	64	69	84	93
Pennington	61	39	37	55	71
Sandmere	81	23	23	56	39
Wolverton	33	62	78	84	57
National	62	59	69	72	71

Note. Results for The Grove should be viewed with extreme caution as numbers were extremely small and sometimes too small for national reporting

National test results of pupils gaining Level 4 or above at the age of 11 years were consulted as one of the three indicators of change discussed in this section. Table 2.1 shows national test results at age 11 for the six schools. (Results for The Grove do not form part of the discussion as numbers of pupils were extremely small.) Two of the three schools where co-ordinators exhibited enthusiasm for the role and clarity of vision at the beginning of the research made early gains in attainment results of pupils at age 11 (the third made a later start, but then steady progress). Schools where these characteristics were not in evidence were slower to make gains. All six schools made gains in the year of the introduction of the National Numeracy Strategy (1999/2000) when extra funding was made available for resources and training (See Introduction). Only two of these schools were able to sustain these gains the following year.

3.7. *Summary*

In this section we have seen that change was perceived at all levels within the *professional community* (headteachers, co-ordinators and classroom teachers), with similar aspects of change being identified particularly by co-ordinators and classroom teachers. The changes that appeared to be most in evidence in the classrooms observed during the research related to the more structural recommendations of the National Numeracy Strategy, such as the three-part lesson and the increased time spent on mental mathematics. Change was attributed to the influence of the co-ordinator in some schools more than others; those co-ordinators appeared to have found successful ways of creating dialogue with the particular colleagues in their schools. Test results at age 11 indicated that changes were associated with improvements in some schools over several years, whereas test results were erratic in other schools.

We focus next on a consideration of those factors arising during the research that appeared to influence the effectiveness of the co-ordinators in carrying out their roles.

4. FACTORS INFLUENCING EFFECTIVENESS

4.1. Characteristics of the people in the role

In terms of "personal resources" (Spillane, 1999, p. 169) the 12 individuals holding the co-ordination role varied widely both in qualifications in mathematics and teaching experience. Within this group of 12, one had a mathematics degree and two had studied mathematics as a main subject in their Education degree. One teacher had studied mathematics up to Advanced Level (age 18), and the rest up to Ordinary Level/General Certificate of Secondary Education (age 16). There were no substantial feelings expressed about lack of confidence in mathematics, although one co-ordinator made it plain that she was not a mathematics specialist. As a group these co-ordinators did not display the feelings of anxiety about mathematics common to many primary teachers (Bibby, 2002). Although some in this study had negative early experiences, these had been superseded by positive later experiences, sometimes through professional development, sometimes by inspiring teaching.

> I needed mathematics coaching at one stage because I had fallen behind and I just did it for a few weeks and she was brilliant and suddenly it all clicked, probably a year before I did my O Level mathematics [at age 16] everything clicked. (Jodie)

As regards professional development, two had completed diplomas in mathematics education and three a long mathematics in-service course (18-20 days). Six of the 12 were experienced in the mathematics co-ordination role, having held the post for several years, either in their current or previous school. Several of these co-ordinators had been teaching for many years. The least experienced co-ordinator was in her second year of teaching. This group of teachers thus had very different sets of circumstances from which to build up the "capacity beliefs" (Leithwood, Jantzi, & Mascall, 1999, p.10) of self-efficacy, self-confidence and academic self-concept described in Chapter 1.

Those co-ordinators who had had a certain degree of choice in becoming mathematics co-ordinator showed a high level of enthusiasm. Contrast these two teachers coming new to a school, both of whom took on the role of mathematics co-ordinator:

> But they did ask me at interview what I wanted to do. I wanted to do mathematics really because I said I had had lots of training in mathematics. I did a 20-day mathematics course as well. (Hannah)

> I applied for it because I wanted to get into a small village school and I wanted to be in a primary school, as opposed to an infant school. ... [Mathematics] was not necessarily part of the – it was a possibility on the application, it said, possibly doing mathematics. I think they were sort of looking for a person, rather than a mathematics person in particular. (Jenny)

All three co-ordinators who relinquished the post before the end of the second year of the research belonged to the group who had had little choice about taking on the role.

Enthusiasm for the role appeared to be linked not only to the way in which they had come into the post, which related to their own personal goals, but also to the extent to which they could envisage a course of action once they had made an assessment of their *situation* and decided what improvements to aim for. "Goals energise action only when a person's evaluation of present circumstances indicates that it is different from the desired state" (Leithwood et al., p. 9). Coming new to a school as a temporary replacement for the co-ordinator, Imogen felt:

> The enthusiasm I think particularly for the mental mathematics is sometimes a bit lacking in comparison to what I've seen ... that's something that I would like to have, you know, seen changed in the time that I've been here. (Imogen)

Another newly appointed co-ordinator described herself as "excited and pleased to be doing it" (Juliet).

The 12 co-ordinators interviewed for this project expressed some contrasting views about mathematics. For example, one co-ordinator regarded mathematics as:

> a nice subject to teach because there's a right and there's a wrong and I think in a way children like that, they know if they've got it right. (Jodie).

In contrast, another co-ordinator expressed approval of changes she was noticing:

> ... people have gradually started to change their belief about what mathematics should and shouldn't be. ... Whereas before, people were expecting themselves to get the right answer in a specific way ... that was in a sense dictating what went on in their own lessons, and consequently they were sometimes fearful of what the children were suggesting, whereas now it seems to be more of a free for all. It's not all the way there yet, but it's happening. (Clare)

This co-ordinator described a key result of her 20-day in-service course being a conviction that "mathematics can be one big wild party".

Although several of the co-ordinators found it difficult to articulate images of a desirable future state for the mathematics in the school, none expressed disagreement with the nature of the National Numeracy Strategy reform they were embarking upon. There was no suggestion that this direction was incompatible with their own goals which was perhaps surprising given their range of views about mathematics.

The responsibility of class teaching, carried by the great majority of mathematics co-ordinators in addition to their subject responsibility, can be a conflicting priority in terms of time and energy and in terms of professional identity. It is a responsibility felt to carry increasing demands since the introduction of the National Curriculum in 1989 (Pollard, Broadfoot, Croll, Osborn, & Abbott, 1994). Not only is a class responsibility seen to be an onerous and time-consuming one, but limited experience of teaching across the whole age-range in a school might be seen to affect the co-ordinator's confidence in her role as 'teacher as educationalist' (Campbell, 1985) and the confidence of her colleagues in advice and expertise proffered. Being a classroom teacher is a core aspect of a primary teacher's identity (Nias, 1989). Co-ordinators are first and foremost classroom teachers; they spend the majority of time with their pupils, experience frustration and achieve satisfaction through their interactions with them. They are judged by others on how successful they are in the classroom.

All of the co-ordinators who participated in this research project faced the demands of responsibility for their own class (there was one exception with a co-ordinator who worked part-time during the later stages). They valued this contact with pupils and used their classroom experience as a basis for helping others. They were aware that they could be regarded as exemplars as regards mathematics teaching. However, without exception, those involved in the project post-1999 felt that the Numeracy Strategy had been beneficial for their own teaching, and most described increased expectations of their pupils following the introduction of the Strategy. In this specific case, therefore, although their classroom responsibilities meant a heavy workload when combined with the co-ordination role, they felt that they were promoting changes in practice with which they were in agreement and were trying to implement in their own classrooms.

We turn now to the wider *situation,* to consider those factors beyond those related to the personal and professional characteristics of the co-ordinators that influenced the way in which they were able to carry out their role.

4.2. Influence of the professional community – the role of the headteacher

A job specification that outlines responsibilities without providing the resources to meet those responsibilities will be a source of strain to a co-ordinator (Campbell, 1985; Nias, Southworth, & Yeomans, 1989). There were contrasts for these co-ordinators in the *situations* in which they found themselves working, in the ways in which they were resourced for the role, both materially, and in terms of support.

In some schools it was noticeable that headteacher and co-ordinator had achieved what we have noted as a 'balanced' relationship where respect for the co-ordinator's judgement and expertise on the one hand was matched by an understanding of the head's priorities and recognition of their support. A situation of *balance* was likely to be associated with a high priority being given to resourcing the co-ordination role. (The role of the headteacher is considered further in Chapter 3.)

Although allocation of funds for the purchase of mathematics equipment and commercially produced materials formed part of the provision of resources, time out of the classroom (non-contact time) for the co-ordinator to observe or work with others was the key resource involved. In three schools priority was given by the headteacher to the provision of non-contact time and although it was sometimes under threat from the need to cover staff absences and other demands, every effort was made to maintain this resource for the co-ordinator. Before the introduction of the National Numeracy Strategy, during the first 18 months of the research in the other three schools, where there was little or no time allocated, the co-ordinators made reference to their lack of knowledge about what other teachers were doing.

> ... we haven't had the opportunity to get out of the classroom to go into other classes to see what they are doing, quite honestly. (Eileen)

> I'm not sure what they do in these two classes here, for mental mathematics. I have heard Sally talk about mental mathematics but I don't know if there's any sort of structure to it. (Jenny)

Where substantial monitoring time was provided, comments were positive and the idea of acting as a 'critical friend' (Osborn & Black, 1994) was suggested by one co-ordinator.

> The 'critical friend'. And going into classes is very much making it clear that I'm here to support as well as monitor, so I make an effort to try and help them with planning and think if I'm going in I make sure I try it with the class. I'm in Year 1 at the moment, I'm trying to work with one group and I'm helping with the planning and trying to take some of the burden off the teacher, so therefore even though I am monitoring there's also the advantage of me being there, taking off some of the workload. So I think that works well. (Jodie)

By the end of the third year of the research (1999-2000) it was observed that resources provided by the Numeracy Strategy had clearly pushed up the priority given to resourcing mathematics and made a difference to the way in which co-ordinators could carry out their role, although these resources were guarded more closely in some schools than in others.

4.3. Influence of the professional community – support from colleagues

During the course of the research the notion of co-ordinating teams was gaining favour in schools, vigorously encouraged by Local Education Authority numeracy consultants, and by the fourth year these teams were firmly established in four out of our six schools. One school was too small for this to be feasible, and the sixth school preferred a model of part-time co-ordinator without a class responsibility. The provision of two places on the Five-day intensive training courses (see Introduction and Chapter 5) meant that colleagues could attend together and mention was made of the value of this in four schools. All four schools with teams (pairs of teachers in three out of the four schools) combined expertise from both Key Stages (ages 5-7 and 7-11) in their teams. The stability of these teams was fragile in some cases, due to temporary contracts and other organisational difficulties, but the benefits of working together were being realised. These colleagues helped to develop the co-ordinator's own *zone of enactment*, providing expertise with other age groups, attending training alongside them and enabling joint reflection to develop ideas and practice. They could also share in the role of 'educationalist' (Campbell, 1985) at meetings and in individual coaching of colleagues. One co-ordinator described her team member being able to monitor and offer advice at Key Stage 1 (ages 5-7), as well as sharing the leadership of Inset sessions. Another had been developing this sharing of responsibility since the previous year.

4.4. Influence of external professionals and policy

The influences of *external professionals* (Local Education Authority advisers and inspectors, National Numeracy Strategy personnel) and the *policy*-makers (those writing and promoting the National Numeracy Strategy since 1997) have been closely interlinked. During the run-up to the Numeracy Strategy in 1997/98, co-ordinators in three schools who were well supported and resourced in their immediate *situation*, were able to take a proactive stance towards preparation in advance for the Numeracy Strategy, and had begun in some cases to use draft copies of the Framework (Department for Education and Employment, 1999) for their in-school planning. The co-ordinators in post in the summer of 1999 attended the initial Three-day Numeracy Strategy training delivered by their Local Education Authority (See Introduction). This training introduced groups of teachers, headteachers and school governors from all schools to the Numeracy Strategy. A Five-day course of training was also provided during 1999/2000 for some teachers in schools judged by the Local Education Authority to be in need of intensive support. One of our six schools was identified as fitting this category, and the co-ordinator and one other teacher attended the Five-day course during this year. In the following year the Five-day course provision was extended to a much broader band of schools and by the end of July 2001, all six schools had received this support that also included time allocated for a consultant (generally five days) to come into school and support the co-ordinator.

Additionally, advisory help from the Local Education Authority that was regularly available was, and continued to be, highly regarded. There were signs that Local Education Authorities that did not provide this help routinely were trying to develop more regular support for co-ordinators. This support generally took the form of afternoon/evening sessions for groups of co-ordinators to meet out of school on a regular basis to discuss issues of common concern and keep up to date with new developments.

The model of numeracy consultant support developed by the National Numeracy Strategy (see Introduction) was also widely appreciated by co-ordinators, who seemed to gain a feeling of security from knowing that there was someone they could contact if they needed advice:

> Yes and she came in and she came for the whole day and in the morning she did mental/oral starters, then she went round the school, she did all the year groups and she did twenty minutes of mental/oral.
>
> Interviewer: That was at your request wasn't it?
>
> Yes and I was finding that we were tending to do the same types of things – tending to use the same equipment as well so we wanted to see variety of work so I went round with her and then at the end she did a staff meeting, so she went through all the games that they'd done and gave us lots of ideas and worksheets and things to make for them. It was very good. (Hannah)

With very few exceptions, it was felt that consultants had fitted in extremely well to these varied schools and supported co-ordinators with great sensitivity. As one headteacher described her consultant's skills:

> ... yes we are still having her now in response to school needs as well as coming along with, because I know the Local Authority are very keen to develop this, this or this and

> the school wants to develop this, this or this and she's very good at gently marrying them together, so she's very good at working with the staff, she's doesn't go and say 'yes, but we are all going to talk about Year 5 questioning skills' or whatever the buzz word is at the time. She'll get her agenda in, but gently. (Headteacher)

With one exception, responses were positive to the work of the numeracy consultants. However, some rather negative messages were coming to the fore in relation to the inspection or monitoring role of Local Education Authority personnel. Co-ordinators felt responsible for the practice of other members of staff and could face criticism if it was found that teachers being monitored by Local Education Authority inspectors or advisers were not following the advice handed down at Inset meetings; in other words, not conforming with the required changes. The co-ordinator in this school described her feelings of accountability.

> Yes because I felt when she [the school development adviser] came in and there was, you know, the planning wasn't done right and I felt quite bad really because I should have been really looking at this and then saying, 'do it like this'. Nobody blamed me but I did feel that I should have done more really beforehand. I just presumed really that what we talked about in the training was happening and, of course, it wasn't in our case. And you think 'oh was that because I didn't explain it properly or was it because they don't care', so that was quite difficult. (Hannah)

Campbell (1985) described the role of "teacher as educationalist" as one "suffused with uncertainty, not because postholders themselves were necessarily uncertain, but because the activity itself was an ambiguous exercise" (Campbell, 1985, p. 68). He pointed to a mismatch between the formal status of co-ordinators (postholders in Campbell's terminology) as curriculum developers, and their actual power as perceived by themselves and their colleagues. A co-ordinator cannot 'make' other teachers adopt a new scheme of work, for example, or a change in practice. "Faced with passive resistance to innovation, the postholder was impotent" (Campbell, 1985, p. 72).

The co-ordinator in another school described two completely different approaches from attached inspectors:

> Well the assigned inspector [from the Local Education Authority] we have now he's very supportive. The one before was very critical. He's got such a way about him to put things across in such a positive way and make even the negative things seem acceptable so that people can still cope despite the fact that they've had a negative outcome at one particular session. [...]
>
> Yes and the good thing about it is giving a reason why, because he justifies himself and you can't really argue with something when the evidence is there and a justification is given. Whereas his predecessor she never gave a reason why, making it more difficult

> for the member of staff to accept. He actually gives a good reason why and supports it from what he sees in the classroom. (Eric)

Other co-ordinators did not report criticism that made them feel inadequate. One described being 'left alone' to get on with things.

Ofsted (2000) have also noted variation in levels and appropriateness of support from Local Education Authorities and have criticised some levels of support quite strongly. The National Association of Educational Inspectors, Advisers and Consultants is currently addressing the need for strong communication skills as part of the role of these professionals, with a new job specification that expects inspectors to be able to "handle emotions so that they facilitate rather than interfere with performance" (Learner, 2001, p. 2).

It was evident from interview data gathered in the fourth year of the project that the morale of some co-ordinators was being eroded by imbalance between pressure and support, whether caused internally or externally to the school. In one extreme case, the co-ordinator expressed the following sentiments:

> I think it's just, I don't know, it's hard to say, I just feel like I did after the week's inspection, just completely drained and just want to get out now. I'm in two minds, I really don't know whether I need to get out or whether I just need to find a different school or just go back to class teacher and nothing else. (Abbie)

4.5. Six linked constructs

The evidence presented in this chapter has drawn on the analysis undertaken for the Focus Project *Whole School Action on Numeracy. Enthusiasm* for the co-ordination role and *clarity of vision* about ways of working with colleagues which we have illustrated here, emerged as important factors promoting change in the six schools and became the first two constructs developed in our analysis. The identification of support from colleagues, the headteacher and external professionals, and the appropriate resourcing of the role, touched on briefly here but developed further in Chapter 3, as other conditions necessary to facilitate change, provided an additional four constructs, listed below and shown in Figure 2.1. These six linked factors appeared to affect the speed and effectiveness with which change (in this case in the development of mathematics) was taken on board (see also Millett & Johnson, 2000a).

Construct 1: *Enthusiasm* for the co-ordination role

Construct 2: *Clarity of vision* about priorities for action and ways of working

Construct 3: *Balance* between headteacher and co-ordinator

Construct 4: *Coherence and consistency* of views within the school community

Construct 5: *High priority given to resourcing* the co-ordination role

Construct 6: *Availability and use of external support*

Based on analysis of qualitative data, combining observation and interview sources from our three groups of participants (headteachers, co-ordinators and classroom teachers), schools were allocated positive or negative positions on these criteria at two points in time during the research. The arrows in Figure 2.1 indicate where links between the constructs were exemplified by the data.

Two of the three schools where a positive position on at least five of the six constructs was identified during the first 18 months of the research made early gains in attainment results of pupils at age 11. Schools that were identified as having negative positions on some of the constructs were slower to make gains.

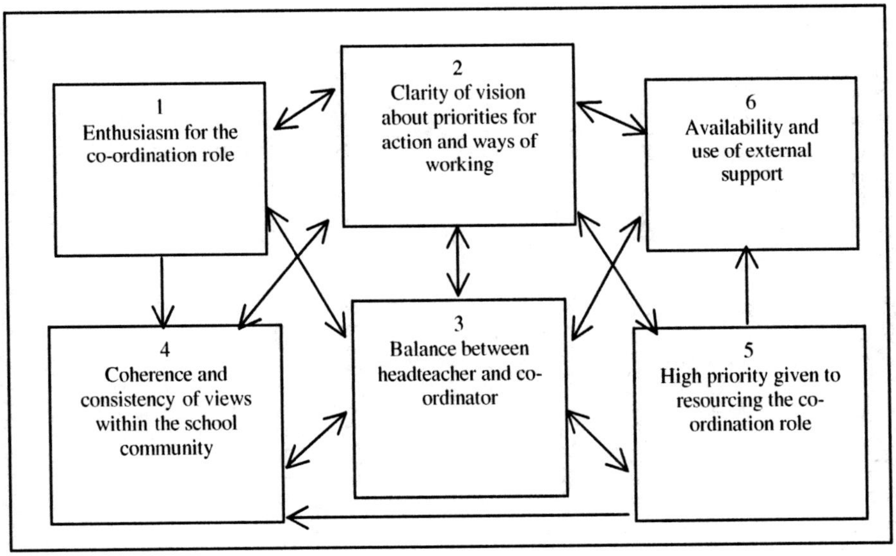

Figure 2.1. Six linked constructs

In three of the six schools there was a negative combination on four of the linked constructs during the run-up to the introduction of the Numeracy Strategy – lack of enthusiasm for the role; difficulty in clarifying goals and ways of working; the absence of balance between headteacher and co-ordinator; failure to prioritise the resourcing of the role. This resulted in three co-ordinators relinquishing the role, two of these in situations of considerable distress. In these two cases, co-ordinators' appointments had been made by a previous headteacher in the school. Headteachers had expectations of the co-ordinator that they felt were not met. Co-ordinators felt unable to take action in an atmosphere of disapproval. Their reactive rather than proactive stance provoked more negative attitudes from the headteacher. The appointment of new co-ordinators in these three schools led to improved situations of *balance*, and positions on the other constructs also began to improve.

5. DISCUSSION

The six constructs identified as critically affecting the co-ordinator's role as an agent of change link closely with the model developed in Chapter 1, being firstly located within the individual's personal resources (Spillane, 1999) (Constructs 1 and 2) and secondly located within the *professional community* and its links with *external factors* (Constructs 3, 4, 5 and 6). In this chapter we have focused particularly on Constructs 1 and 2, the co-ordinators' *enthusiasm* for the co-ordination role, and their *clarity of vision* about ways of working with colleagues. (In Chapter 3 the focus will shift to Constructs 3, 4, 5 and 6.)

We now return to the question posed at the beginning of this chapter. How can co-ordinators, working in their capacity as providers of in-school support, make a difference to the ability of classroom teachers to engage with change? We discuss first the effects of the work of co-ordinators on teachers' *zones of enactment* and then ask whether these effects would satisfy Spillane's criteria for the conditions necessary to promote the implementation of reform. We look at the role of the mathematics co-ordinator as currently conceived in England as a source of professional development, and conclude by raising the issue of whether the core of teachers' practice has been addressed by the attempts of mathematics co-ordinators to act as agents of change.

5.1. The influence of the mathematics co-ordinators on teachers' zones of enactment

In our six schools change initiatives were mediated through the mathematics co-ordinator. Initially these initiatives were developed within the school, but became synonymous with the requirements of the National Numeracy Strategy as the research progressed. This mediation was indeed part of the design of the Strategy's training and implementation. However, although all co-ordinators could be said to be mediators, not all were catalysts of change. In some schools change began to happen sooner than in others, with co-ordinators being attributed a key role in this.

Several teachers in our study attributed new ideas to formal or informal interactions with the co-ordinator. It is important to note here that these were not one-off actions; they were repeated over time and mentioned in subsequent interviews during the course of the research. Learning was occurring within the ongoing working practices of the community (Stein & Brown, 1997). Elements of the capacity to develop rich *zones of enactment* in others were apparent in the practice of about half of these co-ordinators. Some were particularly skilled at making decisions about whether to approach people individually or collectively; some were particularly effective in creating interactive and lively discussion at meetings; some were more confident leaders of classroom practice than others. However, realising rich *zones of enactment* for groups of diverse colleagues was not something that could be accomplished easily. One co-ordinator in our study recognised that she had not been able to touch the practice of one member of staff who was resistant to the Numeracy Strategy; another was trying and failing to keep up with the professional development of a high turnover of staff; another could initiate rich discussions about working with older pupils, but did not have sufficient expertise to do the same for younger pupils. There was also a realisation that certain teachers clung to individualistic ways of working, and co-ordinators were not always successful in breaking down these barriers.

The tensions between a monitoring and evaluating role in acting as an agent of change and a role as a critical friend (Osborn & Black, 1994) were constantly present for these co-ordinators during the four years of the research. However, a critical factor in whether the co-ordinators were able to encourage their colleagues to work in different ways appeared to be their own *clarity of vision* about ways of working – their ability to work appropriately and successfully with individuals or groups; their positioning of themselves as leading learners alongside their colleagues; their willingness to put their own practice up for examination and criticism; their recognition of mutual or disparate aims. Teachers interviewed in four out of the six schools talked positively about the approachability and expertise of the co-ordinator in providing subject guidance. This peer coaching did not appear to depend upon extensive knowledge of mathematics or even on the pursuit of professional development, but rather on sensitivity to the needs of others (an essential constituent of what we have included in *clarity of vision*). There were, however, undercurrents of dissatisfaction. In one school it was felt that the co-ordinator was so concerned to be seen to be promoting government-approved policy, that she was unable to countenance any discussion.

The *situations* in which the co-ordinators were working were clearly highly influential in terms of facilitating professional development through the role. As McNamara and Corbin (2001) also illustrate from one of the co-ordinators in their study:

> I think if you are mathematics co-ordinator you can change the culture ... with the support of the head teacher and the deputy who also wanted to change, if it had been me – one lone voice in the school – with the teachers who had been teaching twice the length of time I had, I don't think I would have achieved so much. (McNamara & Corbin, 2001, p. 275)

5.2. The role of the co-ordinator as a source of in-service training

We now consider how the role of the co-ordinator stands up to scrutiny as a source of in-service training. Several characteristics of what is regarded as successful professional development can be provided by the co-ordination role: it makes use of ongoing rather than 'one-off' intervention (Rowley, Gervasconi, Clarke, Horne, & McDonough, 2001); it provides peer coaching (Joyce & Showers, 1995); it benefits from support, stimulation and resources from the wider school environment (Joyce & Showers, 1995); it can orient teacher education around the practices of teaching and learning (Lampert & Ball, 1999); it can incorporate external advice and support to sustain the quality of discussion (Hawley & Valli, 1999). It possesses a further characteristic by which, in a sense, it stands or falls: in contrast to externally provided in-service training, it is facilitated by a network of established personal and professional relationships that have been built up over time. The attraction for us of Spillane's notion of *zones of enactment* is that this personal element is seen within the context of the wider social interactions at school level.

As mentioned in Chapter 1, models of professional development that featured social interaction with colleagues and also addressed teacher learning (e.g. Lave & Wenger, 1991; Tharp & Gallimore, 1988) were felt to more appropriately reflect the conditions in which teacher learning took place (Stein & Brown, 1997). Chapter 3, which looks in greater depth at the *professional community*, the whole-school setting, will return to ideas of 'learning communities' (Collins, 1998).

As a model of professional development the role of the co-ordinator would appear to have considerable potential to affect teacher learning. Some of the co-ordinators in our study have demonstrated their ability to enhance teachers' *zones of enactment* through choosing appropriate ways of working with individuals and groups to initiate change. What we must question now is whether the work done by the co-ordinators in these six schools facilitated change in the core of teachers' practice, or whether the change identified remained largely superficial.

5.3. Change to the core of teaching

Harris and Anthony (2001) draw a distinction between "collegial interactions that helped produce an emotionally supportive work environment, and collegial interactions that truly engendered significant professional development" (p. 384). All the classroom teachers interviewed for this research identified some changes in their practice, although these were not always confirmed through observation. Most of these changes related to the structure of lessons and the content and planning of the curriculum, including the use of materials and resources, and there was evidence that teachers perceived that their use of the promoted artefacts had increased, although observation did not support this perception to any great extent. We must question to what extent these formal and informal collaborations with colleagues had enabled teachers to get "beyond surface dimensions of practice to appreciate the implications the reforms had for the core of their teaching" (Spillane, 1999, p. 161). The degree to which the new materials and artefacts contributed towards teachers' and pupils' understanding of mathematics reforms they were trying to implement was not clear. Nor was there evidence to support the view that changes in beliefs accompanied changes in practice.

It may well be the case that the actions of the co-ordinators created the potential for affecting the core of teachers' practice, but that this potential was not realised in many cases. Whether the changes identified go beyond the superficial and become a recognisable part of future practice will need a longer research project to ascertain. The degree to which these could be considered to be "deep" change (Earl et al., 2000, p, 39) is considered in Chapter 9.

6. AFFILIATIONS

Professor David C. Johnson is an emeritus Professor at the Department of Education and Professional Studies, King's College London, having recently retired as Shell Professor of Mathematics Education.

7. NOTES

[1] Millett, A., & Johnson, D. C. (2000a). The role of the maths co-ordinator and the National Numeracy Strategy in England. *Teacher Development, 4*(3), 393-410. Copyright © 2000; Teacher Development. Material reproduced here by kind permission of Triangle Journals Ltd., publishers of Teacher Development.

8. REFERENCES

Bibby, T. (2002). Shame: an emotional response to doing mathematics as an adult and as a teacher. *British Educational Research Journal, 28*(5), 706-721.

Campbell, R. J. (1985). *Developing the primary school curriculum*. London: Holt, Rinehart & Winston.

Collins, A. (1998). Learning Communities: A Commentary on Chapters by Brown, Ellery and Campione, and by Riel. In J. G. Greeno & S. V. Goldman (Eds.), *Thinking Practices in Mathematics and Science Learning* (pp. 399-405). Mahwah, NJ: Lawrence Erlbaum Associates, Inc.

Department for Education and Employment. (1999). *The National Numeracy Strategy: Framework for Teaching Mathematics from Reception to Year 6*. London: Department for Education and Employment.

Earl, L., Fullan, M., Leithwood, K., Watson, N., with Jantzi, D., Levin, B., & Torrance, N. (2000). *Watching and Learning. OISE/UT Evaluation of the implementation of the National Literacy and Numeracy Strategies. First annual report*. Toronto: Ontario Institute for Studies in Education, University of Toronto.

Hargreaves, A. (1992). Cultures of teaching: a focus for change. In A. Hargreaves & M. Fullan (Eds.), *Understanding teacher development* (pp. 216-240). London: Cassell.

Harris, D. L., & Anthony, H. M. (2001). Collegiality and its role in teacher development: perspectives from veteran and novice teachers. *Teacher Development, 5*(3), 371-389.

Hawley, W. D., & Valli, L. (1999). The Essentials of Effective Professional Development: a new consensus. In L. Darling-Hammond & G. Sykes (Eds.), *Teaching as the Learning Profession. Handbook of policy and practice* (pp. 127-150). San Francisco, CA: Jossey-Bass.

Joyce, B., & Showers, B. (1995). *Student achievement through staff development*. NY: Longmans.

Lampert, M., & Ball, D. L. (1999). Aligning Teacher Education with Contemporary K-12 Reform Visions. In L. Darling-Hammond & G. Sykes (Eds.), *Teaching as the Learning Profession. Handbook of Policy and Practice* (pp. 33-53). San Francisco, CA: Jossey-Bass.

Lave, J., & Wenger, E. (1991). *Situated Learning: legitimate peripheral participation*. Cambridge: Cambridge University Press.

Learner, S. (2001, 24 August). Warm and friendly – this is the new school inspector. *Times Educational Supplement,* p. 2.

Leithwood, K., Jantzi, D., & Mascall, B. (1999). *Large-Scale Reform: What Works? Submitted as part of the first annual report: External Evaluation of the UK National Literacy and National Numeracy Strategy*. Ontario: Ontario Institute for Studies in Education, University of Toronto.

McNamara, O., & Corbin, B. (2001). Warranting practices: teachers embedding the National Numeracy Strategy. *British Journal of Educational Studies, 29*(3), 260-284.

Millett, A. (1996). *Using and Applying Mathematics: innovation and change in a primary school.* Unpublished PhD Thesis, King's College, London.

Millett, A., & Johnson, D. C. (2000a). The role of the maths co-ordinator and the National Numeracy Strategy in England. *Teacher Development, 4*(3), 393-410.

Millett, A., & Johnson, D. C. (2000b). Dancing to whose tune? Conflicting priorities for primary schools. *Education 3-13, 28*(3), 24-31.

Nias, J. (1989). *Primary teachers talking: a study of teaching as work*. London: Routledge.

Nias, J., Southworth, G., & Yeomans, R. (1989). *Staff relationships in the primary school*. London: Cassell Educational.

Office for Standards in Education. (1994). *Handbook for the inspection of schools (1994 consolidated edition)*. London: Her Majesty's Stationery Office.

Office for Standards in Education. (2000). *The National Numeracy Strategy: the first year*. London: Office for Standards in Education.

Osborn, M., & Black, E. (1994). *Developing the National Curriculum at key stage 2: the changing nature of teachers' work*. Birmingham, UK: National Association of Schoolmasters Union of Women Teachers.

Pollard, A., Broadfoot, P., Croll, P., Osborn, M., & Abbott, D. (1994). *Changing English primary schools? the impact of the Education Reform Act at key stage one*. London: Cassell.

Rowley, G., Gervasconi, A., Clarke, D., Horne, M., & McDonough, A. (2001). *The Early Numeracy Research Project: Using interviews to monitor growth in mathematics*. Paper presented at the British Educational Research Association Conference, 13-15 September, University of Leeds.

Spillane, J. P. (1999). External reform initiatives and teachers' efforts to reconstruct their practice: the mediating role of teachers' zones of enactment. *Journal of Curriculum Studies, 31*(2), 143-175.

Stein, M. K., & Brown, C. (1997). Teacher Learning in a Social Context: Integrating Collaborative and Institutional Processes with the Study of Teacher Change. In E. Fennema & B. S. Nelson (Eds.), *Mathematics Teachers in Transition* (pp. 155-191). Mahwah, NJ: Lawrence Erlbaum Associates, Inc.

Tharp, R., & Gallimore, R. (1988). *Rousing minds to life: Teaching, learning and schooling in social context*. Cambridge: Cambridge University Press.

ALISON MILLETT AND DAVID C. JOHNSON

CHAPTER 3

THE ROLE OF THE SCHOOL IN DEVELOPING MATHEMATICS

Abstract. Focusing mainly on the mathematics co-ordinator, the preceding chapter nevertheless drew attention to the importance of the *situation* within which the individual works and makes decisions. In this chapter we move from the mathematics co-ordinator to look at the ways in which the wider school context – the role of the headteacher and the role of school policies – influence opportunities for professional development. We draw on case-study data to illuminate the six linked constructs that appear to have facilitated effective development in mathematics. How a school responds to policy initiatives, how it views and resources the roles of professionals, how it responds to external pressure and support, how leadership is characterised, are all considered. This case-study data is then set in a wider context through an examination of the characteristics of schools from the large-scale longitudinal study in the Leverhulme Numeracy Research Programme that have been successful in achieving improvements in the mathematics attainment of their pupils over the course of the research programme. The ability of schools to promote a collective capacity for reform by supporting dialogue and discussion, recognising and applauding professional expertise and providing opportunities for collaboration and learning, forms a key focus of the discussion.

1. INTRODUCTION

In the Introduction to this book we described the national and international context for the research and introduced the reader to the influences and constraints under which primary schools in England were operating at the beginning of the Leverhulme Numeracy Research Programme in 1997. In Chapter 1 we outlined our reasons for choosing a model for discussing professional change that encompassed the individual, the *professional community* within the school and a range of external influences. In this chapter we need our model in its entirety to investigate what we have learned from this research that enables us to address the question – how can schools make a difference in encouraging individual classroom teachers to make (and sustain) effective changes in their practice?

Alison Millett, Margaret Brown and Mike Askew (eds.), Primary Mathematics and the Developing Professional.

1.1. The Research

The Leverhulme Numeracy Research Programme set out to address a range of factors that might be associated with low attainment in numeracy. School-level factors featuring among this range of factors formed the focus of *Whole School Action on Numeracy* (see Introduction/Annex 3). This case-study project was concerned with the effect of whole-school action in the area of numeracy within the ever increasing demands of government policies – from a school inspection by the Office for Standards in Education (Ofsted), to the more recent National Numeracy Strategy (see Introduction). The case-study research focused on six primary (elementary) schools as they prepared for, experienced and followed up a school inspection carried out by Ofsted during 1998. It continued for a total period of four years (1997-2001), during which the National Numeracy Strategy was introduced in September 1999. The need to develop mathematics had been identified in all six schools before the implementation of this major national intervention began, and they were attempting to meet this need in a variety of ways.

Judgements were made about the existence and effectiveness of change from:

- perceptions of those in the schools established through ongoing interviews
- observation of a selection of lessons and meetings over the course of four years
- trends in the schools' national test results at age 11.

The views of a Local Education Authority senior primary adviser were sought towards the end of the project on the strategies that schools were using to raise attainment, and on the factors emerging from the research as important in facilitating the implementation of change.

The first part of this chapter draws on the work with six case-study schools that also formed the basis of our reporting on the role of the mathematics co-ordinator in Chapter 2. From these case studies we present selected findings and a summary of developments drawn from the six schools, and then take one of the schools to illustrate these findings in more depth.

In the second part of the chapter, continuing our focus on the way in which different characteristics at whole-school level can affect a school's ability to promote reform, we look at data from the Core longitudinal project, *Tracking Numeracy* (see Introduction and Annex 1), to provide a wider comparative context for our case-study data.

1.2. Selected findings from Whole School Action on Numeracy

In Chapter 2, we presented selected findings that related closely to the mathematics co-ordinator and her work with individual teachers. Here, we present findings from the case-study research that relate to whole-school actions or characteristics.

- some schools took a proactive approach to external constraints and influences; some a more pragmatic, waiting role
- some schools seemed able to satisfy the need for both autonomy and accountability and pursue their own priorities for mathematics development despite competing demands
- the research indicated that six linked factors (shown in Figure 3.1) were of particular importance in facilitating the development of mathematics in the schools. The presence or absence of these were deemed to be of major importance (See also Chapter 2)

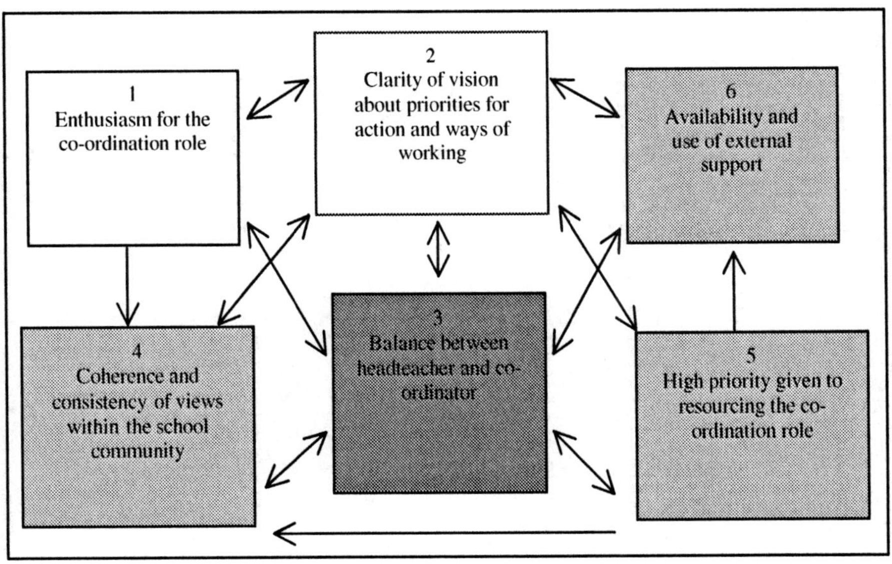

Figure 3.1. Six linked constructs

- of these constructs, the central and critical one appeared to be *balance* between headteacher and mathematics co-ordinator (as illustrated by the shading in Figure 1. The more lightly shaded constructs indicate the other three that we will be considering most closely in this chapter)
- a positive position on one construct could facilitate action on others

- in two of the three schools where positive positions on most of these constructs were identified, co-ordinators were empowered to take a proactive stance towards co-ordination and improvements in attainment began to be made (as indicated by national test results at age 11 (see Table 3.1) between 1997 and 1998). The third began to make improvements from 1998 onwards
- in three schools where these constructs were initially not well developed, their lack could be seen to inhibit the development of the mathematics. However, the introduction of the National Numeracy Strategy in 1999 affected the development of several of these constructs in a positive way, and improvements in attainment were noted in all six schools during 1999/2000 (see Table 3.1)

Table 3.1. Percentages of pupils attaining Level 4 or above in national tests at age 11 in comparison with national averages

School	*1997*	*1998*	*1999*	*2000*	*2001*
Woodbury	46	47	62	84	79
The Grove	43	88	50	81	78
Maple	78	64	69	84	93
Pennington	61	39	37	55	71
Sandmere	81	23	23	56	39
Wolverton	33	62	78	84	57
National	62	59	69	72	71

Note. Results for The Grove should be viewed with extreme caution as numbers were extremely small and sometimes too small for national reporting

- two schools were able to sustain improvement over a further year (2000/01)
- it appeared to be the case that the way in which schools took action or used certain strategies to raise attainment was more important than the actual strategies adopted.

1.3. Summary of developments in the six case-study schools

We look now at the relevance of these constructs to the role of the school in engaging teachers in change. From the data collected during the first 18 months of the research (September 1997-March 1999), it appeared that there was well-defined clustering of the six schools on some if not all of these constructs. Positions relative to the constructs were supported by interview and observation data. *Woodbury,*

Maple and Wolverton schools showed characteristics judged to be positive on at least five of the six constructs. Co-ordinators were enthusiastic, and were able to articulate ways of working with colleagues to pursue certain courses of action (Constructs 1 and 2). The headteachers gave co-ordination a high profile, resourced it accordingly and respected the expertise of their co-ordinator (Constructs 3 and 5).

Outside help was used if regularly available and sought out if not (Construct 6). Other members of the school community did not express divergent or conflicting views when interviewed about the mathematics action being undertaken (Construct 4). Of these three schools, *Maple* was not able to maintain the resources for co-ordination at the level originally intended.

In contrast, the other three schools, *The Grove, Pennington and Sandmere*, showed less positive positions. Co-ordinators had not made a positive choice of role, were not able to articulate clearly thought out ways of working and did not appear to be respected for their expertise; resourcing did not include non-contact time and there was less delegation of responsibility. This was an unsettled time for some of these schools, with new headteachers coming to *The Grove* and *Pennington.*

It appeared that those schools clustering towards the positive end of the six constructs were able to empower their co-ordinator to take a proactive stance towards co-ordination and towards preparing well in advance for the Numeracy Strategy. In those schools clustering at the less positive end of the constructs, co-ordinators appeared hesitant in making decisions and following them through. The two schools most consistently holding positions at the positive end of these constructs (*Woodbury* and *Wolverton*) showed early improvement (1997/98) in attainment results, one marginally and one substantially. (The pupil numbers in The Grove were too small to provide a reliable comparison with the other schools.)

A similar analysis was conducted a the end of three years of the project, after another 18 months. During this time the National Numeracy Strategy training had begun, and the first year of implementation undertaken. Several schools had experienced major staffing changes. The headteacher of *Sandmere* changed and mathematics co-ordinators for *Woodbury, The Grove, Pennington and Sandmere* had also changed. It is perhaps significant that in the three schools where co-ordinators seemed to be exhibiting a lack of control over actions and were not well-supported by their headteachers, new co-ordinators had taken over the role. All six co-ordinators were now enthusiastic about their role and all six indicated that their enthusiasm included the Numeracy Strategy and the requirement that they should be spreading its message. Funding from the National Numeracy Strategy had made provision for monitoring, although this provision was regarded as sacrosanct in some schools, but not in others. External support in the form of intensive training and consultant support had also been funded for a year for one school (Sandmere) and was just beginning for the other five. Personal and professional relationships had changed, sometimes for the better in terms of *balance* (*Pennington* and *Sandmere*), sometimes for the worse in the case of *coherence and consistency* among members of the *professional community*. The attainment results, as measured by national test results at age 11, of all six schools rose during 1999/2000. Change was reported and observed in the all six schools during the course of the research (see Chapter 2).

Final data collection from the six schools revealed some encouraging evidence of the maintenance of improvement. As can be seen from Table 3.1, two schools maintained their upward trajectory in mathematics national test results, two recorded a slight dip, but managed to maintain a level above the national target for 2002 of 75%. Two schools recorded a drop. Headteachers were generally realistic about changes in cohort affecting the detail of year-on-year test results and preferred to place emphasis on trends over several years.

2. THE SIX LINKED CONSTRUCTS IN WOLVERTON SCHOOL

We have chosen one of our six schools to provide an in-depth case-study of the characteristics and factors which seemed to us to be of importance in initiating whole-school development in mathematics[1].

2.1. *Wolverton School*

Wolverton School made the most dramatic strides of all the six schools in the improvement of attainment in mathematics based on national test results at age 11 over the first three years of the research. To do this it employed a range of strategies and exhibited a positive position on all six constructs defined above. *Wolverton* Primary School is situated in an inner-city area that is socially and ethnically mixed, with high proportions of pupils entitled to free school meals and who come from homes where English is not the first language. There is substantial pupil mobility. The headteacher in post during the research came to the school in 1996, and the school was inspected by the Office for Standards in Education (Ofsted) shortly after he had taken over. The report was not positive. Although the school was said to be improving, a third of the teaching in 1996 was found to be unsatisfactory.

The story of mathematics in *Wolverton* School in recent years has been one of improvement. This is not only the judgement of those who work in the school, it is the judgement of Ofsted inspectors and is reflected in national test results (most commonly referred to by teachers as SATs). By 1998, no unsatisfactory teaching was identified in the school's subsequent Ofsted inspection. Table 3.2 shows percentages of pupils attaining Level 4 or above from 1997 to 2001.

Table 3.2. Percentages of pupils at Wolverton School attaining Level 4 or above in national tests at age 11

School	*1997*	*1998*	*1999*	*2000*	*2001*
Wolverton	33	62	78	84	57
National	62	59	69	72	71

In 1999 and 2000 the school's national test results at age 11 in mathematics exceeded the national average and were well above average compared with schools with similar pupil intakes. Those working in the school based their judgements about improved attainment not only on national test results, but also on evidence of pupils' work and attitude to mathematics. The mathematics co-ordinator, the headteacher and the two other teachers interviewed identified change in a range of areas. Higher expectations of pupils were noted at all professional levels in the school. Other positive developments noted by either co-ordinator or teachers were changes in mental mathematics, more detailed planning with a focus on learning objectives, increased confidence and enthusiasm on the part of pupils. (See Section 2.5. for comment on test results for 2000/01.)

2.2. Balance

The central construct that will be addressed through the case study of *Wolverton* School, and its effect on the presence or absence of other constructs, is that of *balance* (Construct 3)[2]. In three of our six schools it was noticeable at the beginning of the research that headteacher and co-ordinator appreciated the importance of each other's roles, and were moving forward together. In two of the other three schools *balance* appeared to develop with a change in co-ordinator. Respect for the co-ordinator's judgement and expertise on the one hand was matched by an understanding of the head's priorities and recognition of their support. This construct implies more than delegation by the headteacher – there is an enabling aspect that includes delegation but also includes support, trust and confidence. When this *balance* was not in evidence it was possible to detect quite critical views of each other between headteacher and co-ordinator, conflicting views about the nature and resourcing of the role, deprecating remarks about expertise and commitment. In a situation of *balance*, the headteachers gave co-ordination a high profile, resourced it accordingly and respected the expertise of their co-ordinator.

The provision made by the headteacher for the co-ordinator to take on a demanding role as subject leader and adviser is a key aspect of *balance*. Bell (1992) found restricted views of the nature of the role amongst headteachers, views which differed from government-sponsored reports available at the time. Moore (1992) described the low importance given by headteachers to subject knowledge, with only a minority feeling that co-ordinators should have authoritative influence on colleagues' teaching. The preference at that time was for:

> the co-ordinator to be a 'helper' and 'fellow worker' rather than a 'school adviser' or a 'decision-maker'. (p.14)

There is more recent evidence, however, of headteachers adopting an expanded view of subject leadership (Webb & Vulliamy, 1996; Bell, 1999). One factor that we have noted as being important in this respect is the creation of the role of 'leading mathematics teacher' through the National Numeracy Strategy. These teachers are identified by local numeracy consultants and Local Education Authority personnel (see Introduction), and their practices are held up as exemplars for other teachers to observe and learn from. This recognition of expertise amongst the staff of a school has been observed to be a source of pride for the school; when the selected teacher is the mathematics co-ordinator it adds to the esteem with which the headteacher regards the subject specialist and thus contributes to a situation of *balance*.

An effective leader "legitimates leadership from members" (Yeomans, 1987, p. 134). This legitimisation involves trust – an area of school management described by West-Burnham (1996) as one "where rhetoric and reality are most widely divergent" (p. 55). The headteachers in this study who exemplified *balance* seemed to have been able to take on this legitimating or enabling role (see also Leithwood, Jantzi, & Steinbach, 1999, writing about leadership and the individual teacher). The quality of leadership exemplified went beyond delegation, it gave co-ordinators the confidence to develop their own specialisms, disagree with their headteacher, argue their own corner. This is not the view of leadership of the current managerialist and rational orthodoxy in the UK (e.g. Teacher Training Agency, 1997), but it fits well with the "values-led contingency leadership" identified by Day, Harris, Hadfield, Tolley and Beresford, (2000, p. 158) as being demonstrated by effective headteachers.

> The heads in the study were centrally concerned with developing their organisation through developing others. [...] The heads in this study involved others in decision-making and had professional trust in them. They cultivated professional dialogue between teachers, placing a high premium upon their own professional development and the professional development of their staff. (Day et al., 2000, p.166)

We have taken the views of the headteacher, the mathematics co-ordinator and two other teachers at *Wolverton* School to illustrate various aspects of this relationship of *balance* that we feel encourages professional development.

Newly appointed at the time of the Ofsted inspection in 1996, the headteacher at *Wolverton* described his first step as clarifying what they were trying to do. He included in his plan for action following inspection the raising of teachers' expectations. Low expectations were identified as a key factor in low attainment by comparing work from the different year groups and assessing the levels of attainment. To raise expectations they looked at what could be achieved at each stage and developed clearer records of achievement.

Teachers already in the school when he arrived who had not been able to cope with the new expectations had not stayed at the school. "It's the expectation that's changed and the people who are still here are taking that on board," the headteacher reiterated. He said that their priorities when employing people had changed. The focus was now unequivocally upon good teaching. Other considerations were of lesser importance. When teaching vacancies occurred, he was firm about the need to employ the best teachers he could find and let them get on with it.

> Employing the best possible people which again is about expectations and about breaking some moulds maybe. Making sure they've got all the equipment to do it and then letting them teach. (Headteacher)

Teachers may not have been selected to fill a vacant co-ordination slot, but much was expected of them when they were given such a role. Jodie was offered the role of mathematics co-ordinator when she had been in the school for a term. She expressed considerable enthusiasm for taking on responsibility for a core subject in the curriculum, admitting that she liked a challenge (Construct 1). Her job specification was demanding and included: monitoring and accounting for national and optional test results; monitoring all teachers' plans; ensuring the implementation of the school scheme-of-work for mathematics (prior to the introduction of the National Numeracy Strategy). Along with other more routine duties relating to resources, she was expected to keep abreast of current developments; act as 'in house' expert and source of information; create finance bids and be responsible for allocated budgets.

Facilitating good teachers to get on with the job meant much more than providing material resources for use in their own classrooms. It also meant providing them with professional support. In this school it meant developing the role of subject co-ordinators to include substantial subject support as well as monitoring duties. This, of course, had to be resourced. Time out of the classroom (non-contact time) meant that co-ordinators could work alongside teachers as a 'critical friend' as well as holding a more supervisory, monitoring role, thus providing opportunities for peer coaching and classroom-based discussion about practice essential to the realisation of *zones of enactment*.

Interviews with the mathematics co-ordinator and the Year 4 teacher, who also held the role of science co-ordinator, provided their viewpoints on the development of their roles. In October 1998, the mathematics co-ordinator spoke about monitoring.

> I mean in staff meetings we monitor all subjects now, we monitor – everyone will bring in their books to one staff meeting and every co-ordinator will monitor their set of books. The history co-ordinator will look through all the history books and I will look through the maths books. I mean I think it puts more pressure on the teachers but I don't think it's necessarily a negative thing because actually if you know people are going to be looking at your work with a critical eye it raises your standards, I think it's an important way. (Jodie)

A year later the science co-ordinator spoke about a concerted effort to make sure that the science profile did not slip too low in spite of the national emphasis on literacy and numeracy.

> And in fact we are, apart from the numeracy staff meetings we have, the last couple of weeks we've got into different curriculum groups to talk about the development of these areas and I've had a group meeting for science and we've talked about the way forward and possible INSET so [the headteacher's] aware of it and is giving me time and has given me money to make sure that it doesn't get squeezed too much which is brilliant and also he's been excellent about the resources that I've had. (Anna, Year 4 teacher, pupils aged 8-9 years, science co-ordinator)

The demands on headteachers as managers in the implementation of the whole raft of innovations emanating from government has made 'running a tight ship' imperative in the face of increased accountability. Headteachers have sometimes developed an almost militaristic approach – planning their campaigns of response to initiatives, keeping one step ahead of the 'enemy'. In some ways, the management of *Wolverton* seemed to fit with this model. The focus was always sharp, the organisation impressive. However, the headteacher had not chosen a hierarchical style of management and did not appear to view his staff as 'the ranks'. He described having chosen a style of management to fit the people within the school. He had no fixed senior management team, but set up groups to work on subjects or aspects of the school as and when needed. Bush (1986) noted: "ambiguity perspectives emphasise that there is fluid participation in the management of organisations. Members move in and out of decision-making" (p. 112). The headteacher was concerned that management style should remain flexible and should always be appropriate for the teachers within the school.

> If I arrived here at this point in time, my headship would be different from when I arrived. And the management structures of the school are based upon the personnel we have. In three years time we might have three newly qualified and suddenly we have senior management and hierarchy. It varies doesn't it. (Headteacher)

The headteacher thought carefully about the roles that individual teachers played both socially and professionally and how the movement of teachers could affect relationships. Knowing the teachers and how they worked was important to him. He encouraged challenge and employed people who would confidently express their points of view. He was also able to sow the seeds of ideas for changes in policies and wait for these to be taken on board by the teachers as their own.

In this school a situation of *balance* appeared to exist, certainly for the mathematics. Jodie described how she saw the support she received:

> ... from my head[teacher] that he's delegated the responsibility for maths to me and from the work I do in the classroom and the training I've been on he lets me make decisions about what are the key issues that I then need to address in staff meetings or with individual teachers. So he's delegated to me a massive amount of freedom to do what I feel is necessary and he's entrusted that, which he does with all his co-ordinators. But at the same time, there are sort of aspects, a minimum that he expects. If a lot of extra work is needed then as I said earlier I've been given time to actually do it, so the work load doesn't become too much. (Jodie)

The headteacher felt that he treated the teachers as professionals and acted on the judgements they made.

> Any amount of time a co-ordinator wants and can justify they can have, which gives you the power and we've got people that don't abuse that. (Headteacher)

Reflecting the other side of *balance*, the headteacher was observed and noted in fieldnotes to be deferring to Jodie's opinion on several occasions, both outside school at the Local Education Authority Three-day Numeracy Strategy training and inside school at in-service training that she was leading.

The Local Education Authority senior primary adviser who provided feedback on the findings of the case-study project was unequivocal in identifying what we have termed *balance* as critical in introducing improvements in a school. Asked about what she regarded as the most important factor in raising standards, she spoke immediately about headteachers, and the way in which they challenged, motivated and resourced members of staff.

> The headteacher is key and I was interested in your report on this school where the headteacher talked about his relationship particularly with the maths co-ordinator and how he gave her her head, if you like, to carry on. Obviously I mean she was a good co-ordinator but he didn't meddle, but was supportive and I think that that is a good approach to have where headteachers have the courage to allow their co-ordinators to lead and to shine, whilst they're are in the background supporting them. But I don't think they leave them on their own. (Senior primary adviser)

She felt that the abilities and expertise of co-ordinators was of growing importance and heads were now prepared to accept that their co-ordinator might well have a greater level of expertise than they themselves had, on which they could draw. Talking about the co-ordinator at *Wolverton*, she said:

> I think she was able to challenge the head and to perhaps lead the head in their private conversations in terms of the mathematics and then he was able to support her in terms of what skills he had in terms of managing the people.

2.3. High priority given to resourcing the role

The provision of time out of their own classroom to go into colleagues' classrooms to observe, monitor and participate (Construct 5) was just one exemplification from the research of the result of *balance* in the relationship between co-ordinator and headteacher, and the seriousness with which the role of co-ordinator was regarded. Monitoring was by this time sufficiently well established in *Wolverton* School for the headteacher to suggest that they did not really notice it any more because it was 'just there'. The construct of *clarity of vision* (Construct 2), documented in Chapter 2, also includes the co-ordinator's choice of ways of working with colleagues. Jodie was convinced about the value of her monitoring role and working alongside teachers as a 'critical friend'. She was also prepared to face questioning and disagreement at meetings so that issues could be addressed in depth and a useful dialogue created.

> Jodie led the meeting quite firmly. Everyone was on task, taking things seriously. I got the feeling that teachers and support staff felt able to make contributions if they thought they would be useful. [The headteacher] deferred to the co-ordinator's expertise several times. He clearly gave the impression that she would be able to advise them how to

> proceed, having had some time in classrooms before Christmas. [...] I felt that both the co-ordinator and the headteacher were a little anxious that there should be so much unhappiness expressed about some aspects of the Framework (in my presence perhaps). I said to her afterwards that I thought it was very interesting that people felt able to raise all these issues – it showed a very informed staff. She said that a couple of years ago, they might have just sat there and said 'OK we'll tick against the key objectives', but now they wanted to get at what these things really meant. (Fieldnotes Inset meeting; comments of the observer)

The teachers valued each other's expertise and referred frequently to asking each other for help with specific problems. Respect for each other's ways of working appeared to have created a feeling of mutual confidence that led to a proactive stance towards outside constraints. In this school there was evidence of this proactive stance in their approach to an Ofsted inspection and subsequently the National Numeracy Strategy. Preparing the staff for inspection at a staff meeting, the headteacher gave clear guidance on what they could expect, and what would be expected of them. He also made it clear that inspectors' attention needed to be drawn to strengths – they wouldn't necessarily find them on their own. There was a need to 'manage' the inspection.

This feeling of taking control through being proactive was also evident in the approach to the National Numeracy Strategy. In the absence of appropriate external support in advance of the Strategy training from their Local Education Authority, both mathematics co-ordinator and headteacher decided to attend a course (paid for out of the school's own resources) by the National Director of the Strategy to ensure that they were well prepared for its implementation (Construct 6). They felt afterwards that this had given them a good grounding upon which to build and had been of more use to them than any of the subsequent training. They felt able to approach the Strategy from a position of strength because their recent rises in national test results gave them some control over how far to take it on board – they could use their professional judgement in coming to that decision.

> No, no we have taken it on but with a view that if after however long, you know, whether people aren't happy with it then we will go back, we are not just going to take it on without consideration that we believe it's good. [...] I think we are all in quite a strong position because of our SATs results. As I said the inspectors who came round [...] the other day put to the headteacher because our results were so good that maybe we didn't need to take it on fully. (Jodie)

Asked in interview about this proactive stance towards external constraints – going out to meet things – the headteacher said "It makes sense doesn't it, it's about keeping control or taking control."

2.4. Coherence and Consistency

Members of this staff group seemed to take collective responsibility and exhibited a 'whole school' (Nias, Southworth, & Campbell, 1992, p. 56) approach. They mentioned each other's roles and work frequently; they talked a lot and appeared to be confident to do so. There was no feeling, still common in many primary schools, of teachers isolated in classrooms. There was plenty of fun in the staffroom, but also very professional discussion. Talking about the greatly improved national test results at age 11 in 1999, Adam, the Year 6 teacher (pupils aged 10-11 years who took the national tests at the end of the year), said:

> ...he [headteacher] said last year I was jumping around saying 'I've done it' and this year I'm saying 'we've done it' and so I think that's true, that's the teamwork.

There was a high degree of consistency between the views of the headteacher and the three teachers interviewed on strategies selected for use by this school to raise attainment (Construct 4), as we have already seen in relation to the high priority given to the co-ordination role. Four further examples are given here: the policy of setting, the importance of good behaviour in the school, the setting of individual pupil targets, the approach to national tests.

2.4.1. Introducing setting

The school introduced setting in three groups across Years 5 and 6 (pupils aged 9-10; 10-11 years) in September 1998. (The policy of setting refers to the teaching of pupils in ability groups for some subjects in the curriculum, most commonly English and mathematics though not necessarily in the same groups for these two subjects. Other subjects are taught within the mixed-ability class unit.) The headteacher did not specifically mention setting as a key factor in raising attainment; but he did feel that the success of a policy depended on the degree to which teachers were committed to it.

> I tried to set up setting when I was first here and the people who were involved didn't think it would work so it didn't work and the second time we did it the people involved wanted it to work and it was very successful. (Headteacher)

The suggestion to extend setting to Years 3 and 4 (pupils aged 7-8; 8-9 years) the following year came, according to the headteacher, from the teachers themselves. The teachers interviewed were all positive about setting. The mathematics co-ordinator's views are given below:

> ... it was the setting that helped improve the SATs [national test] results. And I've now taught all three groups, I've taught the average middle group last year sort of the Level 4

> group/Level 5 group and I felt very happy with how they benefited [...] so I think it's worked for all the children actually. (Jodie)

2.4.2. 'Sorting' the behaviour

'Sorting' the behaviour, according to the headteacher, also helped to facilitate teachers getting on with the job of teaching. Achieving high and consistent standards of behaviour management was no easy task, but these standards seemed to have become part of the culture of the school, so much so that teachers were aware of the consistency rather than the policy. Asked about a behaviour policy in the school, the Year 6 teacher referred to common aims and expectations rather than formal policies.

> I'm not sure if it's formalised like that I'm not sure. I mean we do have a behaviour policy but I can't remember when I last read it or in fact if I've read it at all but yes, there's a shared understanding of what is right and what is not right and, of course, that does, you know, when you, if they're nose to the grindstone for an hour it's much better than three hours of sporadic work isn't it? (Adam, Year 6 teacher, pupils aged 10-11 years)

2.4.3. Setting targets

The headteacher also regarded setting individual national test targets for pupils as an important factor in raising attainment. Pupils were allocated individual target levels to achieve, and progress towards these targets was monitored. The headteacher felt that teachers were now very focused on what they were trying to achieve. He felt that there was a unity of purpose across the staff that this was important and accepted, whereas it hadn't been considered acceptable in the past.

> Whereas beforehand the rules weren't so clear, a number of people wouldn't have been as happy to be – to push as hard. People are quite like-minded I think, I don't know if you find that when you talk to them, they are different characters but there is sort of a desire and an expectation that our children can achieve and I think there may have been a time when there was a feeling that because they were from a variety of backgrounds that this was the level, this is the level you'd expect at Wolverton. Whereas I think the level we expect at Wolverton has changed. (Headteacher)

2.4.4. Teaching to the tests

Teaching to the national tests (referred to by teachers as SATs) was openly admitted and justified in terms of 'playing the game' that had been imposed upon them.

> What we did, you see, we did the forecasts very specifically on those things which come up in the SATs. So I know that year after year, percentages come up, angle, in a specific way, etc., etc. So the forecast [planning], which I've got taped to my desk here, this is set up with those things that I know always come up. So to a certain extent we are teaching, but we are also, can't deny it, we are focused on SATs. Because we've had poor results in the past and we don't want that to happen again. (Adam, Year 6 teacher, pupils aged 10-11 years)

This teacher said later in the interview that he was worried about judgements being made on national test results, and felt that it wasn't fair, but if that was the game they were playing they must play it to the best of their ability, and not pretend that they were being judged on anything else. The national test results were the first thing that Ofsted school inspectors looked at, he said. After their inspection he said that he had been quite prepared to tell inspectors that he was limiting the curriculum to focus on national tests. The mathematics co-ordinator said:

> But there is a degree of teaching to the test and we do do that. I mean we coached in Year 6, we are coaching children maybe giving them lots of practice SATs papers. I mean it's again when we played the game. (Jodie)

2.5 Sustaining change at Wolverton

The headteacher of *Wolverton* School described the pressure to sustain improvement.

> The hard thing here will be to sustain and I don't think you can sustain indefinitely because of the quality of staff. You are not always going to have – there's key people, key staff, and there's already a movement. Too small an organisation ... to say confidently you will make it. If it was twice as big you could take a few changes but every person you change or leaves here has a significant effect. (Headteacher)

During the final year of the research, the co-ordinator, Jodie, was away from the school on maternity leave, two other key members of staff moved on through promotion, and the headteacher himself left to take up responsibility for a larger school. It was also recognised that a lower attaining cohort of pupils had contributed to a drop in attainment results at age 11.

3. ALTERNATIVE PERCEPTIONS

From our analysis relating to the six constructs, *Wolverton* maintained a very positive position throughout the first three years of contact. For them the strategies adopted appeared to be working.

However, this does not mean that the specific strategies adopted by *Wolverton* school could be successfully adopted in all schools. *Wolverton* school has been doing what all schools in this country are being asked to do – raise standards in the core subjects (in this case mathematics), with measurement of success being judged by levels of attainment in the national tests at age 11. To do this, it has employed certain strategies which are viewed critically by some educationalists and teachers – teaching to the tests and setting according to ability. Although other schools in this study expressed reservations about both these strategies, it appeared that with the arrival of Booster Classes (government funding for extra preparation of borderline pupils before the national tests) came an increased focus on one of these, preparing for the tests, particularly at age 11.

The policy of setting, although being promoted heavily by the Office for Standards in Education (Ofsted, 1998), is not encouraged by the National Numeracy Strategy (Department for Education and Employment, 1999) as it has not been shown to be effective in narrowing the range of attainment. (The efficacy of setting will be addressed in Volume 2 of this series in relation to the full sample of schools.) Research has also identified certain groups of children who can be disadvantaged by setting (Boaler, 1997). During 1999, the mathematics co-ordinator at *Wolverton* School had done some analysis of assessments and discovered that the least able children in each set of Years 5/6 (ages 9-10; 10-11 years) made slower progress than expected. Jodie described this as worrying and said it was something they would need to focus on during the year 2000.

From other case-study schools in our research, it had become apparent that schools were dealing differently with the pressure upon them to raise standards. Some schools disapproved of the use of strategies such as setting, and either refused to take it up at all, or discarded it as inappropriate. It was also the case that other case-study schools made positive use of other strategies, such as the establishment of co-ordination teams, while *Wolverton* moved towards a model of co-ordination in the later years of the project where the co-ordinator worked part-time and had no class responsibility.

As already indicated, a senior primary specialist in a different Local Education Authority was sent the fuller version of the *Wolverton* case study (Millett & Johnson, 2003) and asked in interview to describe from her own experience what she considered to be the main factors at work in consistently raising standards. She was also asked to comment upon the strategies used by this school. The adviser admitted to having initially felt quite "angry and dismissive" on reading the *Wolverton* document and her reasons for this became apparent as the interview progressed.

Firstly, she was very uncomfortable with the acceptance of the need to 'teach to the test'. This went against her ideas about what would benefit the children, although she recognised that schools were being pushed heavily in this direction and had to be tough to fight against this trend.

Secondly, she was worried about the move away from considering the whole child, and going back to 'skills' in the morning and 'frills' in the afternoon. She thought that the focus on literacy and numeracy (by implication too heavy) would have to be rethought. But on the other hand, it would depend on what Ofsted were emphasising in their inspections. She felt that some heads were able to promote 'creative' teaching within the confines of the strategies and that this was the direction that things should be going. She was worried about the long-term effects of recent developments on pupils' experiences of school. What would they be like at the end of their school careers – only concerned about levels and grades and afraid to be experimental and take the initiative?

Thirdly, she was anxious that, as part of the self-evaluation process, schools should enlarge their focus to include soft data (such as classroom ethos, or quality of discussion about teaching) as indications of improvement as well as hard data (in the form of test scores), although she recognised that this was difficult for them to do under current pressures. But some good heads were able to do this, she felt. It remained to be seen whether the powers-that-be were prepared to accept such data – for example whether Local Education Authority and Ofsted inspectors would give other indicators credence.

Having expressed these feelings quite strongly, the primary adviser reflected that she should read the *Wolverton* story again and not be quite so dismissive, because the reality that schools faced was unrelenting pressure to raise national test results. However her concern about the effect on children remained.

> I wonder what the long -term effect of that is going to be in terms of this very high focus, thinking about the whole curriculum, you know, but I do appreciate the reality of league tables and that's the way outsiders judge the school, as I think several people said, 'so we are playing the game'.

4. CONCLUSIONS FROM THE CASE STUDIES

In Sections 2 and 3 of this chapter, we have used one of our six schools to illustrate the presence of the six constructs that emerged from *Whole School Action on Numeracy* as important factors in facilitating development in mathematics. From the *Wolverton* story it can be seen that these constructs are closely interlinked.

These links could be identified in other schools. A situation of *balance* between co-ordinator and headteacher, where the headteacher recognised and respected the enthusiasm and expertise of the co-ordinator, appeared to be linked to appropriate resourcing for the role. Choice by the co-ordinator of suitable ways of working with other teachers either individually or in groups appeared to lead to greater consistency of views within the *professional community*. The confidence that came from professional respect appeared to lead to proactive action in approaching reforms and taking up opportunities for external support. These factors appeared to be more important than the actual strategies adopted. Indeed in some cases the strategies used by *Wolverton* had been discarded by other schools. For example, *Woodbury* school, where attainment in national tests also rose considerably during the course of the research, exhibited strong positions on the six constructs but had discarded setting and tried to resist pressure to teach to the test in its drive to raise attainment. The way that schools operated appeared to be more important than the specific strategies they chose to adopt.

5. WHOLE SCHOOL FACTORS – THE WIDER PICTURE

Analysis of the case-study data from *Whole School Action on Numeracy* led to the identification of six constructs that appeared to make a difference to the ability of schools to make changes in their mathematics teaching and raise levels of attainment as measured by national tests at age 11. As can be seen from details given in Annex 3, these six schools had different characteristics, populations and starting points in terms of pupil attainment.

Schools work within the context of certain 'givens' or background variables (Hopkins, 1994). What they do with those 'givens' appears to make the difference between successful and unsuccessful development. At any one point in time, a school has a certain set of pupils with socio-economic characteristics that generally reflect the area in which the school is situated (we do not include here those primary schools that have some element of choice over their intake). Levels of pupil attainment on entering school, levels of pupil mobility, the teaching staff currently employed at the beginning of some development initiative, can also be regarded as 'givens'. The level of basic resourcing from the Local Education Authority is also something over which the school has little, if any, control. Do these factors affect the ability of schools to change practice and raise attainment?

To address this question, we turned to the large-scale Core Project, from the Leverhulme Programme, *Tracking Numeracy* (see Introduction and Annex 1), to which two of our case-study schools also belonged (*Woodbury* and *Sandmere*), to give us a wider picture of the factors involved in successfully encouraging classroom teachers to implement change.

We selected subsets of schools to exemplify schools judged to be *more successful* and *less successful* in providing value-added gains in numeracy attainment for their pupils, measured by the assessments developed for the Leverhulme Numeracy Research Programme. These were administered towards the beginning and end of each school year 1997-2002 for two cohorts of pupils (see Introduction). We must stress here that we have not based our criterion of success on levels of attainment (as would be indicated by levels in national tests) but rather by gains made over time, whatever the initial starting score in 1997, in order to address our question posed at the beginning of this chapter – how can schools make a difference?

We based our selection of schools on: 1) the mean percentage gain made by Cohort 2 pupils in each school over the period 1997-2000 i.e. pupils who were in Year 4 in October 1997 and in Year 6 in June 2000, and 2) the mean percentage gain made by Cohort 1 pupils in each school over the period 1999-2002 i.e. pupils who were in Year 2 in October 1999 and in Year 4 in June 2002. (We have used Year 2 figures as we consider them to be more robust than Year 1 figures for 1998/99.)

We used these gains in two ways: 1) we combined the mean percentage gains and ranked the schools; 2) we ranked each set of mean percentage gains and combined the rankings. We then selected the eight schools that emerged in common at the top end of the rankings as *more successful* and eight schools as *less successful* at the lower end of this ordering. We investigated three factors over which schools had little control that might have contributed towards these different outcomes:

- levels of attainment at the beginning of the research
- socio-economic factors
- pressure and support from outside the school.

We then considered three factors over which schools might be said to exert more control:

- provision for continuing professional development
- attitudes towards reform and the National Numeracy Strategy in particular
- movement of staff.

The only one of these factors that can be said to be specific to the current situation in England is the response to the particular reform of the National Numeracy Strategy. The other factors are common to schools worldwide, and our research can thus inform an international discussion of the role of the school in the implementation of change.

5.1 Levels of attainment at the beginning of the research

Table 3.3 shows the 16 schools (eight *more successful* and eight *less successful*), an indication of baselines for the two cohorts as indicated by the mean percentage starting scores of their pupils in Year 4 (aged 8-9 years) and Year 2 (aged 6-7 years) at the beginning of the timespans chosen (1997-2000; 1999-2002).

Table 3.3. Mean percentage scores in October 1997 and October 99, together with a ranking on mean % gains 1997-2002 for 16 schools from the Core sample

School	*Mean % score Oct. '97 (Year 4 pupils, aged 8-9 years)*	*Mean % score Oct. '99 (Year 2 pupils, aged 6-7 years)*	*Rank on mean % gains 1997-2002*
Talltrees	Below average	Below average	1
Mountain Ash	Broadly average	Broadly average	2
Greenacres	Below average	Below average	3
Windsmoor Infants and Juniors	Above average	Broadly average	4
Kirkshaw	Broadly average	Above average	5
Elmtree	Below average	Below average	6
Redshore	Above average	Broadly average	7
Hawesmere	Broadly average	Broadly average	8
Firsdown	Below average	Broadly average	28
Sandmere	Above average	Below average	29
Bournside	Above average	Broadly average	30
Birchcroft	Broadly average	Broadly average	31
Rowan	Above average	Above average	32
Kirkend	Broadly average	Broadly average	33
Clearwater	Broadly average	Above average	34
Juniper Street	Broadly average	Broadly average	35

The mean starting scores were categorised as: broadly average, (between the 25th and 75th percentiles); above average (above the 25th percentile) and below average (below the 75th percentile).

It can be seen from Table 3.3 that in 1997, the distribution between categories was fairly similar between the *more* and *less successful* schools. There is, however a slight tendency for *more successful* schools to have low starting scores than *less successful* schools, particularly at Year 2 (pupils aged 6-7 years). This could be because there is more potential for schools to make a difference if scores are low.

5.2. Socio-economic factors

Table 3.4. Levels of deprivation for the 16 selected schools, together with pupil eligibility for free school meals

Rank on mean % gains 1997-2002	*School*	*Ranking on Townsend deprivation index of enumeration district of school*	*Pupil eligibility for free school meals*
1	Talltrees	Very high	Above average
2	Mountain Ash	Middle	Above average
3	Greenacres	Middle	Below average
4	Windsmoor Infants and Juniors	Low	Below average
5	Kirkshaw	Low	Below average
6	Elmtree	Middle	Above average
7	Redshore	Very low	Below average
8	Hawesmere	High	Above average
28	Firsdown	Very high	Much above average
29	Sandmere	Very high	Much above average
30	Bournside	Very low	Broadly average
31	Birchcroft	Very low	Broadly average
32	Rowan	Very low	Below average
33	Kirkend	Low	Above average
34	Clearwater	Very low	Below average
35	Juniper Street	High	Much above average

Note. Schools with the most deprived intakes are likely to be ranked 'very high' on the Townsend index and 'much above average' on pupils' eligibility for free school meals

Census data from 1991 was consulted for information on the level of deprivation in the enumeration districts in which the schools were situated (Townsend Index of deprivation). We used five categories to simplify this data: a very high ranking on the Townsend index of deprivation (above 2.8); high (0.08 to 2.8); middle (-1.59 to 0.08); low (-2.94 to -1.59); very low (below -2.94).

As can be seen from Table 3.4, there are schools from a wide range of levels in both more and less successful categories. However, there is a slightly different profile for *more successful* as opposed to *less successful* schools. The *more successful* show a more even spread amongst the categories of deprivation. The *less successful* schools are more likely to be in areas at the extremes of either very high or very low deprivation.

Turning to a consideration of pupil eligibility for free school meals, we used Office for Standards in Education classifications for primary schools (Office for Standards in Education, 2001). These classifications range from much below average (below 2.0%); below average (2.0%-7.4%); broadly average (7.4%-18.8%); above average (18.8%-41.2%); much above average (above 41.2%). The schools in our sample were categorised using data obtained as near to the beginning of the research as possible, and some classifications may have changed since that time.

Table 3.4 shows that eligibility for free school meals is slightly greater amongst *less successful* schools, with three of the eight schools having the highest level of eligibility for free school meals, compared with none of the *more successful* schools. However, *Talltrees*, the most successful school in terms of our ranking of mean percentage gains, is situated in an area of very high deprivation and has above average pupil eligibility for free school meals.

Overall, therefore, there was no clear indication that socio-economic status might be an important factor in influencing gains in pupil attainment in mathematics.

5.3. External pressure and support

We looked at the experience of the 16 schools in terms of Ofsted inspections. All the schools had been inspected at least once during the timespan of the research (see Tables 3.5 and 3.6). Two of the *more successful* schools (*Elmtree and Redshore*) had experienced considerable trauma as a result of their inspections, one of them being placed in the category of 'special measures' (see Table 3.5). This category is synonymous with 'failing' the inspection and schools frequently have to contend with uncomplimentary articles in the local press and considerable anxiety and loss of support from parents.

Table 3.5. Results of Office for Standards in Education (Ofsted) inspections for the eight more successful schools during the span of the research project

Rank on mean % gains 1997-2002	*School*	*Results of Office for Standards in Education (Ofsted) inspections during the span of the research project*	*% teaching judged by Ofsted*
1	Talltrees	After a troubled history, improvements in this school were noted. In 1999, the school was now well placed to make progress. Standards in mathematics at age 11 were above average	1999 83% satis+ 21% v. good+
2	Mountain Ash	In 2000, the school was found to be very effective with high standards in mathematics by age 11	2000 95% satis+ 31% v. good+
3	Greenacres	In 1999, standards in mathematics were found to be not high enough, but there had been satisfactory improvement since 1996	1999 95% satis+ 10% v. good+
4	Windsmoor Infants and Junior	Both Infants and Juniors were found to be good schools. In 2001, the Junior school enabled pupils to achieve excellent results. In 2002, standards of attainment in the Infant school were high. Pupils did well in mathematics	Infants 2002 96% satis+ 25% v. good+ Juniors 2001 96% satis+ 35% v. good+
5	Kirkshaw	In 2000, this was regarded as a very good and effective school. Standards in mathematics at age 11 were sometimes very good	2000 100% satis+ 30% v. good+
6	Elmtree	1997, school put into 'special measures'. Removed in 1999. 2001 – improving steadily; although standards still below national average	2001 97% satis+ 27% v.good+
7	Redshore	1999 report – insufficient progress, high level unsatisfactory teaching in mathematics; standards in mathematics below similar schools	1999 86% satis+ 6% v. good+
8	Hawesmere	In 2001, this was found to be a very effective school with high expectations and achieving high standards	2001 100% satis+ 47% v. good+

Note. 'Satis+' means at least satisfactory; 'v. good+' means at least very good. Teaching was assessed in these grades by Ofsted across all subjects

Table 3.6. Results of Office for Standards in Education (Ofsted) inspections for the eight less successful schools during the span of the research project

Rank on mean % gains 1997-2002	*School*	*Results of Office for Standards in Education (Ofsted) inspections during the span of the research project*	*% teaching judged by Ofsted*
28	Firsdown	1998, attainment well below the national average, but broadly in line with similar schools. Unsatisfactory progress since last inspection, but weaknesses outweighed by strengths	1998 95% satis+ 33% v. good+
29	Sandmere	In 1998, the majority of pupils were found to be making good progress in mathematics, but attainment was below average compared with similar schools	1998 97% satis+ 14% v. good+
30	Bournside	School put into 'special measures' in 1996. In 1998 removed from this category, standards were good and rising	1998 100% satis+ 67% v. good+
31	Birchcroft	In 1998, this school was found to be well managed and happy, with sound levels of attainment in mathematics, in line with national average	1998 91% satis+ 25% v. good+
32	Rowan	In 1998, this was described as a good school with a clear route to become very good. Attainment above the national average	1998 100% satis+ 33% v. good+
33	Kirkend	In 2000, standards in mathematics were found to be well above average and teaching was good	2000 100% satis+ 38% v. good+
34	Clearwater	In 2000, this school was found to have improved over the past four years and to be a very effective school with rising standards	2000 100% satis+ 45% v. good+
35	Juniper Street	2000, standards in mathematics improving and now above average compared with similar schools. However there were serious weaknesses and underachievement of many pupils	2000 84% satis+ 12% v. good+

Note. 'Satis+' means at least satisfactory; 'v. good+' means at least very good. Teaching was assessed in these grades by Ofsted across all subjects

Another of the more successful schools, *Talltrees*, was already regarded as needing additional support by its Local Education Authority, and although not categorised as in 'special measures', its inspection in 1999 noted unsatisfactory progress since the last inspection. They also noted, however, that the school was now well placed to make progress.

It can be seen from Table 3.6 that two of the schools in the *less successful* category had also received highly critical Ofsted reports. One of these, *Bournside,* had been placed in 'special measures' before the research began and the other, *Juniper Street,* was regarded as having serious weakness, although not in mathematics. These two schools would also be the recipients of an increased level of monitoring and support. *Firsdown*, in addition, was receiving extra help from its Local Education Authority.

Interestingly, the majority of schools among our *less,* as well as our *more successful* schools (identified on the basis of gains), received positive Ofsted inspection reports and were regarded as providing a good or very good education for their pupils. These schools with positive reports all had national test results (at age 11) at or above the national average in the year previous to their inspection. The underachievement of high attaining pupils does not appear to have been recognised by Ofsted inspections. It is possible that less pressure is put on schools that have test results at or above the national average. Correspondingly, schools which are very successful and achieve high gains in relation to our data, but still have relatively low attainment in relation to national norms, are less likely to receive the recognition they deserve.

It can also be noted from Tables 3.5 and 3.6 that quality of teaching as judged by Ofsted inspectors in the schools' most recent inspection appears to differ little between the *more* and *less successful* schools. Two of the *more successful* schools have less than 90% satisfactory teaching, compared with one of the *less successful* schools. More of the *less successful* schools were judged by Ofsted to have no unsatisfactory teaching at all.

5.4. Provision for continuing professional development

The information in Tables 3.7 and 3.8 comes from interviews with headteachers and mathematics co-ordinators over the five years of *Tracking Numeracy.* We make no claims that this is a comprehensive list of professional development activities in mathematics for each school, but represents what the school itself considered to be the most important.

Table 3.7. Involvement in continuing professional development of the eight more successful schools

Rank on mean % gains 1997-2002	*School*	*MC to 20/10 day, diploma course, Masters module*	*Teachers to Five-day National Numeracy Strategy Course*	*Support from Numeracy Consultant*	*Information from the schools about professional development activities*
1	Talltrees	√	√	√	MC to co-ordinator meetings Mathematics adviser in to school MC is LMT
2	Mountain Ash	√			MC runs courses in authority MC is LMT
3	Greenacres		√	√	MC to co-ordinator course
4	Windsmoor I and J	√	√	√	MC to co-ordinator meetings Mathematics adviser into school MC is LMT
5	Kirkshaw	√			MC to courses Mathematics adviser into school
6	Elmtree	√	√	√	School in 'special measures' Mathematics advisory teacher in
7	Redshore	√	√	√	MC to courses Mathematics adviser into school
8	Hawesmere		√		MC to courses

Note: MC – mathematics co-ordinator; LMT – leading mathematics teacher; I – Infants; J – Juniors

Intensive help from the National Numeracy Strategy in the form of the Five-day course and five days of support from a numeracy consultant were made available to schools according to need. By 2001/02, most schools had been able to take advantage of the Five-day course, but had not necessarily received the same amount of consultant support in school.

Table 3.8. Involvement in continuing professional development of the eight less successful schools

Rank on mean %gains 1997-2002	*School*	*MC to 20/10-day, diploma course, Masters module*	*Teachers to Five-day National Numeracy Strategy Course*	*Support from Numeracy Consultant*	*Information from the schools about professional development activities*
28	Firsdown	√	√	√	MC runs courses for authority Staff to range of courses
29	Sandmere		√	√	MC to co-ordinator meetings MC to BEAM course
30	Bournside		?	√	In 'special measures' Support from authority MC to course
31	Birchcroft		√	√	Two teachers to courses
32	Rowan	√	√		MC to co-ordinator course. 2 LMTs Mathematics advisory teacher in BEAM courses and University support
33	Kirkend		√		MC – course. Advisory teacher in
34	Clearwater	√			Some teachers to courses
35	Juniper Street	√	√	√	BEAM courses

Note. MC – mathematics co-ordinator; LMT – leading mathematics teacher; I – Infants; J – Juniors; BEAM – private sector provider of in-service training

We can see from Table 3.7 that the *more successful* schools appeared to be making more use of their Local Education Authority advisory personnel, whether they were receiving consultant support or not. It was also the case that a higher proportion of the mathematics co-ordinators from the *more successful* schools had attended either a long mathematics course (20-day course; 10-day course; diploma course; Masters course module) than those from the *less successful* schools. In both groups, outside consultants from the private sector had provided in-service training in the schools. There were therefore some differences, but these were not overwhelming.

5.5. Attitudes towards reform and the National Numeracy Strategy

Responses to the National Numeracy Strategy introduced in September 1999 were generally positive. One school, *Rowan*, elected not to adopt the Strategy and was allowed to 'opt out' as the attainment levels of its pupils were above average and on an upward trajectory. We noted that two of the *more successful* schools, *Mountain Ash* and *Hawesmere,* were proactive in their approach to the reform, organising training and consulting draft materials well before the Strategy was introduced. Although we could detect some differences in take-up of opportunities for teachers to attend the Five-day course, this could be for a variety of reasons, not necessarily related to the willingness of the school to release teachers from classroom duties. For example, one authority had released the dates of the course so belatedly that the school was not able to take up the opportunity. In general, these schools were grateful for the opportunity of extra training and positive about its results. By 2002, one of the *more successful* schools was commenting on a loss of some of the more investigative work, and on children becoming confused by being shown so many methods (both attributed to the introduction of the Strategy), but such negative comments were rare.

5.6. Movement of staff

From data collected over the five years of *Tracking Numeracy*, we looked at the number of years in each school in which there had been disruption either in the role of mathematics co-ordinator or in the role of headteacher. We have categorised this factor as something over which schools have some degree of control in as much as staff mobility may be the result of strong professional development and due to promotion outside the school; in other cases, mobility might be due to the conditions within the school acting as a disincentive to new teachers to take up permanent positions in the school.

It can be seen from Table 3.9 that although there were no striking differences, there was a tendency for *more successful* schools to have fewer years of disruption in terms of headteacher and mathematics co-ordinator replacement than the *less successful* schools. The *more successful* schools suffered 12 disrupted years between them; the *less successful* schools suffered 17 disrupted years between them.

Table 3.9. Major staff movements affecting mathematics co-ordinator or headteacher

Rank on mean % gains 1997-2002	*School*	*Major staff movements affecting mathematics co-ordinator or headteacher. Years affected during the five years of the project (score/5; score/3 if Infant only school, pupils 5-7 years)*
1	Talltrees	3/5 New headteacher and two new mathematics co-ordinators
2	Mountain Ash	1/5 Headteacher seconded to another school Mathematics co-ordinator acting head
3	Greenacres	1/5 New mathematics co-ordinator
4	Windsmoor Infants and Juniors	Infants: 1/3 New headteacher Juniors: 0/5 Nothing to report
5	Kirkshaw	1/5 Mathematics co-ordinator on long -term sick leave
6	Elmtree	1/5 New headteacher
7	Redshore	2/5 Two new mathematics co-ordinators
8	Hawesmere	2/5 Two new mathematics co-ordinators
28	Firsdown	2/5 New headteacher. Mathematics co-ordinator left Headteacher covering co-ordinator role
29	Sandmere	1/5 New mathematics co-ordinator and new headteacher
30	Bournside	3/5 Two new mathematics co-ordinators. New headteacher who is now taking on co-ordinator role
31	Birchcroft	3/5 Two new mathematics co-ordinators New headteacher
32	Rowan	1/5 New mathematics co-ordinator
33	Kirkend	1/5 Headteacher seconded to another school part time
34	Clearwater	3/5 Headteacher seconded to another school. Two mathematics co-ordinators left, headteacher now occupying role
35	Juniper Street	3/5 Two new mathematics co-ordinator New headteacher

5.7. In conclusion – large-scale data from Tracking Numeracy

From updated summaries of yearly visits to these 35 schools, we could report a picture of great variation. Aspects of the six constructs identified during our case-study work appeared to be in evidence. However, in contrast to the ongoing analysis and data collection permitted by case-study work, we found that large-scale data collection clearly did not allow us the same intimate knowledge of schools (based as it was on yearly visits) and did not enable us to make discriminating judgements on the six constructs.

Large-scale quantitative data did allow us to suggest three conditions which might be associated with higher gains over time in pupils' numeracy attainment:

- low starting scores
- higher take-up of external support
- lower levels of staff movement.

Indications, however were small, and there were exceptions amongst both the *more* and the *less successful* schools. The high gains produced by some schools working in areas of high deprivation and with high proportions of pupils eligible for free school meals support our contention that the factors that contribute most forcefully towards effecting change in the practice of a school's teachers, and thereby the attainment of its pupils, lie within the personal control of those working in the immediate school *situation*, by enabling change through the realisation of teachers' *zones of enactment*, a notion susceptible to identification and illumination through in-depth data collection over time, rather than large-scale data collected at less frequent intervals.

6. DISCUSSION

In this chapter we have drawn on data from the Core Project in the Leverhulme Numeracy Research Programme, *Tracking Numeracy*, and from one of its linked projects – *Whole School Action on Numeracy*. In terms of our model, described in Chapter 1, the focus in this chapter has been on the *situation* and some of the *external factors* that have been impacting on schools over recent years. We return to the question that framed this chapter – how can schools make a difference in encouraging individual teachers to make (and sustain) effective changes in their practice?

Hopkins (2001) draws attention to the failure in some school effectiveness research to recognise what he terms the "differential effectiveness" of schools (p. 162). Schools at different stages of development require different strategies to enhance their capacity for development. We would like to point to three important messages to emerge from our research:

- pupil intakes from areas of high deprivation, or intakes with low starting scores, are not necessarily inhibitors of progress, when other actions in the school are enhancing development. Our research has spanned an extremely interesting time in that the reform initiative coming in the middle of that span has been common to virtually all schools in England – a national programme of reform that has not been targeted at specific schools with certain identified needs, although some schools have received more input than others

- findings from our case-study schools indicate that schools already in a positive position on the six constructs identified in the research were able to be proactive in taking innovation on board. As noted in Chapter 2, those in a less positive position were helped by the introduction of support from the National Numeracy Strategy to develop those constructs that seem to us to be of importance to the initiation and implementation of change
- these schools could be considered to be at different "growth states" (Hopkins, 2001, p. 162).

Our focus on the construct of *balance* places the growth state or culture firmly within the *professional community*, that part of the school's situation where attitudes to, and resources for, continuing professional learning are developed and enriched through enlightened leadership.

6.1. A rich situation – a learning culture

The development of Spillane's ideas (Spillane, 1999) into our model for discussing change necessitated, in our view, the addition of a mediating layer between the individual and external factors – the *situation*, consisting of the *professional community* of colleagues and the *pupils* attending the school. Others researching different aspects of the educational process have increasingly placed importance on the school site in discussing professional development and the implementation of change (e.g. Joyce & Showers, 1995).

In our writing about the mathematics co-ordinator in Chapter 2, we described rich deliberations as part of the development of *zones of enactment* that enabled individual teachers to take change on board. In this chapter, we have focused on the ability of one school in particular to provide a rich *situation* that draws on contributions from different members of the *professional community* to facilitate development of *zones of enactment*, despite the range of external pressures constantly impinging upon it.

The notions of "transformational leadership" promoted by Leithwood, Jantzi and Steinbach (1999, p. 4) or "values-led contingency leadership" described by Day et al. (2000, p. 158) attribute great importance to the professional growth of those for whom the leaders have responsibility. Our six constructs, which emerged through data collection and analysis rather than through being imposed on the data, illustrate three in particular of Leithwood, Jantzi and Mascall's constituents of a school situation that promotes learning (Leithwood, Jantzi, & Mascall, 1999, p. 17):

- Expectations that teachers are responsible not only for the quality of instruction in their own classrooms but for department and school-wide decisions likely to influence their classroom practices, as well

- Structures in the school that minimize teachers' isolation and foster dialogue and discussion

- Norms and opportunities for teachers to learn from others not only inside their school but outside, as well.

Our construct of *balance* reflects the emphasis on extended professional responsibility and through its linked constructs illustrates a situation where concern for this professional growth leads to high expectations coupled with the support and resources to enable those expectations to be met. In the case of subject co-ordination, other constituents are implicit – the need for dialogue and discussion to promote subject consultancy; the rejection of isolationism and the promotion of collaborative judgements about practice; the utilisation of expertise from inside and outside the school. All these are prerequisites for the realisation of teachers' *zones of enactment*, where reform ideas are discussed, activated, reflected upon, discarded or adopted, and must be resourced and given priority.

An organisation providing a rich *situation* for its members would be one that, in Leithwood et al.'s terms, exhibited collective capacity and infrastructure for reform – an infrastructure that fostered both individual motivation and capacity (Leithwood, et al., 1999). We feel that a rich *situation* would also include what Nias et al., (1992) have described as a culture of collaboration that values both the individual and the collective contribution and provides the security for differences in views to be openly expressed. C*oherence and consistency* (Construct 4) result from the existence of such a culture.

The first two reports of the government-commissioned evaluation of the National (Literacy and) Numeracy Strategies (Earl et al., 2000; Earl et al., 2001) describe the Strategies as having the potential for "deep" change to occur (Earl et al., 2000, p. 39). However, the evaluators are forthright about the difficulties involved in sustaining change and stress the necessity of creating 'learning cultures' at both school (King & Newmann, 2000) and local district level. Although the use of regular advisory, rather than inspectorial, support from the Local Education Authority emerged as one of our six important constructs in the development of mathematics, a more general study of the influence of the Local Education Authority on the school was not part of our research. However, the importance of strong and appropriate participation in the implementation of reform from local administrators has been emphasised by others (Fullan, 2001).

6.2. *A learning community*

To acknowledge the school as an agent of change implies that its collective capacity is greater than the sum of the individual capacities of those within it. This extra capacity is created through collaborative interactions such as those described in some of the schools in our research. Stein and Brown (1997) use two examples of a socio-cultural perspective on teacher change that relate particularly to our research. The first of these is Lave and Wenger's (1991) concept of moving from "legitimate peripheral participation" to "full participation in the socio-cultural practices of the community" (p. 29). For Stein and Brown (1997), the direction of change for "newcomers" was provided by "old-timers who were seen as the master practitioners of these reform ideas" (p. 171), in their case implementation of the reforms of the Professional Standards for the Teaching of Mathematics (National Council of Teachers of Mathematics, 1989). In our case the individuals bringing greater expertise and broader perspectives relating to the National Numeracy Strategy would be the mathematics co-ordinators, leading mathematics teachers and members of a mathematics co-ordination team.

The second concept of relevance to our work is that of "chains of assistance" (Tharp & Gallimore, 1988, p. 83) where:

> ... those in supervisory positions are responsible not only for providing assistance but most importantly for using their authority to create the time, resources, and incentives for teachers to participate in activity settings where effective assistance can occur. (Stein & Brown, p. 173)

Including the headteacher or principal in the group "provides teachers with organisational support for professional risk-taking and instructional change" (Nelson, 1997, p. 408). In the situations of *balance* that we have described in this chapter, headteachers, co-ordinators (and in some cases classroom teachers) can be seen to have different roles and responsibilities, but a common understanding that each can provide resources of use to others.

6.3. *Sustaining change*

The six case-study schools on which we have mainly drawn in this chapter were successful to different degrees in initiating and implementing change in the teaching of mathematics (based on recorded levels of attainment in national tests at age 11 and the perceptions of those working in the schools). However, the pressure of maintaining good results can be as great or greater than that of achieving them in the first place. As we have seen from our large-scale Core Project, *Tracking Numeracy*, mobility of staff is one factor that may affect a school's ability to implement and sustain change. The greater the professional development teachers experience as part of a rich *situation*, the more likely they may be to move on through promotion. Difficulties over recruiting new staff, currently a problem in England, can exacerbate this situation. Pupil mobility; differences in pupil cohorts and parental support; changing personnel at Local Education Authority level and in those professionals providing the support associated with the National Numeracy Strategy; the timing of further Ofsted inspections, are some of the other internal and external influences on sustainability. During the years in which schools in England were facing initiatives on both literacy and numeracy, they were permitted to allocate less time to other subjects in the primary curriculum (Department for Education and Employment, 1998). External policy initiatives, such as the removal of this moratorium on the foundation subjects in place during the emphasis on literacy and numeracy in 1998 and 1999 and the new resourcing of Information and Communications Technology as a priority for in-service training, have been noted by all our case-study schools as affecting their ability to sustain developments in mathematics.

A combination of some or all of these factors has meant that only two of our six case-study schools were able to sustain consistent improvement over four years and, as we have seen, *Wolverton* is not included here. Given its recent trajectory, further improvement would be likely to be far less dramatic. Two of our case-study schools, *Woodbury* and *Sandmere*, were also in the Core Project, *Tracking* Numeracy. It is interesting that *Woodbury,* whose progress over four years was substantial, just failed to be included in the eight most successful schools in *Tracking Numeracy. Sandmere,* despite making progress in the year of the introduction of the Numeracy Strategy, when improved positions on the six constructs were noted, did not maintain this progress over time.

Researchers contributing to Success Against the Odds – Five Years On (Maden, 2001a) returned to eleven schools (four of which were primary schools) that had previously been found to be succeeding in difficult environments. A critical constituent of the failure to maintain change in one school was a change in leadership after which the existing culture of the school was not maintained. Maden (2001b) reflects that:

> It is probable that 'school capacity' is the single most important matter in trying to identify how and why some schools maintain and sustain improvement (p. 320).

Gray (2001), in his introduction to the same book, discusses how 'culture' has given way to 'capacity' in school improvement literature – cultures by their nature being more difficult to change, capacities being more "malleable" (p. 27) and lending themselves to improvement. Malleability implies flexibility, an ability to adapt to changing conditions. Perhaps it also implies an ability to adapt external influences to suit the needs of the school – "colonising" external reforms (Sofer, 2001, p. 71) rather in the way that two of our case-study schools "defused conflict" (Millett & Johnson, 2000b, p. 29) by addressing the key issues in their Ofsted inspection reports through their own priorities for development.

Maden (2001b) describes some elements of an organisational capacity or school culture which secures continuous improvement:

> The spelling out of values and core beliefs is important. This isn't the slick business model of a touchy-feely 'mission statement' – even if this latter term is deployed. Rather, it is a clearing-out process, of all the inessentials and diversions which clutter up the works and are sometimes imposed from elsewhere. (Maden 2001b, p. 321)

6.4. How the school can make a difference

In this chapter we have seen that some schools appear to have affected pupils' attainment levels in the short term, but we have also raised questions about the conditions necessary for sustaining change over the longer term.

We return here to Leithwood, Jantzi and Mascall's (1999) reference to a state of disequilibrium in a school as a possible prerequisite for change, mentioned first in Chapter 1. Complacency about existing attainment or progress will militate against reform. A state of disequilibrium can be caused from inside or outside the school. Dissatisfaction can come from within the *professional community*, for example from a new headteacher or mathematics co-ordinator whose vision for the way ahead cannot be realised without change. Alternatively, the shock of a negative external inspection report, either from local or national personnel can stimulate a discussion within the school. In the case of *Wolverton* school, both these conditions were in operation. We have seen from our Core data that schools with very different sets of 'givens' can make similar improvements.

It seems to us that enlightened and determined leadership in a school can create a "growth state" (Hopkins, 2001, p. 162), starting the "clearing-out process" (Maden, 2001b, p. 321) from quite unprepossessing beginnings, and that this itself can be seen as a staged process. In order to answer the question posed at the beginning of the chapter, we return to the stages of development through which the headteacher of *Wolverton* School guided the members of the school's *professional community*:

- dissatisfaction with the status quo
- clarification of objectives

- promoting the acceptance of aims and objectives leading to coherence and consistency of views within the professional community
- raising expectations of the professional roles within the school
- resourcing these accordingly through both internal and external provision
- expecting ongoing learning from all members of the professional community
- resisting complacency in order to sustain change.

The following quotation from the mathematics co-ordinator at *Wolverton* illustrates this last point without further explanation:

> Yes it's hard to keep, I think it's hard to keep the momentum going. I know after Ofsted the teachers were very much feeling that. [The headteacher] went on a course and we all had to do, he did these evaluations of what he felt and we all felt like we'd achieved, what we wanted to achieve and quite honestly, you know, we would have just plateaued there but he didn't let us, and he kept taking it further ... so he definitely kept the school moving forward. (Jodie)

Listing the stages in this way inevitably depersonalises what to us is an intensely personal process that makes the way in which actions are decided upon and taken more important than the actions themselves. It is the combination of the personal and the organisational which, we feel, builds up a rich *situation* in which the development of *zones of enactment* becomes part of routine school practice with the expectation that ongoing professional learning is both a prerogative and a duty of all members of the school community.

7. AFFILIATIONS

Professor David C. Johnson is an emeritus Professor at the Department of Education and Professional Studies, King's College London, having recently retired as Shell Professor of Mathematics Education.

8. NOTES

[1] A fuller version of this case study appears in Millett, A. & Johnson, D. C. (2003). Raising attainment in mathematics: the story of Wolverton School. *Education 3-13, 31*(1), 26-36.

[2] Previous writing on the six linked constructs has appeared in Millett, A. & Johnson, D. C. (2000a). The role of the maths co-ordinator and the National Numeracy Strategy in England. *Teacher Development, 4*(3), 393-410. Copyright © 2000; Teacher Development. Material reproduced here by kind permission of Triangle Journals Ltd., publishers of Teacher Development.

9. REFERENCES

Bell, D. (1992). Co-ordinating science in primary schools: a role model? *Evaluation and Research in Education, 6*(2&3), 155-171.

Bell, D. (1999). *Subject leadership in the primary school. Views of headteachers.* Paper presented at the British Educational Research Association, University of Sussex.

Boaler, J. (1997). *Experiencing School Mathematics.* Buckingham: Open University Press.

Bush, T. (1986). *Theories of Educational Management.* London: Harper & Row.

Day, C., Harris, A., Hadfield, M., Tolley, H., & Beresford, J. (2000). *Leading schools in times of change.* Buckingham: Open University Press.

Department for Education and Employment. (1999). *The National Numeracy Strategy: Framework for Teaching Mathematics from Reception to Year 6.* London: Department for Education and Employment.

Department for Education and Employment. (1998). *Blunkett strengthens curriculum focus on basics. Press release 006/98.* London: Department for Education and Employment.

Earl, L., Fullan, M., Leithwood, K., Watson, N., with Jantzi, D., Levin, B., & Torrance, N. (2000). *Watching and Learning. OISE/UT Evaluation of the implementation of the National Literacy and Numeracy Strategies. First annual report.* Toronto: Ontario Institute for Studies in Education, University of Toronto.

Earl, L., Levin, B., Leithwood, K., Fullan, M., & Watson, N. (2001). *Watching & Learning 2: OISE/UT Evaluation of the Implementation of the National Literacy and Numeracy Strategies. Second annual report.* Toronto: Ontario Institute for Studies in Education, University of Toronto.

Fullan, M. (2001). *The new meaning of educational change. 3rd Edition.* New York, NY: Teachers College Press.

Gray, J. (2001). Introduction: building for improvement and sustaining change in schools serving disadvantaged communities. In M. Maden (Ed.), *Success Against the Odds – Five Years On* (pp. 1-39). London: RoutledgeFalmer.

Hopkins, D. (1994). School improvement in an ERA of change. In P. Ribbins & E. Burridge (Eds.), *Improving education: promoting quality in schools* (pp. 74-91). London: Cassell.

Hopkins, D. (2001). *School improvement for real.* London: Routledge.

Hopkins, D., Ainscow, M., & West, M. (1994). *School improvement in an ERA of change.* London: Cassell.

Joyce, B., & Showers, B. (1995). *Student achievement through staff development.* New York, NY: Longmans.

King, B., & Newmann, F. (2000). Will teacher learning advance school goals? *Phi Delta Kappen, 8*(8), 576-580.

Lave, J., & Etienne, W. (1991). *Situated Learning: legitimate peripheral participation.* Cambridge: Cambridge University Press.

Leithwood, K., Jantzi, D., & Mascall, B. (1999). *Large-Scale Reform: What Works? Submitted as part of the first annual report: External Evaluation of the UK National Literacy and National Numeracy Strategy.* Ontario: Ontario Institute for Studies in Education, University of Toronto.

Leithwood, K., Jantzi, D., & Steinbach, R. (1999). *Changing leadership for changing times.* Buckingham: Open University Press.

Maden, M. (2001a). Further lessons in success. In M. Maden (Ed.), *Success Against the Odds – Five Years On* (pp. 307-339). London: RoutledgeFalmer.

Maden, M. (Ed.). (2001b). *Success Against the Odds – Five Years On.* London: RoutledgeFalmer.

Millett, A., & Johnson, D. C. (2000a). The role of the maths co-ordinator and the National Numeracy Strategy in England. *Teacher Development, 4*(3), 393-410.

Millett, A., & Johnson, D. C. (2000b). Dancing to whose tune? Conflicting priorities for primary schools. *Education 3-13, 28*(3), 24-31.

Millett, A., & Johnson, D. C. (2003). Raising attainment in mathematics: the story of Wolverton School. *Education 3-13, 31*(1), 26-36.

Moore, J. L. (1992). The role of the science co-ordinator in primary schools. A survey of headteachers' views. *School Organisation, 12*(1), 7-15.

National Council of Teachers of Mathematics. (1989). *Curriculum and evaluation standards for school mathematics*. Reston, VA: National Council of Teachers of Mathematics.

Nelson, B. S. (1997). Learning about teacher change in the context of mathematics education reform: where are we going? In E. Fennema & B. S. Nelson (Eds.), *Mathematics Teachers in Transition* (pp. 403-419). Mahwah, NJ: Lawrence Erlbaum Associates, Inc.

Nias, J., Southworth, G., & Campbell, P. (1992). *Whole school curriculum development in the primary school*. London: Falmer Press.

Office for Standards in Education. (2001). *National Summary Data Report (PICSI and PANDA Annexes for 2001/2002 reports containing 2001 data)*. London: Office for Standards in Education.

Office for Standards in Education. (1998). *Setting in primary schools*. London: Office for Standards in Education.

Sofer, A. (2001). Columbia Primary School. In M. Maden (Ed.), *Success Against the Odds – Five Years On*. London: Routledge/Falmer.

Spillane, J. P. (1999). External reform initiatives and teachers' efforts to reconstruct their practice: the mediating role of teachers' zones of enactment. *Journal of Curriculum Studies, 31*(2), 143-175.

Stein, M. K., & Brown, C. (1997). Teacher Learning in a Social Context: Integrating Collaborative and Institutional Processes with the Study of Teacher Change. In E. Fennema & B. S. Nelson (Eds.), *Mathematics Teachers in Transition* (pp. 155-191). Mahwah, NJ: Lawrence Erlbaum Associates, Inc.

Teacher Training Agency. (1997). *National Standards for Headteachers*. London: Teacher Training Agency.

Tharp, R., & Gallimore, R. (1988). *Rousing minds to life: Teaching, learning and schooling in social context*. Cambridge: Cambridge University Press.

Webb, R., & Vulliamy, G. (1996). *Roles and responsibilities in the primary school. Changing demands, changing practices*. Buckingham: Open University Press.

West-Burnham, J. (1996). Quality and the primary school curriculum. In J. O'Neill & N. Kitson (Eds.), *Effective curriculum management. Co-ordinating learning in the primary school* (pp. 52-61). London: Routledge.

Yeomans, R. (1987). Leading the team, belonging to the group? In G. Southworth (Ed.), *Readings in primary school management* (pp. 128-139). Lewes: Falmer Press.

VALERIE RHODES AND ALISON MILLETT

CHAPTER 4

THE MEDIATING ROLE OF TEXTUAL MATERIALS IN TEACHERS' RESPONSE TO CALLS FOR CLASSROOM REFORM

Abstract. This chapter examines how the introduction of the National Numeracy Strategy impacted on planning for mathematics at the level of the whole school and the individual teacher. In its initial training the Strategy encouraged schools nationally to open up their planning to include a wider range of materials. It is argued here that decisions about the choice of materials to use when planning the daily mathematics lesson had the potential to act as a conduit for professional development. On an individual level for a few teachers this proved to be case. At a collective level this potential was realised for some teachers planning collaboratively, but not where issues of efficacy in terms of time and duplication of effort were felt to militate against joint planning activities. Despite an initial push by government to encourage teachers to plan from a range of materials, the subsequent publication of ready-made lesson plans, available electronically on the web, brings government's commitment to promoting planning as a professional development opportunity into question.

1. INTRODUCTION

In this chapter we turn to the third question posed in Chapter 1: how can the use of textual materials contribute towards the realisation of rich *zones of enactment* that enable teachers to take change on board? We consider what we have learnt from our research about the impact of a major national reform initiative on the ways in which materials provided for the teaching of mathematics are used, and how their use can affect teachers' professional development. We draw on the model described in Chapter 1 in terms of the *person*, the individual teacher working within her *professional community* and providing lessons for her *pupils* within the context of national policy reform in England. This reform initiative, the National Numeracy Strategy, has not only published its own materials to support the teaching of mathematics, but has also affected the use of commercially produced mathematics

Alison Millett, Margaret Brown and Mike Askew (eds.), Primary Mathematics and the Developing Professional.

materials – illuminating links in our model with *policy* and *private sector* external factors.

By considering this range of factors, we reflect Stray's historical view of the textbook as:

> ... the intersection of several relationships involving teachers and pupils, producers and consumers, institutions and the state. (Stray, 1994, p. 24)

We frame the chapter round the following questions:

- what is the national and international context for the use of published materials for the teaching of primary mathematics
- what do we mean by textual materials within the context of this research
- how has the introduction of the National Numeracy Strategy in England in 1999 affected the use of published materials
- how are decisions made about the use of materials, what influences these decisions and what reasons are given for these decisions
- what examples of professional development through the use of materials have been evident in this research?

2. THE NATIONAL AND INTERNATIONAL CONTEXT FOR THE USE OF PUBLISHED MATERIALS

The use of published materials in the form of textbooks or commercial mathematics schemes as a main resource for the teaching of mathematics in England has long been common practice. The word 'scheme' implies a structured set of published materials for pupils and teachers used predominantly by primary teachers which may include children's textbooks, teachers' books, assessments and resource materials, and which span the primary age range. Evidence suggests that this use of commercially produced materials is a world-wide phenomenon (Robitaille & Garden, 1989; Miwa, 1991; Zhang, 1991). Countries differ in the degree of choice allowed to schools in the selection of textbooks, with, for example, Pacific Rim countries requiring that texts are subject to ministry approval (Foxman, 1999).

In England, common practice has been less centrally determined; schools have been completely free to select and buy their materials from commercial publishers who work within an extremely competitive market. For some years, it has been suggested that English classroom teachers can become over-reliant on commercial schemes or textbooks and this practice has been viewed with concern. This concern has generally been based on two quite different beliefs:

- that heavy reliance on commercial mathematics schemes is not in the best interests of pupils' mathematical development

- that heavy reliance on commercial mathematics schemes restricts the professional development of teachers in that they are not researching, comparing and selecting the materials to use for their teaching.

Prior to the introduction of the mathematics National Curriculum in England and Wales (Department of Education and Science/Welsh Office, 1989), the Cockcroft Report (Department of Education and Science/Welsh Office, 1982) in discussing primary mathematics, warned that any textbook should be used with discrimination and should not be expected to provide a complete course to meet the needs of all children. After the introduction of the National Curriculum, the Office for Standards in Education (Ofsted) (1993), reporting on the teaching and learning of number in primary schools, focused on the first of the concerns identified above:

> In over a third of classes there was an over-reliance upon a particular published scheme which usually led to pupils spending prolonged periods of time in which they worked at a slow pace, often on repetitive, undemanding exercises, which did little to advance their skills or understanding of number, much less their interest and enthusiasm for mathematics. (p. 16)

Her Majesty's Inspectorate (1992) focused on the second concern, noting that teachers in all Key Stages (Ages 5-7; 7-11; 11-14; 14-16), in both primary and secondary schools, were relying on schemes rather than undertaking detailed planning of their own from the curriculum documents.

The Evaluation of the Implementation of National Curriculum Mathematics undertaken at King's College London 1991-1993, identified two contrasting types of scheme use, noting differences between *scheme-driven* planners, who turned to the scheme as the first avenue for their planning and took more than 50% of the work for their pupils from the scheme, and *scheme-assisted* planners, who used a scheme as just one of a range of resources (Askew et al., 1993; Millett & Johnson, 1996). In some *scheme-driven* classrooms children worked independently through textbooks at their own pace, whilst in others teachers and children worked through books together. In both cases the order in the book was generally followed. In contrast in *scheme-assisted* classrooms teachers followed a school scheme-of-work using textbooks or other commercially produced materials as additional resources. We make the distinction between published 'schemes' and 'schemes-of-work'; the latter are schools' own tailormade curriculum documents that generally include ideas for teaching and assessment activities as well as curriculum content. Schools are expected by inspectors to have schemes-of-work even if they are following closely a published scheme.

Askew et al. (1993) noted that the anxiety caused by the introduction of the mathematics National Curriculum in 1989 had led some schools to spend large amounts of money on buying in new versions of commercial schemes, although there were delays for a few years in the production of appropriate materials as publishers came to terms with new developments that included three different versions of the National Curriculum in quick succession (Department of Education and Science/Welsh Office, 1989;1991; Department for Education, 1995). Local Education Authority mathematics advisers interviewed at the time were, on the whole, not happy with the trend to plan directly from a scheme rather than choosing activities from a wider range of materials from a variety of sources. Their advice to schools was generally to promote *scheme-assisted* practice, although they recognised the demands on mathematics subject knowledge that the National Curriculum brought with it. Some Local Education Authority advisers were able to take advantage of a situation where schools were looking to change their schemes, providing them with a structured approach to making an informed choice and thereby raising awareness of positive features as well as possible pitfalls and inadequacies of different commercial materials (Millett & Johnson, 1996). There was some acknowledgment, however, of the potential benefits of scheme use for teachers who lacked knowledge of, or confidence in, mathematics.

In the late 1990s the mathematics curriculum in English primary schools was marked by a radical new initiative, a National Numeracy Strategy introduced in September 1999 (see Introduction). The National Numeracy Strategy documentation advocated a number of key principles including a structured daily mathematics lesson consisting typically of three parts, a focus on direct teaching and interactive oral work and an emphasis on mental calculation. Many of the changes the Strategy advocated required teachers to make changes at a structural level such as in the format of the lesson, the organisation of pupils, and the organisation of the curriculum. However teachers were also being encouraged to make changes to their practice at a deeper level by focusing on the mathematics they were teaching and the methods they were using. The first step of the change for teachers was to make changes in the way they planned lessons.

The introduction of this major national intervention in primary mathematics foregrounded once more schools' decisions about materials. The Framework for Teaching Mathematics from Reception to Year 6 (Department for Education and Employment, 1999a) gave a termly programme of objectives and was intended to be used as a day-to-day reference point. Although prescriptive and specific about mathematical teaching objectives and learning outcomes, the Framework does not fill the gap between these two, and schools were once again searching for helpful materials. The National Numeracy Strategy notes for locally appointed consultants acting as trainers (Department for Education and Employment, 1999b) clearly promoted *scheme-assisted* planning, with an initial focus on the learning objectives laid out year-by-year in the Framework.

The script urged trainers to:

> [m]ention that many publishers of primary mathematics schemes are beginning to link their publications to the Framework. So, for example, teachers who are planning work on, say, reading and writing numbers in figures and words, can look in the published teachers' books and readily find pages with suggestions for activities, including references to children's books. Schools in the National Numeracy Project who have worked in this way have welcomed becoming 'scheme-assisted' rather than 'scheme-driven'. (p. 107)

As had been the case with the introduction of the National Curriculum a decade earlier, the inevitable outcome of the introduction of the Framework was a mismatch between the mathematics presented in the commercial schemes published previously and the new curriculum. This was seen, however, as an opportunity to encourage teachers to move away from over-reliance on a scheme to structure their teaching and persuade them to focus down on to the mathematics. There were only a few months between the final publication of the objectives in the Framework and the national implementation of the Strategy. The result was that several of the first sets of new materials available were published hurriedly and were not generally of a high quality.

3. MATHEMATICS MATERIALS IN THE CONTEXT OF THIS RESEARCH

The commercially produced schemes being used in schools during this research fell into two broad categories, those written in line with the National Curriculum before the introduction of the National Numeracy Strategy, and those revised and/or published after. In the case of some of the latter schemes the original materials had been rewritten, in other cases the materials were completely new. With a few exceptions, the schemes aimed to provide a complete package of materials including, for example, teachers' books, scripted lessons suggesting questions teachers should ask at appropriate times, children's textbooks, assessment and resource materials and homework ideas. The provision of scripted lessons are a particular characteristic of some of the new schemes, following the publication by the Numeracy Strategy itself of a collection of sample lessons, and were rarely found in commercial schemes before the Numeracy Strategy. A notable feature of many new schemes was that they claimed to provide 'everything you need for a Successful Daily Mathematics Lesson' through use of their 'comprehensive teacher and pupil material'. Whilst at one extreme, one such scheme had no textbooks included, it was prescriptive in so far as it provided daily lesson plans and termly planning sheets. Another popular scheme on the other hand, aimed to "support" teachers in implementing the Strategy. Although it provided a wide range of materials it also allowed teachers some flexibility by providing only three rather than five structured lesson plans a week.

In addition to these commercially produced materials, we include in our consideration the key materials provided by the Strategy itself. The introduction of the Framework document with its termly objectives (Department for Education and Employment, 1999a) was closely followed by a set of Sample Medium Term Plans for each year group (Department for Education and Employment, 1999c), introduced to all schools during the Three-day course at the beginning of the training, for each year group. These set out a sequence of topics for each half term, with the number of lessons to be allocated and the objectives to be covered. These outline plans then had to be fleshed out within schools to create the detailed lesson plans for everyday use that were required under the Strategy and monitored by national and local school inspectors. Other smaller publications relating to such areas as Calculator Use (Department for Education and Employment, 1999d) and Reasoning about Numbers (Department for Education and Employment, 1999e) were distributed nationally as part of the Five-day course (see Introduction). The most recent development, starting in 2001, was the production of individual lesson plans for Year 4 (pupils aged 8-9 years) and Year 6 (pupils aged 10-11 years) distributed from the Department for Education and Employment website. At the time of writing, these lesson plans were being produced for other age-groups.

4. THE RESEARCH

For the purposes of this chapter, we shall be discussing data collected in the course of our work on the Core Project, *Tracking Numeracy*, Focus Project *Teachers' Knowledge, Conceptions and Practices* and Focus Project *Whole School Action on Numeracy* of The Leverhulme Numeracy Research Programme (see Introduction/ Annexes 1, 2 and 3). During the first year of *Tracking Numeracy* headteachers and mathematics co-ordinators were interviewed at length. Annual visits then enabled the research team to track changes through shorter update interviews with key personnel. Classroom teachers of the pupils in Cohorts 1 and 2 in *Tracking Numeracy* were interviewed each year.

In *Whole School Action on Numeracy*, the mathematics development and action taken in six case-study schools (two of which were also Core schools) were followed over the course of four years (see also Chapters 2 and 3). *Teachers' Knowledge, Conceptions and Practices*, which began two years later in 1999, followed 12 teachers in four schools (two of which were also Core schools). (See also Chapters 5 and 6.)

Analysis has considered the use made of commercial mathematics schemes, or elements of these schemes, as part of a range of materials used in the planning and teaching of mathematics. Also included in this range were documents provided by the National Numeracy Strategy. We have taken three periods of time as critical in this analysis – before the introduction of the National Numeracy Strategy (1997/98; 1998/99), during the initial year of implementation (1999/2000), and after this initial year (2000/01; 2001/02). We have focused primarily at school level, taking our description of how a school uses materials from the mathematics co-ordinator and the headteacher. However, we did not assume that having decided upon a policy it was adopted uniformly throughout a school; some primary schools chose to adopt one model in Key Stage 1 (5-7 years) and another way of working in Key Stage 2 (7-11 years). One school which did not follow the Numeracy Strategy has been omitted from the analysis as has one infant and one junior school for which data were incomplete. The findings being tracked here are based on data from 41 Core schools; infant schools (pupils aged 4-7 years) and junior schools (pupils aged 7-11 years) were treated separately for this purpose. As the children in the infant-only schools moved into junior schools in September 2000, the analysis for the infant-only schools is based on data up to this period only.

4.1. Reviewing our analytical criteria

In this chapter we have defined schools prior to the National Numeracy Strategy as *scheme-driven* if headteachers and mathematics co-ordinators made no mention of drawing on a school or Local Education Authority scheme-of-work (curriculum document), but only referred to their commercial scheme and the National Curriculum. A definition of a primary school as *scheme-driven* required that teachers of pupils across the whole primary age range were following this practice.

During and after the introduction of the Strategy, *scheme-driven* schools in the original sense no longer existed as the Framework document with its medium-term plans had for all become an intermediary in the planning process. For the timespan following the introduction of the Strategy we have developed a new category of *scheme-dependent* to describe those schools where scheme use was heavy and provided plans and resources for lessons across the age range, but where the objectives in the Framework would usually be referred to.

Scheme-assisted schools made use of a range of materials, but their own or a Local Education Authority scheme-of-work was central to their planning prior to the

Strategy, with the Numeracy Framework initially taking the place of these schemes-of-work. The definition is a broad one, however, as the range of resources available could vary from one or two commercial schemes in some schools to a whole bank of books and materials in others.

During the period just before the Numeracy Strategy was introduced, 11 *schools* out of 41 in the Core Project, *Tracking Numeracy*, were categorised by us as *scheme-driven*, just over 25%. This is similar to findings of previous surveys although the levels of analysis were different. In 1993, Ofsted's figure of just over a third related to primary *classes* where there was judged to be over-reliance on schemes. The categorisation as *scheme-driven* by the Evaluation of the Implementation of National Curriculum Mathematics (Millett & Johnson, 1996, p.59) related to four out of 20 primary *teachers* (20%), so although direct comparisons are not possible, it would seem likely that before the introduction of the Numeracy Strategy, heavy reliance on a single commercial mathematics scheme for both curriculum planning and teaching activities affected pupils in about a quarter of primary schools.

5. THE IMPACT OF THE NATIONAL NUMERACY STRATEGY ON THE USE OF PUBLISHED MATERIALS

The introduction of the National Numeracy Strategy required changes from previous ways of working in three main aspects of planning:

- planning had now to be objectives/outcomes led rather than in relation to a specific set of class activities
- planning was now required for the three individual parts of the new three-part lesson (mental/oral starter, main teaching activity, plenary), rather than for the lesson as a whole
- the model of the curriculum changed from one where mathematics topics, for example shape and space, might be taught for several weeks and then not referred to again during the course of a year, to one of more frequent revisiting of topics throughout a year.

The detailed lesson plans that resulted from the planning process were intended to constitute schools' own individual schemes-of-work.

With the introduction of the National Numeracy Strategy, schools were forced to re-examine the merits of the materials they were using and make decisions about whether or not to invest in a new commercial scheme or to begin to work with a range of materials.

Table 4.1. Method of planning reported in the Spring Terms of 1998 and 2000/02 in primary and junior schools (n=34) and in the Spring Terms of 1998 and 2000 in infant schools (n=7)

Use of scheme/s	*Method of planning* 1998 → 2000/02	*Number of schools* primary/junior	infant	*Total*
Change	Scheme-driven ---> scheme-assisted	3	2	5
	Scheme-assisted ---> scheme dependent	7	2	9
Little or no change	Scheme-assisted ---> scheme-assisted	20	1	21
	Scheme-driven ---> scheme-dependent	4	2	6
	Total	34	7	41

Note. Final data from infant-only schools was in 2000, as the cohort we were following then moved up to the linked junior schools

The research described here, which spanned the introduction of the National Numeracy Strategy, observed shifting patterns of scheme use in some but not all schools. Overall, the percentage of schools defined as *scheme-assisted* fell between 1997 and 2002 (73% to 63%) and the percentage of those defined as *scheme-driven* or *scheme-dependent* rose from 27% to 37%. Patterns of use of materials in the 41 schools fell into two broad categories:

- schools where there was a distinct change in practice (*scheme-driven* to *scheme-assisted*; *scheme-assisted* to *scheme-dependent*)
- schools where there was little or no change (*scheme-driven to scheme-dependent* and *scheme-assisted* to *scheme-assisted*, see Table 4.1).

The National Numeracy Strategy proved to be a catalyst for change in some schools whilst others maintained the status quo. There was a distinct shift in practice in 14 schools, five of which had opened up their planning by starting to use a wider range of published materials; nine of which had chosen to focus down to a position of reliance on a core scheme. The advent of the Strategy appeared to have had no or relatively little impact upon scheme use in more than two thirds of schools (n=27). The majority of these were already using commercial scheme materials in the way advocated by the Strategy, that is as one of a range of resources.

We now illustrate the four patterns with vignettes of school practice. As the examples below indicate, the journey was not always smooth, and decisions could be influenced by a number of priorities which changed over time.

5.1. Scheme-driven ---> scheme-assisted (five schools)

In some schools the Strategy proved to be a liberating influence and encouraged teachers to search for teaching materials from a range of sources.

In *Hawesmead* school before the introduction of the Numeracy Strategy (1997/98), mathematics work was centred around a commercial scheme which had been acquired before the arrival of the current headteacher some three years previously. Teachers also referred to National Curriculum documents in their planning. The new headteacher was aware, however, that the scheme was not adequate as it met neither the statutory requirements of the time nor the needs of the children who were not being stretched sufficiently and consequently were underachieving. It was clear that alternative resources would need to be explored before the Numeracy Strategy was introduced and mathematics, along with literacy, was deemed to be an area which needed to be developed. The school began to acquire more resources the following year and a new mathematics co-ordinator was appointed shortly afterwards. As he explained, staff were now:

> ... tak[ing] resources as they saw fit to pick and mix, rather than before where we were reliant on one specific scheme.

One of the new schemes purchased by the school was particularly popular with staff as it allowed teachers greater discretion over what they taught, unlike the scheme in use before the Strategy which had been unduly confining and restrictive. Teachers were actively encouraged to use their professional judgement when deciding what to use when. According to the mathematics co-ordinator, resourcing had become "very open … very teacher-led" and teachers were described as "doing much more with their maths". New materials were bought as a support and were not intended to be used as a scheme in their own right.

5.2. Scheme-assisted ---> scheme-dependent (nine schools)

Other schools faced with the demands inherent in implementing the Strategy chose to reduce their workload by becoming increasingly dependent on the use of one scheme to frame their planning.

In September 1997, *Larkhall* school was in the final year of developing a new school scheme-of-work (curriculum document). Based on Local Education Authority guidelines and policy, the scheme-of-work had been adapted to meet the specific needs of the school. The school's scheme-of-work, which was an "ongoing document", was supported largely, although not exclusively, by a recently published commercial scheme which teachers adapted as necessary for use in the classroom.

When the Numeracy Strategy was first implemented teachers continued to use a variety of resources but soon realised that seeking them out and matching them to objectives was very demanding of their time and energy. As the headteacher/ mathematics co-ordinator explained:

> My Year 3 teacher who is probably one of the strongest people for planning on the staff ... superb planning. And she's coming in and saying you know 'I'm sat round and I'm just thinking don't give me another book because I just, you know to get my head round where I'm going to get the work from'. It's a very worrying issue. And I don't believe that you should be spending more time planning than delivering. That can't be right.

In order to alleviate teachers' justifiable concern over planning it was decided to buy another commercial scheme, even though it was very expensive. This was well received by staff as it gave them "something to hang things on". But by the following year (Spring 2001), the school had purchased yet another new commercial scheme chosen because it followed the Numeracy Strategy closely. Staff were pleased with this scheme as it provided a comprehensive range of materials that the previous scheme had not provided. Although staff continued to "dip into" other schemes, the headteacher reported that the latest scheme was being taken on board by staff and was rapidly becoming adopted as the school's official scheme-of-work.

> Our school scheme-of-work is based on the use of [name of latest commercial scheme]. This scheme is fully in line with the NNS [National Numeracy Strategy] and incorporates all elements required to deliver the strategy. (excerpt from Larkhall's mathematics document written in June 2001)

By the following year, commercial scheme use had become established throughout the school. However, although the headteacher/mathematics co-ordinator followed it very strictly in his own teaching, he expressed some concern that some staff had begun to be more critical about its use and felt that they wanted to supplement it with other materials. He, however, believed this would break down the "momentum" of the Strategy.

5.3. Scheme-assisted ---> scheme-assisted (21 schools)

Within this well-populated category there were, of course, variations in practice. Some schools appeared settled in their practice, whereas others were widening their range of materials. Others again, for instance *Clearwater*, had become *scheme-dependent* for a while before reverting back to a more *scheme-assisted* approach for younger pupils.

Prior to the introduction of the National Numeracy Strategy, teachers in *Clearwater* school worked from their school scheme-of-work, using a commercial scheme for pupils aged 7-11 years and referring to the National Curriculum and other purchased materials. Although the commercial scheme formed a "base" in terms of content, less than half the mathematics work was actually textbook based. They began to use the Framework for their planning in 1999/2000. Teachers of younger children (5-7 years) continued to use a range of resources whilst teachers of 7-11-year-olds continued to draw from the commercial scheme "fitting" it in where possible. However, whilst they had previously used additional resources to supplement the scheme, they found it increasingly difficult to find suitable materials. According to the mathematics co-ordinator:

> … if we were using an area of the Strategy which isn't covered in [name of scheme] then it becomes more difficult to cover exactly or find the right materials for.

They also bought in other mental mathematics materials during this time. By 2000/01, the school had purchased a new commercial scheme for all age groups from Reception to Year 6. The headteacher described how their choice was influenced by the fact that lesson plans were all set out:

> ... idiot's guide to teaching maths, it is really. But also it tells you what resources to use, there are other back-up resources and there's good extension stuff as well.

The commercial scheme in question included a teachers' guide, long, medium and short-term plans, children's workbooks, copiable extension, support and homework materials, a games pack and CD Rom. The content of each lesson was closely tied to the Strategy. The teachers' notes provided clear guidance giving not only the objectives, key vocabulary and highlighting key teaching points but also giving step-by-step instructions on how to conduct the lesson. This included what to write on the board and questions to ask, as well as detailing additional resources within the scheme. As the headteacher explained:

> They're using both, but they're using the [name of scheme] more than the Numeracy Strategy materials. In a sense it supersedes it because it ties in so well with the Numeracy Strategy.

However, he did add that they still needed a range of materials and that one scheme did not answer everything, and that teachers of pupils aged 5-7 years were not finding the scheme as easy to implement as those of pupils aged 7-11 years.

The mathematics co-ordinator felt that the latest scheme was a "bit scripted", but that at the moment, they needed continuity. She felt they would have the confidence to move away from it as the years went by and come back to the Framework. She said:

> I sometimes look at the Strategy, but not as much as I did before we used the scheme, but it is closely tied.

Concerns about the scheme's suitability for use with the younger children did not abate, however, as teachers found that its coverage of the curriculum was "too narrow". Consequently by 2002, older schemes had been re-introduced for use with pupils of 5-7 years and were used alongside the new scheme to provide a "good range" of materials.

5.4. Scheme-driven ---> scheme-dependent (six schools)

In the initial stages of implementation, the Framework was used as a focal point for planning by almost all schools. Some schools in which the mathematics had been aligned to a commercial scheme found they were no longer able to use these older materials in the same way, so searched for a suitable replacement. Although the Framework was still a first point of reference, there was evidence that in some schools reliance on a commercial scheme had never stopped and was actually increasing over time.

At the start of the research, *St Luke's* mathematics work was heavily textbook-based throughout the school, from Reception (pupils aged 4-5 years) to Year 6 (pupils aged 10-11 years). Committed to raising standards, the headteacher had initiated a policy some years earlier whereby the majority of children worked from the book intended for the year group above. The staff felt secure in teaching the subject and had found from experience that this way of working was highly effective as measured by children's success in national tests. Whilst very satisfied with the scheme that they were using, with the implementation of the Numeracy Strategy it became apparent that it did not always match the content or schedules advocated in the Framework. It was decided therefore to look for a new commercial scheme which would meet the new requirements.

> I feel we've got an excellent scheme with the [name of current scheme] but some of the new methods and examples really require some fresh ides so we are currently looking to find a scheme which is compatible and we are thinking of [name of scheme] there. (Mathematics co-ordinator)

After reviewing a number of schemes and consulting with colleagues in other schools, a new commercial scheme was chosen which compared favourably with the original scheme. According to the headteacher, teachers, having become familiar with its structure, were increasingly becoming more dependent on the scheme. As she explained, she preferred the staff to follow one scheme rather than have access to a range of resources as it ensured curriculum coverage and made planning less time-consuming.

> You see I'm loath to have teachers choosing between two and three schemes because otherwise things might get missed out or something like that. I prefer them all to be following one scheme rather than many. I also think if you've got too many resources ... the time it takes for teachers to go about looking at this one and that one and the other one and deciding which one, is just time consuming. You know so I think that could be a problem, having too many resources.

As the new scheme became embedded teachers felt less need to refer to the Framework. As the mathematics co-ordinator explained:

> ... teachers are so busy they haven't got time to keep going back to it [the Framework]. I mean myself I tend to go more towards the scheme than the Framework.

We use here the example of Aden, a Year 6 teacher (pupils aged 10-11 years) at *St Luke's*, to illustrate how the use of materials could change over time. The arrival of the National Numeracy Strategy resulted in a fundamental change forcing him away from reliance on textbooks and leading him to take a more proactive role in the planning process.

> ... I felt myself because of the Numeracy hour moving away from actually using the textbooks and relying more upon board, blackboard teaching [...] but then the way to teach it isn't really in it there [the Framework] I mean you find your own ways of teaching it.

However for Aden this change was relatively short-lived. The following year the school had bought a new commercial scheme which was followed by all teachers. Subsequently, when web-based lesson plans became available he started to use them and found them so comprehensive and useful that by the Summer of 2002 he said that he felt that he no longer really needed to use the scheme adopted by the school, as the web-based lesson plans provided everything he needed.

5.5. Summary

Three main stages encapsulate what we have learnt from our research about the effect of the introduction of the National Numeracy Strategy on the use of published materials for teaching mathematics.

1) In its early stages the National Numeracy Strategy clearly promoted a policy of *scheme-assisted* planning with the intention that this would contribute to teachers' professional development. The Sample Medium Term Plans (Department for Education and Employment, 1999c) provided an outline for the detailed planning of day-to-day mathematics lessons that were to be built up into schools' own schemes-of-work.

2) As the availability of commercially produced materials grew, there was a tendency for schools to drop *scheme-assisted* practice in favour of heavier reliance upon prescriptive scheme materials to deliver implementation of the reform. Thus the introduction of the National Numeracy Strategy has not resulted in major changes in the use of commercially produced materials to promote professional development.

3) During the year 2000/01, web-based lesson plans for Year 4 and Year 6 pupils were piloted, and made available to a limited number of teachers initially. By the Autumn of 2001 they became more generally available and could be freely downloaded from a government website. The production of web-based lesson plans directly contradicted the original policy relating to the use of materials. Little was left for the teacher to do apart from adding:

> ... to the oral and mental starters a variety of other questions relating to work from the previous couple of weeks and rehearsing aspects that teachers know children have not yet mastered. (http://www.standards.dfes.gov.uk/numeracy/unit_plans, p. 2)

The vignettes of practice illustrate the different trajectories that schools have taken in response to the introduction of the National Numeracy Strategy. Whatever their practice before the Strategy, all schools appeared to go through a period when the Framework became the focus for their planning, however briefly, and when they cast around for materials to help them. An important factor in determining the extent of scheme use appeared to be the presence or absence of a school scheme-of-work. Before the introduction of the National Numeracy Strategy, those schools identified as *scheme-assisted* were using either a school scheme-of-work, or one bought in from a Local Education Authority to fill this need. In the second year of the Strategy's implementation, there was substantial pressure on co-ordinators from numeracy consultants and training materials to develop schemes-of-work, tailored to the needs of their own schools, from the detailed planning that the introduction of the National Numeracy Strategy required. Some schools were receiving in-school consultant help to do this. However, producing a school scheme-of-work was a time-consuming activity, and given the additional workload many teachers were saying that they did not have time to do everything. Others do not appear to have received such strong messages about developing their own planning documents, and were moving towards loosening their ties with the Framework, and tightening their ties with the commercial scheme. The ability and speed with which schools were able to produce their own schemes-of-work was likely to be an important factor in whether schools retained their independence from the constraints of a commercial scheme, but the recent provision of prescriptive lesson plans may have stopped this drive towards schemes-of-work and may have discouraged schools from investing in a new commercial scheme if they had not already done so.

Comparing the current situation with the introduction of the National Curriculum in 1989, there are many similarities: schools have felt the need for more materials to help them implement the new curriculum; advisers and consultants have cautioned against becoming too dependent on a commercial scheme; schools have been under pressure to produce their own scheme-of-work (also the case in the early days of the National Curriculum, but taken up more fully by some schools than others). However, the Numeracy Strategy goes further than the National Curriculum in prescribing not only content, but also the pedagogy, in terms of the three-part lesson and interactive whole-class teaching (Brown, Millett, Bibby, & Johnson, 2000). Commercial schemes, and more recently the government-produced web-based lesson plans, attempt to fill the gap between teaching objectives and learning outcomes, with some commercial schemes providing actual scripts for teachers to use in their interaction with the whole class.

6. MAKING DECISIONS ABOUT THE USE OF PUBLISHED MATERIALS

6.1. How decisions were made

From our work with schools and teachers over the five years of the research, we have identified five main ways in which decisions were reached about the use of published materials. Some schools appeared to use only one way, some a combination of ways. As we shall see, there was a range of influences on these decisions, and we return to our model described in Chapter 1 to describe the source of these influences. The school vignettes given in the previous section are examples of different *situations*. They illustrate different decisions taken for different reasons by different people in different *professional communities*. In some cases, the locus of control was largely with one individual – be it headteacher, mathematics co-ordinator or a knowledgeable other – and most teachers barely participated. In others, decisions were undertaken jointly, although the depth of these deliberations varied from just looking through materials to making informed judgements based on classroom trials.

6.1.1. Executive action by headteacher or mathematics co-ordinator

In some schools the decision about which scheme to buy was essentially an executive decision. At *Larkhall,* although the final choice of scheme was undertaken jointly with staff, it was influenced greatly by the headteacher, not least because of the financial incentive. He liked the chosen scheme because:

> ... it was very reliant on the Strategy [...] I mean it is just a total script for delivery in maths ... that frees you up because once you've got that knowledge of 'this is what concepts you'll be teaching' and this approach to it, you can then add flair ... .

In other schools it was accepted that deciding which scheme to buy was part of the mathematics co-ordinator's role. Aware that teachers were spending an inordinate amount of time searching for suitable materials to support the Strategy, the mathematics co-ordinator at *Greenacres* looked through a range of schemes at the local teachers' centre before choosing one which she felt was "most user-friendly and most adaptable".

Schools where the locus of decision-making rested with one or two individuals exemplified *professional communities* that placed less importance on the reaching of collaborative decisions than others appeared to do.

6.1.2. Suggestions sought from knowledgeable others

Other schools sought advice from knowledgeable others, usually co-ordinators at neighbouring schools or numeracy consultants. For instance, the mathematics co-ordinator at *Firsdown* discussed the pros and cons of various schemes with other teachers at a numeracy support centre before trialling one particular scheme which she liked and decided to buy.

> We had co-ordinator cluster meetings in [Local Education Authority] and I went to a few of those where you met other people who had bought various schemes and just sort of gauged other people's opinions.

At another school, *Birchcroft*, a scheme was recommended by the local numeracy consultant.

Here we can see the influence of *external professionals*. It has already been noted that Numeracy Strategy personnel were promoting *scheme-assisted* practice in the early days of implementation. This perspective sometimes influenced the advice given to schools. Some consultants were more likely, for example, to recommend commercial schemes with a smaller degree of prescription.

6.1.3. Whole-staff meetings with publishers' representatives

In some cases publishers' representatives were invited to staff meetings to inform the debate.

> So we got a lot of different companies and organisations and reps to bring in their things and pretty much they came in during staff meetings so the staff had a chance to look at resources. (Mathematics co-ordinator)

Commercial schemes designed to match the requirements of the Strategy have been produced by educational publishers (the *private sector* in our model). Sometimes pressure can come from the 'hard sell' emanating from the publishing companies themselves. At *Larkhall* for example, which had purchased a number of schemes over successive years, the choice of yet another scheme (Spring 2001) was strongly influenced by the fact the new scheme was heavily discounted because the school had purchased a mathematics scheme from the company in the recent past.

6.1.4. Whole-staff meetings comparing materials

Some schools compared a number of schemes during staff meetings before making a final decision.

> … I much prefer [name of new scheme] and most of the staff did – it was an overall, you know sort of went to the vote and overall […] we looked through the teacher's folders, it was a staff decision. (Mathematics co-ordinator)

6.1.5. Trialling and repeated discussion over a period of time

A few schools made informed choices based on experience of using a scheme in the classroom rather than relying on the judgement of others or just looking through materials.

> … Guy is using [name of scheme] and he's trialling that. One or two people have trialled [name of second scheme] … some people had heard that this one was going to be a good one with the Strategy. (Mathematics co-ordinator)

Similarly, staff at *St Saviour's* trialled two schemes and then met to discuss their pros and cons. Although the mathematics co-ordinator knew both schemes well, she was adamant that the choice of scheme rested with all the teachers, not with her.

> I did know the structure of them quite well … and I did say to people when we had a meeting … that I wasn't biased in any way but it's completely up to them.

6.2. Reasons for reaching the decisions made

It was difficult to distinguish reasons for reaching the decisions made, as many responses refer to more than one, and in any case, there were strong links between them. However, the following were identifiable as contributing to the decision-making:

- a desire to reduce workload
- a wish to implement required reform in a pain-free way
- a need to address teachers' lack of confidence in mathematics
- a concern to perpetuate practice perceived as successful in terms of pupil attainment
- a wish to provide teachers with the opportunities to exercise professional judgement in choice of textual materials.

In the next section, we turn our attention to the small number of examples from our research where we can point to the use of textual materials being involved in the process of professional development.

7. EXAMPLES OF PROFESSIONAL DEVELOPMENT THROUGH THE USE OF MATERIALS

7.1. Teachers working individually

We look first at examples from the research of occasions where teachers have spoken about their own personal learning through planning.

Consequences of a school policy promoting *scheme-driven* practice before the introduction of the National Numeracy Strategy were described graphically by two teachers interviewed for *Teachers' knowledge, conceptions and practices.* Comments from these teachers illustrate an oppressive side to over-reliance, in some cases related to an acceptance within these teachers' schools that the scheme provided the mathematics and had to be followed, whether the teacher understood it or not.

> 'Cos with things like the [scheme] maths and the schemes they were very set and very structured and if you didn't understand it, you didn't understand it and teachers didn't teach any other way and therefore if you didn't understand it you [had to] carry on. (Year 4 teacher, pupils aged 8-9 years)

Rather than being enabling, the use of a commercial scheme can mean that decisions about curriculum content or appropriate activities are taken away from individual teachers, leading to a lack of thought on their part about the mathematical experiences that they are providing for their pupils.

> For a start I knew I had a scheme. I didn't ever think about it very much, I didn't have to take an hour and a half to do it and then do an hour photocopying. I'd head into a week, I'd sit with my partner for two minutes, 'what chapter are we covering', OK. Sometimes I thought 'this is isn't good enough' and I'd do it on Friday afternoon and think what resources do I need so I'd only go a step further and get the resources ready for the week. (Year 6 teacher, pupils aged 10-11 years)

For these two teachers, the benefits of giving up the commercial scheme and moving to a wider range of materials included higher expectations of pupils and greater professional involvement.

> When I left college, when I started teaching they used the [named] maths scheme ... that was a good thing because it was page after page after page after page, you just went through the book [...] it was set and it was structured and this is how you teach it and so it was easier for somebody like me who didn't like maths anyway. So when the Numeracy Strategy came in I was panicking, I was thinking 'oh my god, you know, I can't do this and I can't follow this [named] maths scheme any more' and when you look at the [named] maths scheme now compared to the Numeracy Strategy for that age group for my Year 4, it's unbelievable how low in level that was for my kids. (Year 4 teacher, pupils aged 8-9 years)

> Before I left [previous school] they started the Numeracy Project, the Numeracy Strategy I should say. Now that's when I started teaching, that is most definitely where I learnt what it is to sit down to differentiate my maths to get the correct activity to have to really look at the Strategy and see what it says. Now you didn't have to do that before and although we had a scheme it really wasn't 100% appropriate. (Year 6 teacher, pupils aged 10-11 years)

For the Year 4 teacher, insecure about mathematics herself, approaching her teaching through the Framework was opening up new learning opportunities.

> Sometimes I look at things and I'll go right, now, I'm not quite sure about that so I'll flick through it [Framework] and I look at it and I'll study it and think 'I've got it, I can do it' and I do hundreds and hundreds at night – 'I can do this', you know, and that's how my confidence has increased because I feel as though I've gone back to my childhood and I'm relearning. (Year 4 teacher, pupils aged 8-9 years)

7.2. Teachers working collaboratively

In this chapter we have so far seen little that could be seen to be influencing teachers' *zones of enactment* as decisions about the use of materials were negotiated and formulated. Despite the fact that advisers were encouraging schools to discuss the need for materials, not all schools had taken this on board. A few schools, such as *St Saviour's* (see Section 6.1.5.), were really talking about what the schemes provided and debating which would best meet the needs of their school, whilst in others such as *Clearwater*, the deliberations were less rich and there was not so much emphasis on the collective decision-making process. While schools may involve all staff in the decision-making process, the actual extent of participation may be superficial. Although staff at *St Luke's* were involved in a review and consultation process, this had a limited impact in practice. Despite the mathematics co-ordinator's preference for a scheme to be used in a supporting role, the headteacher was adamant that continued reliance on a scheme was the only way forward.

In *Wolverton* school, staff had worked closely together on choosing a commercial scheme which they considered to be:

> ... the most appropriate scheme for getting children to think in different ways. Sort of approaching a new topic or area from different angles ... [r]ather than some of the other schemes which are just sort of pages and pages of sums, this was actually a practical approach to maths first. (Mathematics co-ordinator)

In this case, the mathematics co-ordinator felt that discussion about scheme use had led on to further discussion focusing on the mathematics.

We turn now to the situation once the choice of materials has been made. We discuss those examples of collaborative planning that have the potential for providing the peer coaching and rich deliberations that can lead to the realisation of teachers' *zones of enactment*.

It is acknowledged that in the early days of the National Numeracy Strategy at least, planning proved to be demanding and burdensome for many teachers. The task was potentially less onerous in schools where there was more than one class per year group. In such schools planning was a potential vehicle for teachers to work together, sharing experience and expertise, where ideas could be cross-fertilised and teachers could start to make the Numeracy Strategy their own, customised to meet their teaching needs and those particular to their school and their pupils.

There were a number of instances, in 16 of the 41 schools, where teachers of parallel classes could have shared the planning. However, only about two thirds choose to do so (see Table 4.2). As practice could differ in different Key Stages (5-7 years and 7-11 years), we have considered these separately. As shown in Table 4.2, there were a total of 27 Key Stage departments with parallel classes in the 16 schools.

Table 4.2. Methods of planning adopted by teachers of parallel classes in Key Stage 1 and Key Stage 2 in 1999-2000

Key Stage	*Number of Key Stage departments where teachers planned together*	*Number of Key Stage departments where one teacher took responsibility*	*Total*
Key Stage 1 (ages 5-7 years)	11 (79%)	3 (21%)	14
Key Stage 2 (ages 7-11 years)	8 (62%)	5 (38%)	13
Total	19 (70%)	8 (30%)	27

7.2.1. Examples of learning through collaborative planning

One of the advantages of planning together was that it gave teachers a forum for thinking about the mathematics and the opportunity to learn from each other. One Year 2 teacher (pupils aged 6-7 years) explained that even though her parallel teacher was less experienced, working together had benefited her, not least because she thought that her partner was a better mathematician.

> … we have been thinking a lot about the mathematics and my partner in the year is probably better at it [numeracy] … despite the fact she is a probationer. Although she is a probationer so that she lacks experience … she does what I don't do she thinks mathematically so it has been quite useful seeing things sometimes from her point of view.

Other teachers also described the advantages of working collaboratively in enabling them to pool ideas and to share their knowledge, especially useful when they differed in experience and expertise.

> The other Year 3 teacher is a newly qualified teacher and I'm new to the school so we started off planning together and then, because I'm the literacy co-ordinator I took literacy and she did the maths … well we've gone back to planning together now. (Year 3 teacher, pupils aged 7-8 years)

> I like to do that [planning] with my colleague … as well just to help her as well, 'cos every day she asked me for some help so I thought well if we sit down and do it together it would be easier to just do it together, show each other our ideas. (Year 3 teacher, pupils aged 7-8 years)

In some schools there were expectations that everyone would participate, share expertise, think about the teaching and think about the children's learning. It was acknowledged that everyone had a valuable contribution to make and had something to learn.

> There's a lot of participation from everyone. Obviously there's an NQT [newly qualified teacher] in our team but she contributes and Alicia … this is her third year in Year 2 so she brings experience of Year 2. I've just moved up from Year 1 so I'm looking for that experience but equally we're all looking in the Numeracy Strategy and learning together … we think what we're going to be asking the children to do, is this real, can we do it, does it make sense, how would we explain it, are there any problems, so it's a lot of planning goes on in that planning session. (Year 2 teacher, pupils aged 6-7 years)

Although teachers put a lot of effort into joint planning sessions, having the support of colleagues and working together was judged to make life "easier" rather than harder for many.

One Year 6 teacher (pupils aged 10-11 years) made the point that interpreting other people's plans could be fraught with difficulties because teachers needed to understand what they were teaching and why they were teaching it and this could only be achieved through joint planning.

> We share it very much between us although Stacey is more literacy-based. I am not a mathematician … but it is very important that we do it together because we both have to understand what we are doing and what we are going through and we find that as with anything if you are trying to pick up on someone else's plans you can't always read into their minds what is there. So we do try very much to plan together and know exactly what we are doing …

7.2.2. Sharing rather than collaborating

In other instances teachers chose to allocate the planning to one person as it shared the workload and increased their "efficiency". Working in this way did not necessarily preclude input from others, but whilst they might discuss things in general terms the detailed planning rested with one individual.

> So we talk together as a year group … we discuss things but after that it is left to me to plan the whole week and what activities we do and how we differentiate and that sort of thing. (Year 2 teacher, pupils aged 6-7 years)

Other schools, however, chose to let one teacher take sole responsibility for the process from the outset.

> … what happens with the maths … is that I do the planning with the maths and she [parallel teacher] follows me and she does the planning for literacy and I follow her. (Year 2 teacher, pupils aged 6-7 years)

In four schools planning was done on a rotation basis with one teacher taking responsibility for one of the main subject areas of numeracy, literacy or science. At *Woodbridge* subjects were allocated with reference to a teacher's particular strength, and whilst this had its advantages in terms of efficiency, it meant that the other teacher did not necessarily need to think about what she was teaching. A Year 3 teacher (pupils aged 7-8 years) for instance, admitted that:

> ... Leone has taken on the maths side of the plan and I follow what I'm given, I'm spoon fed if you like ... .

If rotated on a regular basis, it was felt that sharing the planning in this way need not necessarily preclude teachers from gaining knowledge and experience of the numeracy curriculum.

> Charlotte and I share the planning ... I do numeracy one week and she does the literacy and then we swap, so I've planned all the numeracy this week, she's planned all the literacy and then we share the lessons. (Year 2 teacher, pupils aged 6-7 years)

Neither did this necessarily mean that there was no discussion between teachers, as a Year 3 teacher from *Kestrel* explained:

> We're still discussing it, we still discuss it, we met yesterday to make sure that we're consistent ... so we take it in turns for going round, we take a core subject like English maths and science and we share that. I think it is very difficult just to ... so you can have one focus and forget about all the others, so we take it in turns to plan and before we plan we evaluate together.

However in some schools, a teacher was more likely to take on the responsibility for a longer period, a term or more. Planning in this way was not necessarily regarded as a negative experience. In a some instances teachers believed that having sole responsibility for the planing of a curriculum area rather than sharing the planning was regarded as a professional development exercise for individual teachers.

> ... it's just that we felt ... professional development-wise it better if we all have an opportunity to plan every subject within our year group, to plan every subject within the national curriculum eventually. So that's the plan, and we are just sort of rotating it around really with what we want to and how we want to and at the speed we want to. (Year 6 teacher, pupils aged 10-11 years)

However, whilst this may have seemed to work for some, it must be questioned as to whether teachers who were not actively involved in planning the lessons they were to teach, always had the depth of understanding they would have had, had they been partners in the process.

At *Woodbury*, some teachers had chosen to divide up the planning between them in this way, much to the dismay of the co-ordinator who could see that opportunities for professional development were being lost.

> Some year groups have split their planning so one person will go and do literacy, one person will do maths, one person will do the topic and then they get together and share.

> [In Year 1 (pupils aged 5-6 years)] we work so that we have a meeting and we all plan everything together. Somebody said to me yesterday, 'oh I haven't picked up the Framework yet, I don't really know what's in it', so I said, 'well how are you doing your planning', she said, 'oh well, he does it for me and then I just do it'. [...] So they don't talk about it and discuss, which isn't just a problem for maths it's a problem for all of it really, which is something that we might have to address. And yes it takes an afternoon out, you know, an evening out to plan, it does take quite a long time but we find – I mean we find it really valuable. (Mathematics co-ordinator)

7.2.3. Circumstances that militated against collaborative planning

In some of these schools teachers found it difficult to plan together either because there was one mixed-age class or children were 'set' for mathematics (taught in ability groups) across year groups. In almost all these instances teachers described how circumstances precluded planning together as the children in the different classes had very different needs. As a teacher of a Year 1 and 2 class (pupils 5-7 years) explained:

> For maths we tend to plan on our own. We are following the same scheme and we are roughly at the same point but you know our classes are quite different, there are more special needs in my class.

This problem was exacerbated where children were 'set' for mathematics. Although teachers of the older children at *Kirkshaw* planned for the medium term together, detailed weekly plans were completed by teachers individually. The teacher of the higher set of pupils aged 10-11 years explained:

> … Mervyn and I, the other Year 6 teacher, do our half-termly plans together … however how I turn that into a weekly plan I do myself because the diversity between the two groups is so huge that we don't really see the point of sitting down together and sort of planning activities with such a wide range of children. Besides you know the children in your class or your set better.

7.3. Summary

For a few individual teachers, following the National Numeracy Strategy had proved to be a liberating influence as it had forced them to search for materials from a range of resources rather than relying on one particular commercial scheme, on occasion enhancing their expectations of what children could achieve.

A minority of schools in *Tracking Numeracy* chose to plan collaboratively. There was evidence that some of these recognised the opportunity for professional development that this provided. Advantages of collaborative planning mentioned by teachers included learning from each other, sharing of expertise, valuing the contributions of everyone regardless of experience and lightening the workload. In other instances, allocating the job of planning to one teacher was believed to be more efficient although other teachers might still have some peripheral involvement. Teachers of mixed aged and setted classes in particular, did not feel that they could plan together because of the difference in age range and ability of children in their classes.

8. DISCUSSION

For at least half of the schools in our research, the choice and use of materials were based on considerations other than a concern to promote professional development – the need for coherence in implementing reform; the need to save teachers' time; unwillingness to change previously successful practice. However, even when the intention to promote professional development was there, it was not enough to simply provide a range of materials, and expect professional development to follow. The motivation to engage with the process was also necessary. The co-ordinator could play a critical role here in promoting the use of the planning process as a basis for discussion about the detail of mathematical activities, rather than just the structure of the lesson.

The more the decisions are based on pragmatic arguments about implementation and the more prescriptive the materials provided, the less the incentive to get involved in the process of mediation and shift the focus from implementing the reform to thinking about the mathematics. As McLaughlin and Mitra (2000) (quoted in Fullan, 2001) discovered:

> The experiences of these three theory-based reforms underscore the point that the relevant "it" that needs to be embedded in practice is not the particular activity structures, materials, or routines of a reform, but rather the first principles. (p. 10)

A group of schools in our research had taken advantage of situations with parallel classes to develop collaborative planning. The mathematics co-ordinators and teachers whose planning was described in Section 7 were helping to realise, through collaborative planning, several aspects of Spillane's notion of a *zone of enactment*. Through discussion of appropriate curriculum materials, there was a sharing of expertise by the mathematically more experienced that was recognised as beneficial. There was a focus on the needs of the pupil in making decisions about the activities to use. There were opportunities to reflect on past practice in a supportive environment and to learn together. As Ball and Cohen (1999) suggest, the need for professional learning to be "centred in practice" (p. 14) does not necessarily imply "situations in classrooms in real time" (p. 14). They argue for the use of documentation of practice, such as students' work, curriculum materials and teachers notes.

> Using such things could locate the curriculum of teacher education "in practice," for they could focus professional learning in materials taken from real classrooms that present salient problems of practice. (Ball & Cohen, 1999, p. 14)

The use of materials provided either by the National Numeracy Strategy or by commercial publishers has resulted in changes in the mathematics curriculum and in classroom practice. From our observations, we would suggest that in many cases the changes made have been those most easy to achieve (structural). We contend that for deeper change to occur, teachers also need understand and internalise the more subtle messages related to the mathematics in order to take 'ownership' of the curriculum.

Long-term, sustainable change requires not only changes in materials but also changes in teaching approaches and teachers' beliefs (Fullan, 2001). Many teachers in this research programme have described how they are to some extent learning through directly engaging with the 'what' set out in the Framework and the exceptional teacher may be studying the Framework in a learner's role, and gaining in knowledge and confidence from that.

The potential of the planning process for providing ongoing professional learning and having a major impact on the realisation of rich *zones of enactment* does not appear to have been realised by many schools. It remains a strong possibility that more and more schools will find *scheme-dependency* increasingly attractive, particularly in a climate where government is committed to cutting teachers' workload – the practical imperatives of which have resulted in a curious dichotomy. Having adopted an initial position which encouraged teachers to think about their teaching and develop their lessons using a variety of materials, government seemingly relented and set its mind to developing detailed daily lesson plans with support materials available online, ostensibly in response to demands from teachers. Although initially the National Numeracy Strategy did not itself provide the detail of the 'how' – the lessons plans in detail – there appears to have been a recent policy decision to enter into these previously uncharted waters.

Adopting these lesson plans, however, may not be straightforward as this section from an interview with another of the teachers involved in *Teachers' Knowledge, Conceptions and Practices* illustrates. Over-prescription of materials can in some ways hinder rather than help the classroom teacher.

> [talking about the lesson plans downloaded from the website] I think there's too much information because if we are to use this as a lesson, a daily lesson plan I've highlighted it so that I can just look at it quickly as a quick reference and teach on it and that hasn't

> helped. I'm thinking way ahead of myself in terms of, you know, what I've got to cover in the whole lesson and moving through your lesson faster than I would probably if I'd written it out. And because these aren't my own examples, I didn't write them, I have to keep looking at them so whereas for me if I write my own plan I know what I've written and I can take exactly what I'm going to do. But where it's somebody else's plan, I have to read it, internalise it, understand it all and then, you know, but it's not my order and it's not the way I speak. So it's all gone, I lose it all. (Year 6 teacher, pupils aged 10-11 years)

With government backing, the Strategy, it would seem, is less likely to be regarded as a potential conduit for professional development through the choice and use of materials. The results of this may be even more worrying in terms of teacher professionalism than reliance on previous schemes, with responsibility taken from the teacher not only about 'what' to teach in giving children questions to do, but also giving them scripts outlining exactly 'how' to teach it.

However, by the end of the research in 2002, there were positive indications from some schools of a more flexible approach both to the Numeracy Strategy and to their commercial scheme materials, with a greater degree of professional decision-making about what is appropriate for pupils being described. As teachers become more confident about new ways of planning, more opportunities for collaborative planning and discussion of materials may be created.

9. AFFILIATIONS

Dr Valerie Rhodes is a Research Fellow in the Department of Education and Professional Studies, King's College London.

10. REFERENCES

Askew, M., Brown, M. L., Johnson, D. C., Millett, A. M., Prestage, S., & Walsh, A. (1993). *Evaluation of the implementation of national curriculum mathematics at Key Stages 1, 2 and 3 volume 1: report.* London: School Curriculum and Assessment Authority.

Ball, D. L., & Cohen, D. K. (1999). Developing Practice, Developing Practitioners: Towards a Practice-Based Theory of Professional Education. In L. Darling-Hammond & G. Sykes (Eds.), *Teaching as the Learning Profession. Handbook of Policy and Practice.* San Francisco, CA: Jossey-Bass.

Brown, M., Millett, A., Bibby, T., & Johnson, D. C. (2000). Turning Our Attention from the What to the How: the National Numeracy Strategy. *British Educational Research Journal, 26*(4), 457-471.

Department for Education. (1995). *Mathematics in the National Curriculum.* London: Her Majesty's Stationery Office.

Department for Education and Employment. (1999a). *The National Numeracy Strategy: Framework for Teaching Mathematics from Reception to Year 6.* London: Department for Education and Employment.

Department for Education and Employment. (1999b). *The National Numeracy Strategy. Three-day course. Notes for course tutors*. London: Department for Education and Employment.

Department for Education and Employment. (1999c). *Sample medium-term plans for mathematics*. London: Department for Education and Employment.

Department for Education and Employment. (1999d). *Calculator activities*. London: Department for Education and Employment.

Department for Education and Employment. (1999e). *Reasoning about numbers, with challenges and simplifications*. London: Department for Education and Employment.

Department of Education and Science/Welsh Office. (1982). *Mathematics Counts: Report of the Committee of Inquiry into the Teaching of Mathematics in Schools*. London: Her Majesty's Stationery Office.

Department of Education and Science/Welsh Office. (1989). *Mathematics in the National Curriculum*. London: Her Majesty's Stationery Office.

Department of Education and Science/Welsh Office. (1991). *Mathematics in the National Curriculum (1991)*. London: Her Majesty's Stationery Office.

Foxman, D. (1999). *Mathematics textbooks across the world: some evidence from the third international mathematics and science study (TIMSS)*. Slough: National Foundation for Educational Research.

Fullan, M. (2001). *The new meaning of educational change. 3rd Edition*. New York: Teachers College Press.

Her Majesty's Inspectorate. (1992). *Mathematics Key Stages 1, 2 and 3: a report by HM Inspectorate on the second year 1990-1991*. London: Her Majesty's Stationery Office.

McLaughlin, M., & Mitra, D. (2000). Theory-based change and change-based theory: Going deeper, going broader. Unpublished paper, Stanford University, Stanford, CA.

Millett, A., & Johnson, D. C. (1996). Solving teachers' problems? The role of the commercial mathematics scheme. In D. C. Johnson & A. Millett (Eds.), *Implementing the mathematics National Curriculum: policy, politics and practice* (pp. 54-74). London: Paul Chapman.

Miwa, T. (1991). School mathematics in Japan and the US: focusing on recent trends in elementary and lower secondary school. In I. Wirszup & R. Streit (Eds.), *Developments in School Mathematics Education Around the World, Volume Three*. Reston, VA: National Council of Teachers of Mathematics.

Office for Standards in Education. (1993). *Mathematics Key Stages 1, 2 and 3, fourth year 1992-93: a report from the office of Her Majesty's Chief Inspector of Schools*. London: Her Majesty's Stationery Office.

Robitaille, D. F., & Garden, R. A. (Eds.). (1989). *The IEA Study of Mathematics II: Contexts and Outcomes of School Mathematics*. Oxford: Pergamon Press.

Stray, C. (1994). Paradigms regained: towards a historical sociology of the textbook. *Journal of Curriculum Studies, 26*(1), 1-26.

Zhang, D. (1991). Some puzzling questions arising from mathematics education in China. In I. Wirszup & R. Streit (Eds.), *Developments in School Mathematics Education Around the World, Volume Three*. Reston, VA: National Council of Teachers of Mathematics.

ALISON MILLETT, MIKE ASKEW AND SHIRLEY SIMON

CHAPTER 5

RESPONSES OF TEACHERS TO A COURSE OF INTENSIVE TRAINING

Abstract. In this chapter, the spotlight is on that part of our model that includes the *person* within their immediate *professional community* responding to an external intervention, and has links mainly with the *external professional* and *policy*. The *policy* in this case emanates from the National Numeracy Strategy in the form of a Five-day course covering aspects of mathematics content and pedagogy, delivered by professionals external to the schools. Twelve teachers in four schools were interviewed and observed to explore their subject knowledge, orientations and beliefs and classroom practice. Eight of these teachers experienced the Five-day course in 2000/01, with three more attending at a later date. This chapter discusses how the first eight teachers responded to this professional development, both initially and over the longer term; how they took influences from the course into their own classrooms; how they prepared to feed back their ideas to their colleagues in school and how this feedback was received. The degree to which this in-service training provided the constituents of effective professional development is also critically examined.

1. INTRODUCTION – EXTERNAL INFLUENCES

In previous chapters, we have considered in turn how the mathematics co-ordinator, the teacher's broader *professional community* and the materials provided for the teaching of mathematics can make a difference to the implementation of change. In this chapter we turn to a national intervention from outside the school site. We look at the responses of a small group of primary (elementary) teachers to a course of in-service training in mathematics for primary schools. Drawing on our model discussed in Chapter 1, *external factors* provide the stimulus for change, taking the form of a government-sponsored course of training, mediated and delivered at local area level. This course of training was established to support the ongoing implementation in England of the National Numeracy Strategy (see Introduction), and was delivered by professionals external to the schools – numeracy consultants

Alison Millett, Margaret Brown & Mike Askew (eds.), Primary Mathematics and the Developing Professional.

and mathematics advisers employed by Local Education Authorities, but ultimately answerable to the Strategy's managers.

1.1. The National Numeracy Strategy

The National Numeracy Strategy was designed to raise standards by changing both the content emphasis and methods used in the classroom (Brown et al., 2000). Introduced in 1999, the Framework for Teaching Mathematics from Reception to Year 6 (Department for Education and Employment, 1999) was distributed to all schools. Although not statutory, the use of the document (commonly referred to as the Framework) was strongly urged. The scheme of work suggested in the Framework lists the curriculum in terms of detailed objectives to be taught separately in a logical sequence. It advocates an approach to teaching based on key principles of a daily three-part lesson, an emphasis on mental calculation and the direct teaching of the whole class or groups (see Introduction). The National Numeracy Strategy was highly resourced in terms of materials and training. An initial Three-day introductory course was focused on mathematics co-ordinators (subject leaders), headteachers and school governors, with packs of prescriptive training materials provided to 'cascade' this training back in schools. Additional training in the form of a Five-day course and consultant support were given to schools identified as in need of 'intensive' support.

1.2. The Five-day course

The Five-day course forms part of the National Numeracy Strategy training. In its first year of provision, this course was designed for those schools deemed in need of intensive help. In the following year, 2000/01, it was offered to a wider range of schools. The aims, according to the participants' handbook (Department for Education and Employment, 2000, p. 1), were to:

- increase your knowledge of how mathematical topics in The Framework for teaching mathematics may be taught effectively
- diagnose and rectify children's calculation errors and misconceptions
- plan and prepare a series of day-to-day lessons
- prepare to provide in-school training and support for your colleagues in school.

The handbook described the first four days of the course as having an emphasis on the teaching of particular mathematical topics (Department for Education and Employment 2000, p. 2): addition and subtraction; problem solving with challenges and simplifications; working with measures; multiplication and division; using a calculator; laying the foundations for algebra; fractions, decimals, percentages, ratio and proportion; teaching mathematics in Reception (ages 4-5 years); numbers and the number system; solving word problems; graphs and charts; shape and space.

The fifth day focused on planning sequences of lessons, taking account of the progress children make, and supporting colleagues. The two Local Education Authorities involved in our research made some changes to the order of the days on which different aspects of the course were presented; to the order of the sessions given in the handbook; to the layout and content of some of the materials. Overall, however, the course in both authorities remained much as outlined in the Department for Education and Employment handbook. The verbal introduction to the course in both authorities included a strong message that the main aim was to improve participants' subject knowledge in mathematics.

The Five-day course was intended for the mathematics co-ordinator (subject leader) and one other teacher from each school selected. A cascade model of feeding back what had been learnt from the course at school level was intended for the co-ordinator and outlined in the course booklet for the fifth day of the course. In the second year of the course (2000/01), the two Local Education Authorities differed as to whether they required the attendance of the co-ordinator for the first four days of the course. In one of the two authorities, this requirement was waived if it was felt that the co-ordinator was highly experienced and other teachers would benefit more from the training. However, the requirement to feed back to others did not appear to have been waived, although in our view this was not made explicit during the first four days of the training.

1.3. Unique features of this example of professional development

International interest in the constituents of effective professional development (Fennema & Nelson, 1997; Darling-Hammond & Sykes, 1999) make a consideration of the effect of this course of training pertinent. The Five-day course was developed for those schools deemed to be in greatest need of support in mathematics when the National Numeracy Strategy was introduced, and was later extended to a wider range of schools; it was not focused on those with identified strengths in mathematics. Some participants were mathematics co-ordinators (subject leaders), but many were not, and had been nominated by their headteacher precisely because they were perceived as lacking confidence in mathematics, or were likely to benefit from input in this subject area. Throughout England, thousands of teachers have now participated in Five-day courses in their local area.

There is much that we might learn from the responses of teachers attending this type of in-service training that would inform the wider discussion on effective professional development. How did the design of the course affect the extent to which messages from the course were mediated or diluted? How lasting were these messages? What effects could be identified on changes in classroom practice? In this chapter, we use data from case studies of a small group of teachers to address these questions and to ask: how can such a course of externally provided training affect teachers' ability to engage with change in the teaching of mathematics?

2. THE RESEARCH

The evidence reported on here is drawn from the study *Teachers' Knowledge, Conceptions and Practices* that explored the nature of teacher change. This study was part of the five-year longitudinal Leverhulme Numeracy Research Programme based at King's College London (See Introduction/Annex 2).

In each of four schools selected, we opted to work with the two teachers who would be undergoing the National Numeracy Strategy Five-day training (eight teachers), and a third teacher who would not be directly engaged in the training (four teachers), making 12 teachers altogether. (One teacher was replaced early on in the research by the teacher who took over her class.) These four schools were not regarded as in need of intensive help in the first year of the Strategy's implementation, but were given the opportunity to send teachers on the course in its second year. In June or September 2000 (depending on availability), baseline data was gathered on the 12 teachers in terms of profiles of their beliefs, knowledge and practices, prior to the Five-day National Numeracy Strategy training. Using methods developed in previous research at King's College (Askew et al., 1997), extended interviews and classroom observations probed the teachers' understandings and beliefs. Each of the 12 teachers was interviewed twice at the beginning of the project: once to explore their beliefs and practices, and once to elicit their understanding of aspects of mathematics and, in some questions, how it might be taught (for more detail of the schools, the teachers and the interviews, see Annex 2). The teachers were also all observed teaching mathematics to establish some, albeit minimal, baseline data on teaching methods, styles of teaching organisation and curriculum emphasises prior to the course of training. They were then observed on four further occasions.

The eight teachers attending the course during 2000/01 were subsequently interviewed immediately prior to and after the course, and then three times more (the final interview corresponding closely with key elements of the initial two interviews). One of these eight was not present for the final interview, having moved schools two months previously. For the four teachers not attending the course initially, the pre-course interview was omitted, and the post-course interview referred to feedback received from those colleagues who had attended it. In the authority that did not require the attendance of co-ordinators, the four teachers in our research (who were not co-ordinators) attended the first four days of the course, and the co-ordinators from the two schools attended on the fifth day. In the other authority, the four teachers (of whom two were also co-ordinators) attended for the first four days, and the co-ordinators alone attended for the fifth day. All five days of the courses in both Local Education Authorities were observed and recorded in fieldnotes by either one or both of the researchers working on this project. (Although three of the additional four teachers attended the course in the subsequent year, the major part of the data reported in this chapter refers to the eight teachers attending the course in the year 2000/01, unless specifically indicated to the contrary.) The findings reported in this chapter draw in the main from interview data over a period of two years (2000-2002) substantiated with observation data over the same period.

We structure this chapter in three main sections. These sections relate to our model described in Chapter 1, focusing on the *person*, the *professional community* and the *zone of enactment*. Using a different terminology, but essentially the same constituents, Joyce and Showers (1995) in the second edition of their much quoted earlier work (1988) discussed four sources of renewal: the individual practitioner, the school site, the district office (in our case the Local Education Authority) and government agencies (1995, p. 4), with a co-ordination of all four sources being required for success. They identified three main variables that affected the transfer of what had been learned into classroom use:

- individual factors
- school factors of pressure and support
- peer-group influences.

We regard a consideration of these three variables as essential in assessing the effectiveness of a professional development initiative such as the Five-day course.

3. INDIVIDUAL FACTORS – THE PERSON

An expectation that professional development should take account of the complex lives and needs of individuals has engaged many writers. Hargreaves (1995) criticised the dominant paradigms of teacher development research and practice as tending to either ignore "the turbulence, excitement and unpredictability of teachers' emotions" or reinscribe them "within rational frameworks where they can be planned or managed in dispassionate ways" (p. 23). Huberman (1992) drew attention to commonalities in career cycles affecting teachers' motivation for taking on changes in practice. Sikes, Measor and Woods (1985) focused on the effects of critical incidents in teachers' lives/careers; Clarke (1997) to the need for personal space to make changes in practice.

Joyce and Showers (1995) used the term "states of growth" (p. 134) to describe the readiness of teachers to take change on board, identifying four main types: gourmet omnivores; active consumers; passive consumers; reticent consumers. States of growth depended on a range of personal motivational characteristics, career choices and trajectories as well as opportunities associated with the workplace, either peer- or school-generated. Joyce and Showers described different levels of activity that were produced by "the individual's orientation toward their environment moderated by social influence" (1995, p. 177). Although not following these classifications closely (Joyce and Showers possessed more information about the personal lives of the participants in their research and included personal attributes in their definitions of states of growth), we have found them useful in considering the starting points, stages in career and motivation of the teachers in our research, emphasising as they do the individual differences that affect responses to professional development.

Whilst also reporting on our participants more generally, we have selected three teachers (Sam, Frankie and Jo) from our group of eight upon whom to focus in this chapter.

3.1. Starting points and expectations

The eight teachers who undertook the Five-day course varied considerably in their length of teaching experience, with Sam being among the least experienced, in the second year of teaching at the beginning of the research, Frankie being among those having two to five years' experience and Jo being among those with more than 10 years' experience. Jo also had secondary teaching experience. The eight teachers all had a full-time class responsibility, with Frankie and one other teacher additionally holding the post of mathematics co-ordinator.

Primary teachers are generalists by the nature of their work, with only a minority having studied mathematics beyond age 16 (Askew et al., 1993). Millett (1996) identified the particular problems with mathematics when teachers collectively lack the confidence to discuss issues in depth and take risks with their practice. Ball and Bass (2000) consider mathematics subject matter knowledge to be fundamental to teaching, arguing that there is a close relationship between ideas and their representation and that, if pupils' methods are to be valued and built upon, then subject understanding is essential. While a mathematics degree does not necessarily translate into good pedagogic practice (Askew et al., 1997; Farah-Sarkis, 1999), inadequate mathematical knowledge can restrict a teacher's ability to reflect on her own teaching and can be a barrier to learning from a course of training (Irwin & Britt, 1999).

Table 5.1. Details of the teachers attending the course 2000/01

Teacher	*Length/main type of teaching experience*	*Mathematics qualification*
Sam	2 years, pupils aged 7-11 years	GCSE
Chris	12 years , pupils aged 4-7 years	GCE 'O' Level
Jo	Over 10 years, pupils aged 3-7 and 11-16 years	GCE 'O' Level
Andy	Over 20 years, pupils aged 7-11 years and 11-16 years	GCE 'O' Level
Jess	7 years, pupils aged 4-7 years	GCE 'O' Level
Frankie Mathematics Co-ordinator	3 years, pupils aged 7-11 years	GCSE Studied mathematics for an additional year post-16
Clare Mathematics Co-ordinator	4 years, pupils aged 7-11 years	GCSE
Toni	2 years, pupils 5-7 years. Now teaching pupils 7-11 years	Access course to higher education as a mature student

A post-16 qualification in mathematics was not held by any of this group of eight teachers, and several described having struggled to acquire a minimum qualification at age 16 (the percentage nationally passing this qualification has varied from approximately 20% for General Certificate of Education Ordinary Level (GCE 'O'

Level), as the post-16 qualification was known until 1985, to approximately 50% more recently with the General Certificate of Secondary Education (GCSE)).

Five of the eight teachers described difficulties with mathematics at school or at college. Maths was "a bit of a mystery" and made one teacher "cry every night" at primary school. Another found that "everyone else seemed to understand what was going on and I was behind and didn't like to ask questions". Having chosen a mathematics specialism in her teacher training, a third teacher admitted that this was for career reasons, having noted the lack of those with mathematics as a specialism, but she subsequently found herself hating her teacher training because it identified how weak she was in mathematics.

Of the three teachers described here in more detail, Sam described finding mathematics difficult at secondary school, of being left to flounder when she didn't understand.

> It was very much if you didn't understand it, tough, you know, they'd explain it once or twice and then it was just like, 'well I've explained it, there's nothing else to explain so if you've not got it now', you know, it was kind of like 'if you've not got it now you never will, you'll just have to keep trying'.

In contrast, Frankie and Jo expressed quite confident feelings about mathematics in their initial interviews, with Frankie especially remarking on enjoying it at school. Frankie was the only one of the group of eight teachers to have studied mathematics beyond age 16, although only for one year. In the mathematics interview, we found that Jo and Frankie's subject knowledge appeared to be relatively strong, with Sam's being less secure (see also Volume 2 in this Series where teachers' subject matter knowledge is addressed in depth).

Only two teachers, one of whom was Sam, had expectations that the course would address subject knowledge. Others, including Jo and Frankie, expected ideas for the classroom suited to the ages of the pupils they were teaching. Some teachers found it difficult to adjust to being told, as soon as they arrived on the course, that subject knowledge was the focus of the course.

To summarise, the eight teachers approached the course from different starting points and with different expectations about its aims and content. In terms of our three teachers selected for a specific focus in this chapter, before the course, Sam was in her second year of teaching, insecure in subject knowledge but expecting the course to address this. Jo had taught for over 10 years, was fairly confident in subject knowledge and was expecting to take back ideas for a class of 5-6 year olds. Frankie had three years' experience, had just been appointed mathematics co-ordinator, was confident in subject knowledge and expected to take back ideas for a class of 8-10 year olds. Evidence from interviews indicated that Frankie showed a proactive attitude to the opportunity of an enlarged role as co-ordinator and to the course of training. Sam gave clear indications of the areas of mathematics she hoped the course would address. Jo, while not appearing reluctant to engage with this professional development, anticipated ideas for classroom practice without specifying any particular needs.

3.2. Initial responses following the course

None of the eight teachers had attended a mathematics course of this length before. This was a cause of delight to some teachers. Jo described it as a luxury:

> Yes absolutely I've never never spent so long on any kind of course before now. It's brilliant to get soaked in the mathematics.

On the other hand, two of the eight teachers were leaving new classes that had not yet settled, and they had rather resented the time spent away, feeling that the length of the course had not really been justified. But in general the responses were ones of enjoyment and satisfaction with the content (having got over the initial adjustment to the focus on subject knowledge rather than ideas for the classroom), the presentation and the general facilities. One teacher had a brief recurrence of the "feelings of dread" that mathematics had aroused at school, but found that she did better than she expected. Another teacher felt that some things went completely "over her head" and made her feel a bit silly. However, all the teachers were complimentary about the sensitive way in which these potential problems had been handled – they had not felt pressurised or put down.

Borko and Putnam (1995) while commenting more generally on changing the teacher's knowledge base, nevertheless took many of their examples from the field of mathematics. Drawing on the work of Shulman and colleagues (Shulman 1986; Shulman & Grossman, 1988), Borko and Putnam distinguished between subject matter knowledge – knowledge *of* mathematics and knowledge *about* mathematics (Ball, 1990) – and pedagogical content knowledge – an understanding of how a subject area can be organised and represented for teaching which included:

- overarching conception of teaching a subject
- knowledge of instructional strategies and representations
- knowledge of students' understandings and potential misunderstandings
- knowledge of curriculum and curricular materials.

These components seem of particular relevance to our consideration of the in-service training experienced by the teachers in our study, as can be seen from the aims of the Five-day course (Section 1.2). Our fieldnotes from the courses indicate some potentially conflicting statements by course presenters as to which aspect of subject knowledge they were addressing. One presenter introduced the session on Fractions, Decimals, Percentages, Ratio and Proportion as an "in-depth look at that area of mathematics". The objectives were "to clarify progression from Reception to Year 6 and to give practical ideas for teaching the topic", which was mainly a topic for pupils aged 7-11 years. However, his next sentence was that "the main purpose was with their own mathematical understanding" (Fieldnotes, Five-day course).

Interviewed shortly after attending the course, all eight teachers felt that they had brought back some ideas for teaching (with Sam and Frankie being particularly positive about these), but not as many as they might have expected.

> Just enlarging things ... having large place-value cards which I hadn't thought of before. We do use them but we didn't have any teacher-size ones and the large money and things like that. (Frankie)

They referred to feeling more confident with more general aspects of the National Numeracy Strategy – aspects such as progression through the entire primary age range; using the Framework to provide differentiation of work; and becoming familiar with a range of new resources.

However, four of the eight teachers felt that they had not gained new subject knowledge, although they spoke positively in terms such as 'revising', 'refreshing', 'reinforcing' what they already knew but had forgotten.

> I think you realise how rusty you become when you don't use mathematics and suddenly like the algebra, you think right yes, and you are thinking back, what, 20 years ... I think you realise just how much you forget. (Year 3 teacher, pupils aged 7-8 years)

> I wouldn't say I came away thinking 'oh I know how to do that now and I didn't know how to do it before' ... it kind of reinforced some of your subject knowledge and it had gone over it but it didn't really seem to be like 'eureka' if you understand, do you know what I mean. (Sam)

Sam had focused particularly on resources that had been suggested. Jo said that the course was a reminder about a lot of things, but was cautious about its effect:

> It's had **some** effect on what I know about mathematics, it's had **some** effect on maybe what I would use in the classroom. (Jo's emphases)

For the four teachers (including Frankie) who did report new subject knowledge, this learning related primarily to coming to an understanding of expanded methods of calculation, mainly for multiplication and division. These methods included what was termed 'chunking' for division, a method that repeatedly subtracts multiples of the divisor (Department for Education and Employment, 1999, p. 6.69).

256 ÷ 7	256	
	- 70	10 x 7
	186	
	- 140	20 x 7
	46	
	- 42	6 x 7
	4	

Answer: 36 remainder 4

For multiplication, the 'grid' method suggested uses an area model as in the example given below (Department for Education and Employment, 1999, p. 6.67).

72 x 38

x	70	2
30	2100	60
8	560	16

$$\begin{array}{r} 2160 \\ +\ \underline{576} \\ 2736 \end{array}$$

In several cases the teachers described these methods as new to them and spoke about them with considerable excitement and enthusiasm.

3.3. Translating to the classroom

Hyde, Ormiston and Hyde (1994) suggest that effective professional development programmes should provide "methods, materials and activities that teachers can try out in their classrooms with initially limited risks" (p. 51). But even when the translation into the classroom is supposed to directly reflect the course, putting new knowledge and awareness into practice is "fraught with dilemmas" (Jaworski & Wood, 1999, p. 132).

Although actual classroom examples in the course materials were limited for some age groups, some teachers did identify immediate effects in the classroom. Frankie described getting to know resources better and extending her repertoire of uses for them. The counting stick she mentions below is a wooden stick, generally a metre in length, with ten divisions marked in alternate contrasting colours.

On the course, the counting stick was used in a range of contexts from chanting multiplication facts to counting along in decimals and fractions.

> The counting stick I thought was good because it was so versatile, because when I first saw the counting stick on a video maybe a year ago, I just thought oh, I saw somebody doing the times tables and I thought that's all you could do. I didn't think of anything else and then, you know, we were mainly using it on the course, we were doing it for everything and it was really good I thought. (Frankie)

Sam mentioned particularly the counting hoop as already being in use in the classroom (this referred to a hoop also divided into ten alternately coloured sections, to be used for counting in a variety of intervals).

> Well it works so much better than the line because it's giving them, I think it helps them to understand that numbers are kind of just ongoing.

Another teacher described how she was feeding back her new knowledge about expanded methods (in this case the grid method for multiplication) into the her work with her 9-10 year olds. This teacher was also quite explicit about how the message she had received from the course about the need for less written work was affecting her practice.

Frankie remarked on an increased emphasis in the classroom on making sure that children knew **why** they were doing things and compared this with learning mathematics when at school herself:

> ... when you multiplied the fraction and you turned it upside down and all these things that we learned that we still do, it's so funny we still do them, we don't really know why we are doing them.

Frankie felt that the numeracy consultants employed through the National Numeracy Strategy were pushing teachers away from using commercially produced mathematics schemes that mediated the curriculum (see Chapter 4), towards generating calculations in other ways, for example, using dice. Having been sceptical about this at first, Frankie was finding it feasible now, although not appropriate on all occasions.

> I do do that with my class now and with digit cards and things like that where they make up [calculations] and they do enjoy it and they are getting much better at it.

Frankie described increased confidence with formal methods, not just for use in the classroom, but also as mathematics co-ordinator, when people came to ask for help and advice.

3.4. Responses after nine months

Talking about the effects of the course nine months further on, Jo said "It fades, it fades", finding that suggested resources were not in use in her classroom, and identifying only a more secure overview of the Framework as a result of the course. Jo referred to the amount of numeracy training they had had before the course, within the school setting, implying that change had taken place in response to that, rather than to the course that came later. One of the eight teachers reported that she had retained her feelings of increased confidence, another felt more confused now than she had before.

Several teachers had retained one or two important messages. Frankie had brought back the importance of the teacher modelling an activity, with pupils then replicating it closely for the section of the lesson where pupils were working in pairs or individually. This continuing of the same task or activity that had been modelled by the teacher was suggested on the course (Approach A) as one way to approach the problem-solving activities in the main teaching session (Department for Education and Employment, 2000, p. 92). (Approach B was to complete an activity during initial whole-class discussion, then follow this by providing different but related tasks.) Approach A was observed in one of Frankie's lessons to be ensuring a smooth transfer from teacher-focused to pupil-focused activity where pupils replicated a whole class activity on identifying the operations between chains of numbers in individual worksheets. This approach was observed in other classrooms, but without the teacher specifically identifying it as having been learnt on the course.

Several of the teachers were talking positively about the effects of the course in terms of increased use of resources in the classroom. Those mainly identified were the counting hoop, the counting stick, number lines, 100 squares as well as such things as timers, new games and individual pupil whiteboards. Observation recorded several occasions where these resources appeared to be contributing appropriately to the lesson. For example, a teacher of four and five year old pupils adapted an idea from the course to make two square boards each containing nine numbers, with those on the second board being ten more than those on the first board.

> Every now and again something will happen and I'll remember something that we did like the number squares I did today. I saw them on the course. [...] I just saw them using the one. Now I'd forgotten about that and then something happened a few weeks ago and somebody must have mentioned something about them and I thought 'oh, I haven't used those that's a good idea'. (Reception teacher, pupils aged 4-5 years)

It was noted from observation of the Five-day course that opportunities were sometimes missed to make links that would be helpful to teachers. For example, in a discussion on partitioning as a mental strategy to multiply 13x15, some teachers suggested that (10x10) + (3x5) was an appropriate response. In trying to address this misconception, no use was made of the 'grid' method, due to appear later in the session, which would have clarified why the response was inappropriate. Occasions were observed during the research where a lack of understanding of the implication of messages from the course appeared to be causing confusion in the classroom when teachers' pedagogical content knowledge or subject matter knowledge were insecure. For example, one teacher of Year 5 pupils (aged 9-10 years) followed a suggestion from the course that differentiation could be facilitated by pupils choosing the size of numbers with which to work. The activity in this case was the use of doubles or near doubles as a mental strategy to facilitate addition. Some pupils chose four-digit numbers which in many cases were not near enough to doubles to be useful, and they were unable to compute these mentally. The teacher was unable to anticipate this in time to prevent substantial confusion and misunderstandings. On another occasion, observation revealed that Sam needed a greater knowledge of the mathematics behind the use of the counting stick as a representation rather than simply a counting device; it seemed that the course had failed to provide this when promoting the use of this resource. In one lesson observed, the end of the counting stick was identified as ten, rather than zero, so subsequent identification of places on the stick was confused by the fact that their position was not equivalent to their value, ie. the halfway point on the stick did not represent 50, but 60.

3.5. Responses after 18 months

This research began during the first year of implementation of the National Numeracy Strategy (1999/2000). However, training (both in school for all teachers and out of school for mathematics co-ordinators and headteachers) had been taking place over the previous year. So although not completely new when we spoke to the teachers for the first time, the Strategy was comparatively new.

All the twelve teachers (the eight who attended the course in 2000/01; the three who attended the course in 2001/02; the one who did not attend the course at all) were already identifying changes in their practice at the beginning of the research (in the first interview), before the course became available to them. These identified changes focused on first impressions of how the Strategy was affecting them as classroom teachers, with the following aspects of perceived change being particularly mentioned:

- their role as teachers in interactive whole-class teaching
- the structure of their mathematics lessons – a daily lesson of three parts
- changes in mental mathematics
- tighter and more detailed planning focusing on learning objectives
- reduced use of a commercial mathematics scheme
- increased pace of lessons
- a requirement for less written work by pupils
- a move towards more formal assessment.

Two years later at the end of the research, and 18 months after the end of the course provided in 2000/01, the teachers were asked to reflect back over the two years of the research and talk again about changes in their practice. They were also asked to identify the major influences behind these changes. By this stage, the total number of teachers had reduced to 11 – one of the original eight had moved schools.

The general feeling was one of increased confidence and enthusiasm. Only one of the original eight teachers did not subscribe to this view and reported feelings of insecurity and inadequacy:

> I don't actually feel I'm a better teacher. Particularly in maths. I feel I'm worse. [...] Some of the things I can do I'm working them out in my head and I'm thinking I'm not confident enough to actually go ahead and do it. Without having gone through. So I won't take that step further which a lot of the children do need, and can cope with. (Year 6 teacher, pupils aged 10-11 years)

Another reported having lost the feelings of increased confidence with which she returned from the course.

The National Numeracy Strategy was regarded as a positive innovation: "better suited to children's learning", according to one teacher. But at that point in time, three years after the National Numeracy Strategy was introduced, the overriding change, for both teachers and pupils it was felt, was having a new repertoire of methods to use. Talking about 'new methods' on returning from the course, the teachers were generally referring to expanded methods of calculation for addition, subtraction, multiplication and division. It was not easy to establish whether teachers who talked about approaching things in different ways, having many routes to the same answer, using different methods to solve problems, being aware of more strategies, giving pupils more options, were all talking about the same thing. Unpacking the examples given helps to exemplify what they meant.

One teacher described a mental strategy that was new to him – when finding 26% of something, to make this up from 10%, 5% and 1%, something which he would never have done before. Another teacher described becoming aware of, for example, 24 as 20 and 4 and being able to use that in calculation. A third teacher talked about many routes to the same answer. The essence seemed to be one of providing variety, and an appreciation that pupils (and teachers) found some methods or strategies easier to understand than others. Teaching a range of methods was more likely to hit the spot with more pupils. Their increased understanding of these new methods formed the principal component of the improvements in their own mathematics reported by the teachers. It was not clear from interview responses whether this range of methods was for an individual pupil or for a class. The point of choosing a method because of its efficiency and effectiveness in addressing a specified mathematical problem did not appear to have been addressed with sufficient clarity on the course to be retained by these teachers as a critical reason for providing a range of methods, as we can see from the following quotation from an interview with Sam:

> Well it's like the multiplication, like today we've looked at multiplication as repeated addition and tomorrow we're going to look at it, multiplication as an array ... and you give them those strategies and once they've got those strategies they can then pick how they want to do it. And because further up the school they do the grid method in multiplication and you give them, there's certain ways that different children work and their minds work in different ways so obviously for some children repeated addition is easier because they know what they are doing with addition and they find that a lot easier. But with others the arrays will be a lot better because they can count and they've got something, more the special needs thing, that works for them better, they seem to like that a lot but other children, because they can see visually, how big something is they can ... so you give them a range.

Although the learning of new methods of calculation and the increased use of a range of resources had been described by several teachers on returning from the Five-day course, the major influence over changes in practice was attributed, both by teachers who had attended the course and by those who had not, to the Framework document itself. "Just doing it" was described by several teachers, with others being much more explicit. The Framework document is referred to variously as 'the Strategy' and the 'numeracy folder' in the quotations that follow:

> ... the best thing really has been actually opening the Strategy, working through that, try and understand what they're getting at, what it's getting at. And actually the practice of it in class. Because I've said to you before I think, a lot of the time it actually didn't click while I was reading, but it actually clicked through the teaching or through the children's responses. (Year 6 teacher, pupils aged 10-11 years)

> ... probably most useful is still the actual numeracy folder, very useful in the early stages but even now still a very useful document for dipping into and checking to see what I should be doing and note all the bits and methods of working as well, that's the thing I use, rely on most of all still. (Year 6 teacher, pupils aged 10-11 years)

In-service training conducted within the school, generally by the mathematics co-ordinator, was the second most important influence noted, with the Five-day course appearing to have less impact than the in-school variety.

Of the three teachers who attended the course the following year (2001/02), two had found it interesting but relatively unmemorable. One teacher, however, attributed substantial changes in practice to the Five-day course, and this was in terms of being forced into really using the Framework document for the first time. Speaking directly after the course, he felt that in particular it had informed his expectations of pupil progression, and subsequent differentiation in the classroom. In the final interview of the research, Frankie, the mathematics co-ordinator from the same school, described the course as "really valuable", not just personally, but for other members of staff who had attended it, but felt that it should have come earlier in the implementation of the Strategy. It should be noted that the school in which both these teachers taught had fallen behind in it's implementation of the Strategy, with some of the initial in-school training being missed. In other schools, messages provided by the Five-day course were felt to have been already transmitted through in-school Inset.

In this section on individual factors, we have seen that although experiences in terms of course provision were similar for the eight teachers who attended the course in the year 2000 (and probably for the additional three teachers who attended in 2001, although these courses were not observed by the researchers) their responses varied considerably and were seen to be affected by their initial expectations; the in-school training they had already experienced; their confidence about mathematics; the roles they held; their attitudes towards the relevance of the course to the ages of the pupils they were teaching, and, as we shall see in the next section, by the school situations to which they returned.

4. SCHOOL FACTORS – THE PROFESSIONAL COMMUNITY

The previous section focused on the responses of individual teachers to their course of professional development, both in the short and in the longer term. We now turn to a consideration of the role played by the school context in which these teachers were situated. The second source of renewal, according to Joyce and Showers (1995), was the school. They remarked on a change of emphasis since their earlier writing: "We have changed in that we emphasize more centrally the position of the school." (Joyce & Showers, 1995, p. xv). In this example of in-service training, the *professional community* (defined in Chapter 1 as the immediate school context in which teachers operate) played a minor role in these teachers' experiences of the training itself. This course was not mediated through the school mathematics co-ordinator, as previous in-school Inset had been. The teachers attended out of school and external professionals – mathematics advisers from the Local Education Authority and/or numeracy consultants appointed as part of the National Numeracy Strategy – provided the delivery. It was when these teachers came back into school, with the expectation that they would be cascading their knowledge down to other members of staff that the school *professional community* came into play.

With cascade models of training, such as that utilised by the National Numeracy Strategy, the outcomes for other teachers are critical to the success of the training. Discussing the cascade model of training, Steadman, Eraut, Fielding and Horton (1995) note that criticism of the model can stem from misunderstanding the key purpose of cascade events.

> Those expecting to be informed rather than trained, and to get sufficient classroom-related experience to be able to identify training needs, were less likely to be disappointed. (p. 34)

The problem with this example of in-service training, the Five-day course, was that the design, or even the existence of the cascade was not clearly defined. For this reason, it would appear, our eight teachers found feedback extremely difficult. Short sessions only had been allocated to them during staff meetings in two schools and the teachers were anticipating having to provide longer feedback at a later date; a whole-staff meeting had been allocated in a third school. One problem they raised was how to condense four or five days of course activities into one or two hours. Another major source of difficulty seemed to be that the course had been 'for them' and they could not translate that into appropriate Inset for the other teachers. One teacher described getting so wrapped up in it that she resented the fact that the headteacher and the mathematics co-ordinator were coming on the final day. Because it was for their own personal development, and to address their own subject knowledge, the teachers who had attended the course appeared to feel that the development, if any, that had taken place was within themselves and not transferable.

> [We] found it very hard to feed back because we didn't really know what to feed back. We had the resources and everything they'd given us but we didn't really feel there was huge amounts to talk about with it. (Sam)

> Just something I did think about training though, and these courses are good for the individual and you store it somewhere in the back of your memory and it comes back, but we were looking at the effectiveness of this kind of a course to impact on the school. I think it is very difficult. (Jo)

In three schools, after brief discussions between the two teachers concerned, they resorted to focusing on resource ideas and how to use them, circulated photocopies of the course materials for teachers to read themselves, and passed back the main messages as they saw them. They were aware that their feedback had been a disappointment to other members of staff, who were "expecting them to come back with all these ideas to show".

The priority given to feedback by those managing staff-meeting time for mathematics (generally the headteachers) clearly differed, but then their *professional communities* differed. Two of the schools had extremely proactive and experienced mathematics co-ordinators who had led the school-based Inset sessions the previous year, and teachers attending the course from both these schools brought the message back that they were "well on" with the implementation of the Strategy in comparison with other schools.

In Frankie's school, the *professional community* had different characteristics. This school had missed several of the National Numeracy Strategy school-based Inset sessions from the previous year because of a lack of a mathematics co-ordinator for several months. It was therefore in a different position from the other three schools, which had completed more of the sessions. Provision for feedback in this case was for a half-day's Inset session with the additional support of the school's numeracy consultant.

5. PEER GROUP FACTORS – THE ZONE OF ENACTMENT

Joyce and Showers (1995) place particular emphasis on the value of peer coaching following in-service training as being critically important in the transfer to the classroom of new knowledge, skills and attitudes. It is not enough for teachers to work privately to make changes in their practice; ongoing support is required for them to be able to do this (Carter & Richards, 1999). Professional isolation is an impediment (Clarke, 1994). Guskey (1995) also stresses the need to recognise change as both an individual and an organisational process. These eight teachers received little, if any, peer support when they returned from the course, nor, in three schools out of four, much organisational support for their feedback.

In Chapter 2, mathematics co-ordinators were seen to have developed carefully thought out ways of working to influence teachers' *zones of enactment* – encouraging valuable dialogue with other teachers and introducing them to a range of resources. Dialogue of quality in relation to the feedback sessions was extremely limited in three out of our four schools, by the teachers' own admissions. Two factors seemed to be playing a part here – a lack of status given to the feedback by others in positions of authority in the school, together with the feeling on behalf of several of the participants that the course had been 'for them' and their subject knowledge, and this was not something that was easy to share. Describing the role of the co-ordinator in providing National Numeracy Strategy in-service training, McNamara and Corbin (2001) observe:

> This required the implicit to be made explicit and shared, through processes of affirmation/acceptance/challenge etc., in order to facilitate the professional reconstruction of colleagues' practices as 'valid'/'reliable' in the light of the 'official' pedagogy. (p. 275)

For six out of the eight teachers, not experienced in conducting mathematics in-service training, these were high-level demands in terms of subject leadership.

It was our interpretation that the lack of organisational support stemmed from poor communication from those running the courses about this secondary level of training. Teachers received contradictory messages about the course being designed to focus on individual subject knowledge on the one hand and yet require them to transfer this to others on the other hand. The coaching experiences regarded as essential by Joyce and Showers (1995) which could have contributed to the development of *zones of enactment* were not part of the Five-day course model. The cascade model required these teachers to attempt to demonstrate their own learning before they had been able to develop it themselves in the classroom, and from subsequent interviews with these teachers there did not appear to have been opportunities for reflecting on course experiences with professional colleagues. Indeed one teacher commenting informally on the cascade model after the completion of the research compared it to the game of "Chinese Whispers" where messages become distorted as they are passed from person to person.

The situation regarding feedback was different in Frankie's school. It was Frankie's first major presentation as mathematics co-ordinator and it was planned very carefully with the help of the local numeracy consultant. Peer support was thus provided from outside the school, but nevertheless from someone familiar with the school and well known to the co-ordinator. The Inset session was entitled 'Developing Mental Calculation Strategies: ideas for using resources in the mental/oral starter', and was not, therefore, an attempt to feedback on the whole content of the Five-day course, but rather to focus specifically on something that would be of use to the staff of the school in their current position. Frankie combined some material provided by the consultant with practical demonstration of resources, many of which had been demonstrated on the Five-day course. Resources had been prepared in conjunction with a small group of volunteer parents who had come in to help.

> I wanted to get across that we've got to teach them ways of doing it on paper so that they can apply that in their heads once they understand it so we did, we looked at lots of ways of using the number line for addition and subtraction and division, you know, I did a couple of demonstrations with that on the board and then just using the resources and I think people, they definitely learnt from it, people came up to me saying they felt it was worthwhile. (Frankie)

The other course participant in this school was extremely complimentary about the Inset, and said that it had been very well received.

> I think [Frankie] was quite nervous that some of the more sort of experienced members of staff had been doing very well thank you for years and might not take too kindly to these new fangled methods but in actual fact, you know, everyone was going 'oh yes, I do that, oh that's a good idea', it was all very well received and positive.

As part of the co-ordination role, Frankie reported following up discussions at this session with individual teachers after they had had time to put some of the ideas presented into practice, providing the opportunity for reflection directly related to classroom experience. For the teachers in this school, there were the opportunities for dialogue centred on classroom practice that Spillane (1999) regarded as essential for the realisation and development of *zones of enactment*.

6. SUMMARY OF SELECTED FINDINGS

6.1. Initial responses to the Five-day course

6.1.1. The eight teachers who attended the course in 2000/01

- all eight teachers described the course as enjoyable and on the whole found it interesting and involving
- four teachers expressed an increase in confidence in teaching mathematics after having attended the course
- four teachers defined learning new methods of teaching calculation from the course as improvements in subject knowledge. The other four felt that the course had 'revised' or 'refreshed' their subject knowledge, rather than giving them new knowledge
- five of the eight teachers described becoming familiar with a wider range of resources
- messages received from the course about the nature of expected feedback in school were mixed, and several teachers found it difficult to condense the course content into short sessions appropriate for their colleagues, thereby limiting the 'cascade' aspect of the training model.

6.1.2. The three teachers who attended the course in 2001/02

- two of the three teachers had found the course interesting but unmemorable. For one teacher the course had changed things 'strategically', through being forced into really using the Framework document for the first time.

6.2. Responses some time after the course

The 10 teachers remaining in the research who had attended the course by April 2002 were asked about the impact of the course within the context of all the National Numeracy Strategy initiatives.

- two teachers regarded its influence as extremely valuable, while one described its influence as providing good ideas. However, the remaining seven teachers did not regard the Five-day course as having been instrumental in influencing practice. In terms of changing practice, they regarded working with the Framework document itself and the effects of in-school Inset training as being of greater importance

- two of the four teachers who had initially felt more confident after the course, had lost those feelings of confidence
- at the end of the research, the teachers indicated that the overriding change, for themselves and their pupils was having a new repertoire of methods to use. The essence seemed to be one of providing variety, and an appreciation that pupils (and teachers) found some methods or strategies easier to understand than others
- the major influence over changes in practice was attributed to working with the Framework document itself. In-school Inset was the second most important influence noted
- all but one of the teachers felt that they would be able to sustain the changes they had already made although they would welcome such things as more resources, in-class support, ICT provision, practical apparatus, ideas for teaching, meetings with other teachers.

6.3. *Changes observed by researchers*

- observations by the researchers did not note marked changes in practice. However, it must be remembered that the research began when some initial major changes – such as the three-part lesson, the increase in whole-class teaching, the use of a new range of resources – were already being implemented
- observation noted the use of certain resources recommended by the Five-day course
- there were indications that some teachers were placing greater emphasis on listening to pupils' explanations of ways of working.

6.4. *Changes in pupil attainment*

- pupils in the classes of all 12 teachers made gains in attainment over both years 2000/01 and 2001/02 as measured by the Leverhulme tests. All classes tested had made gains in their test scores from the beginning to the end of the school year of at least 6% and sometimes as much as 32%. When these results were compared with those of the larger sample in the Core project (NB in most cases for a different school year), well over half of the gains were found to be above the averages for the larger sample. High and low gains were made in the classes of teachers who had been on the course, and those who had not. Classes of some teachers made high gains one year and lower gains the following year. The classes of other teachers made higher gains in the second year.

7. DISCUSSION

As a model of in-service training, the Five-day course, originating at government level (the Department for Education and Employment/National Numeracy Strategy), delivered and mediated at Local Education Authority level, could not be said to demonstrate a co-ordination of the four sources of renewal defined by Joyce and Showers (1995) – the individual practitioner, the school site, the district office (in our case the Local Education Authority) and government agencies. The design of the model of training did not incorporate ongoing opportunities for trialling and supported reflection on suggested classroom activities (Joyce, Calhoun, & Hopkins, 1999) – either in the form of repeated sessions over time (as in the 20-day model of mathematics training undertaken in England during the 1990s (Ofsted, 1993)), or in the form of in-school provision after the course. This in turn meant that the three variables of individual, peer group and school factors that appear to impact on classroom practice were not addressed.

Change was identified initially as emanating from the course, but for many of the teachers it related more to general feelings of confidence in mathematics, than to specific areas of improved subject knowledge, although effects on pedagogical content knowledge (eg. the teaching of different methods of calculation) were noted. Observational evidence from the research indicates that the major influence upon pupils might be in an increased range of resources intended to be used as representations of different mathematical ideas, although a lack of understanding of the representations implied by different resources, such as the use of the counting stick illustrated earlier, must limit their usefulness.

As the data have identified, attitudes towards the course, and responses following the course, were personal and individualistic. With differing personal characteristics and at varying stages of career, some of these teachers were more active than others in their approach to the opportunity of training. This approach may also have reflected the fact that the reasons behind the decision on their school's part to release them for the course were not always made explicit. It did appear to be the case that the teacher, Frankie, who appeared to have derived the greatest benefit from the course approached it initially with more vigour and enthusiasm than other teachers, describing activities as "interesting" and a "challenge". This teacher was able to articulate several aspects of learning from the course as being practised in the classroom. In this new stage of career, the role as mathematics co-ordinator enabled

Frankie to view the course as not only a personal professional learning experience but also as resource for learning about what was appropriate for colleagues teaching different age-groups. Sam, although returning from the course enthusiastic, could only point to her increased use of certain resources as a lasting outcome. Jo, starting from a lower level of enthusiasm, felt that the course had not resulted in changes in practice although it had resulted in a better overview of the National Numeracy Strategy documentation. Our initial interviews had also identified individual differences in the confidence of these teachers in their mathematical subject matter knowledge when working on mathematics problems (see Volume 2 of this series).

Could the course have been said to address these individual differences? The Local Education Authorities deviated little from the model they were given by the Department for Education and Employment. As already indicated, there was some potential conflict between the stated aims of the course, particularly the first of these – "to increase your knowledge of how mathematical topics ... may be taught effectively" (Department for Education and Employment, 2000, p. 1) – and the verbalised aim at the beginning of both courses, that the course was aiming to increase the teachers' own subject knowledge. However, the use of the term 'subject knowledge' appeared to fit more closely with what might be termed 'pedagogical content knowledge' rather than 'subject matter knowledge' (See Borko & Putnam, 1995), as the 'subject knowledge' was exemplified through the mathematics curriculum identified in the National Numeracy Strategy. There were mixed messages here. It seemed that, although encouraged to think of the course as providing mathematics 'for themselves', it was also for their pupils, or at least for pupils aged 7-11 years. The course aims and content matched closely the four aspects of pedagogical content knowledge outlined by Borko and Putnam (1995) (see Section 3.2.). During the following year, the course in one Local Education Authority was tailored for teachers of different age-groups (e.g. teachers of pupils aged 7-9 years and teachers of pupils aged 4-7 years), suggesting a shift away from subject matter knowledge to pedagogical content knowledge.

If aimed at subject matter knowledge, the task was huge. The range of mathematical knowledge and confidence among these eight teachers indicated by our interviews, if replicated across all course participants, would certainly be felt to necessitate differentiation if this was a classroom situation. No assessment was made of this range. To a certain extent the course activities could be said to provide for differentiation by outcome, but the same material was presented to all the participants – a 'one size fits all' model applied to teachers in this case, rather than pupils. It is interesting that one of these two Local Education Authorities has since made training provision for teachers self-identified as having low levels of confidence in mathematics.

Although responding to the course as individuals with different histories, it is likely that teachers were also affected by the quantity and quality of the in-school Inset that they had already experienced and by the roles they held. Positive mediating influences of peer-group and school-site variables (Joyce & Showers, 1995), the *professional community* in our model, were only clearly in evidence after the course in one school where one of the teachers attending the course was also the mathematics co-ordinator, and who was, in turn, supported both by management and the local numeracy consultant. In Chapter 6 we look in greater depth at ways in which reform ideas and the Five-day course affected the classroom practice of two of the eight teachers who attended the course in 2000/01.

The design of the Five-day course provided some of the constituents of effective professional development (Clarke, 1994): it was long enough to address issues in depth, as opposed to the 'one-off' sessions so commonly criticised; it made provision for more than one teacher to attend from each school facilitating discussions with colleagues. In terms of specific factors relating to those presenting the courses observed in the two authorities, course providers were generally regarded as effective in delivery and personally approachable, and the activities presented provoked interest and enthusiasm. However, it was our view that several essential constituents relating specifically to the mathematics were missing:

- some of the aims and objectives of the training had not been clarified and made explicit
- the use as mathematical representations of some of the suggested resources had not been sufficiently addressed
- useful mathematical connections were not always identified
- general principles underlying reform were not explicit.

However, even if the course had addressed these issues with the individuals attending, it is unlikely that these mathematical ideas could have been transferred into the classroom, let alone to an audience of colleagues without substantial iteration of trial, discussion and repeated practice in a supportive environment.

In this book we are suggesting that a critical element in the effectiveness of professional development is the enrichment and expansion of each teacher's *zone of enactment*, "that space where reform initiatives are encountered by the world of practitioners" (Spillane, 1999, p. 144), where innovations in practice and new knowledge can be mulled over, discussed with others, tried out in the classroom, reflected on again in an iterative process that results in changed, rather than amended practice. The cascade model of training implies by its very nature the creation of learning opportunities for a wider group of teachers than those individuals who undertake a course of training. Those promoting cascade models of training need to think carefully about providing these opportunities through collaborative investigation and organisational support within the *professional community* after the course itself is over.

8. AFFILIATIONS

Dr Shirley Simon is Lecturer in Science Education at the Institute of Education, University of London

9. REFERENCES

Askew, M., Brown, M. L., Johnson, D. C., Millett, A. M., Prestage, S., & Walsh, A. (1993). *Evaluation of the implementation of national curriculum mathematics at Key Stages 1, 2 and 3 volume 1: report.* London: School Curriculum and Assessment Authority.

Askew, M., Brown, M., Rhodes, V., Johnson, D., & Wiliam, D. (1997). *Effective teachers of numeracy: Final report.* London: King's College.

Ball, D. (1990). The mathematical understandings that prospective teachers bring to teacher education. *Elementary School Journal, 90*, 449-466.

Ball, D. L., & Bass, H. (2000). Interweaving content and pedagogy in teaching and learning to teach: knowing and using mathematics. In J. Boaler (Ed.), *Multiple perspectives on mathematics teaching and learning*. Westport, CT: Ablex Publishing.

Borko, H., & Putnam, R. T. (1995). Expanding a teacher's knowledge base: a cognitive psychological perspective on professional development. In T. R. Guskey & M. Huberman (Eds.), *Professional development in education: new paradigms and practices* (pp. 35-65). NY: Teachers College Press.

Brown, M., Millett, A., Bibby, T., & Johnson, D. C. (2000). Turning Our Attention from the What to the How: the National Numeracy Strategy. *British Educational Research Journal, 26*(4), 457-471.

Carter, R., & Richards, J. (1999). Dilemmas of constructivist mathematics teaching: instances from classroom practice. In B. Jaworski, T. Wood, & S. Dawson (Eds.), *Mathematics teacher education: critical international perspectives* (pp. 78-90). London: Falmer.

Clarke, D. (1994). Ten Key Principles from Research for the Professional Development of Mathematics Teachers. In D. B. Aichele & A. F. Coxford (Eds.), *Professional Development for Teachers of Mathematics 1994 Yearbook*. Reston, VA: National Council of Teachers of Mathematics.

Clarke, D. M. (1997). The changing role of the mathematics teacher. *Journal for Research in Mathematics Education, 28*(3), 278-308.

Darling-Hammond, L., & Sykes, G. (Eds.). (1999). *Teaching as the Learning Profession. Handbook of policy and practice.* San Francisco, CA: Jossey-Bass.

Department for Education and Employment. (1999). *The National Numeracy Strategy: Framework for Teaching Mathematics from Reception to Year 6.* London: Department for Education and Employment.

Department for Education and Employment. (2000). *National Numeracy Strategy Five-day course. Course handbook.* London: Department for Education and Employment.

Farah-Sarkis, F. (1999). Inservice in Lebanon. In B. Jaworski, T. Wood, & S. Dawson (Eds.), *Mathematics teacher education: critical international perspectives* (pp. 42-48). London: Falmer.

Fennema, E., & Nelson, B. S. (Eds.). (1997). *Mathematics Teachers in Transition*. Mahwah, NJ: Lawrence Erlbaum Associates Inc.

Guskey, T. R. (1995). Professional development in education: in search of the optimal mix. In T. R. Guskey & M. Huberman (Eds.), *Professional development in education: new paradigms and practices* (pp. 114-131). New York, NY: Teachers College Press.

Hargreaves, A. (1995). Development and Desire: a postmodern perspective. In T. R. Guskey & M. Huberman (Eds.), *Professional development in education: new paradigms and practices* (pp. 9-34). New York, NY: Teachers College Press.

Huberman, M. (1992). Teacher development and instructional mastery. In A. Hargreaves & M. Fullan (Eds.), *Understanding teacher development* (pp. 122-142). London: Cassell.

Hyde, A., Ormiston, M., & Hyde, P. (1994). Building professional development into the culture of schools. In D. B. Aichele & A. Coxford (Eds.), *Professional development for Teachers of Mathematics 1994 Yearbook* (pp. 49-54). Reston, VA: National Council of Teachers of Mathematics.

Irwin, K. C., & Britt, M. S. (1999). Teachers' knowledge of mathematics and reflective professional development. In B. Jaworski, T. Wood, & S. Dawson (Eds.), *Mathematics teacher education: critical international perspectives* (pp. 91-101). London: Falmer.

Jaworski, B., & Wood, T. (1999). Themes and issues in inservice programmes. In B. Jaworski, T. Wood, & S. Dawson (Eds.), *Mathematics teacher education: critical international perspectives* (pp. 125-147). London: Falmer.

Joyce, B., Calhoon, E., & Hopkins, D. (1999). *The new structure of school improvement: inquiring schools and achieving students*. Buckingham: Oxford University Press.

Joyce, B., & Showers, B. (1988). *Student achievement through staff development*. New York, NY: Longmans Inc.

Joyce, B., & Showers, B. (1995). *Student achievement through staff development*. ew York, NY: Longmans.

Lampert, M., & Ball, D. L. (1999). Aligning Teacher Education with Contemporary K-12 Reform Visions. In L. Darling-Hammond & G. Sykes (Eds.), *Teaching as the Learning Profession. Handbook of Policy and Practice* (pp. 33-53). San Francisco, CA: Jossey-Bass.

McNamara, O., & Corbin, B. (2001). Warranting practices: teachers embedding the National Numeracy Strategy. *British Journal of Educational Studies, 29*(3), pp 260-284.

Millett, A. (1996). *Using and Applying Mathematics: innovation and change in a primary school.* Unpublished PhD Thesis. King's College, London.

Office for Standards in Education. (1993). *The teaching and learning of number in primary schools*. London: Her Majesty's Stationery Office.

Shulman, L. (1986). Those who understand: knowledge growth in teaching. *Educational Researcher, 15*(2), 4-14.

Shulman, L. S., & Grossman, P. (1988). *Knowledge growth in teaching: a final report to the Spencer Foundation (Technical report of the Knowledge Growth in a Profession Research Project)*. Stanford, CA: School of Education, Stanford University.

Sikes, P., J, Measor, L., & Woods, P. (1985). *Teacher careers: crises and continuities*. London: Falmer Press.

Spillane, J. P. (1999). External reform initiatives and teachers' efforts to reconstruct their practice: the mediating role of teachers' zones of enactment. *Journal of Curriculum Studies, 31*(2), 143-175.

Steadman, S., Eraut, M., Fielding, M., & Horton, A. (1995). *Making school-based INSET effective*. Brighton: University of Sussex Institute of Education.

SHIRLEY SIMON, ALISON MILLETT AND MIKE ASKEW

CHAPTER 6

THE DYNAMICS OF TEACHER DECISION-MAKING: CASE STUDIES OF TEACHERS RESPONDING TO THE NATIONAL NUMERACY STRATEGY

Abstract. Drawing on the data from the study outlined in Chapter 5, *Teachers' Knowledge, Conceptions and Practices*, this chapter includes case studies of teachers in order to examine more closely the 'space' between the *pupil*, the *person* and the *policy* within the classroom, hence the core of teachers' classroom practice. Teachers' choice of tasks and modes of interaction result from decision-making both prior to the lesson and moment-to-moment within the classroom, these choices and actions reflecting teachers' underlying beliefs and perceptions about pupils and their learning. The chapter draws on interview and classroom observation data from the study to provide evidence of teachers' views about teaching and learning and how these relate to decisions made in the classroom in terms of children's activities and classroom discourse. Informed by previous work on teachers' belief systems, in particular their implicit theories of learning, case studies of two teachers' enactment of the National Numeracy Strategy Framework within the classroom focus on changes in practice over time. The findings show that the teachers have different initial beliefs about teaching mathematics and respond to the messages of the same in-service training in different ways. Though some changes are apparent in teachers' discourse and use of resources, the core of practice, influenced by underpinning theories of learning, does not change for either teacher. More fundamental changes would need to be stimulated by training that focuses more on how children learn in classrooms, and how teachers' implicit theories of learning can be addressed and enhanced.

1. INTRODUCTION

This chapter presents case studies of two teachers as they implemented the National Numeracy Strategy. These teachers participated in the Focus Project *Teachers' Knowledge, Conceptions and Practices*, and were part of the group of eight teachers forming the basis for discussion in Chapter 5. (See also Annex 2.) The studies focus on the ways in which the teachers' views and practices changed as they adopted the National Numeracy Strategy Framework for Teaching Mathematics from Reception

Alison Millett, Margaret Brown and Mike Askew (eds.), Primary Mathematics and the Developing Professional.

to Year 6 (Department for Education and Employment, 1999), and in particular on the impact of the Five-day in-service training course that took place during the second year of the Strategy (see Introduction). The analytical framework for the studies builds on previous work on teachers' theories, models of practice and orientations (Askew et al., 1997; Murphy, Davidson, Qualter, Simon, & Watt, 2000; Pollard, 2002) and rests on the premise that teachers' implicit theories about knowledge and children's learning are manifested in their classroom practice (Elmore, 1995). Previous studies have shown how teachers' deeply held beliefs and sustained practices are resistant to change, even when reforms promote quite different views of learning and practices (Spillane, 1999).

The research examines the degree to which the model of teaching presented in the National Numeracy Strategy Framework, and its underpinning assumptions about learning, challenges teachers' existing beliefs. It was possible that if the teachers in the study held views that were already commensurate with the ideology of the National Numeracy Strategy, they would adopt new practices without necessarily having their underlying beliefs questioned. Alternatively, it was possible that through changes in practice, teachers would begin to perceive new possibilities for thinking about children's learning or even, that reform recommendations would be interpreted to fit with existing beliefs and practices resulting in little deep change to either.

A major concern of the wider Leverhulme Numeracy Research Programme was the effectiveness of teachers' practice with respect to children's learning outcomes. It was therefore of some interest to consider how teachers' orientations (Askew et al., 1997), and the changes observed, could be considered to facilitate effective, purposeful learning. Rather than make experimental measures of progress with small numbers of children, the indicators of effectiveness are taken from observations of purposeful engagement in classroom activity.

The research began when the teachers had been implementing the National Numeracy Strategy for a period of one year. The case studies focus initially on the ways in which the teachers perceived they had changed their practice as a result of this implementation, and through early observations and interviews, existing orientations towards teaching and views of learning are identified. The studies then focus on changes that occurred after the teachers experienced the Five-day in-service training for the Strategy, drawing on observations made after the training, and teachers' own perceptions of their change.

2. TEACHERS' ORIENTATIONS TOWARDS TEACHING AND THEORIES OF LEARNING

Decisions made within classrooms, in terms of activities and teaching approaches, reflect the ways in which teachers view knowledge, how they should teach, and the process of learning. Though external policy requirements and contextual factors within schools play an important role in shaping teachers' practice, it is their personal experiences and underlying beliefs about teaching and learning that influence moment-to-moment decision-making in classrooms. The case studies presented here draw on previous studies of the ways in which teacher' beliefs and views of learning have been linked to effective practice in primary mathematics and science (Askew et al., 1997; Murphy et al., 2000).

The project *Effective Teachers of Numeracy* (Askew et al., 1997) identified three models of sets of beliefs that emerged as important in characterising, and helping to understand, the approaches teachers took towards the teaching of numeracy. The three models are described in terms of orientations towards teaching mathematics, and are referred to as *connectionist*, *transmission* and *discovery* positions. Connectionist teachers would characteristically focus on the connections between mathematical ideas to strengthen understanding and would view learning as the building up of a network of ideas as children are challenged and struggle to overcome difficulties. They also worked hard at connecting their teaching to children's existing understandings. Teachers with a transmission position would teach ideas separately, and believe that children need to be taught step by step to secure knowledge before moving on. Children's prior understandings were of secondary importance to the act of teaching for such teachers. A discovery orientation would be characterised by teachers presenting ideas separately for children to make their own connections and by the view that children learn new ideas only when they are ready. For these teachers, learning took priority over teaching. The study showed that teachers with a more strongly connectionist orientation had classes that made the greatest gains in performance. Yet because each of these orientations is idealised, teachers did not fit exactly into any one of them. The case studies reported here use the framework presented in the *Effective Teachers of Numeracy* study (Askew et al., 1997) to identify main orientations, but also draw on other perspectives (e.g. Murphy et al., 2000; Pollard, 2002), to inform our analysis of how teachers' beliefs do or do not change to become potentially more effective in the climate of the Strategy.

In the case studies presented here, the framework developed by Askew et al. has underpinned our analysis by focusing our attention on teachers' views of learning and how these are reflected in what children are asked to do and talk about. The case studies analyse how teachers' engagement in the National Numeracy Strategy may, or may not, have enabled them to develop a deeper understanding of children's learning and its relationship to teaching. In other words, the research addresses the question of whether a national strategy, presented and supported in the way it has been, can help teachers to develop practice that is underpinned by theoretically sound ideas about learning.

3. TEACHERS' RESPONDING TO SYSTEMIC REFORM

Previous studies of teachers changing their practice in response to systemic reform provide useful analytical frameworks for making sense of the changes portrayed in these two case studies. Our analysis of change draws primarily on the work of Spillane (1999) and his concept of the *zone of enactment* of a reform, that is the space in which teachers make sense of, and operationalise for their own practice, the ideas advanced by reformers. Spillane found that differences in teachers' enactment zones were key in understanding their efforts to change the core of mathematics instruction (see Chapter 1). In the case studies discussed here, of teachers adopting the systemic reform of the National Numeracy Strategy, the concept of the *zone of enactment* is used to discuss the extent of, and differences in, the changes observed. The study of change presented here also draws on Leithwood, Jantzi and Mascall's framework for analysing the success of large-scale reforms (Leithwood et al., 1999), with reference to the 'will', 'capacity' and 'situation' of teachers, as discussed in Chapter 1.

3.1. The National Numeracy Strategy Five-day course

Key to the analysis of change presented here is the impact of the Five-day course experienced by the teachers in our sample during the summer and autumn of 2000. The aims of the Five-day course were to increase teachers' knowledge of how mathematical topics may be taught effectively, to help teachers diagnose and rectify children's errors and misconceptions, to help plan and prepare lessons, and to prepare teachers to provide training and support for colleagues. The structure of the three-part lesson introduced in the Framework provided the context for studying the teaching of particular topics, which are covered in some depth in the course (see Chapter 5). The course included reference to children's common problems and difficulties in these topics and several ideas for teaching strategies.

4. CASE STUDIES

At the beginning of this research, the teachers had been implementing the National Numeracy Strategy Framework (Department for Education and Employment, 1999) for a period of one year. The first interview, conducted in the summer of 2000, was intended to establish background information about the teachers, drawing on their memories about learning mathematics, accounts of teaching and assessing in mathematics and views on how the National Numeracy Strategy had changed their practice. The analysis of these interviews, together with videoed observations of practice at this time, focused on teachers' existing beliefs and practice. The first part of the case-study accounts therefore provides a synopsis of the existing views of the two teachers, in terms of teaching, knowledge, learning and differentiation (meeting individuals' needs).

After these initial data were collected, the teachers attended the Five-day training course in two Local Education Authorities. The teachers were interviewed immediately after they attended the course, and subsequently observed and interviewed on three occasions over a period of 18 months (see Annex 2 for more details on the schools, the teachers and the data sources). The analyses of these data focused on ways in which beliefs and practices appeared to change as a result of the Five-day course.

We were very grateful to the teachers in this research project for granting us access to their classrooms. We would emphasise that, in the case studies that follow, the focus is on assessing the influence of the course rather than on criticising teachers' practice. The two teachers whose lessons have been studied in some detail were committed, hardworking teachers whose pupils over the two years appeared to enjoy their mathematics lessons and made gains in attainment as measured by the Leverhulme tests. The teachers were selected because of interesting differences in their beliefs about teaching and learning, and in their response to the course.

4.1. Andy

Andy recalled enjoying mathematics at secondary school, remembering particularly one inspiring teacher. She had been teaching in her primary school for nine years at the beginning of the study, and was teaching a class of Year 3/4 pupils (pupils aged 7-9 years). She also had secondary teaching experience, but not in mathematics.

4.1.1. Andy's existing views and practice

Andy planned at three different levels. At a strategic, weekly level, she planned with a friend, who had a similar class in a different school. They discussed types of lessons that 'work' and worksheets they could use. These plans followed the objectives in the half-termly plans from the Framework. Andy discussed her plans with a colleague at school to fine-tune the activities to be used and then planned from day to day by herself. Thus her planning was driven by a need to cover objectives for the class as a whole, rather than for individual progression in learning.

Andy expressed the view that teaching should include good explanations. She recalled being frustrated by mathematics in primary school because she was expected to work at her own pace on problem-solving questions rather than be 'taught'. She described herself as the sort of person who likes to be "taught properly", meaning she liked to have things "explained properly". This view of *teaching as explaining* was reflected in how Andy referred to herself as a teacher. She talked about "teaching" as taking place in whole-class or group situations, where she was either asking questions, getting the children to work on problems, or explaining procedures. Her preferred approach to teaching involved leading a session to focus on an aspect of mathematics, which children would then use to work on their own problems:

> The main teaching activity, I try to use as much visual aid as I can, whether it's on the board or with number lines. I involve the children as much as I can in the main activity, get them coming up, you know, asking them questions, getting them to explain answers, talk about it because obviously that's important, and I have them all together when I do that, both year groups, and I probably spend about another 10, 15 minutes, it varies, it just depends on the activity and how they are grasping it. I send them away and relate the work to that obviously and that's – I have the children working individually, in pairs, or groups depending on the activity. It tends to be individual a lot of the time but I always relate it in.

All the lessons observed were structured in this way. Andy preferred to keep children all together, so that she could take on this 'teacher as explainer' role.

Andy believed that the curriculum should be structured for the teacher to follow and made many references to knowledge being "built up", demonstrating a view of *knowledge as hierarchical and sequential*. She also talked about learning as children *grasping* things, saying that she was "never sure whether they've grasped it or not". Her planning was driven by a need to cover objectives for the class and was informed by a general inability of children to "grasp" what she was providing, in which case she went over things again.

Andy used individual work mostly, with some paired work, because she felt she could evaluate children's performance more easily that way, and keep the noise under control. She did not use group work unless it was a practical session and in interview she queried the meaning of 'collaborative work'. Andy's references to children and their learning were mostly as a collective group, rather than as individuals, which led to a view of *differentiation as extension*. Her whole-class introduction was undifferentiated, as was the main activity for the majority of the class, but she prepared a selection of easier work for one group, and extension work for another group. When talking about this aspect of her decision-making, Andy said she was not able to predict how children would perform, she relied on formal assessment to gain knowledge of individual children's progress. She primarily described *assessment in terms of marking*, from which she was able to see whether the children understood what they had been taught.

Andy's views about teaching and learning would appear to demonstrate a predominantly transmission orientation (Askew et al., 1997) towards teaching, in that the teacher 'teaches' and the children 'grasp' what is taught. However, Andy showed a desire to be effective and a concern for children's learning. She also welcomed new ideas. She had found a course on children's misconceptions valuable because she began to look at "how children were thinking" and through teaching less able children had begun to think more deeply about children's learning. She also had an intuitive feel for the benefits of peer learning, as expressed in her view that "they learn a lot from each other when they talk about things". These insights indicate that Andy was concerned about children's learning but she lacked an awareness of how to adopt an approach involving careful elicitation, informed differentiation, planning guided by formative assessment and well-designed collaborative activity. Would the Five-day course help her?

4.1.2. Andy's practice before the Five-day course

Andy's practice before the course demonstrated certain key features. There was a strong reference to time and an emphasis on curriculum coverage. There was a tendency to close episodes with answers from high-achieving children and there was limited exposure of a range of children's strategies. Overall, Andy's approach demonstrated a transmission orientation through her use of cued elicitation (Mercer, 1995), though there were clear episodes where she wanted children to discover answers for themselves. On some occasions she included potentially useful peer discussions, but did not draw on the outcomes of these.

At the beginning of the lesson Andy had drawn on the board two three-by-four grids. She began by telling the children that 'we are going to look at our times tables again today' and that she was going to use her stopwatch 'to see if we can get a better time'. The children had sheets with several examples of full and empty grids.

1	4	7
6	10	8
11	5	3
9	2	12

Andy then explained that she was going to choose a number, and that the children were to 'take the number, times it by whichever number I tell you' and to write their answers down in their own grids. These instructions were given very quickly. Andy then wrote down the number 2 and said 'go'. The first child finished in 43 seconds. Children alerted her as they finished so there was a ripple of 'finished' every few seconds and Andy shouted out the number of seconds. There appeared to be no observation on Andy's part as to whether the children's grids were correct or not. The video showed that some were not.

Though this task was to enable practice of using tables, the main focus was on the speed at which pupils were working. Pupils duly focused on speed, sacrificing accuracy in the process. Andy's concern was on the filling in of grids to indicate the completion of the task, rather than on accuracy as she scanned pupils' work.

As most people finished, Andy reminded them they had to 'double your number'. She waited for all to finish, those who finished quietly chatted. She reached a point where she said 'we'll stop there, don't worry if you've not quite finished, we'll come back'. She then said 'let's put some answers in', and directed her questions at different children. She asked pupils who gave her correct answers for the first two numbers in the grid, she filled these in on her first grid as they did so. Her third choice was a boy who took rather longer, but he gave the correct answer, 14. Each time Andy asked someone, she said 'x times two?' for whatever number it was. One child gave her answer correctly as 12, for 'six times two?', even though she had written 16 in her own table. Many pupils could be seen writing down their answers as Andy went around the class. Everyone she asked gave a correct answer. (Video observation notes)

This opening work appeared rather easy for those who could do it and misunderstood by those who were struggling, although appropriate for some pupils. The discourse norms focused on speed, rules, and filling in the right answers. There was no discussion of strategy for achieving accuracy, or diagnosis of those who were going wrong. It was hard to see how this task served to enhance children's knowledge and understanding of their tables, though it did provide some practice. There was a very quick transition to the next episode.

> This episode involved division sums, which had to be matched to pictures of shopping items, for example, two trays of six eggs. The task involved more than procedural knowledge, as children had to transform pictures into abstract numbers. In presenting an example for the children to follow, Andy was clearly aware that she needed to assist many children with understanding what was required of them. The first two answers for simple division problems showed children's limited understanding of the task. Andy then used the answer of an able child as a means of demonstrating to the others the right answer. (Video observation notes)

For many children this is enough for them to see what is being asked. For others, demonstrating the correct answer is no help if they do not understand how it has been derived. There was no attempt to go over the strategy used by the child answering correctly, nor an attempt to ask children whether they could see how to work it out. It appeared that part of the task was for children to work out the strategy for themselves, as exposing it would be like telling them the answer. Shaping tasks in this way is like pseudo-'discovery' learning and begs the question of the purpose of the task.

There followed three short episodes where Andy gave the children problems to do for a few minutes after which she went through the answers as a class. During two of these episodes Andy asked children to work with their partner, "to discuss and talk about what you think your answer is and how you are going to get to your answer". Thus she introduced opportunities for children to use talk to enhance their learning. Her whole-class teaching did not draw specifically on these discussions, but involved formal question and answer to get individual children to show how they had carried out the problem. One problem was:

> Mrs Smith needs 45 eggs from the supermarket to make a special meal for her family. Eggs are sold in boxes of six. How many boxes does she need to buy? The dialogue proceeded as follows:
>
> One child said that he went to 72 and shared it into six so Andy asked him why he went to 72. He said that he went down in sixes, she asked how many boxes he got in the end, he said eight. Andy asked why he went to 72 when Mrs Smith only needed 45 eggs, he said he was counting down. Andy asked if he thought he should have started at 72 (indicating this was incorrect) and where should he have started, he said six. Andy suggested that then he would have counted up. She asked another child to help him, who said she went to the six times table, found 48, took away one (six) and got 42. Andy went back to the boy and told him he would not have started at 72, and asked him where he would have started, he looked confused. Andy asked how many eggs Mrs Smith needed, he said 45, she asked so how many did she need, he said 10. Andy then

> told the boy she would correct him, just this time, and that he would have counted down from 45, or gone up in sixes to get the answer. (Video observation notes)

Andy found she had no way of helping this boy to articulate the answer she was looking for so she had to 'correct' him, which from her tone was unusual. She seemed to believe that to tell children the answer or correct procedure was not what she should do in whole-class question and answer sessions, yet she ran out of alternative strategies.

This lesson then included an extended period where children worked from differentiated worksheets. The lesson ended with a plenary focusing on examples from the easy worksheet, where Andy asked some children to explain their strategies. This was a useful metacognitive learning experience for those describing their strategies, but there was no specific task for those listening.

The observation served to confirm that Andy's predominant orientation was transmission, where children would listen to her, or to an achieving child, and grasp understanding through explanation. It also demonstrated an element of discovery (Askew et al., 1997), as Andy simultaneously held the view that children should construct their own learning, as evidenced by the tendency not to want to correct children but encourage them to discover strategies and answers for themselves. She also had some intuitive recognition of the value of social learning, as evidenced by the encouragement of discussion, but this lacked clarity of purpose, and hence focus and direction.

4.1.3. The initial impact of the National Numeracy Strategy

In the initial interview, Andy talked about the National Numeracy Strategy and how it had influenced her since its implementation a year previously. Three key features were noted in her account of the National Numeracy Strategy. The first was the way in which the structure required by the Framework resonated with Andy's preferred way of working, so she could adopt a teaching approach that suited her. The second was the way in which Andy welcomed some of the new ideas which would mean she could make changes she felt comfortable with. The third was the way in which she described her deliberations with others, which indicated the way in which her *zone of enactment* was constructed. These three features are described below in more detail.

Andy welcomed the National Numeracy Strategy as it heralded a change from following a published scheme to using a more structured framework. Prior to the Strategy she had experienced a tension between her preferred way of working, which was to "keep them all together", and the scheme, where children worked at their own pace. The structure and detail provided by the Framework helped her to become more confident in her planning.

With reference to new ideas, Andy emphasised the mental work, and how she had become more aware of the different ways in "how we go about working out". This latter feature had a big impact on Andy throughout the period of the study. She had gained insights into ways of "breaking things down" for children, and found that the idea of exploring alternative strategies with children "really stimulates your thinking".

The success of reforms reported by Spillane showed that ongoing deliberations with colleagues as well as experts were central to teachers' reform efforts (Spillane, 1999). Andy often shared ideas with others, for example, planning her week's work with a friend, discussing individual lessons with the teacher in the room next door and evaluating how well lessons "work". However, though she believed that her approach was similar to other teachers in the school since implementing the National Numeracy Strategy, because everyone had adopted the Strategy and were positive about it, when asked about other teachers' comments she was unsure of what others might have said. It is possible she worked in relative isolation within her *professional community*, though she clearly valued opportunities to discuss issues with colleagues:

> I think just sitting down as a staff discussing it and looking at different things was useful and reassuring, maybe that you were on the right track as to how it should be going… . I mean I think there's always bits you can pick up but I think it's chatting to other teachers as to where things are going and how they are finding it, I found that probably as useful as anything really.

Thus Andy's main *zone of enactment* was constructed by herself, drawing on her own will and capacity to take on the reform, with only limited support from colleagues. She recognised at this point in time that she had much more to learn and perceived that she would benefit from more training on differentiation and misconceptions, particularly if she moved out of her current age group.

4.1.4. Andy's response to the Five-day course

When interviewed about what she had learnt from the Five-day course Andy was reluctant to expand without her notes, indicating that she was aware she had noted down much more than she was able to remember (Joyce & Showers, 1995). She appreciated that the course was about subject knowledge, but her conception of courses was "to get out as much as you can for your age group". When she first arrived on the course she wondered why all the Year 3 (pupils aged 7-8 years) teachers were not grouped together to discuss good ways of teaching (she was now teaching only this age group). Even when she appreciated the subject knowledge goals and was made aware of areas where she was "rusty", she still questioned the relevance of the content to her own teaching. She felt that her lack of recall of detail was due to the lack of relevance, because as soon as she returned from the course she was focusing on her own age group.

Andy perceived that the Strategy was saying the "same old thing" about ways of teaching, and she identified two main messages: an emphasis on the importance of differentiation and using a variety of strategies. She therefore did not see the Strategy as promoting anything new, rather, as reinforcing her existing beliefs and preferred practices. For example, she described the practice of getting children to come to the board and explain their strategies as a little idea that she tended to use anyway. Her memory of the value of this practice had been refreshed by the course video. Andy focused on ideas, such as the use of jottings as an aid to mental and written calculations, which were strategies she perceived were useful. She thought that when using a mental strategy, time limits on tasks prevented useful mental jottings:

> You are so focused on the test and it's five seconds, five seconds, five seconds that they wouldn't have time to do mental jottings ... and I think it's a jolly good idea to get them to actually do that.

This comment reflects a change from practice identified at the beginning of he study, where Andy was preoccupied with speed rather than accuracy. Andy also liked the idea of using jottings on white boards as a means of helping her to see what children do when "talking and sharing with their partners". Thus jottings were not only useful for children's thinking, but also important for her as a teacher to "see where they are coming from to get their answer".

The impact of the course was influenced by Andy's expectation, which was to pick up tips for teaching and how she saw these illustrated through the video. When asked about messages for children's learning and misconceptions, she had made notes but had not internalised them sufficiently to be able to talk about them. The course did not impact on Andy at a level deeper than in providing tips she thought might help her as a teacher to see where children were coming from. Yet in as much as it did this, changes in practice were perceived. The course was too intensive for Andy to retain much of what was covered. It needed reinforcement through subsequent feedback sessions. The interview for the project acted on Andy in this way, because when she was asked what she would feed back from the course to others she went through the process of thinking aloud to come up with her own main messages for teachers. These were to do with problem solving, in particular getting children to read the questions, underlining key words in word problems and checking answers to see whether children recognise it's a reasonable answer.

Andy felt that the course and the Strategy had given her more confidence in herself as a teacher. The strategy has provided her with structure and approaches, and the course emphasised the fact that she could teach these.

> You wonder if you are good enough to actually do it. Now you know you could, and I think on the course you say, yes I could do that and I think because the Numeracy Strategy is now in place, there's plenty of guidelines there and strategies that you can follow to teach and I think that is something that is good, you know.

4.1.5. Influences on Andy's practice

A focus of Andy's teaching after the course was an emphasis on children "working out and thinking with their own strategies". She used children's individual whiteboards frequently after the course, so that she could see "where the children are coming from" and identify those who understood what she was asking them to do. From the course she had learned that children use different strategies for the same question, which she now recognised as being legitimate. However, though she showed signs of coming to terms with children's ideas, she was anxious about them and retained her view of what she considered an approved style. She did not really use the children's strategies.

4.1.6. Limitations to Andy's change

When asked about how she handled transitions from whole-class teaching to individual work, Andy's answer indicated a continuing emphasis on providing instruction and a reliance on her explanation as the main mode of learning, that is transmission. She was, however, aware that not all children "get the message", and followed up her whole-class instructions with checks in small groups to make sure children understood.

Andy was conscious of different children's needs, particularly the most able in her class, for whom she devised individual work, and those with special needs. In trying to explain her rationale for paired work, Andy exposed tensions in her beliefs about learning and her role as a teacher. She believed that "they do learn from each other a lot and I think more and more we should realise that", yet her practice did not reflect this espoused belief.

Andy did not change her overall process of planning. There was little indication that planning would take into account any ongoing assessment and evaluation of children's learning, rather, it was about teachers structuring the contents of the required curriculum. The Strategy served to reinforce this basis for planning.

4.1.7. Indication of potential change

When interviewed at the end of the study, 18 months after going on the course, Andy's comments confirmed her previous perception of how the course had most impact. She was "far more aware that there are many routes to the same answer". Whereas she tended in the past to teach one strategy to get an answer she now included as many different ways as possible. Though Andy changed her pedagogy, the changes did not necessarily indicate an alteration in her fundamental beliefs about how children learn mathematics. Rather, they served to provide a wider range of legitimate strategies for children to achieve different ways of getting right answers. Andy offered no clear rationale (in terms of children's learning) for why she perceived these different methods to be legitimate – there may be better pedagogical reasons than she is aware of, for example, choosing a method that is appropriate to a problem, rather than allowing any method a child chooses. Andy may have appeared to have developed a broader educational discourse (Mercer, 1995), but her efforts may not achieve outcomes in terms of enhanced educated discourse, that is, children may not know which methods are appropriate for particular problems.

Andy had begun to perceive value in different patterns of classroom interaction. She did not elaborate how it helped the children (hence demonstrate any great change in beliefs about how they learn), but she felt it enhanced her evaluation of their learning. She said she was more aware of their learning because she was listening to them more and she placed more emphasis the importance of "chatting it through". Though the last observation showed an attempt by Andy to have some paired discussion, the "chat" was not used in any way to enhance cognition.

> Andy introduced a problem: Three adults pay £27 all together to see a match. What was the cost of each ticket? Children's tickets are half the price of adult tickets, what would be the cost of two adult and three children's tickets to go to the match?
>
> Andy used cued elicitation to get the answer to the first part of the problem (the cost of each ticket). One child told her how he would do the next part (he was correct) and Andy said with a laugh, 'don't pre-empt me'. She went through the problem stepwise. At the point where all calculations had been completed apart from the last, she asked the children to speak to the person next to them and work out the two totals. The time given for this was very brief. When she asked for an answer she was given £21.50 by one child then £31.50 from another. She asked the children how she might check it, referring to 'two ways I've got in my head'. (Video observation notes)

The lesson showed Andy had retained her mainly transmission orientation towards teaching.

4.2. Frankie

At the beginning of the study Frankie was in her third year of teaching. The Year 5 children in her class of Year 4/Year 5 pupils (aged 8-10 years) were of low ability, therefore she was working towards the objectives for Year 4 pupils in the Framework. Her main subject at college was English. Frankie's recollection of college mathematics was that it was insufficient to help her prepare lessons. She learnt more on Teaching Practice than she did at college. Frankie considered herself to be quite strong at mathematics and she had always been in the top set at school. She recollected a good mathematics teacher, whom she described as understanding each person – "it was like she was just teaching *you* because she gave us so much time". Frankie took on the role of mathematics co-ordinator in her school in July 2000.

4.2.1. Frankie's existing views and practice

Frankie planned by herself each week using the Strategy planning sheet, but adjusted her plans according to the progress made, taking longer than suggested on things in order to suit her own children:

> I find that if they don't understand something and I have to go on and do two days on something pretty different I don't like it so I do yes, I'm always adding days.

Thus Frankie adjusted her planning according to the perceived needs of the children.

Frankie's existing practice included episodes of board work where children go up to the board to show how they work things out. She explained that she liked children to do this because it was good for them and it enabled other children to see what they were doing. She clearly valued the exposure and comparison of different strategies for working things out, shown by her example of how she encouraged children to consider different methods. Observations showed prolonged episodes in Frankie's practice of children carrying out their methods of working in front of the whole class. Frankie was clearly aware of the limitations of this practice. There was a tension in her practice of *teaching as demonstrating* and her awareness of individual needs for understanding, which she analysed as time constraints:

> I found in the past where I spent a long time on the plenary sometimes it can go on a bit too long, you know, and you feel like you should sort out all their problems that they don't understand and then suddenly you've lost loads of time, that's what I find so difficult, time constraints.

So Frankie aimed for understanding but used whole-class strategies that were time-consuming. However, by asking children to check their answers using the alternative methods they observed from their peers, she was encouraging them to use the different problem-solving strategies demonstrated. Frankie made other comments emphasising her view of teaching as demonstrating:

> The main teaching activity that is, you know, teacher-led whole-class discussion about how to do something and children coming up and demonstrating. Me showing them different ways of doing something, discussing how they work something out, how different children work things out and then using what they've learnt in that part of the session to then go on and do something on their own.

When Frankie asked children to work on the board, there was an assumption that the 'doing' was facilitating their learning, and that for the others, learning took place through observation. Frankie saw *knowledge as connected*, rather than sequential. Though she perceived *learning as understanding*, she thought this took place through children observing and listening, reflecting a transmission orientation. She believed that children should not struggle to overcome difficulties, indicating that she was unaware of the notion of learning through cognitive conflict, or challenge. When asked how she organised the children, Frankie emphasised her use of whole-class teaching. She perceived her whole-class teaching as "everybody taking part". She asked those children whose minds she thought were wandering to use the board. She did not seem to place much emphasis on the value of paired working:

> The whole class dominates the first half of the lesson really with everybody taking part and I think that works great. I'm happy with that as long as I'm constantly on at the children that I know whose minds wander, but they are the ones who I often get up to the board, which works fine. Now where you say group, they sit in a group but they might be working individually on independent tasks. They don't often, if they are doing something like measuring or something very practical then they would work together as a group to work something out, but if it's independent written work where they are doing, working out calculations then it would be individual. But then I often get them to mark their own work by sitting with a partner so if they've got the same answers, as long as they haven't copied, and they've both checked them then they do that so that would be a pair situation.

Frankie built differentiation into her teaching in different ways. For problem-solving work she might ask children to make up their own problems, which would be different for different children. On other occasions she would structure work for three different groups by *differentiation according to complexity.* Sometimes Frankie used mixed-ability groups but she found similar-ability groups easier. She thought that she probably should do more mixed-ability teaching, but felt that her whole-class teaching sufficed:

> You hear that you should be doing more like paired, mixed-ability work but I sometimes find that if I do that then the less able ones just get lost really and they don't – they are not really working at their own level so I think because we do so much whole class, you know, at the board everybody is taking part, everybody is looking at how other people are working things out and all that I think that compensates then for the abilities, splitting them into the ability groups.

Thus her strategy for showing working on the board was a result of the tension she felt with respect to mixed-ability teaching.

When asked about assessment, Frankie talked about half-termly tests, either constructed by herself or taken from published materials. She also referred to her ongoing assessment using the planning sheets which encouraged teachers to note which children did not achieve the objectives. She found these limiting in that she was putting the same names down each time for extra help, so she would add other information about children's needs. She would also note down topics where children didn't understand something.

4.2.2. Frankie's practice before the Five-day course

Early observations of Frankie's practice showed consistent lesson structures which included 15 minutes of mental activity, followed by an episode of about 20 minutes of interactive whole-class teaching to introduce the main activity, 20 minutes of individual work and about 10 minutes plenary. Thus the amount of whole-class teaching was extensive.

The first mental warm-up we observed focused on practising the five and 10 times tables and the division facts that go with them. The episode was conducted at a moderate pace and was punctuated by reminders about certain rules that the children could apply. Digit cards were used, and the children held them up when they knew the answer. This style of 'interactive whole-class teaching' was typical of Frankie's practice. The following passage describes this episode.

> Frankie asked the children to remember the patterns in the five times table, using the question 'what can you tell me about the numbers in the five times table, what do they always end in?' to which a child answered 'a five and a zero'. She asked for a similar rule for the 10 times table and got the answer 'they always end in a zero'. She then reinforced this by asking the children that when she called out a sum from the five or 10 times table, 'what will your number have to end in, what will your answer have to end in when you hold up the correct answer?' Children put their hands up and someone answered five or zero. Frankie then said that she may ask them a division fact – and asked whether someone could give an example of a division fact. A child answered 12 times five to which Frankie replied that she had to use a division fact, so after a pause for thought the child gave '60 divided by five'. Frankie accepted this answer, saying

'the reason you said 12 is that the answer is 12 isn't it? So 60 divided by five and the answer would be 12.'

Frankie then called out sums. The first was five fives. She asked them to hold up digit cards and then say the answer all together, which they did. She asked for another way of saying five times five, as they had done this recently, at which one girl said five squared. Frankie reinforced this by saying that when you square a number, you have to multiply it by itself. The next sum was six times five, most held up cards, Frankie said everyone together, and they chanted '30'. Next was nine times five, followed by six times 10, though not all children held up answer cards or chanted the answer. Frankie then asked a group seated round one table to give an answer for three times five. Someone had nine, Frankie said this was three times three, someone else had 30, Frankie told her this was three times 10, she asked them to check and someone else had the correct answer, 15.

Frankie then went on to say she would do division ones and asked the whole class for 70 divided by 10. She asked someone who held up the correct answer to say it and praised her when she gave it. She then gave 80 divided by 10, again targeting someone with the correct answer. Frankie asked the children to put their hands up if they found it easy to work out the division facts of the 10 times table. Several children (in view) put up their hands and Frankie asked one why she found it easy. The child said 'If you do something times 10 all you have to do is put a zero on, if its division, if you divide something by 10 you take off the zero.' Frankie rephrased this 'if the number gets 10 times smaller the zero disappears, so for example when it's 80 divide by 10, you just get rid of the zero, the number gets 10 times smaller and it's eight'. Frankie reinforced the idea of the zero disappearing by demonstrating it on the board. She then asked if everyone was ready and she gave 90 divided by 10, 100 divided by 10. Frankie then switched to the five times table. She asked for 60 divided by five, re-wording as 'how many fives are there in 60?' She got the children to chant answers as before. She went on to ask children on another table on their own, 40 divided by five. (Video observation notes)

The rapidity with which children held up their answers suggested that the sums were quite easy for most of them. However, the small group that were asked to work out three times five were clearly challenged. Frankie used this opportunity to see the children's errors and correct them. She did not explore why they had reached their different answers. As the mental warm-up proceeded, a method for dividing by five by first dividing by 10 and then doubling the answer was introduced and encouraged as follows:

Frankie gave the children the sum of 70 divided by 10 on the board (with pupil input) and asked for 70 divided by five. Some pupils had difficulty. Frankie asked if someone could explain what they had just been trying to do. She chose a girl who had been giving answers quickly:

Frankie: S, can you explain what we've just been talking about?

Pupil: ... we had to do 70 divided by 10, and we had to add up s...

Frankie: [interrupts] then we were gong to work out what 70 divided by five was, and what did we say that the answer was going to be?

Pupil: seven

Frankie: When you divide it by 10 it's seven, but when you divide it by five what do you have to do to get the answer? You have to ..

Pupil: Got to add seven

Frankie: Yes you've got to seven add seven is (she wrote this on the board), what's that word beginning with 'd' that D used? You've got to do what to seven, you've got to dou...

Pupil: Divide

Frankie: Not divide

Pupil: Double it

> Frankie then asked for the answer, repeating the strategy, and more pupils got it correct. Finally she asked them to work out 90 divided by five. There was a chant of 18 and she asked someone to explain how he got an answer. He did this clearly, repeating the strategy. Frankie asked the children to suggest another way of saying double nine, and someone said times, prompted by Frankie as to say times by what, he said two. (Video observation notes)

Frankie's warm-up showed that she aimed to include as many children as possible in her whole-class teaching. She distributed her questions widely and used resources that would involve all the children. She also differentiated by asking different groups of children questions with varying levels of difficulty. She continuously made connections for children between the sums they were doing and rules or number patterns. But the lesson lacked representations that might make the connection stronger, for example, the link between dividing by 10 and deriving the answer to dividing by five was not supported by any pictures or diagrams. At the end of the mental warm-up Frankie asked one child to explain what the class had been doing, thus she also included metacognitive reflection. These aspects of her practice reflect a view of teaching as connectionist (Askew et al., 1997). However, Frankie's whole-class teaching showed that many children were relatively passive or unchallenged for extended periods. Frankie clearly valued the importance of teaching for understanding but she did not like children to struggle, instead she preferred to demonstrate how to use procedures so that children could then feel secure in how to works things out for themselves. Her approach therefore also reflects a transmission orientation, with a limited awareness of *how* children construct their knowledge and understanding.

Frankie's main activity in this lesson continued to show evidence for this mixed set of views:

> The theme of the lesson was decimal fractions, and she used a number line on the board to demonstrate the position of fractions and decimal fractions along the line, from zero to one. She gave out cards to some children, bearing the fractions or decimal fractions that were to be included. Much of the task involved children coming up to stick on their card while the others watched. Once the first few cards were up, the task seemed very straightforward and unchallenging, as the children followed the number sequences for their style of card. Most children were watching as the sticking up of cards involved less than half the class. Frankie continued to help make connections, by relating both fractions and decimal fractions to money values. The exercise was very visual. After all the tenths and decimal tenths were in position, Frankie asked for 0.25 and 0.75, and she asked particular children to convert these to fractions. This clearly challenged many others, but rather than be put into a position where they had to try and resolve it, those who *could* answer the questions *did* whilst the others watched (the video shows more lack of attention at this point). Once Frankie went back to ask less difficult questions of the whole class and distributed the questions around, the whole class sat up and took notice. (Video observation notes)

4.2.3. The initial impact of the National Numeracy Strategy

Frankie's main perception of the Strategy was that there was a lot of emphasis on mental and oral work, with whole-class teaching where the children were involved. She also perceived that having key objectives was good in that it helped to know what needed to be done, and also what the children had achieved.

Frankie's perception of how her practice had changed related to pacing. She said she used to be quite slow with the children because she wanted to make sure everyone understood. However, through speeding up her questions she had found that she got the children's minds working more quickly. Thus the benefits she perceived from the National Numeracy Strategy were to do with pace and learning rather than lesson structure and coverage. Frankie was finding that her episodes of individual work were shorter, but believed that children were doing the same amount in less time. However, this shift raises questions as to the nature of the children's experience. Lengthy periods of listening and observing were still a feature of Frankie's lessons, where the children were somewhat passive. However she was concerned with lack of engagement in individual work, and felt that children were engaged as they listened and observed during whole-class teaching:

> I think the whole interactive whole-class thing I've got better at doing, you know, just having the children up all the time and, you know, I'm always asking questions really quickly, right who wants to come do this, you know, quickly, you know, it's all like that all the time whereas before I couldn't even have done it like that because I was worried about the consequences of the behaviour if someone's up at the board and the others weren't listening or, you know, that kind of thing, so I think it always just comes with experience.

Frankie thought that she had learnt new ways of doing things from the Strategy, for example ways of adding. Because there had been no mathematics co-ordinator in her school until she herself took on the role, she felt that numeracy had not been tackled in the way that it should have been, at the beginning. She had also felt somewhat isolated. There was little chance to observe each other's classes in the school and the staff had not talked to each other about how they were getting on. In becoming responsible for creating opportunities for dialogue with colleagues through her role as co-ordinator, Frankie's *zone of enactment* took on a different dimension.

4.2.4. Frankie's response to the Five-day course

From the Five-day course Frankie was able to see different methods of doing calculations and valued the emphasis on being clear about the reasons for working in different ways. She also gathered different ideas for using resources, for example the counting stick, which she had discovered could be used in different ways. She felt that the course had helped her with her own subject knowledge, for example using algebra, because she learnt from discussing different approaches with others on the course. She found some things quite difficult, like a method for doing long division that she had not done recently, but did not feel threatened or pressurised whilst on the course. She also developed her knowledge of fractions, decimals, percentages and ratio. Frankie became more aware of the purposes of different methods:

> I think it's important for us to be able to see so that when we are teaching the children, and I do this more and more now ... make sure that they know *why*, you know. Sometimes it's frustrating because they still don't, no matter how much you explain it they still kind of find it hard but I think at least we are aware of it that they need to know why.

With respect to the teacher's role, Frankie thought the course was good in terms of demonstrating and modelling, and had incorporated this into her feedback to her colleagues after the course:

> I think it was good in terms of how we demonstrate things and it made it very clear that we are there to be the model, to model what the children are going to do. I think that was a really clear message which is what I sort of, you know, I was saying to people on the Inset [in-service training] day, as that you're standing up there demonstrating exactly then what the children are going to do.

Her focus on this aspect reflects her underlying belief of *teaching as demonstrating*. When asked whether the course helped her to understand how children learn, Frankie said that it did because they looked at different ways of approaching things. She related this to learning as an adult:

> ... we did look at errors and different ways of approaching things. I think when you do it as an adult and you look at what other adults do it's good to be able to think about how the children will pick up things in different ways... .

It is possible that Frankie's view of learning could have developed through her own experience of learning on the course, which she referred to frequently, rather than through any explicit message about children's learning. If the course had made explicit that relationship and how to use it to enhance practice, Frankie could have developed a more connectionist orientation with respect to how children learn.

4.2.5. Influences on Frankie's practice

The course prompted Frankie to emphasise, in her teaching, different methods children use for reaching solutions. She described how she used more resources and encouraged children to generate their own sums, talk about their sums and "to come up to the board and demonstrate what they've done and talk it through". She had practised this before, but was more aware of doing it after the course. Her evaluation of what the course had provided for her was in terms of how children responded to her use of resources such as place-value cards, digit cards and number lines, showing understanding and enjoyment. Observation of a lesson after the course showed Frankie adopting the practice of children demonstrating their methods on the white board.

> The lesson began with exercises to add a two-digit number to a multiple of 10. On the board Frankie had drawn two circles, enclosing first the two-digit numbers, second the multiples of 10. Frankie told the children she would choose a number from each box and they would have to add them together. She said they could do the sum in their heads and write down the answer on their white boards, or they could use their boards to write down how they were doing it. She named three methods, horizontally, vertically or using a number line. The first example was 13 plus 10: most children in view got this correct – different methods were used. Frankie asked children to put their hands up if they had done it: most put their hands up. She then asked individual children to say how they had done it and she illustrated their methods on the board.

> The next sum was 48 plus 30. Some children did this very quickly, yet others did not get an answer. The video observation focused on one child who wrote out the sum and drew a row of 16 zeros beneath it. She quickly rubbed these out and covered the whiteboard with her hands when Frankie asked who else had got 78. This observation demonstrates the uncertainty of what children are doing in the whole-class scenario. Again Frankie asked children who may have used different methods to describe them. She then asked them to put their hands up if they felt confident, and most put their hands up. (Video observation notes)

Following this warm-up, Frankie wrote a problem on the board:

> 'Kerry has 63 stickers in her book. Her friend gives her another 25. How many does she have now?'. Frankie then asked the class how they might do this. She emphasised that there were different ways of doing it and that it did not matter, as long as they got the right answer. Frankie then asked children to come and write out their methods on the board and emphasised that those who were not confident should watch. The first child used a vertical method, two others were chosen who had used a horizontal method and a number line. It took each child several minutes to write up his or her example. (Video observation notes)

By sharing strategies in this way Frankie was implementing the recommendations of the course, but the practice included long periods of passive watching, and the approach was underpinned by an assumption that the children who lacked confidence would learn through observing. Shared strategies would work if children were trying to solve a problem or construct an idea, and by listening to another child they themselves gain understanding. Yet it was not clear how many children were gaining in this way from the lengthy demonstrations; there would be little benefit to those for whom the sum posed no difficulty, or for those who could not relate the methods being observed. Some children may have seen and learnt to use a new method, indeed the observation focused on some children using their whiteboards to work out the sum whilst the demonstrations were occurring. However, the demonstrations were not supported well by verbal explanations to aid social learning, children said very little during their demonstration as they concentrated on writing on the board. Frankie asked them to talk about their strategies, but children's explanations were minimal.

Frankie discovered the limitations of spending large amounts of time having children demonstrate their methods one at a time whilst the others listened. When interviewed after the lesson she said:

> There were parts of it that I was quite disappointed with actually because the mental bit was fine because everybody understood what they were doing and I think that encouraged them all and that was quite good. Once we started getting into looking at different ways of adding because the ability is so varied in the class, you know, the more able ones, they were brilliant because they sat and listened, but I could tell that

> they knew it all and they'd seen it and it didn't really stretch them... . When you've got the whole class there you can't spend too long going through every child's different ways of doing things so in that way it was a little bit frustrating because I knew that, well really ideally I'd have liked to work closely with each group of children for quite a long period of time and that was something I felt from the lesson.

Thus Frankie was conscious of the limitations within that lesson for individual children's learning, and she had already resolved to change this approach for her subsequent lesson. Her emerging awareness of children as individual, purposeful learners was making her question the value of spending such large amounts of time on this approach.

One aspect of whole-class teaching that Frankie thought had changed as a result of the course and which she was confident would be sustained was that of modelling. The course focused on "modelling what the children have to do", and this was "constantly repeated", so Frankie did this every day in her main teaching activity. She liked this idea because it fitted well with her view of teacher as demonstrator.

4.2.6. Sustained change

Observations of Frankie's practice in the 18 months following her attendance on the course revealed some changes in her practice, but little indication of a fundamental change in beliefs about teaching and learning. The length of time spent where children demonstrated different methods on the board was reduced. The amount of time spent on whole-class teaching remained high, and showed a continuing commitment to modelling the children's activity. It also continued to become more interactive, although she retained her view of teacher as demonstrator as indicated by the final lesson observed:

> Frankie told the children they were going to add multiples of 10 to other numbers. She had a large 100 square on the wall behind her and referred to it as she got the children to generate numbers for adding together. She had a large dice and invited children, one at a time, to come to the front to roll it. As the dice cast a number, it was multiplied by 10, and the children were asked to add this to a two-digit number given by another child. Using her large number square, Frankie prompted the children to say how they would use it to find the answer. Children all had laminated 100 square grids for writing on. They were encouraged to circle the first number and then find the resulting addition. After a few addition sums, Frankie said they were going to do subtraction and asked the children which way they were going to move from the number. With these additional resources, the children were actively engaged in listening to numbers, circling them and trying to find the answer. Frankie also asked some children to explain how they arrived at them and one child was asked to write her method on the board. An episode of individual work showed the children using differentiated worksheets. The plenary involved a child coming up to the board to show how he worked out 74 take away 43.

> Frankie encouraged the class to see how he did this. He wrote up his method without saying anything and Frankie praised the class for watching so carefully. (Video observation notes)

At this time Frankie herself felt as though her practice was constantly developing:

> The more you're teaching in that way, the more you can see what works and what doesn't work. So even though there have been lots of changes, some of those changes might not work and we still might feel that we're struggling with them. So I mean you sort of adapt it again and again, so yeah I think. I think it will only get better, I think. That's very optimistic but I think, you know, I do think it will.

Observations of her practice reveal small but constant changes, thus leading to an interpretation that Frankie is a continually changing teacher. As such she would be amenable to training that made her aware of different ideas and practices. She had seen the value of change and was therefore more open to change. However, though she now expressed a view that would seem to reject a transmission view of teaching: 'It's not just you standing there teaching them something and them all listening', her underlying beliefs had not really changed, as her approach remained fundamentally the same. She continued to express connectionist views about teaching mathematics for understanding, but retained transmission views about how children learn.

5. SUMMARY

5.1. Context

To explore in detail how individual teachers responded to the Strategy and the training the data for two teachers were analysed and written as case studies. The case studies focused on the ways in which teachers' existing practice reflected their implicit theories about learning and whether there were any signs that these underlying theories were changed after the National Numeracy Strategy training. The analysis drew on the models of teachers' beliefs and practice, or orientations towards teaching mathematics, that were developed in the earlier Effective Teachers of Numeracy Project (Askew et al., 1997). These orientations are:

- connectionist
- transmission
- discovery.

5.2. Case study – Andy

Andy's existing practice showed features that reflected a transmission orientation, characterised by views of:

- teaching as explaining
- knowledge as hierarchical and sequential
- learning as grasping
- differentiation as extension.

Andy's accounts of teaching and learning reflected these views, and observations of her practice served to confirm this interpretation. Children were expected to listen to their teacher, or to an achieving child, and grasp understanding through explanation. However, Andy's practice also demonstrated an element of discovery, as she simultaneously held the view that children should construct their own learning; she did not always to want to correct children but to encourage them to discover strategies and answers for themselves. She also had some intuitive recognition of the value of social learning, as evidenced by the encouragement of discussion, but this lacked clarity of purpose, and hence focus and direction.

In response to the Framework, Andy welcomed using a more structured approach; she liked the mental work and different strategies for "working things out"; she valued opportunities to discuss issues with colleagues because she worked in relative isolation within her *professional community*. However, she did not perceive the Framework as providing anything new – she saw it as reinforcing her existing beliefs and preferred practice.

After the course there was an emphasis on children "working out and thinking with their own strategies". Andy used children's individual whiteboards frequently after the course, so that she could see "where the children are coming from" and identify those who understood what she was asking them to do. From the course she had learned that children use different strategies for the same question, which she now recognised as being legitimate. However, though she showed signs of coming to terms with children's ideas, she was anxious about them and retained her view of what she considered an approved style. She did not really use the children's strategies.

Though Andy changed her pedagogy, the changes did not necessarily indicate an alteration in her fundamental beliefs about how children learn mathematics. Rather, they served to provide a wider range of legitimate strategies for children to achieve different ways of getting right answers. She offered no clear rationale (in terms of children's learning) for why she perceived these different methods to be legitimate.

5.3. Case study – Frankie

Frankie expressed views that demonstrated a more connectionist view of learning.

- teaching as demonstrating
- knowledge as connected
- learning as understanding
- differentiation according to complexity.

She clearly valued the exposure and comparison of different strategies for working things out, but she included prolonged episodes of children carrying out their methods of working in front of the whole class where most children were passive and classroom dialogue was limited. Frankie was clearly aware of the limitations of this practice. There was a tension between the view she had of teaching as demonstrating and her awareness of individual needs for understanding. She clearly valued the importance of teaching for understanding but she did not like children to struggle, instead she preferred to demonstrate how to use procedures so that children could then feel secure in how to works things out for themselves. Her approach therefore also reflected a transmission orientation, with a limited awareness of *how* children construct their knowledge and understanding. Her emphasis on understanding did lead her to differentiate by providing a range of different activities with varying degrees of challenge, rather than extension materials on top of a common core.

Frankie's main perception of the Strategy was that there was a lot of emphasis on mental and oral work, with whole-class teaching where the children were involved. She focused her attention on developing her whole-class teaching, believing the increased pace of her questions enabled children's minds to work more quickly.

From the Five-day course Frankie was able to see different methods of doing calculations. She also gathered different ideas for using resources, for example the counting stick, which she had discovered could be used in different ways. However, her practice still included long periods of passive watching, and the approach was underpinned by an assumption that the children who lacked confidence would learn through observing. It was not clear how many children were gaining in this way from the lengthy demonstrations; there could be little benefit to those for whom the sum posed no difficulty, or for those who could not relate the methods being observed. Frankie was conscious of the limitations for individual children's learning, and she had already resolved to change this approach for her subsequent teaching. Her emerging awareness of children as individual, purposeful learners was making her question the value of spending such large amounts of time on this approach. She continued to express connectionist views about teaching mathematics for understanding, but retained transmission views about how children learn.

6. DISCUSSION

The National Numeracy Strategy provided Andy with the structure she craved in her teaching and therefore she took to that aspect of it very well. She became more motivated to teach to National Numeracy Strategy objectives, using her energy to trawl sources, make resources and discuss her plans with friends and colleagues. Though she was aware of individual difficulties, Andy did not fundamentally adjust her teaching approach to accommodate them and remained predominantly in a transmission orientation. She still included her 'teacher as explainer' episode to the whole class, with an expectation that they would all listen and gain something, though with a realistic awareness that all did not. This dilemma is common to many teachers who plan within a structure, for curriculum coverage, and who believe that children learn by grasping what is being explained to them. They are aware of individual differences, but do not have the knowledge or confidence to fundamentally change their practice. Andy's questioning of the value of the course for her own classroom practice suggests that it needed to be more explicit about the links between concepts to enhance both teachers' holistic understanding of the subject and the nature of progression within it.

The Five-day course provided Andy with insights into the possibilities of alternative methods in the way children worked things out. This awareness became more obvious in her practice. The course also provided her with more confidence that what she was doing was right and her approach after the course reflected this confidence. Yet her fundamental beliefs had not altered. For a teacher to change deep-seated beliefs, it is our opinion that training must tackle these more overtly.

Like Andy, Frankie reported that the course reinforced what she had done before. Yet what was being reinforced was different for each teacher. One interpretation from this finding is that teachers focus on practice they have previously experienced or considered, and find legitimacy for that in the multiple messages bound up within an intensive course. They then focus on that message, possibly to the exclusion of other messages that come thick and fast. Frankie showed herself to have a connectionist orientation in the way she talked about numeracy and mathematical ideas, but her transmission view of problem solving and learning showed her limitations of understanding how children develop reasoning. She did not value the process of being challenged, resolving conflict and hence constructing new knowledge. Her practice was therefore an attempt to demonstrate and use children's strategies to connect ideas, but because her approach did not challenge children's thinking and reasoning, it fell short of its aims. For Frankie, the course needed to focus more on the nature of children's development of reasoning and how that could be achieved in practice. Because she showed continuous change in terms of refining her whole-class teaching and using resources, and a willingness to change, a course designed to raise her awareness of children's learning would be appropriate.

In Chapter 5 we saw how responses to a course of in-service training were influenced by a range of individual and organisational factors. Our two case studies illustrate in greater depth the ways in which teachers' individual attitudes and beliefs about teaching and learning can affect what they take from a course of professional development. Courses designed to change teaching need to be more diagnostic about teachers' underlying beliefs if they are to be more effective, otherwise teachers will take from a course what they are familiar with and develop it, or incorporate it into existing practice, rather than changing practice fundamentally.

7. AFFILIATIONS

Dr Shirley Simon is a Lecturer in Science Education at the Institute of Education, University of London.

8. REFERENCES

Askew, M., Brown, M, Rhodes, V., Johnson, D., & Wiliam, D. (1997). *Effective Teachers of Numeracy. Report of a study carried out for the Teacher Training Agency 1995-96 by the School of Education, King's College London.* London: King's College.

Department for Education and Employment. (1999). *The National Numeracy Strategy: Framework for Teaching Mathematics from Reception to Year 6.* London: Department for Education and Employment.

Elmore, R. (1995). Getting to scale with good educational practice. *Harvard Educational Review, 66*(1), 1-26.

Joyce B., & Showers, B. (1988). *Student Achievement Through Staff Development.* White Plains, NY: Longman.

Leithwood, K., Jantzi, D., & Mascall, B. (1999). *Large-Scale Reform: What Works? Submitted as part of the first annual report: External Evaluation of the UK National Literacy and National Numeracy Strategy.* Ontario: Ontario Institute for Studies in Education, University of Toronto.

Mercer, N. (1995). *The Guided Construction of Knowledge.* Clevedon: Multilingual Matters.

Murphy, P., Davidson, M., Qualter, A., Simon, S., & Watt, D. (2000). *Effective Practice in Primary Science. Report of an exploratory study funded by the Nuffield Curriculum Projects Centre.* London: Nuffield Foundation.

Pollard, P. (2002). *Reflective Teaching.* London: Continuum.

Spillane, J. P. (1999). External reform initiatives and teachers' efforts to reconstruct their practice: the mediating role of teachers' zones of enactment. *Journal of Curriculum Studies*, *31*(2), 143-175.

DAVID C. JOHNSON, JEREMY HODGEN AND MUNDHER ADHAMI

CHAPTER 7

PROFESSIONAL DEVELOPMENT FROM A COGNITIVE AND SOCIAL STANDPOINT

Abstract. The primary Cognitive Acceleration in Mathematics Education (P-CAME) research focused on the impact of an intervention, a programme of 24 lessons for children, taught regularly over a two-year period in Years 5 and 6 (pupils aged 9-11 years), that drew upon developmental psychology. Of particular relevance to this chapter were, first, the interactions and collaborative activities of the research team as a source of professional development for the teachers involved in this team. Second, in the main field-study phase of the research, a professional development programme was implemented to support the new teachers in trialling P-CAME Thinking Maths lessons. These professional development sessions were in fact a set of three or four activities (each of about one hour), each modelling the approach the teachers were to use in their own teaching and included engagement by the teachers in discussions linked to developing an understanding of the theoretical basis of the design of the lessons. As with the pupils' lessons, the intent was that the shifts in 'personal professional development' would be cumulative over the two-year period. Planned cycles of practice and shared reflection on the practice were essential ingredients in the professional development model.

1. INTRODUCTION

In previous chapters we have seen how the *situation* in which individual teachers were working, defined in Chapter 1 as being made up of the *professional community* and the *pupils*, generally comprised the immediate school environment. In this chapter we shift the location of the *professional community* as we report on research in which teachers came out of school to become part of a different *professional community*, a working group that included classroom teachers, university researchers and a Local Education Authority mathematics adviser. Through this working group, specifically set up for the research project, they experienced an intensive form of professional development that had certain unique features.

Alison Millett, Margaret Brown and Mike Askew (eds.), Primary Mathematics and the Developing Professional.

This chapter reports on two aspects of the project, Cognitive Acceleration in Mathematics Education in primary schools (P-CAME) – part of the Leverhulme Numeracy Research Programme (see Introduction and Annex 4). The main focus of P-CAME was on teaching lessons designed to promote cognitive development, i.e., increasing the level of thinking of children, through and in the subject domain of school mathematics. The approach involved responsive mediation of pupils' engagement with advanced concepts in activities planned to lead to general cognitive development. The P-CAME intervention was carried out through a programme of 24 Thinking Maths lessons that supplemented the normal curriculum, on average one lesson every two/three weeks.[1]

In the first part of this chapter we exemplify the process of developing a framework through which the theoretical premises of the approach are made explicit in the planning of the lessons and the lesson guidance for teachers. This is achieved through descriptions of the activity of the research team in developing one of the CAME Thinking Maths lessons – Pegboard Symmetry. The descriptions illuminate the idea of the *zone of enactment* (see Chapter 1) in relation to the teacher-researchers and indicate the key elements in this construct – ongoing deliberations, using experts from inside and outside, grounded in day-to-day attempts to enact change.

The P-CAME lesson framework was then used to provide a central element in the professional development activities in Phase 2 of the project, when the research was extended to include new teachers in 10 schools (19 classrooms with about 600 pupils, see Annex 4). The work here provided the opportunity to examine further the interactions of the research team and within it the role of the teachers as developing professionals, their *zones of enactment*, and the impact on their classroom practice.

2. P-CAME – DESCRIPTION AND METHODOLOGY

In October 1997 a team comprising four primary school teachers, designated as 'teacher-researchers' from two schools, a Local Education Authority mathematics adviser, and a team of four university researchers, began work on a three-year project on the feasibility of a cognitive acceleration programme of lessons in mathematics in Years 5 and 6 (pupils aged 9-11 years). Work in the first phase of the project was structured around classroom-based activities and fortnightly whole-day seminars of the full research team. The main elements in this phase were:

- central seminar/workshops where the team discussed plans of new lessons or the adaptations of existing CAME secondary Thinking Maths lessons (Adhami, Johnson, & Shayer, 1998a) for the primary classroom. Altogether, eight new lessons and 10 existing Thinking Maths lessons were 'simulated' and discussed in detail in the first year, both for the purpose of trialling in the classroom and as a means for the elaboration of the approach as a whole

- trialling of lessons, with more than one 'iteration', by members of the research team (the teacher-researchers, the adviser and the university researchers), observed and supported by colleagues. This activity continued into the second year, albeit not as intensively, as the main focus of the work of the team was now on implementing the programme on a larger scale with 19 new teachers in nine schools
- production of notes and documentation for reflection and sharing in the workshops and seminars. This included initial drafts of guidance for the teachers participating in the second phase of the research. One outcome of the work was a booklet containing introductory material and detailed lesson guidance for 24 lessons (Johnson et al., 2003).

The focus of the second phase was on investigating both the impact of the lessons and the feasibility of a professional development programme which was intended to mirror the approach taken with children in the primary classes. The professional development programme for teachers in the second phase was built around a model of six half-day central seminars each year, using the written guidance produced by the research team, and school visits by members of the research team. The impact of the lessons on children's attainment over the two-year period (Years 5 and 6) was monitored through the use of pre- and post-tests which assessed children's attainment in relation to Piagetian levels (administered in both P-CAME trial, i.e., experimental, and control schools). Two tests were administered, one a general measure of cognitive development, referred to as the Piagetian test, and the second specific to mathematics or mathematics reasoning ability as described in cognitive terms. For reasons of difficulties in administration of the post-test for mathematics reasoning ability, the results for this instrument were deemed unreliable. However, the results for the Piagetian test indicated statistically significant differences between experimental and control schools/classes in favour of the experimental classes ($p<0.01$).

The description and evaluation of the professional development programme was based upon:

a) the data from the tests, which provided information about the pupils' gains in the assessments of Piagetian levels;

b) the field notes and reports of the professional development sessions; and

c) the less rigorous, but regularly discussed, impressions of the team based on schools visits and conversations with the teachers.

The discussion of the professional development in the second part of this chapter draws mainly on a small subset of the data from (b) and (c).

3. RESEARCH AND THEORY

P-CAME is an extension of the CAME work in lower secondary school in the period 1993-1999 (Adhami, Johnson, & Shayer, 1998a; 1998b; 1998c). CAME Secondary was in turn an extension and adaptation of earlier programmes of research. In matters of theoretical background and overall programme design the work has drawn from the programme of work in Cognitive Acceleration in Science Education (Shayer & Adey, 1981). The Cognitive Acceleration in Science Education (CASE) programme of research spans a period of almost two decades and the positive long-term effects on performance are well documented in the literature (Adey & Shayer 1994). For CAME, the Piagetian/Vygotskian theoretical basis for Cognitive Acceleration in Science Education is extended to include the mathematical aspects in the research in Piagetian and neo-Piagetian developmental psychology, along with the developments in the areas of constructivism (e.g. Davis, Maher, & Noddings, 1990), and social constructivism ('socio-mathematical classroom norms' e.g. Cobb (1994) and Cobb, Boufi, McClain, & Whitenack (1997)).

The Piagetian element is used to describe the underlying difficulty of tasks in the same terms in which it describes the cognitive developmental level of pupils (Mok & Johnson, 2001). The focus from social constructivism is that of linking the nature of the classroom environment, socio-mathematical norms, and children working 'like mathematicians' (Lampert, 1990; Brown, Collins, & Duguid, 1989) on mathematical activities which are challenging in terms of the planned increases in cognitive demand. Thus the approach can be described as drawing together aspects of 'good practice' with particular attention given to the use of research and theory to connect and link elements of such practice.

On the substantive side of the cognitive agenda of mathematical activities in lessons or topics, CAME drew heavily on the literature in the areas of pupils' strategies, conceptions (or misconceptions) and understanding of school mathematics. This includes the programme of work conducted by researchers at Chelsea (now part of King's) College, University of London (Hart, 1981; Booth, 1984; Johnson, 1989; Brown, 1992). The main conceptual strands or mathematical 'ideas' in CAME were those found to be most difficult for children. The core strands for both primary and secondary CAME are those of multiplicative relations, number properties, estimation, generalised number (early algebra) and measure (including data handling) (Adhami et al., 1998a).

As indicated above, the implementation of CAME can be seen to have both cognitive and socio-cultural dimensions. In the cognitive dimension the research is based on a model in which the lessons are intended to be a component of the curriculum, with one Thinking Maths lesson replacing one ordinary mathematics lesson every two to three weeks over a two-year period. This relatively sparing, but steady rate of cognitive intervention (and challenge) reflects the focus on intellectual development which is taken to be a slow process – the building up of thinking, or processing, ability over an extended period of time – as contrasted with the direct teaching and learning of specific knowledge and/or skills which can sometimes be achieved through concentrated practice.

The socio-cultural dimension of the programme takes into account the fact that at any given point in time pupils in the same class are likely to be at widely different levels in their cognitive development and in their motivation to engage with the lesson challenges. In terms of lesson structure and delivery, the programme was designed to pragmatically optimise the chances of pupils engaging in, and benefiting from the approach in different contexts, at different times and at different levels of attainment. That is, outcomes for different pupils will in turn be different – the mathematical agenda can be described as *planting seeds* rather than mastery of some specific content objective. The cognitive agenda in P-CAME is that of moving all the children to higher levels of thinking or reasoning.

The challenge for the secondary CAME teachers has been to attend to the socio-cultural aspect in the approach and to integrate it with the shift of focus towards cognitive development. This integration might be described as *socio-cognitive* pedagogy. Apart from the cognitive match and challenge in the lesson agenda, this pedagogy involves the conduct of lessons through the four phases of *preparation*, *construction*, *sharing* and *reflection*, repeated in two or three successive episodes in a lesson. It also involves the development of a classroom learning culture embodied in whole-class and small-group interactions informed by the notions of *reflective discourse* and *collective reflection* (Cobb et al., 1997). The attention to cognitive demand in Piagetian terms represents an elaboration of the construct of *a shift in the object of attention* mediated by the teacher or by a fellow pupil in the discourse.

The model for working with the teacher-researchers in the first phase of P-CAME was built on the premise that one means of illuminating the approach would be for the teacher-researchers to have the opportunity to participate in the role of pupils in a CAME lesson – a 'lesson simulation'. After the reasoning agenda of a lesson had been explored by the teacher-researchers in a lesson simulation and through discussion within the research team, they then trialled the lesson in their schools.

This mode of working within the research team led to the consideration and development of a model or framework for communicating the approach, firstly within the team and ultimately for working with the new teachers in the second phase of the research. This framework was further refined in the second phase – the professional development programme for the new teachers.

4. FORMULATING THE AGENDA OF A LESSON – THE PROFESSIONAL DEVELOPMENT OF THE TEAM

The account which follows focuses on the main steps in the formulation of the cognitive agenda of a primary Thinking Maths lesson and how this led to a way of working within the research team. It is noted that the opportunities for professional development for the members of the research team were enhanced by the time which was made available by the Leverhulme funding for trialling lessons and meetings. It was also a case of each individual engaging with the work at a level consistent with their own motivation and perceived needs. The interactions and collaboration of the members of the team were seen to provide evidence of change and development, but as indicated in Chapter 8, there was noticeable variation in their level of engagement.

The story here also illustrates how the CAME agenda might be communicated to generalist teachers to illuminate both the lesson structure and the links with cognitive demand. The trajectory, or chronology, of how the final framework evolved is based on an analysis of fieldnotes from central research seminars/workshops, tape recordings of discussions between team members, transcripts (taped and transcribed) and notes of individual interviews and classroom observations.

We propose to illustrate the developments in this initial phase of the project through an analysis and synthesis of the data specific to only one of the 24 Thinking Maths lessons, Pegboard Symmetry. Here we have nine sets of notes linked to the activity (taken as data in the analysis). The full chronology of the development of Pegboard Symmetry shows the complex collaborative process of formulating the cognitive agenda of a Thinking Maths lesson where both classroom teachers and researchers are involved. This was largely a process of ongoing negotiations and discussions between the application of the cognitive acceleration theoretical approach by the university researchers on the one hand, and the perceptions and practices of the generalist primary teachers (the teacher-researchers) on the other. The chronology shows how the four teacher-researchers (pseudonyms Ursula, Alexandra, Lisa and Henrietta) and the Local Education Authority adviser (pseudonym Rhoda), in their initial period of involvement with the approach, focused primarily on using it as a powerful tool to deliver the curriculum, and their pressure for plain and friendly guidance material to that purpose – *seeing the curriculum potential of the cognitive approach*. At the same time, the university researchers (pseudonyms Nadir, Samuel, Donald and Henry) attempted to find how an area of the curriculum might be used as a context for more general cognitive development (for the children) as well as looking for ways of communicating the subtleties involved in an appropriate format for teachers – *seeing the cognitive potential of the curriculum focus*.

Within the research domain, the story exemplifies a process of elaboration of the cognitive demands of the various mathematical concepts and skills involved – *charting the appropriate range of cognitive challenges*. The outcome of this process was the identification of a range of cognitive challenge points appropriate to the age cohort of the children and the type of mediation required by the teacher in a typical classroom. This kind of elaboration was witnessed in all Thinking Maths lessons that had their beginning as curriculum activities that were felt to be 'promising' in terms of their potential for some exemplification of different levels of cognitive challenge or demand. Hence the account described here is illustrative of an outcome of more general import, providing a framework for communication and planning within the research team as well as serving as a basis for simulation, planning and reflection with and by the new teachers who participated in the second phase of the research, thus *communicating the agenda to generalist teachers*. We provide some detail on the process of lesson development to illustrate the close involvement of all the members of the research team in both lesson design and trialling. (All quotations in the sections that follow are from fieldnotes, except where specifically indicated.)

4.1. Seeing the curriculum potential of the cognitive approach

The activity Pegboard Symmetry was suggested by Rhoda, who:

> saw the possibilities in the lesson to link co-ordinates, reflection, symmetry and number relationships.

The first notes on the activity were not specifically written for a Thinking Maths lesson, but rather were intended as notes for a teacher in-service session on a curriculum activity that was felt to be promising. The notes highlighted key mathematical language and questions without a specified order. While this was viewed to be in line with 'good practice' in the other curriculum and professional development schemes, it did not provide a structure for enabling teachers to make decisions as to when to use the questions – how they relate to each other and, more importantly, how they relate to children's constructions.

The focus of the activity was for the children, firstly, to notice that the sum of the x co-ordinates of pairs of points reflected in a vertical line is a constant, and secondly, to generalise this for other reflection lines. Figure 7.1 gives the case of x=5, where the x co-ordinates of pairs of reflected points sum to 10.

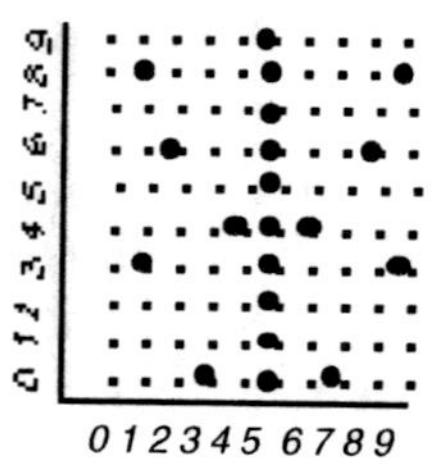

Left pair	Right pair
(3,0)	(7,0)
(1,3)	(9,3)
(4,5)	(6,5)
(2,6)	(8,6)
(1,8)	(9,8)

Figure 7.1. Pegboard and co-ordinates

Here we now have an illustration of the facilitation of activity in the teachers' *zones of enactment*. At this time, Alexandra and Ursula proposed additional lessons giving the same rationale of intuitively felt richness of activities and possibility of structuring them through some analysis of the cognitive demand as exemplified in the Thinking Maths approach (these also went through a development process similar to that for Pegboard Symmetry). The perceived richness of a proposed activity stemmed either from the way it engaged the children in mathematical talk in general or from the fact that it addressed and linked different parts of the curriculum. Rhoda saw Pegboard Symmetry as a practical activity leading to a clear number pattern that can be generalised; an active route to achieving a given learning objective. At the same time, the breadth involved in the range of (connected) topics was viewed as a kind of a desirable openness.

Rhoda and Ursula also saw the process of devising new lessons as experimental:

> part of the thing is when you try out a lesson you find out the possibilities.

4.2. Seeing the cognitive potential of the curriculum focus

Steering the activity in light of theory involved firstly shifting the focus in the learning objective from 'closed' to 'open', and secondly, including a range of outcomes at different levels of attainment as described in the (Piagetian) model for cognitive development (i.e., different levels of progression in an identifiable reasoning strand). These are the two dialectical aspects of the principle of 'acceptance of lack of closure' implied in the CAME pedagogy.

In one of the project's central seminars, Nadir (university researcher) suggested criteria for lesson development such as 'low floor', 'high ceiling' and 'range of informal methods'. He suggested that Pegboard Symmetry is framed so that most children access it through first working on reflection on one axis. At the higher levels they move to present the generalisation as a number equivalence sentence.

> Symmetry ... There is clearly a potential here .... . And attention to 'lowering the floor', 'raising the ceiling' and widening the range of informal methods would help. The activity can be made more accessible by first using one axis only ... . For advanced pupils the procedures can be shown in a number sentence, proving that (15+7) + (15–7) = 2x15 [mirror line at x = 15] and its generalisation.

Sometime later Rhoda produced a sketch of teacher guidance on the activity and included questions and key language in a sequential order as well as 'why does this happen?' In the two trials of the lesson that followed, taught by Rhoda and Henrietta, the focus of the activity remained the same as before. However, there was no guidance for the teachers to develop further the cognitive and social agendas for themselves or with children. Part of the problem here was that the notes on the activity were part of a lengthy document including other general comments. Our previous experience in teamwork with teachers indicates that written texts without discussion are open to a range of interpretations. Teachers who are used to working firmly within the 'curriculum delivery' mode could interpret the openness implied by 'widening the range of informal methods' as referring to breadth across topics rather than to depth within a reasoning strand, a critical element in a Thinking Maths lesson.

As for the 'lower floor', the teacher-researchers seemed to be convinced that working with Cartesian co-ordinates would be relatively straightforward for Year 5 pupils (aged 9-10 years) because of prior experiences with this topic, and there was no felt need to begin the lesson at some lower level. Similarly, the 'ceiling' in the activity seemed to be natural as this was viewed as merely linking the two number patterns in a table (the sum of the two x co-ordinates of reflected pairs is equal to twice the x co-ordinate of any vertical reflection line). The suggestion for expressing that generalisation in a number equivalence sentence, and 'proving' that generalisation seemed unnecessary in the curriculum delivery mode.

A crucial step forwards was made by Samuel after observing one of the trial lessons also observed by two other members of the team. Samuel placed the activity within the reasoning strand of generalised number, and then drafted a comprehensive plan for the lesson. This document was based on a detailed analysis of both the mathematical content and the cognitive agenda. An indirect result of this step was to emphasise the principle that the potential of an activity could not easily be recognised through a thought experiment, and that a classroom trial was of crucial importance.

4.3. Charting the appropriate range of cognitive challenges

The full team meeting discussed researchers' suggestions on *working toward a reason for the rule (Proof).* Rhoda explained later that she:

> ... originally moved from reflection in the x=5 line, and the children noticing that the two co-ordinates add up to 10, to look at and compare reflections in other x=10 and y=5 lines.

whereas researchers Samuel and Donald wanted

> *children to look at why did they add up to 10?*

Rhoda produced a revised sketch for teacher guidance taking account of the background document, and this sketch was the basis for another trial, this time by Ursula. In the full team meeting, and informal contacts which took place in the month prior to the meeting, there was more discussion around the fundamental lesson aims. Donald suggested that transformation rather than symmetry should be the focus, to avoid confusing teachers and pupils using the edges of the pegboard as reference points as had occurred in one of the trial lessons. The researchers also highlighted the complexity of using the co-ordinates as a context for the number generalisation:

> Samuel: … this is quite complex …[should we] shift mirror [line] to zero?
>
> Donald: There is an absolute system … how do I represent it in the reference system … don't want them to change the mirror to zero … [we want the children to observe the difference as if the mirror line was at x=0, but without doing the actual transformation, hence the question for children is] how do I represent this transformation in the absolute system in this relative agreed system?

Samuel, in response to 'calls' from the teacher-researchers for some visual/pictorial description of what was to happen, revised the background notes, and produced a new abstract showing the flow of the lesson together with an indication of the thinking levels required at different points of the lesson. This abstract used quotations from earlier lesson notes as illustrations of children's thinking. It also included a corresponding column on relevant National Curriculum statements and levels.[2] Such correspondence in a topic strand had been used before in CAME Secondary and the difference here was that it was now being used for a single activity. One feature of the diagram at this stage was the lowering of the starting level (cognitive demand) in the preparation phase – looking at the reflection on a number line and construction of the zero point/line as was suggested earlier. The co-ordinate system is viewed as the combination of horizontal and vertical number lines.

At this point the lesson was accepted as one of the first set of lessons to be used in the main study. Rhoda produced a new sketch of teaching guidance to go with the background notes and the pictorial representation. These now also contained some of the key questions for children:

> Why does this happen? How is this 10 connected with the x=5? (double) … predict their reflected co-ordinates … How did you know this would happen? … What would happen if the line was through x=12? (the x co-ordinates would add up to 24) … How do you know? How does this link to the idea of double 12? How could you express what you know as a sum? (12-2)+(12+2)=24. (Pegboard Symmetry Draft Teaching Notes)

The emphasis was clearly on *'looking for a reason for their generalisation'*, although this was still to be achieved through the consideration of several reflection lines. This differed from the notes and abstracts of Samuel in which the focus was on the x=5 reflection line. It is noted here that the team's way of working meant that further clarification, including argument and negotiation, was necessary.

PEGBOARD SYMMETRY

An activity on the co-ordinate grid. It combines two mathematical strands: a) constructing and using the co-ordinate system for mirror reflection, and b) exploring the number relations involved, up to the use of generalised number.

This activity is in two episodes, each with introduction, construction and sharing phases. It ends with a 'looking back' phase that should be conducted however far the pupils have reached in the activity.

Episode 1. Constructing the co-ordinate system and generating tabulated results.
Children first label a row of dots into a number line, including zero position. They move to the two co-ordinate system, place a 'mirror line' and record two dimensional reflection of points. They write co-ordinate pairs of points reflected in the mirror line from either side, tabulating these, recognising the sameness of one co-ordinate and then attempting to describe the constant addition relationship of the other. The sharing phase ends with checking the rules, and posing the question as to why that happens.

Episode 2. Looking for reason and ways of describing general relationships.
Pupils are likely to either a) relate points and their images to the mirror line co-ordinate, e.g. in (4, 6) and (6, 6) the 4 is one less and the 6 one more than the 5 of the mirror line; or b) recognise that the x co-ordinates in each pair always add up to 10. In either case they move on to describe the relationship mathematically using brackets. In words or symbols they approach either $(5-x) + (x+5) = 10$, or $x + (10-x) = 10$. They are asked to explain 10 in relation to the mirror line, and begin to think about other mirror lines.

Reflection: Awareness of the mathematics and logical reasoning involved.
Pupils review their steps of reasoning, and verbalise the way generalisations are made from the consideration of a number of individual cases.

Before you teach

This activity is not intended as practice with co-ordinates. Rather, the co-ordinate system is used as a context for children to explore and generalise number relationships. Hence it is important that children have had some prior experience with co-ordinates and reflection.

Figure 7.2. Pegboard Symmetry abstract (textual)

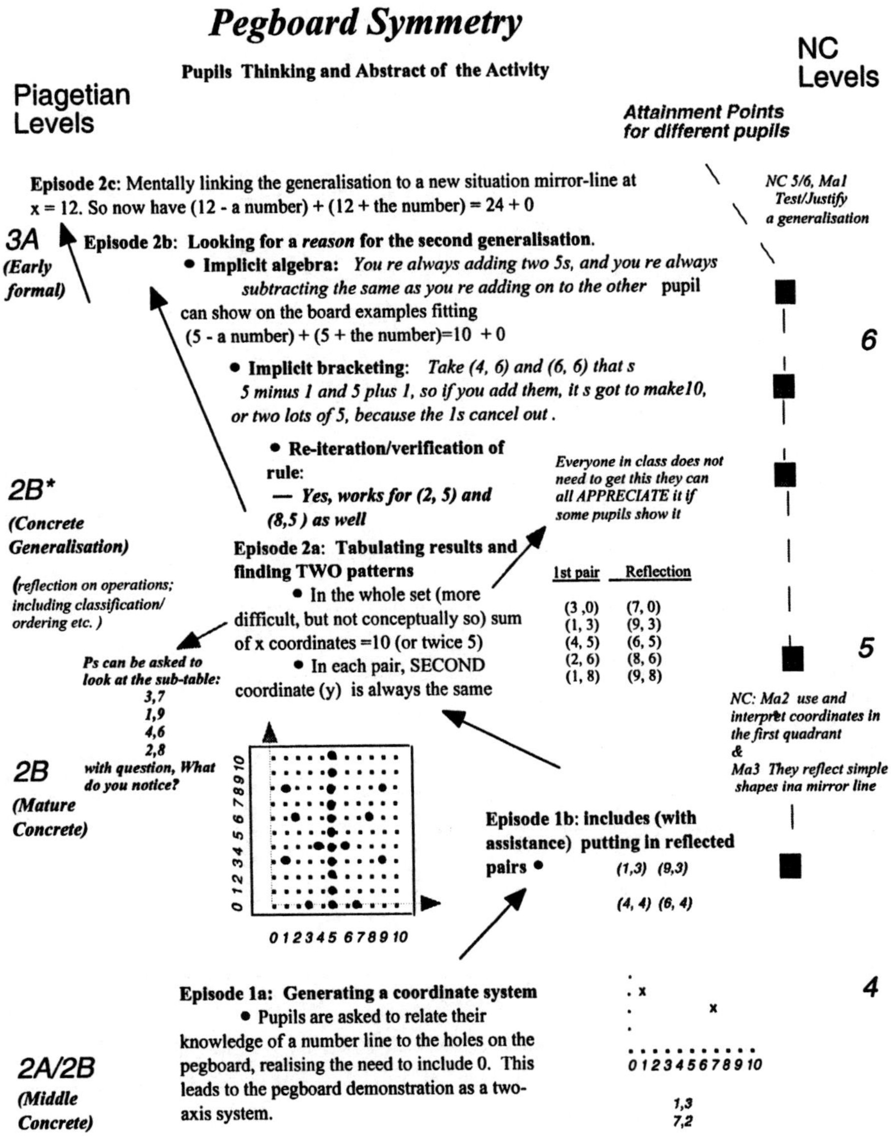

Figure 7.3. Pegboard symmetry abstract (visual)

PEGBOARD SYMMETRY

CAME Aims

- Finding the relationship between the co-ordinates of reflected points
- Discussing the relationship between the *x* co-ordinates for points and the vertical mirror line

Resources:	**Organisation:**
• Pegboards (one between two) • Coloured pegs • Photocopies of pegboard notesheet • Labelled grid on board or OHT	• Near ability pairs on mixed ability tables • Coloured counters on Blu Tac are useful for showing pegs when working on the board
Vocabulary: co-ordinates mirror line axis/axes line of symmetry reflection points	**National Curriculum Reference:** Co-ordinates Number patterns Symmetry

1

Whole-class preparation: (about 5-10 mins)

- *We are going to do some thinking work with co-ordinates*
- Reminder of the convention of labelling axes and co-ordinates (along the path and up the ladder)
- *Put a green peg in (1, 3). Check with others on the table. Now put a blue peg in (7, 2)*
- *What mistakes could people have made?* (Mixing up x's and y's, forgetting to count 0)
- *What things must we remember?* (along the path and up the ladder)
- Repeat with other colours in other positions
- Draw some coloured pegs on the board grid and get children to record co-ordinates
- *Place pegs in (5,1) (5,7) (5,9) (5,4). What do you notice?* (They are in a line).

Figure 7.4. Pegboard Symmetry two-page teaching sketch (1)

2

Paired work: (5-10 mins)

- *Place a variety of coloured pegs anywhere on your board to the left of your mirror line, record their co-ordinates*
- *Reflect the pegs in the mirror line and record the co-ordinates after reflection (keep reflected pegs the same colour to avoid confusion)*

What do you notice about the numbers before and after reflection?

- After a few minutes, model a recording system on the board

Colour	Old Peg	New Peg
Green	(1,3)	(9,3)

4

Paired work: (10-15 mins)

- Ask pupils to explore their ideas further and formulate answers to: *What did you notice about the numbers with mirror line at x=5? How would you express what you know as a sum on the page?* (5-1 + 5+1 = 10; 5-3 + 5+3 = 10; etc.)
- *What is happening here?* 5 – (a number) + 5 + (the number) = 10 + 0
- *How is this 10 connected with x = 5?* (double)

3

Class sharing: (about 10 mins)

- Orchestrate the feedback
- Individuals draw their before and after co-ordinates on the pegboard OHT and record their co-ordinates on the class recording system
- *What if an original co-ordinate was (4, 7)? What is the reflected co-ordinate?*
- *What do you notice about the pairs of numbers?* (y co-ordinate stays the same, x co-ordinates add up to 10)

5

Class sharing: (10-15 mins)

- Discuss results from the paired work – looking for a general rule in words or symbols
- If time permits follow with a 'mental' task (without the pegboard): *What would happen if the mirror/vertical line was at x=12? Without doing it, think about what would happen if we put a peg in at (10,3), what is the reflection? what about (1,5)? How would you express what you know as a sum? How does this relate to the case when the mirror line was at x=5?*

12 - (a number) + 12 + (the number) = ?

Figure 7.5. Pegboard Symmetry two-page teaching sketch (2)

It was deemed essential that some 'shared' view was accepted by the research team. Here, there was a strong emphasis on professional development for all involved with the project. There was also a need for consistency in ways of working as it was the case that the final documentation for lessons would now include a two-page teaching sketch, prepared by the teacher-researchers, and background notes, developed by the university-researchers.

It was decided that the background notes would include the visual representation, i.e., the diagram showing the increasing levels of cognitive demand, as well as a related textual description of the flow of the lesson. The latter would give more attention to the notion of episodes in the lesson and some aspects of the classroom management (e.g., group work and whole-class discussion). The textual and visual presentations were thought desirable in that they would:

> provide the teachers with more than one point of access into the theoretical and practical aspects of the approach. (Ursula (edited), Central seminar)

The final version of the background notes, i.e., the abstract and textual and visual forms of the flow of the lesson, and the teaching sketch are given in Figures 7.2, 7.3 7.4 and 7.5. These now provided the framework for the final form for all the lessons. The materials were laid out as two sets of 'facing pages' – the first pair being the two presentations of the abstract or lesson description and the second pair the lesson notes. Other items to be included were some more general statements regarding planning and materials as well as further pointers to other mathematical links (e.g., vocabulary) and the National Curriculum.

4.4. Communicating the agenda to generalist teachers (preparing for phase two)

The format of guidance for teachers was identified as an important issue early on in the project. In terms of support during the actual teaching the teacher-researchers pressed for a simplified two-page teaching spread with sketches similar to that which is used in other popular teacher resources. Here, the decision taken was to have the background notes, i.e., the general textual and the more detailed visual presentations, in a section which preceded the two-page sketch. Other background information provided indicated that since these may have little meaning prior to the actual teaching of the lesson, teachers may only wish to glance through, or even ignore, the material before teaching a lesson for the first time and come back to these later. The plan for supporting the new teachers in the second phase included some consideration of all the background materials for each lesson in the central professional development sessions. These were time-tabled to precede classroom implementation – with some discussion and feedback on the lesson experiences in the following central session.

5. THE RESEARCH TEAM – A COMMUNITY OF PRACTICE

The focus in the previous section has been on the professional peer group, the research team, and their deliberations as to a form for presenting the lessons – for sharing amongst themselves and for future use with new teachers. We suggest that the discussion in Section 4 provides examples and insights as to how the teacher-researchers individually and collectively came to grips with the theory and practice which underpinned the CAME approach. There were many such instances, not merely the story of the pegboard lesson, where the influence of the *external professional*, the *pupils*, and *the professional community* is illuminated in the personal professional development of the teacher-researchers, and their activities. This theme is not elaborated on here as it is a major focus in Chapter 8.

We now propose to go on to a consideration of the professional development of the new teachers in Phase 2. Here, we first describe how the CAME approach, embodying both the cognitive and the social, and the notion of episodes and phases in lessons, was adapted for working with the new teachers. This is then followed by a more general discussion of the key elements in the CAME professional development, and how particular models of support can make a difference in what the teachers say and do (Spillane, 1999).

6. THE PROFESSIONAL DEVELOPMENT PROGRAMME – COGNITIVE AND SOCIAL PERSPECTIVES

As indicated previously, the experiences in Phase 1 led to the model to be used in the professional development programme in Phase 2 of the research[3]. The model is underpinned by the same theory as that for the pupils. Here, the social emphasis provides a central component in the programme. Within the professional development sessions it includes teacher-teacher and teacher-tutor interactions and the use of small-group and 'whole-class' discussion. It was also the case that the notion of the cognitive demand of tasks, while defined more in terms of pedagogy and a consideration of the pupil's mathematical thinking rather than items of mathematics (as in the case of the pupils), was also a central component. In addition, the notions of *preparation* (common introductory experiences for all participants), *construction*, *sharing* and *reflection* were central for the planning of the session activities.

Basically, the model begins with a situation in which the teachers participate in a lesson simulation, taught by one or two of the teacher-researchers (now acting as tutors). This was considered by all participants, the research team and the new teachers, to be a crucial component in the programme. The teachers then go on to teach the lesson in their own schools. In the second year of the professional development programme, this was actually on the same day as the central session, with the professional development in the morning and the teachers team-teaching the lesson in the afternoon observed by two or more members of the research team. Finally the teaching was followed with some brief discussion of the experience.

With the teachers, the lesson simulation is initially considered as a 'CAME professional development lesson' in itself even if it is part of a longer session of about three hours. That is, it is considered to include the usual components of the CAME approach (from *preparation* through *construction* and finally *sharing* and *reflection*). However, when the experience of the simulation is taken along with the actual classroom teaching, this then serves as preparation for a further professional development 'lesson' (again part of a longer session) involving two episodes. Each episode starts with concrete preparation, focusing on a particular aspect of the theory. This is followed by small-group work and then whole-class discussion or sharing. The two episodes are each considered to include a progression in terms of increasingly higher level challenges, i.e., cognitive demand.

- one episode focuses on the mathematical development; the teachers are asked to share their insights and experiences. What mathematical ideas evolved? How might they characterise the children's mathematical constructions? etc. After teaching the first few lessons, the teachers were also asked to include a consideration of the lesson abstract, in particular the Piagetian analysis, in their discussions. This in turn also provided opportunities to consider further general issues in terms of misconceptions or naïve strategies and how these might be addressed
- the second episode involves the teachers working on the task of sharing their insights and experiences in regard to the social aspects of the children's lesson. How did the children engage with their peers? Did the children listen to one another? How did the children share ideas? Was there really discussion taking place between the children? What techniques did they as teachers employ to facilitate this aspect of the agenda? etc.

This model was followed for all sessions (with two new lesson simulations in each professional development session and the appropriate follow-up on these at the next professional development session). Note that there were other components in the sessions. For example, at selected points in the programme we considered sets of lessons to look at how progression might be interpreted in one of the core strands, and at other points we returned to more general discussions of the theory.

7. COMMUNICATING THE AGENDA OF A P-CAME LESSON IN THE PROFESSIONAL DEVELOPMENT PROGRAMME

In order to focus down on specific aspects of the components of the professional development programme as described above we propose to look at these in the context of one P-CAME lesson – again Pegboard Symmetry. The discussion will include selected aspects of two professional development sessions rather than any comprehensive look at a full single half-day session. We will first look at the lesson simulation. Note that the framework described in the first part of this chapter has been designed to communicate the approach in terms of children's involvement in the activity, in particular the two-page teaching spread. Here we go on to describe what happened with the new teachers and we propose that this in turn will serve to illustrate further some of the key features in the lesson.

7.1. A lesson simulation in the professional development programme – Pegboard Symmetry

Fifteen teachers were present at the session which was the second in the first year of the programme. It should be noted that the teachers involved generally had no specific mathematical background, although some had responsibility as mathematics co-ordinators (subject leaders) in their schools. The vignettes below illustrate how these teachers found the mathematical tasks involved in Pegboard Symmetry challenging. The complete lesson simulation, which also included some discussion of teaching points, lasted 55 minutes.

We propose to illustrate how teachers may develop their understanding and ownership of the lesson framework as well as providing some sense of the 'social' aspects in the CAME approach. In doing so we will refer to the constructs of socio-mathematical norms (Yackel & Cobb, 1996), reflective discourse, shifts in the focus of attention and collective reflection (Cobb et al., 1997). We stress here that the following analysis and discussion is based on just one lesson simulation which was early on in this group of teachers' engagement with the CAME approach. We accept that teacher change is complex, difficult and long-term. Our earlier experience with secondary (upper middle) school teachers is that the process of teacher development takes a period of years, and even then does not always have visible results. Engagement with the process of collective reflection as suggested in the vignette reported here is planned to take place over a two-year period and in addition to lesson simulations will involve reflection during and after teaching lessons, discussions with CAME teacher/tutors and formal reflection sessions at subsequent professional development sessions.

7.1.1. Experiencing and resolving cognitive conflict through collaboration

Rhoda began the simulation by highlighting the dual purpose of doing and reflecting upon the mathematics.

> Do make notes and do write down some of the things I say, some of the questions I use. Now I'm going to treat you very much as a class of kids.

All the teachers were observed to be making detailed notes and highlighting sections of their copy of the Teaching Notes in the guide throughout the simulation. Many teachers annotated their own mathematical work and attached this to the notes. It is a feature of the Teaching Notes that plenty of space is left for teachers' own notes and annotations.

The first vignette focuses on the cognitive step in the first phase of the first episode in the lesson, the construction of co-ordinates on the pegboard. Two teachers (Faride and Grace) were observed working together to locate (1,3) on the pegboard,

> Faride: Does it go here? [placing the peg at (0,2)].
>
> Grace: No, that's the zero, so you need to count zero, one along and zero, one, two, three up. There.
>
> Faride: [consults the Teaching Notes] Oh, I was forgetting about the zero. These are the axes, aren't they. We've got to emphasise the axes.
>
> Faride highlights this phrase in the Teaching Notes: What mistakes could people have made? … forgetting to count 0.

We would suggest here that Faride experienced cognitive conflict. She resolved this collaboratively with Grace by recognising the need for zero. She then used the Teaching Notes as a framework to link this recognition to the notion of axes and further to reflect on her role as a teacher of the lesson.

The same two teachers were later observed reflecting points in x=5 line. Rhoda intervened to shift the focus of teachers' attention from the action of reflection to the possibility of patterns across these reflections:

Rhoda [to the whole group]: Write down any rules that you've noticed.

Faride: [to Grace] What rules? .. Oh, look [she points and reads from the teacher's guide] what do you notice about the numbers before and after reflection.

They continue to check and record the points.

Grace: The y co-ordinate stays the same, doesn't it? Look [and shows this happens]

Faride: Oh yes.

Grace: Because you just move it across.

It is worth noting how Faride used the Teaching Notes to support the cognitive shift implied in Rhoda's question. Grace then noticed and justified a pattern.

Faride: Look, this isn't right [indicating (7,4); the incorrectly placed reflection of (2,4)] it should be here. [She counts the empty pegs from (2,4) across to mirror line and repeats this on the other side placing the peg at (8,4).] We counted from the outside.

Grace: Oh, yeah.

Faride and Grace have again resolved a conflict collaboratively. However this resolution appeared to require more than a simple correction and Faride provided an apparently unprompted justification. We suggest that the lesson framework establishes the need for explicit justification, corrections on their own are not enough. Further, this kind of small-group collaboration provided an important rehearsal for both teachers' participation in the subsequent episode of reflective discourse and provided the conditions for collective reflection.

7.1.2. Sharing experiences

The next vignette is from the first sharing phase in the lesson. Rhoda collected details on the co-ordinates of points and their reflections from the groups. We note here that Rhoda, in a research-team meeting held prior to the professional development session, asked Ursula and Henry to include typical children's mistakes in their inputs to the small-group work with the teachers, e.g., the error Faride and Grace corrected above – counting from outside or looking for 'symmetry' within the pegboard rather then reflecting in the mirror line. As part of the small-group contributions Henry offered (0,0) and (9,0) as the reflection. Rhoda asked him to check this with the others on his table.

> Faride: [counts pegholes to mirror line] The distance isn't the same.
>
> Henry: Oh.
>
> Rhoda: Has somebody sorted out the mistake that Henry made. What happened there?
>
> Faride: The distance between the – the reflected image and the real image is not the same – from the mirror line.
>
> Rhoda: Right. So you need to make sure that you are counting. Now which one did you put in first?
>
> Henry: Zero, zero but we had a problem with the board, because ... [Laughter – the correct reflection point (10,0) is off the pegboard.]
>
> Rhoda: If your board was larger, what should that point actually be?
>
> Henry: What should that be?
>
> Faride: [counts pegs] 10 – 10, zero.
>
> Rhoda: If your board was big enough to continue, what would that be?
>
> Henry: 10, zero.
>
> ...
>
> Samuel: You don't have 10.
>
> Rhoda: You don't have 10, but Henry has sort of imagined.

Rhoda planted the error and highlighted in practice the potential use of cognitive conflict as a way of challenging pupils' constructions. In this case, the points and their reflections were not symmetrically placed within the pegboard. It is worth noting that Faride's justification had become much more mathematically precise when presented publicly. We suggest that her earlier collaboration on, and resolution of, a similar cognitive conflict provided an important rehearsal for her participation in reflective discourse and for the initiation of collective reflection on the socio-mathematical norm of what constitutes mathematical explanation. Changing teachers' conceptions of mathematical explanation is a long-term aim of the professional development programme and will be revisited on many occasions in the two-year period. Finally in this episode, Rhoda shifted the focus of discourse from co-ordinates as place-markers on the pegboard to the mental construction of Cartesian space beyond the physical confines of the pegboard.

7.1.3. A shift in the object of attention – increasing the level of cognitive demand

Rhoda asked for patterns that teachers had noticed: the *y* co-ordinate always stays the same; the difference between the pairs of *x* co-ordinates is always even; and the sum of the pairs of *x* co-ordinates is always 10. She then again shifted the focus of attention, to a higher level of cognitive demand – from the generalisation of patterns to looking for reasons for the generalisations (see Figures 7.4, 7.5).

> Rhoda: What about this one? Why is the y co-ordinate or the second number, always the same? Why is that true?
>
> Grace: That's because it's a mirror image. You go across. The two pegs are opposite each other. They're in the same row.

Grace's justification has become more mathematically precise compared with her earlier 'you just move it across'. Again we note the importance of her earlier collaborative rehearsal. Rhoda then asks why the difference between the pairs of *x* co-ordinates is always even.

> June: The distance to the mirror line is always the same and so the difference is like doubling this distance to the mirror line.
>
> Rhoda: It's always doubling.
>
> Nadir: This is a very important point. You are always doubling the distance to the mirror line.
>
> Samuel: You're always adding two of the same things.
>
> Rhoda: OK. Did anyone play around with why the x co-ordinates always add up to 10?
>
> Ivan: I played around with it but I found it quite distressing.
>
> Nina: Why is it always even?
>
> Rhoda: It's always even because as June said the gap to the mirror line on the first side is the same as the gap from the mirror line to the reflected point on the other side. The two gaps are the same.

> Ivan: **So on one side it's a certain amount bigger than five and on the other it's a certain amount smaller than five. They sort of cancel each other out**. (authors' emphasis)

Although Ivan found this cognitive shift difficult, during the discourse, he appeared to recognise the implicit bracketing as in (5+2) + (5-2). We suggest that Nina's request for clarification of the previous justification constituted a shift in the focus of attention. Attention was drawn not only to the doubling or addition of equal gaps, but more crucially to the possibility of a connection between the justifications. The results from the previous activity had now become an object for reflection.

Following Ivan's recognition of implicit bracketing, Rhoda again shifted the focus of attention to expressing this in formal algebraic terms.

> Rhoda: What if it was, you know, a, b? What's it going to be on the other side?
>
> [Pause.]
>
> Teacher: Something .. b.
>
> Rhoda: Something .. b. What's this 'a' going to be on the other side?
>
> Another teacher: It's got to add up to 10.
>
> Rhoda: It's got to add up to ten. So what's it going to be on the other side?
>
> A third teacher: 10 minus 'a'.

The cognitive shift here is towards generalised number and through participation in the reflective discourse the teachers have begun to produce a series of number sentences. We note again that it is not intended that this level of understanding should be reached by all participants, teachers or children. The additional vignette is included here only to illustrate what might, and did, happen with the teachers.

7.1.4. Teachers' participation in the lesson simulation

In these vignettes we have illustrated how the teachers' participation in reflective discourse contributed to their own professional development. Repeated shifts in the focus of attention and hence acts of collective reflection were supported by the lesson framework. At the same time a discourse concerning mathematical explanation was initiated. We are not claiming that the teachers' conception of mathematical explanation was fundamentally changed nor that the socio-mathematical norms concerning acceptable mathematical explanation were developed through this limited experience. However, we do note here the importance of rehearsal in earlier collaborative activity – a lesson simulation – as an important catalyst for this reflective discourse. We further suggest that the annotation of the Teaching Notes creates the possibility for teachers to remember the reflective discourse and crucially the cognitive shifts they themselves have participated in. It is our contention that through participation in reflective discourse and acts of collective reflection the teachers will 'come to know' what is behind Thinking Maths lessons and teaching as a social process, and thus to take on *ownership* of the lessons and the framework.

7.2. Teachers discussing their experiences in teaching – the social and mathematical agendas

The next professional development session, the third in the programme, took place almost two months later, and there was the Christmas period in between. One of the activities in this session was the discussion of the social and mathematical aspects of Pegboard Symmetry in terms of teachers' experiences in teaching the lesson.

The main element in the discussion was the sharing of experiences in small groups and some interesting points were made – for example, a contribution from Fauzia that there was a need to "give children time to think at appropriate points" (in particular when studying the table of values and deciding what numbers to ignore). However, due to lack of time many of these points were not able to be shared in 'whole-class' discussion on this occasion.

There were however other instances of some useful and insightful contributions arising in the 'whole-class' sharing and reflection component in the professional development. For example, in the social discussions, teachers agreed that careful attention was needed to avoid giving answers. Conversations with individual teachers indicated that they felt the benefit of sharing their experiences in the two theoretical domains of the social and the mathematical and this in turn has provided a focus for their thinking about the approach and the lessons overall.

8. GENERAL FEATURES OF REFLECTION SESSIONS IN THE CAME PROFESSIONAL DEVELOPMENT PROGRAMME

The CAME professional development programme is structured as cycles of shared practice and reflection on such practice. Reflection is integral to all professional development components, based on the principle that teaching experience and intuition cannot be translated into expertise without generalisation and links with secure bodies of pedagogic, psychological and curriculum knowledge.

In all cases the reflection on classroom practices is focused on a given Thinking Maths lesson that has been recently taught. As indicated above, this reflection is structured in two parts, designated as the cognitive and social. This forces the teachers to move away from simple global judgements, or generalities, to consider the two dimensions separately before consciously integrating them. There is a developmental trajectory over the duration of the professional development programme with a gradual shift of emphasis from the more specific features of a particular lesson, to the more general, i.e., across lessons.

The issues handled in the reflection sessions may either be raised by the teachers and groups or by the tutors based on their observations and interactions with teachers.

8.1. The cognitive dimension

Teachers in early professional development sessions are asked to recount some interesting instances related to the mathematical ideas and ways of working. This tends to elicit fragments of observations related to their own reactions to the way the lesson flowed. A typical example in the Pegboard Symmetry lesson would be:

> I was surprised that Paul and Hassan, both normally low attaining boys, came up with the idea of the left and right differences before the more able kids, who were looking for the pattern in numbers.

In the plenary the specifics on insights and levels of thinking are generalised. In particular, the reason why the focus on oral reasoning sometimes allows the seemingly low attaining children to arrive at insights in unexpected ways, while seemingly high-achieving children are held back by their concern with minor features. This in turn is linked to the difference between a reasoning level and a level of achievement. Distinctions between reasoning and achievement levels are made within a topic area, e.g. co-ordinates, so the opportunity arises of exploring different features of the mathematics curriculum. Teachers come to recognise that learning involves both a set of linked concepts and formalisation, and processes of construction based on linking of perceptual experience and use of natural language.

In early professional development sessions some teachers raised concerns about the fact that they were not completing the full agenda of the lesson as it had taken place in the simulation. In the Pegboard Symmetry lessons many classes did not get beyond recognising that the two x co-ordinates added up to 10. Colleagues needed to be assured that it is not expected that a Thinking Maths lesson is ‘fully delivered’, but rather a fruitful challenging classroom activity is conducted in which children are engaged at different levels. The teacher needs to be responsive to the particular class, mindful of the need for challenge and pace, and also for providing the opportunity for a full exploration of concepts and reasoning appropriate to the range of thinking skills in the class. Related to that is the appreciation by the teacher of ways of simplifying logistics, or 'busy work', allowing more time for key questions. Other teachers raised the opposite concern: the lesson did not seem to take much time at all, i.e., the class understood the formula (x-5) + (x+5) =10 even when the 5 (the value for the vertical line) was changed to another value. For these teachers the discussion suggested that the pupils had been 'taught' by following teacher's explanation of the reasoning. Here the question becomes one of whether this is of equal value to pupils struggling to construct the concepts or relationships themselves.

With accumulated experience in the cognitive dimension teachers come to recognise the subtleties of the approach in assessing the difficulty, or cognitive demand levels, in the activity, how this is related to the cognitive potential of individual children, and how this is in turn linked with achievement levels. The teachers also gradually become more confident in describing the agenda of the lesson to colleagues. They can see the Thinking Maths lessons as deeper experiences which allow for genuine differentiation, thereby avoiding the notion of a single common objective or learning outcome to be achieved by all pupils.

8.2. The social-interactions dimension

The social interaction of the pupils is the focus of another CAME 'reflection on practice' session. The main foci here are the opportunities for interaction and argument. These are again first shared by teachers in small group work and then generalised in a plenary session. General pedagogic issues emerge on different types of teacher-pupil and pupil-pupil interactions, on ways of grouping children for optimum engagement of all individuals, and on focus and pace. These pedagogic issues are often the first to be recognised by teachers as relevant to the rest of their teaching. The theoretical foundation of the approach helps in various ways. For example, issues of placing children in groups, whether fully mixed-ability or by avoiding mixing extremes, are approached from the perspectives of what is socially desirable, and also cognitively effective, i.e., when communication between children is to be meaningful.

8.3. The culture-of-learning dimension

Teachers' accumulated experience through the professional development programme in structured reflection in the cognitive and social dimensions lead ultimately to the handling of a third area – the 'culture of learning' dimension. Positing such a dimension is deemed necessary to account for the attitudes and values in the class towards learning and towards mathematics itself. Whilst the classroom culture of learning is a complex phenomenon involving several factors, including, for example, the school itself, family and youth cultures, etc., the teacher should be aware of their own contribution in this domain. This includes the way the CAME approach itself can contribute to a more positive culture in regard to the learning of mathematics. In the latter stages of the professional development programmes teachers have often commented on the shifts they have noted in their classes and their own general teaching practices (see also Chapter 8). Seen in this light the 'culture of learning' dimension is a derivative of both the cognitive and social dimensions, or rather a product of their interaction. It is also the more difficult dimension to discern, and hence is approached and handled less explicitly in the early stages of the programme.

9. DISCUSSION

The account given of the process of formulating and communicating the agenda of Pegboard Symmetry as a Thinking Maths lesson for the primary classroom served to demonstrate key aspects of the framework for the development of Thinking Maths lessons in general. As illustrated in the first part of this chapter, the process starts with recognising the potential of a curriculum activity for the range of cognitive levels expected by the Piagetian and neo-Piagetian theory for the given age cohort. The selection of the curriculum tasks is informed by a global view of the school mathematics curriculum and the application of Piagetian developmental psychology to describe the underlying difficulty of a task in the same terms used to describe the cognitive level of children.

Following the recognition of the cognitive potential of the activity, there is the stage of identification of sub-tasks as reasoning steps, each of which, on its own, may span a range of cognitive levels. The part of the account related to this detailed cognitive demand analysis has shown that it:

- required empirical validation and could not be achieved merely through a 'thought experiment'

- involved selection, closing and opening of lines of work in light of the need for focus and increasing demand, and
- involved negotiation between several intuitive and implicit models for analysing cognitive demand.

Once the cognitive potential is delineated, the key issue then becomes one of communication of the agenda and the pedagogic guidance for implementation in the classroom – here we are focusing on the use of the lesson guidance materials in professional development sessions, initially within the research team (Phase 1) and then in the formal professional development programme (Phase 2).

The experiences of the research team would suggest that in the case of the CAME approach:

- written guidance on its own is not sufficient – there is a need for negotiation with teachers, a lesson simulation prior to the teaching and sharing and reflection specific to the lesson agendas afterwards
- the written guidance and lesson plan for a specific lesson come to take on (some) meaning after an initial trial by the teacher, and
- the process of coming to a more complete understanding evolves over an extended period of time, i.e., it is not a case of communicating the multiple features of the approach/model through one or two professional development sessions and some similar number of classroom experiences.

The analysis of the constructs of reasoning strands, reasoning steps and phases seem to lead to a notion of the centrality of teacher decisions on the optimal lesson flow. Further, this is dependent on the particular lesson and class and there is a need for careful guidance, at least in the initial phases of the implementation of the approach.

The role of the researchers and tutors is crucial for the professional development programme. The key aspect in their work is responsiveness to individual teachers over the period of the programme. The issues they must address apply to any long-term teacher-centred professional development, as distinct from a professional development focused on new curricula, resources, technology, or assessment procedures.

Tutor responsiveness to teachers in professional development involves adjustment to individual motivation to engage in the new approach, and to a relatively slow rate of change, akin to that of any change of adult lifestyle. Teacher engagement is obviously greater where there is the prior innate recognition of need on the one hand, and where sufficient management support and resources are present on the other. It was clear in the CAME research at both primary and secondary levels that personal motivation may be a more significant factor than management support. That was evident in cases where heads of the participating schools were all supportive, but there was still considerable variation between teachers in terms of, for example, attendance at professional development sessions, in readiness to arrange tutors' school visits, and in the scheduling of the teaching of the Thinking Maths lessons. Without the voluntary engagement of teachers one can expect forms of superficial adoption, conscious or unconscious, together with what might be seen as exaggerated perceptions of practical difficulties, in lieu of real engagement.

In summary, our experience so far indicates that normally two to three years are required for significant shifts to occur in beliefs and practices of most teachers. Some teachers, however, may be inherently more predisposed to the approach than others. Nevertheless, certain conditions must also be present:

- time is essential not for its own sake but for **cycles of practice and reflection on the practice** to take place. Without reflection *experiences* may not turn into *expertise*
- individual reflection is problematic because of the circular praxis effect: you analyse your practice in terms of the concepts you used in that practice, so that you may only recognise the problems you know about. Hence the need for **collective reflection**, in which other points of view illuminate the shared experiences
- collective reflection however without **clear theoretical perspectives** may have the same limitations and haphazard nature as those which take place in the staffroom or over social drinks in a bar in the evening.

Hence the CAME approach relies on the programme of cycles of professional development through shared practice and collective reflection from both the social and cognitive perspectives.[4] The mode of operation in the professional development sessions are meant to be as near as possible to the conduct of the CAME lessons themselves, with analogous features. The implications of this are that much of the work in sessions is open-ended, there is potential for continuous refinement of the materials, and the evolution of the approach is ongoing. This also provides a model for the concurrent development of all involved with the approach – the pupils, teachers, tutors and researchers.

Looking back at our model described in Chapter 1, we can see that the P-CAME approach to professional development links the *professional community* of the working group of teacher-researchers, university researchers and advisory personnel in the first phase of the programme to the *situation* back in school of the teachers in the second phase, through the use of the teacher-researchers as tutors. The P-CAME approach appears to provide the essential constituents defined by Spillane (1999) for the realisation of *zones of enactment* – ongoing deliberations in a social setting, using external and internal expertise, and grounded in day-to-day attempts to enact change. We pursue this discussion in Chapter 8 where we look in depth at a case study of two of the teacher-researchers to discover what other factors might be involved in enriching the quality of *zones of enactment*, in turn facilitating "deep" change (Earl et al., 2000, p. 39).

10. AFFILIATIONS

Professor David C. Johnson is an emeritus Professor at the Department of Education and Professional Studies, King's College London, having recently retired as Shell Professor of Mathematics Education.
Jeremy Hodgen is a Lecturer in Mathematics Education at the Department of Education and Professional Studies, King's College London.
Mundher Adhami is a Research Fellow at the Department of Education and Professional Studies, King's College London.

11. NOTES

[1] One may wish to contrast this work with that of the Cognitively Guided Instruction, CGI, project in the US (see, e.g., Fennema, Carpenter, Franke, Levi, Jacobs, & Empson, 1996) with particular attention paid to the degree to which the construct of 'cognition' is made explicit from a theoretical standpoint in each of the projects. However, whilst in CGI the focus is on developing teachers' knowledge of children's thinking, CAME takes a broader approach placing teachers' and children's cognition in the context of pedagogy and didactics.

[2] The mathematics National Curriculum levels in England and Wales have been formulated to identify achievements linked both to the range of abilities in a particular age group as well as some expected average. In this regard, Level 2 is that which would be expected for the average child at age 7, and Level 4 is that for the average child at age 11, the end of primary school (Year 6).

[3] As noted earlier, the schedule for the professional development programme was for two half-days per term for each of the three school terms – six sessions per year, 12 over the two years. All Year 5 teachers (of pupils aged 9-10 years) in the experimental schools attended and these teachers went on to teach the Year 6 lessons (pupils aged 10-11 years) in the second year of the two-year programme of lessons (24 lessons).

[4] The cyclical and developmental nature of curriculum development and the research base for such work is also a central feature in the work of Gravemeijer and others in the Realistic Mathematics Education (RME) movement in the Netherlands (see, e.g., Wubbels, Korthagen, & Broekman, 1997) and the work of Simon (1994).

12. REFERENCES

Adey, P. & Shayer, M. (1994). *Really Raising Standards*. London: Routledge.

Adhami, M., Johnson, D., & Shayer, M. (1998a). *Thinking Maths: The Programme for Accelerated Learning in Mathematics*. Oxford: Heinemann Educational Books.

Adhami, M., Johnson, D., & Shayer, M. (1998b). Cognitive development and classroom interaction: a theoretical foundation for teaching and learning. In J. D. Tinsley & D. C. Johnson (Eds.), *Information and Communication Technologies in School Mathematics* (pp. 205-213). London: Chapman Hall.

Adhami, M., Johnson, D., & Shayer, M. (1998c). Does CAME work? Summary report on phase 2 of the Cognitive Acceleration in Mathematics Education, CAME, project. In *Proceedings of the British Society for Research into Learning Mathematics Day Conference, Bristol, 15 Nov. 1997*. London: British Society for Research into Learning Mathematics, 26-31.

Booth, L. (1984). *Algebra: Children's Strategies and Errors*. Windsor: National Foundation for Educational Research-Nelson.

Brown, J., Collins, A., & Duguid, P. (1989). Situated cognition and the culture of learning. *Educational Researcher, 18* (5), 32-42.

Brown, M. (Ed.). (1992). *Topic Criteria Handbook* (in the Graded Assessment in Mathematics (GAIM) pack). Walton-on-Thames: Thomas Nelson & Sons.

Cobb, P. (Ed.). (1994). *Learning Mathematics: Constructivist and Interactionist Theories of Mathematical Development*. Dordrecht, Netherlands: Kluwer Academic Publishers.

Cobb, P., Boufi, A., McClain, K., & Whitenack, J. (1997). Reflective discourse and collective reflection. *Journal for Research in Mathematics Education, 28* (3), 258-277.

Davis, R., Maher, C., & Noddings, N. (Eds.). (1990). *Constructivist Views on the Teaching and Learning of Mathematics*. Reston, VA: National Council of Teachers of Mathematics.

Earl, L., Fullan, M., Leithwood, K., Watson, N., with Jantzi, D., Levin, B., & Torrance, N. (2000). *Watching and Learning. OISE/UT Evaluation of the implementation of the National Literacy and Numeracy Strategies. First annual report*. Toronto: Ontario Institute for Studies in Education, University of Toronto.

Fennema, E., Carpenter, T. P., Franke, M. L., Levi, L., Jacobs, V. R., & Empson, S. B. (1996). A longitudinal study of learning to use children's thinking in mathematics instruction. *Journal for Research in Mathematics Education, 27*(4), 403-434.

Hart, K. (Ed.). (1981). *Children's Understanding of Mathematics: 11-16*. London: John Murray.

Johnson, D. (Ed.). (1989). *Children's Mathematical Frameworks 8-13: a Study of Classroom Teaching*. Windsor: National Foundation for Educational Research-Nelson.

Johnson, D., Adhami, M., Shayer, M., Hodgen, J., Hafeez, R., Dubben, S., Longfield, A., Harvey, L., Hindshaw, J., & Davidson, M. (2003). *Primary Thinking Maths Lessons*. London: BEAM Education.

Lampert, M. (1990). When the problem is not the question and the solution is not the answer: mathematical knowing and teaching. *American Educational Research Journal, 27*(1), 29-63.

Mok, I. & Johnson, D. (2001). Reasoning algebraically with IT: a cognitive perspective. *Mathematics Education Research Journal, 12*(3), 286-303.

Shayer, M., & Adey, P. (1981). *Towards a Science of Science Teaching*. London: Heinemann Educational Books.

Simon, M. A. (1994). Learning mathematics and learning to teach: Learning cycles in mathematics teacher education. *Educational Studies in Mathematics, 26*, 71-94.

Spillane, J. P. (1999). External reform initiatives and teachers' efforts to reconstruct their practice: the mediating role of teachers' zones of enactment. *Journal of Curriculum Studies, 31*(2), 143-175.

Wubbels, T., Korthagen, F. A. J., & Broekman, H. (1997). Preparing teachers for realistic mathematics education. *Educational Studies in Mathematics, 32*, 1-28.

Yackel, E., & Cobb, P. (1996). Sociomathematical norms, argumentation, and autonomy in mathematics. *Journal for Research in Mathematics Education, 27*(4), 458-477.

JEREMY HODGEN AND DAVID C JOHNSON

CHAPTER 8

TEACHER REFLECTION, IDENTITY AND BELIEF CHANGE IN THE CONTEXT OF PRIMARY CAME

Abstract. The focus of this chapter is on how the potential for professional change encapsulated by a teacher's *zone of enactment* can be realised through reflection. The discussion is set in the context of the case study of two teachers involved as teacher-researchers in the Primary CAME project. The notion of identity is used to emphasise teachers as active agents in their own professional change. A critical factor in facilitating reflection was the mathematical heterogeneity of the teachers' *zones of enactment* reflecting the teachers' multiple identities as teachers, lesson-developers, tutors and researchers. Reflection occurred in situations in which the teachers had no choice but to respond.

1. INTRODUCTION

Reflection is a much used idea in teacher professional development. Many mathematics teacher education programmes have, therefore, formally allocated time to enable teachers to reflect. However, as Clarke (1994) argues, enabling teachers to reflect is not a simple task and, in order for reflection to take place, teachers need motivation and to have resources with which to reflect. In this chapter, we discuss these issues in the context of the Primary CAME Project (see also Chapter 7).

Reflection is a key aspect of the CAME approach to professional development. However, whilst there were many formal opportunities for the teachers to reflect, deep and explicit reflection was an infrequent occurrence. Nevertheless, when it did take place, such reflection did appear to be a significant event for the teachers.

A further aim is to extend and develop Spillane's (1999) notion of *zone of enactment* (See Chapter 1). Spillane's analysis is important in highlighting the role of teachers' wider professional and social networks in their change, and in particular the ways in which policy and curriculum initiatives are mediated by these *zones of enactment*. As has been noted elsewhere in this volume, he argues that teachers'

Alison Millett, Margaret Brown, Mike Askew (eds.), Primary Mathematics and the Developing Professional.

involvement in "rich deliberations about the substance … a practising of reform ideas with other teachers and reform experts includ[ing] material resources or artefacts that support [these] deliberations" (p. 171) is crucial for qualitatively significant changes in teachers' beliefs and practices to take place. However, his concern is at a policy level and his approach, as it stands, appears to lack the fine tuning necessary to explain differential change amongst teachers with opportunities to realise rich, broad and extensive *zones of enactment.* For example, despite an unusually favourable and extended professional development setting in which they had access to both rich deliberations in the form of regular discussions with other teachers and academics together with teaching resources supporting these deliberations, only two of the six teachers in the study reported here appeared to change significantly. In short, the *zone of enactment* provides a description of the potential for change, but it is less helpful in analysing how this potential is realised or actually enacted by teachers.

To develop the notion of the *zone of enactment*, we draw on theories of identity in order to analyse both the nature of reflection and the role of teachers as active agents in their own change. Our focus is on the case of the two teachers for whom change was clearly demonstrated and their changing beliefs about mathematics and mathematics education.

2. THE RESEARCH

The research reported here is based on a four-year longitudinal study into the professional change of the six teachers involved as teacher-researchers in the Primary CAME research team. (See also Chapter 7 and Annex 4.)

The fieldwork was conducted between November 1997 and July 2001. Data collection was qualitative using multiple methods, including observations of seminars, lessons and professional development sessions, semi-structured interviews with individuals and groups, and structured mathematical interviews. Our own roles were as participant observers. Analysis was conducted using techniques drawn from grounded theory (Strauss & Corbin, 1998) and social constructivist approaches (Kvale, 1996).

From its inception, the project research team consisted of four researchers, four primary teachers and the Local Education Authority mathematics adviser. During the school year 1997/8, the research team met fortnightly to assess the feasibility of the approach and to develop Thinking Maths lessons specifically for primary children in the age range 9-11 (Years 5 and 6 in England). Two more teachers were added to the research team in the second year, making six teachers in all

During Phase 2 of the project, over the school years 1998/9 and 1999/2000, a further group of teachers from seven more schools joined the project to begin implementing the Thinking Maths lessons more widely.[1] The Primary CAME professional development for the Phase 2 teachers was a two-year programme consisting of twice-termly central seminars and a package of teaching materials. In Phase 2, the Phase 1 teachers acted as tutors to the new cohort of teachers as well as continuing to develop lessons, leading central professional development sessions and visiting teachers in their classrooms to observe, team-teach and reflect with them on Thinking Maths lessons.

2.1. The two teachers: Alexandra and Ursula

As we have noted in the introduction to this chapter, we will focus on two of the six teachers, Alexandra and Ursula.[2] The choice of these teachers was based on the criteria that the two case studies provided substantial documentation on individuals for whom change was judged to be extensive. In terms of Spillane's analysis, both teachers had a *zone of enactment* with all the characteristics required for extensive change:

- both were experienced teachers
- both had participated in extended professional development in mathematics education
- their school had an investigative approach to teaching mathematics, and
- they had a close professional relationship and personal friendship and had worked collaboratively for a number of years, planning and team-teaching classes together.

We note that at least one of the remaining four teachers, Lisa, had a similarly extensive *zone of enactment*. However, a key difference was that Lisa's *zone of enactment* appeared to facilitate her professional change in relation to her role as a manager rather than as a primary mathematics teacher.[3]

2.2. CAME professional development

The teachers' professional development was somewhat unusual in that it was integrated within the project's wider developmental work: the teachers learnt by working alongside the other members of the research team. During the first year of the project the research team met fortnightly for day-long seminars. A typical meeting included one or two lesson simulations, a session reflecting on lessons taught and discussion on an aspect of the CAME approach or theory. The seminar agendas were flexible and much of the discussion was open-ended and wide-ranging. Alexandra, for example, described meetings as having "several conversations going on at once" (Seminar, June 1999). Throughout the first year, a discussion paper was circulated prior to each team meeting. Although the King's researchers made some formal presentations to these Phase 1 teachers, these were relatively infrequent. Team meetings were lively with heated debates about the nature of teaching and learning and the applicability of ideas and activities to the primary classroom.

Alongside the research seminars, the teachers taught Thinking Maths lessons. Initially, these lessons were taken exclusively from the secondary materials, in order to communicate key aspects of the CAME approach. As the project developed, the teachers themselves suggested new contexts for Thinking Maths lessons. Many of these lesson development trials were either team-taught or taught with other research team members observing.

2.3. The fractions lessons

Our discussion is focused on the teachers' experiences of lesson development and Phase 2 tutoring in the context of two fractions lessons: Share an Apple, and Halving and Thirding (Johnson et al., 2003). These two lessons were initiated by Alexandra and Ursula themselves. The events we consider took place over three academic years. (See Table 8.1, for a timetable of this process.)

In Share an Apple, the focus is on representations and comparisons of fractions. So, for example, children are asked to consider various ways of representing and comparing the magnitude of simple fractions of everyday objects. In Halving and Thirding, the focus is on developing and connecting different representations for the multiplication of fractions, including repeated multiplication by $^1/_2$ and $^1/_3$. Halving and Thirding concludes with the children tackling a multiplication problem in the context of mixing different coloured paints. (This problem is a revision of the Whisky and Water problem discussed in the case study below.) See Hodgen (2002) for further information on the development of these lessons.

Table 8.1: The fractions lesson development timescale.

1997-1998	The two fractions lessons trialled, discussed and re-worked by research team.
199-1999	The first fractions lesson, Share an Apple, taught by Phase 2 teachers with tutoring support from Alexandra, Ursula and the other teacher-researchers.
1999-2000	Alexandra and Ursula write and present paper about the fractions lessons at two academic conferences.
	The second fractions lesson, Halving and Thirding, taught by Phase 2 teachers with tutoring support from Alexandra, Ursula and the other teacher-researchers.

3. REFLECTION IN MATHEMATICS TEACHER EDUCATION

Reflection is something of a ubiquitous idea within teacher education. Many commentators highlight the crucial role that reflection plays in mathematics teacher education (e.g., see reviews by Clarke, 1994; and Grouws & Schultz, 1996). However, this apparent consensus conceals some differences in meaning. Grimmett (1988), for example, lists several different conceptions of reflection, including:

> thoughtfulness about action ... to 'apply' research findings to practice, ... deliberation and choice amongst competing vision of 'good teaching', [and] reconstructing experience, the end of which is the identification of a new possibility for action. (p. 12)

Since our focus is on significant change, we are concerned with the last and strongest of these definitions: reflection as the reconstruction of experience and knowledge.

The work on this strong conception of reflection draws largely on two distinct theoretical strands: on the one hand, constructivism and the work of Piaget; and, on the other, the work of Schön (1983) and his notion of a reflective professional. From a constructivist perspective, Wood and Turner-Vorbeck (1999) argue that reflection is central to teacher education. Mathematics teacher learning, they argue:

> involves interpretative constructions and reconstructions in thinking through processes of reflection on the activity of self and others. (p. 174)

Working within a similar tradition, the cognitive acceleration approach conceives of reflection in terms of metacognition or "becoming conscious of [one's] own thinking" (Adey & Shayer, 2002, p.6). Indeed, Adey and Shayer argue that such reflection can only take place after the action being reflected upon:

> The requirement for consciousness means that it is a process that must take place *after* a thinking act, since at that time a student is engaging in a problem-solving activity their consciousness must be devoted to that. ... The value of this type of metacognition [is] in making general thinking processes explicit, and thus more readily available for use on other occasions. (p. 6, original emphasis)

Schön (1983) also notes the importance of explicit reflection after the act of teaching, which he terms reflection-on-action. However, in contrast to the cognitive acceleration of Adey and Shayer, he sees reflection-*on*-action as leading to reflection-*in*-action, a deeper and more developed form of reflection taking place explicitly and consciously during the process of teaching. Nevertheless, Schön emphasises the role of reflection-on-action and thinking about action after the event as a precursor to reflection-in-action.

In practical terms, reflection remains a somewhat elusive concept. It is unclear how teachers' reflection can be facilitated or encouraged. Indeed, there is considerable evidence that enabling teachers to reflect is a far from simple task. Cooney (1994), for example, argues, "no magical way exists to promote reflection" (p.16). Several authors (e.g. Clarke, 1994) argue that substantial time should be allocated within professional development programmes for reflection. However, whilst the provision of time may be a necessary condition for reflection, it is not a sufficient one. Cooney (1994) highlights the crucial importance of teachers' own motivation to reflect. He argues that simply telling teachers that reflection is a good thing is unlikely to be universally successful: "they must see that for themselves" (p19). In a similar vein, Clarke (1994) argues that reflection is an active not a passive process. It is dependent on teachers perceiving a "need to become articulate, to be communicative, or to use thoughts as objects of systematic attention with their colleagues" (p. 44). Goldsmith and Schifter (1997), however, argue that motivation is a particularly neglected issue within research in mathematics teacher education.

Given the concern with reflection *on* one's own activity, it is perhaps unsurprising that several authors use physical metaphors of distance to convey the difficulty of this process. Wood and Turner-Vorbeck (1999), for example, highlight the difficulty and complexity of 'decentering'. Cooney and Shealey (1997), indeed, link these physical metaphors to the notion of a teacher's willingness to reflect:

> A precondition for the act of reflection is the ability of the person to decenter and view his or her actions as a function of the context in which he or she is acting. Schön's (1983) reflective practitioner, a notion that enjoys so much credence in the field of education, cannot exist unless the individual is willing to step out of himself or herself and view his or her actions from a relativistic perspective. (p. 100)

The arguments for reflection and the metaphor of distancing are persuasive. Indeed, as we have already noted in the introduction to this chapter, the teachers' reflections, although infrequent, did appear to be significant events in their professional change. Our aim in this chapter is to analyse several of these reflective events and to place these within the social context of teachers' identities. In doing so we address the following questions: How does reflection actually take place? What motivates teachers to reflect? Building on the metaphor of distance, how can teachers 'step outside' themselves in order to reflect on their own change?

4. TEACHER BELIEFS ABOUT MATHEMATICS

In terms of the teachers' changing beliefs about mathematics, we focus on three interrelated areas: beliefs about authority in mathematics; beliefs about mathematics as a connected discipline; and, mathematics without closure, a set of beliefs promoted by the CAME project.

4.1. Authority in mathematics

We draw on Povey's (1997) re-working and development of Belenky, Clinchy, Goldberger and Tarule's (1986) work on ways of knowing in the context of mathematics to focus on two positions in relation to mathematics: *external authority* and *author/ity*. External authority is a way of knowing where teachers perceive knowledge to be validated by experts and as fixed and absolute. In this position teachers are "deeply dependent on others, especially authoritative others" (Povey, Burton, Angier, & Boylan, 1999, p. 234). Author/ity, in contrast, is a position where teachers understand mathematical knowledge as negotiated and co-constructed with others. In coining the term, Povey (1997) relates this position explicitly to authorship in mathematics:

> Author/ity links back together two words that have a common root, but which have come to be read very differently from each other. An author is one who brings things into being, who is the originator of any action or state of things. Authority is linked with power and the validity of knowledge. Linked together they lead to the construction of an epistemology which recognises each of us as the originator of knowledge. (p. 332)

In contrast to the position of external authority, where authoritative sources, textbooks or expert mathematicians, for example, are relied upon, in the position of author/ity such authorities are critically evaluated.

4.2. Connections in mathematics

Here, we refer to the work of Askew et al., (1997), who found teachers with a connectionist orientation to mathematics teaching and learning to be more effective teachers of numeracy than those with either discovery or transmission orientations. The connectionist orientation was characterised by amongst other things beliefs about teaching mathematics as a connected discipline. This perspective has similarities to what Cobb et al., (1997) refer to as a *mathematizing orientation*, by which they mean engaging in the discourse of mathematics. In her work on elementary teacher knowledge, Ma (1999) extends the notion of connections by identifying four aspects of teacher mathematical knowledge: an understanding of the *connectedness* between simple and more fundamental ideas in mathematics; consideration of *multiple perspectives* and different approaches to mathematical ideas; knowledge about the *basic ideas* underlying the mathematical curriculum; and, knowledge of the entire elementary, or primary, mathematical curriculum and its *longitudinal coherence*.

4.3. Mathematics without closure

We use *mathematics without closure* to refer to a distinctive set of beliefs promoted by the CAME Project. A key element of this is that children's learning is seen as *without closure*. Thinking Maths lessons are not closed: there is not generally a *common* end point or learning objective to be achieved by all children. The lessons are seen in terms of 'sowing seeds' for later work in mathematics. However, it was in relation to a teachers' knowledge of the school mathematics curriculum as a whole that CAME appeared to be distinctive. The academic researchers stressed the importance of teacher knowledge of key mathematical concepts, or 'big ideas', in order that she can "frame … the specifics of each task so that 'the road ahead' does lead in the right direction" (Adhami et al., 1998, p. x).

Hence, by mathematics without closure, we refer to beliefs about the importance of children's long-term and conceptual mathematical development over the short-term achievement in particular mathematical activities or lessons, together with beliefs about the importance of teacher knowledge of big ideas in mathematics. This knowledge, although similar to Ma's (1999) longitudinal coherence, goes beyond the primary curriculum.

5. IDENTITY, THE ZONE OF ENACTMENT AND PROFESSIONAL CHANGE

Underlying this analysis is Wenger's (1998) conception of identity as located in communities of practices and his understanding of development in terms of an individual "building an identity" (p. 2). Schifter (1996) conceives of teacher change in terms of teachers constructing "narratives of professional identity" that draw on their experiences in local communities (p. 2). She stresses the plurality of teacher professional identity:

> These teachers enact multiple identities: as mathematical thinkers, as managers of classroom process, as monitors of their students' learning, as colleagues, and as

> members of the wider education community. "Identities" in this sense – more a matter of what one does than who one thinks one is – are constructed in and realised through practices. (p. 2)

It is important to note here that, whilst Schifter sees these different aspects of identity as constructed through practices, these identities cut across the communities of practice a teacher participates in. Thus, in contrast to the notion of identity as membership of a distinct community, this conception of a teacher's identity might be as a mathematical thinker, for example, which could be enacted in a variety of distinct communities, including the classroom, planning sessions with colleagues, the wider school, community, professional communities and more. Like Schifter's teachers, the teachers in this study, at the same time as participating in the research team, were developing different aspects of their identity as primary teachers, including their identities as mathematical thinkers, for example. And, like Schifter's teachers, this went beyond the strict confines of their participation in the immediate professional development initiative. Through their participation in Primary CAME, they were developing their identities as lesson-developers, as tutors, and as teacher-researchers. However, these wider aspects of their identity drew on a variety of practices and, thus, provided a link between their membership of different communities. For example, in developing an identity as a tutor, both Alexandra and Ursula drew on experiences and practices within school, as well as their CAME tutoring work.

Schifter's approach to identity is similar to that of Holland, Lachicotte, Skinner and Cain (1998) who distinguish between figurative and positional aspects of identity:

> We make an analytic distinction between aspects of identities that have to do with figured worlds – story lines, narrativity, generic characters, and desire – and aspects that have to do with one's position relative to socially identified others, one's sense of social place, and entitlement. These figurative and positional aspects of identity interrelate in myriad ways. Sometimes they are completely coincident; sometimes one dominates over the other. (p. 125)

Figurative identity refers to aspects of identity that span and make sense of the discontinuities between the positional aspects of identity and, thus, reflect the teachers' participation within wider, more dispersed and plural discourse communities, which Wenger (1998) refers to as "a complex social landscape of shared practices, boundaries, peripheries, overlaps, connections, and encounters" (p. 118). Hence, any teacher's *zone of enactment* is a multiplicity of social spaces that are riven with discontinuities. The key issue for professional change is the extent to which this multiplicity affords opportunities and the extent to which a teacher recognises and acts upon these opportunities.

Hodgen discusses elsewhere ways in which the discontinuities between the different positional aspects of the teachers' identities were crucial in how the teachers' engaged with and interpreted new practices (Hodgen, 2003). However, it appeared to be these wider and more figurative aspects, and the fact that they encompassed the teachers' practices across different communities, that enabled the teachers to step outside themselves and thus reflect. Being a tutor, or a lesson developer, or indeed simply engaging with a colleague in collaborative team-teaching enabled the teachers to distance themselves from their identity as a classroom teacher or a doer of mathematics and become aware of and reflect upon their activity and, thus, explicitly reconstruct their knowledge. Yet whilst such social interaction was relatively frequent, deep reflection occurred infrequently. This raises the question of what were the particular features of these infrequent occasions that enabled the teachers to reflect deeply and thus actively develop their beliefs about mathematics and mathematics education.

6. THE CASE STUDY: REFLECTION AND PROFESSIONAL CHANGE

We will now develop this analysis through a discussion of four examples of reflection. All are in the context of the fractions lessons that we have discussed above. In the first example, we briefly give an example of reflection in the context of lesson development. In this case, reflection took place as part of, rather than separate to, the teacher's practices of lesson development. In the second, we explore reflection in the context of a team-teaching experience. Here, we focus on the notion of distance and suggest that the presence of another teacher was a crucial factor in locating and grounding the reflection. In the third example, we will explore the opportunities for reflection in the formal reflection sessions during the research seminars. Whilst learning did take place, the role of explicit and conscious reflection in these sessions was limited. However, reflection did take place later, but was prompted by the two teachers' experience of writing a paper for an academic audience. In the fourth and final example, we will look more closely at Alexandra's beliefs about school mathematics. The discussion focuses on an informal and impromptu discussion between the researcher and Alexandra that took place immediately after a Phase 2 tutoring visit. Again, in contrast to the formal 'reflection' sessions, reflection did appear to take place, as part of, rather than separate to, the activity of tutoring. Moreover, the transformation of Alexandra's beliefs was in this case very significant in terms of school mathematics. We describe how reflection was enabled by the opportunity provided by the experience of tutoring for Alexandra to 'step outside' her identity as a teacher of mathematics.

6.1. Lesson development: reflection as part of practice

In drafting the final lesson materials for Halving and Thirding, Ursula commented on the earlier teaching notes, which she herself had written 18 months previously:

> They're too led. It's too much about getting an answer. The point is to get children thinking around the issues, about what fractions mean, to open up what's quite a standard school activity. These are too much like get to answer in each episode, then go on to the next one. (Research Team, October 2000)

Thus, the experience of revising and reviewing lesson materials enabled Ursula to reflect on her own change. The lesson materials provided a record of Ursula's previous thinking, thus enabling a distancing from her previous practice, in this case teaching that was "too led," whilst at the same time providing a prompt for reflection. A further factor was, we suggest, that her role in the project as a lesson developer enabled her to locate her previous practice within a wider perspective; this experience of lesson development provided the opportunity for Ursula to 'imagine' a teaching practice different to her own previous experiences (Wenger, 1998).

Although this reflection took place at a research seminar, we stress that it was made during small-group work on lesson development and thus took place as part of the 'authentic activity' (Lave, 1991) of writing lesson materials rather than in a separate formal reflection session. Indeed, a second key aspect for reflection, alongside the opportunity to distance oneself, was the teachers' engagement with practice. Indeed, the reflection that was observed generally took place during, or shortly after, the teachers' engagement in authentic activities, like teaching, lesson development, or tutoring, rather than in formal reflection sessions.

6.2. Team-teaching: imagination, engagement and the other teachers

Here, we consider a team-teaching experience, in which Lisa, another of the teacher-researchers, had opted out of teaching the lesson Share an Apple with Ursula. Shortly after the lesson, Lisa commented: "I don't see the value of this lesson." This in turn prompted Ursula to say: "This is a Thinking Maths lesson. It's making us think. ... It's like Picturing Numbers in that it opens up a closed activity." (Fieldnotes, October 1999). Thus, the experience enabled Ursula to link her insight about the Share an Apple lesson itself to a lesson she had up until that point expressed a very strong antipathy to, as for example in this previous comment: "It's like what I would normally do, but closing it down" (Research Team, June 1998). For Ursula, Picturing Numbers, a lesson about models of addition, had signified all that was confusing about CAME. She constantly referred to the lesson when talking about the difficulties she had in grasping what was special about CAME. She described the lesson at various times in somewhat contradictory terms as "airy-fairy", "not special", "too difficult", "too easy", "not my cup of tea", "too closed", and "just what I normally do" (Interview, March 1998; Research team, December 1997, March, May & July 1998). Indeed, this was the first time she had made a positive comment about this lesson. Moreover, in highlighting opening up of a closed activity, she placed her earlier contradictory descriptions of the lesson within a key aspect of CAME's *mathematics without closure* approach. Hence, this was, we suggest, a very significant reflective event in her professional change.

There were two critical factors involved in this reflection. Firstly, this lesson took place as preparation for the first Phase 2 professional development session. Hence, a key concern was the issue of how to present the ideas to the Phase 2 teachers. The experience of team-teaching and the consequent movement between teaching and observation – as a tutor rather than as a teacher – enabled Ursula to step outside her identity as a teacher. Hence, she was able to both engage with the teaching and imagine how the teaching could be different. Wenger (1998) argues that this "combination of engagement and imagination" is very powerful:

> Such a practice combines the ability both to engage and to distance – to identify with an enterprise as well as to view it in context, with the eyes of an outsider. Imagination enables us to adopt other perspectives across boundaries and time … and to explore possible futures … [and thus] trigger new interpretations. In turn, engagement provides a place for imagination to land, to be negotiated in practice and realized into identities of participation. (p. 217)

A second factor was the presence of Lisa as an observer and that Lisa's reaction was very similar to Ursula's own initial reaction to Picturing Numbers. Not only was Lisa's comment about the value of the lesson similar to Ursula's early comments, but, like Lisa, who had opted out of teaching Share an Apple, Ursula had opted out of teaching Picturing Numbers because "I just couldn't get into it", leaving the teaching to Rhoda (Research Team, December 1997). Lisa's presence, we suggest, enabled Ursula to remember, locate and thus reflect on her previous practice.

6.3. An audience: the imperative to reflect

6.3.1. Preparation

During the first year, there were three formal 'reflection' sessions during the research team seminars in which the discussion focused on the teachers' experiences of teaching the fractions lessons. These discussions generated considerable excitement amongst the King's researchers about the value of the lessons as Thinking Maths lessons.

However, despite this very positive validation of their work, both Alexandra's and Ursula's reactions to these reflection discussions were largely negative. A particular focus for the teachers' criticisms was the academics' attempts to introduce a more explicit theoretical base to the lessons. During the second reflection discussion in January 1998, the university researchers led a discussion about children's errors, strategies and misconceptions in the area of fractions. This discussion largely focused on distinguishing part-part and part-whole relationships, children's difficulties with fractional notation, and different meanings of fractions. A further discussion in May 1998 was focused on mathematical background notes produced by Nadir, one of the academics. In these notes, which were essentially a summary of the January 1998 discussion, Nadir discussed the mathematics in both lessons.

In March 1998, Ursula commented that the January discussion was "way beyond" her needs in developing the lesson:

> I mean the input we've had into fractions so far has been an argument about, I don't know, some mathematical term or whatever between them [the academics] that hasn't been helpful to Alexandra and I in developing the lesson at all. One-off chats with Nadir have, because they've been about developing the first part of the Year 5 lesson. But then what we've had actually at the meetings has not been helpful, because it's too high powered and it's not related to the task necessarily from my eyes. It's way beyond it. (Interview, March 1998)

Indeed, a year later she still remembered this discussion as a "nightmare". Similarly, during the second discussion, Alexandra commented that she felt this explicit research base was unnecessary, because "these background notes, unless you've got somebody who's particularly interested in the sort of mathematical side of it, this is too complex", a comment which Ursula had also affirmed: "Yes, far too complex, Nadir." (Research team, May 1998)

The two teachers were unspecific about what exactly was too "high powered" or "complex." However, they had themselves highlighted children's difficulties with fractional notation and representation in their initial presentation of the lesson.

Whilst the academics certainly focused on a more theoretical understanding of these issues, the only extra issue that the academics had added were part-part and part-whole relationships. Therefore, it would seem that the teachers' perception of difficulty lay in relation to this, which Nadir presented as follows in his background notes:

> In both lessons the distinction is explored between the part-whole relationship expressed in fraction, such as 1/3, and the part-part ratio relationships within the whole, '1 to 2', which we at this stage avoid to express and leave implicit. It is a fact that in the 1/3 example we prefer, as adults, to relate the one part to a constructed or original total of three parts while we *see* only two parts, one of which is twice (or half) the other. It is curious that the ratio 1:2 is a more concrete representation of the outcome of finding a third of something. The fraction notation, however, is more elegant in the sense that it preserves the action, and allows easier manipulations of several fractions. A clash is evident between a perspective that looks at what is here and now, and one that is geared to subsequent use of notation. (Project memo, May 1998, Original emphasis)

In this document, Nadir certainly took something of an idiosyncratic position on the relative difficulty of part-part and part-whole relationships and his writing style was at times dense. Moreover, in each of these reflection discussions, there was considerable disagreement between the academics about the particular difficulties children face. Nevertheless, the characterisation of ratio and proportion, or indeed any of the issues raised in these discussions, as way beyond the teachers' needs in developing this lesson is somewhat strange, and suggests that, at this point, these teachers did not appreciate the importance of Ma's (1999) longitudinal coherence that "teachers are not limited to the knowledge that should be taught in a certain grade" (p. 122). Indeed, ratio and proportion do feature in many standard textbooks on mathematics for primary teachers (e.g., Williams & Shuard, 1994) and the topics are now introduced at Year 4 in the National Numeracy Strategy (Department for Education and Employment, 1999). Certainly these issues are inherently no more challenging than the multiplication of fractions at the heart of the Halving and Thirding lesson: $^1/_2 \times {}^1/_2$, $^1/_3 \times {}^1/_3$ and $^1/_2 \times {}^1/_2 \times {}^1/_3 \times {}^1/_3$.

6.3.2. Writing for an audience

In August 1999, 18 months later, writing a paper to present their lesson development work to an academic conference, Alexandra and Ursula took a rather different position in relation to the mathematical background. In this paper, entitled 'Being a teacher and doing research', they discussed the development of the two fractions lessons. Their comment about the mathematical background was as follows:

> [The agenda for] the finalised Year 5 lesson, Share an Apple (see attached background notes for clarification) [Nadir's original background notes] ... can be summarised as:

> meaning of fractions; notation; adding simple fractions; comparing size of fractions. ... [The Y6 lesson] naturally follows within the spiral curriculum of the CAME lessons. Like Share an Apple, it deals with exploring the distinction between the part-whole relationship expressed in a fraction, and the ratio relationships between the parts that make up the whole. (Academic paper, August 1998)

Alexandra and Ursula referred explicitly to the content of the mathematical discussions, including the issue of part-part and part-whole relationships, which they had previously described as "too high powered". Moreover, they referred to Nadir's mathematical background notes as clarification: notes which they had earlier described as "too complex." Significantly, the researcher later observed Alexandra and Ursula lead discussions with primary teachers using this more explicit knowledge of children's learning difficulties. At the lesson simulation of Halving and Thirding, the Year 6 lesson, in February 2000, Alexandra used their joint paper together with the academics' mathematical background notes as the basis of a presentation on children's difficulties with fractions. In June 2000, Ursula led what she described as a challenging discussion on the mathematical meanings of ratio and proportion at a National Numeracy Strategy training session. Hence, whilst their initial reactions to these ideas were negative, they did later appear to come to appreciate at least implicitly the value of what they perceived at the time to be mathematically a very challenging and complex discussion.

Certainly, then, professional change in terms of their beliefs about longitudinal coherence had taken place, although we note that in using the original background notes unchanged they were still referring to Nadir as a mathematical authority. However, our focus in this discussion is on how they learnt it, and in particular what role, if any, reflection played in this learning. We reiterate that, despite the emphasis placed on reflection within the CAME approach, at no point in the formal discussions did we observe the teachers explicitly reflect. Of course, the fact that we did not observe reflection take place does not mean that such activity was completely absent. However, our observations of the teachers' frustration together with the teachers' comments suggest that little learning of a substantial or transformative nature took place within the formal reflections sessions.

In contrast, the writing of the academic paper appeared to be a prompt for the teachers to reflect. Ursula sent the researcher a draft of the paper with the following comment:

> Another 'one in the morning' job over a bottle of wine and plenty of disagreements! We actually looked back over Nadir's notes and found them useful. Made everything fall into place. (Ursula, Personal communication, 5 August 1999)

The imperative for a considered analysis was a critical factor in enabling significant changes in their mathematical knowledge for teaching, although we note the additional factor of the passage of time. The two teachers had to produce an academic paper and an academic paper very powerfully required them to resolve some of their previous difficulties with the mathematics in the lesson. It is significant that they referred to Nadir's notes as enabling everything to "fall into place," since they had judged these earlier as "far too complex."

A further feature of this event was the way the teachers themselves appeared to be catalysts in their own learning. Whilst not entirely spontaneous, since it was prompted by writing the paper, the teachers were themselves working together and separate from the wider research team. Moreover, in taking place until late into the night, at Ursula's home and socially over a bottle of wine, there were very strong similarities with their existing collaborative practices of inter-linking the professional and the personal. So, whilst they were engaged in the practice of academic writing, they were distanced not only from their own initial engagement as teachers but also from their position as teacher-researchers within the research team. Nevertheless, they could draw on their existing ways of working in order to engage with the practice of academic writing.

6.4. Tutoring: reminders of oneself as a learner

The examples that we have discussed so far involve one-off examples of reflection. In the following example, we explore a series of reflections that enabled Alexandra to begin to transform her beliefs and knowledge about school mathematics. In the main, this discussion draws on the reflection discussion at the first seminar in January 1998, a discussion following a tutoring visit between Alexandra, another teacher from Alexandra's school and the researcher in January 1999, and an interview in March 1999. The starting point for these reflections was the following Whisky and Water problem which, restated in terms of blue and yellow paint, was the focus of the Halving and Thirding lesson:

> I have two glasses. One glass contains whisky, whilst the other contains water. If you pour half of the whisky into the water, mix it up, then pour half of that quantity back into the original whisky glass, which glass now has more whisky?

6.4.1. Solving the problem

In January 1998, Alexandra and Ursula presented the Whisky and Water problem to the research team. Each of the academic researchers solved the problem using an algebraic solution. In contrast, Alexandra solved the problem using diagrams. (See Figure 8.1 for an example of a diagrammatic solution similar to Alexandra's.)

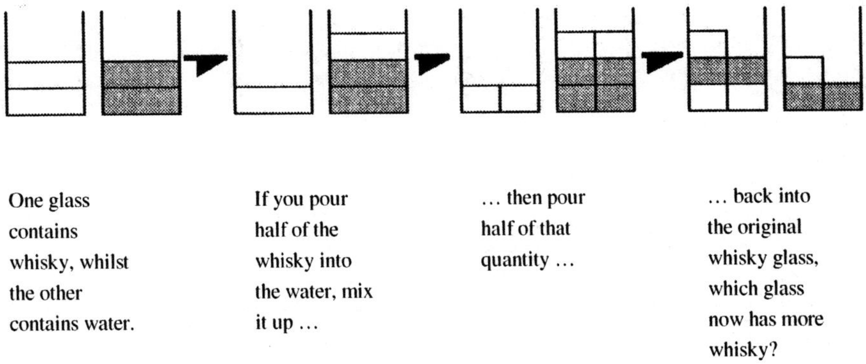

Figure 8.1. A diagrammatic solution of the Whisky and Water problem similar to Alexandra's approach.

When sharing this solution, Alexandra argued that it was "not scientific". We suggest that she believed that her solution, although perfectly appropriate for everyday problem solving and despite producing a convincing solution, was not truly mathematical, because it used diagrams and that it could not form the basis of a truly mathematical argument.

Alexandra's diagrammatic solution is both mathematically elegant and rigorous. In her solution she assumed that, although each solution of whisky and water was mixed completely, she could still separate out the whisky and water in each glass in order to solve the problem. This is the same reasoning step that is needed for an algebraic solution.[4] Indeed, in many ways her diagrammatic solution mirrors the algebraic solution, using an area model to illustrate the multiplication of fractions. In this particular example, in which the original quantities of whisky and water are equal, the diagrammatic solution is more efficient than an algebraic solution in generating answers to a variety of related questions regarding the problem.[5] For example, the ratio of whisky to water in each glass, and hence the strength of the two mixtures, can simply be visually read off the final diagram. In contrast, the algebraic solution requires further manipulation to answer this second question. Alexandra's solution was indeed judged a mathematically better solution in this case by the teachers and, significantly for Alexandra, by the King's researchers. Moreover, such solutions are an important element both of mathematical problem-solving (e.g. Polya, 1957) and of mathematical proof (e.g. Waring, 2000).

Alexandra was pleased and excited at the academics' positive reaction to her solution, exclaiming "Oh, yes!" in a loud voice (Research team, January 1998). This pleasure and excitement did not in itself result in a fundamental shift in her mathematical thinking. Indeed, she subsequently described her solution as "just my little way of doing it" (Fieldnotes, May 1998), a description which strongly suggests that she did not fully value her method as a *mathematical* solution. However, the experience did appear to provide the basis for a further reflection.

6.4.2. Reflection

A year later, following a tutor visit to a Phase 2 school in January 1999, Alexandra appeared to experience a sudden insight about the mathematical validity of diagrams. Alexandra had taught another Thinking Maths lesson, Pegboard Symmetry, with the teacher observing. Pegboard Symmetry is a lesson in which children explore number relations in the context of a reflection in the line $x = 5$, using pegboards to model the Cartesian co-ordinate system. The transformation is, then, represented algebraically. Hence, like the two fractions lessons, connections are made between algebraic and diagrammatic representations, although the context in this case is relationships between numbers. (See Chapter 7 for further detail on this lesson.)

After the lesson, Alexandra had had a long discussion with the Phase 2 teacher in which she had to justify the context of the co-ordinate system in a CAME lesson in response to the teacher asking: "What's difficult about co-ordinates?" A particular focus of Alexandra's response was to emphasise "counting the zero" in identifying the co-ordinates of a point. These issues had themselves been discussed during the reflection sessions at research seminars. Alexandra and the researcher then returned to her own school to discuss the visit.

Later the same day, at her own school, Alexandra initiated a discussion with another teacher about number lines and their mental images of numbers with: "You know, the way I picture numbers is in steps. Steps of 1 up to 20, then steps of 10 up to 100, then steps of 100." The researcher then suggested that this linked to her discussion with the Phase 2 teacher about the co-ordinate system. Alexandra responded as follows:

> But it's different isn't it. On the number line you're counting steps, but with the co-ordinates you're counting the zero, aren't you. So it's different. You're counting steps on the number line and you're counting points with the co-ordinates [Long pause] No, it isn't. They're the same thing really. I've just realised that. Counting the zero means you're counting the steps. ... Co-ordinates are like a 2D number line. (Fieldnotes, January 1999)

This appeared to be a very intense experience for Alexandra. The researcher's fieldnotes record it as follows: "It felt like ideas slotting into place there and then. … like an 'ah-ah' moment, where this suddenly occurred to Alexandra." Indeed, this was one of the few times that we observed any of the teachers experience a conscious and explicit revelation of this type.

Whilst she expressed this in a slightly clumsy way, the connection Alexandra made between number lines and the co-ordinate system is a very significant one, since, as she recognised here, Cartesian co-ordinates are formed by two perpendicular number lines. Although the immediate prompt for this was the researcher's comment, Alexandra's discussion with the Phase 2 teacher was, we suggest, more crucial. The Phase 2 teacher had confronted her with a problem for which she had no set response. Yet as a CAME tutor, she expected herself to be able to respond. However, in constructing her response, she drew on earlier research seminar discussions. This link between Cartesian co-ordinates and the number line had been made very explicitly during these seminars. Indeed, Nadir had earlier introduced a preparation activity in which points on a number line were reflected in the point $x = 5$ (Draft lesson materials, September 1998). Yet, despite these prolonged discussions in which she took an active part, it appeared that she had not fully grasped this connection until this reflection.

What appeared to be crucial to Alexandra making the connection for herself, was the necessity to justify the challenge of the lesson in her role as a tutor. In her role as a tutor, she had been forced to communicate articulately with the Phase 2 teacher, requiring her to justify the importance of co-ordinates. As a tutor, she was able to step outside and reflect on her identity as a learner and doer of mathematics. In addition, it seems likely that, as in Ursula's Share an Apple experience discussed above, the presence of the Phase 2 teacher enabled Alexandra to vividly remember and thus engage with her earlier experiences in the research seminars. Hence, as in the reflections discussed earlier, the distancing from herself as a teacher afforded by her identity as a tutor, was accompanied by a reminder of her own previous engagement and difficulties.

This first reflection itself prompted Alexandra to reflect further:

> Alexandra: Thinking about that, it was something no-one really made clear to me at school. You know that something like quadratic equations have a spatial meaning. No-one made the connections between the spatial and the number system.
>
> Researcher: A bit like Whisky and Water.

> Alexandra: Yes, like at school we just did fractions using fraction notation, you know using the procedure to multiply and add fractions. No-one ever made it clear that diagrams were just as mathematical. (Fieldnotes, January 1999)

Here Alexandra linked her earlier insight into the co-ordinate system to the grander notion of linking spatial and numerical, or algebraic, representations. Indeed, in invoking the iconic notion of quadratic equations, she makes the link to algebra very clear. School experiences of learning mathematics were very important to Alexandra. Indeed, she often referred to the absence of a connectionist approach in her own school mathematics. However, up until this point, her references to the notion of connections were largely general and unspecific. When prompted to make a connection with the Whisky and Water problem, she linked her diagrammatic solution very explicitly to the standard procedures for the multiplication of fractions. Her comment that diagrams are "just as mathematical" is very different to her earlier description of this as "just my little way of doing it." In contrast to her earlier pleasure at her diagrammatic solution being judged acceptable by 'experts', here she appeared to understand the mathematical validity of diagrammatic solutions for herself.

6.4.3. Further reflection

A further reflection took place at an interview in March 1999, when the researcher asked Alexandra to comment on an earlier and less developed version of the analysis in Section 6.4.2. above, which particularly focused on the mathematical validity of her diagrammatic solution. She responded as follows:

> I would say now, it's using one preferred learning style to achieve an outcome and it's partly about that, isn't it … I'm going off at a tangent now, but do you remember when we were talking about number lines and I was explaining my convoluted number line that I had in my head. It never occurred, I know this sounds really stupid and pathetic, but … I'd never thought about the fact that you'd have a number line in your head or [another teacher] wouldn't be able to visualise a number line in her head and … those shared experiences or lack of experiences depending your particular learning style. It's made … me think more … about … the intellectual processes that kids go through to get somewhere. (Interview, March 1999)

Although much less intense than the earlier reflection, this emphasises the shift she has made. Indeed, her link back to the discussion about images of number evokes the beginnings of her revelation. Moreover, she expressed this in terms of learning styles, an area in which she felt herself to be pedagogically strong. Thus, she embedded these new beliefs by interpreting them through her existing practices.

The 'new' mathematical knowledge that Alexandra demonstrated here is, in terms of specific concepts and skills, relatively small. She has not learnt to use diagrammatic solutions, since she could do these previously. Moreover, during the development of lessons, she demonstrated on many occasions an arithmetical proficiency that would suggest she would have been able to successfully perform the algebraic solution used by the academic researchers. However, in terms of her beliefs about school mathematics, the shift in her thinking is highly significant. In viewing her own invented and informal solution as just as valid as an algebraic solution, she appears to be developing a mathematizing orientation and her shift towards Povey's (1997) sense of author/ity in mathematics is considerable. Beliefs about how mathematical ideas can be represented or are judged valid are crucial to the teaching of mathematics (Yackel & Cobb, 1996). Indeed, as Wagner and Parker (1993), for example, note, algebra and geometry are often taught completely separately. Without an understanding of the validity of diagrams in mathematical argument, it is difficult to see how a teacher could promote a connected understanding for children. Moreover, she has developed an understanding of the importance of multiple perspectives: an appreciation of the "different facets of an idea and various approaches to a solution, as well as their advantages and disadvantages" (Ma, 1999, p. 122). She does this both in pedagogical terms, through the link with learning styles, and mathematically, through her recognition of the validity of mathematical diagrams. In addition, through the connection she makes to quadratic equations, she was continuing to develop her beliefs about longitudinal coherence.[6]

6.5. The case study: a summary

In the above case study we have examined reflection in four settings:

- lesson development, in the writing of teaching materials for Halving and Thirding
- teaching, in the context of Share and Apple with another teacher-researcher observing
- academic writing, in the context of the teachers' joint paper, and
- tutoring, where Alexandra made connections in the mathematics across two lessons.

In each of the settings the teachers themselves appeared to be catalysts in their own learning. We note the teachers' different roles and multiple identities here as lesson-developers, teachers, researchers and tutors. Of further note is the setting of these reflective events as integral to the teachers' practices as teacher-researchers. We emphasise again that reflection of this kind was rarely observed in formal reflection sessions.

7. DISCUSSION

In each of the above examples, we have described how distancing was enabled by these teachers' different and developed roles within the project. Key here was not simply the teachers' engagement with CAME, but the depth of this engagement. Here we refer to the teachers' development of wider, substantive, figurative identities that cut across their membership of particular communities: their identities as tutors, lesson-developers and researchers. Through these different roles, the teachers were able to step outside their identity as a teacher or as a learner of mathematics, for example, and thus, 'decenter' and distance themselves (Wood & Turner-Vorbeck, 1999).

In writing the joint paper, for example, Alexandra and Ursula were able to deliberate upon their earlier difficulties. In particular, they reflected on the earlier research team discussions, which Ursula remembered vividly as a "nightmare". Their own vivid memories of the discussions, together with the written materials as an aide-memoire, provided them with the mathematical language in which to frame this subsequent reflection. However, these discussions in themselves did not appear to be the setting for radical reflective transformations in the teachers' mathematical beliefs – rather the discussions supplied the material, in the form of mathematical artefacts and tools, for subsequent transformative reflection. A further critical factor was that Alexandra and Ursula were engaged in this activity as teacher-researchers. This distancing enabled them to reflect on their activity as teachers. Thus, the act of writing, and the consequent need to analyse their earlier work, provided both the possibility and the necessity to step outside their identities as teachers of primary mathematics.

Thus, the distancing afforded by their different identities was accompanied by vivid reminders of the teachers' own early engagement and attempts to make sense. This combination of distance and proximity enabled the teachers to "imagine" different practices, whilst at the same time "anchoring" these imagined futures in terms of their past experiences (Wenger, 1998, p. 217).

In all the examples that we have analysed, the teachers were faced with situations to which they had to respond. In relation to the writing of the lesson materials, for example, Ursula was forced to re-evaluate her earlier approach to teaching in order to move on and revise the materials. In the example of the academic writing, both Alexandra and Ursula had no choice but to reconcile and resolve their earlier difficulties with the mathematics, since an academic position required this. Holland et al.'s (1998) argument about the necessity of authorship is particularly appropriate here: "the world demands a response – authoring is not a choice." (p. 272). In each of these cases, the teachers reflected not because they chose to in isolation, but rather because circumstances required them to. We stress, however, that this is not a deterministic analysis with teachers solely governed by wider forces and structures. Indeed, in each of these cases the teachers had authoring and improvisational choices. In the case of the tutoring, for example, it was Alexandra herself who raised her own mental images of number thus enabling her to reflect on the Cartesian system.

A key feature in facilitating reflection was that these circumstances required the teachers to look across lessons and contexts and thus take a broader view. However, reflection, whilst characterised by sudden insights or clear-cut breaks with past practice, was dependent on the teachers drawing on existing practices in order to interpret and make sense of new practices.

In this analysis, we have emphasised the importance of the teachers' identities. However, we note that these identities were themselves fostered through Alexandra's and Ursula's participation in different but related communities of practice. In other words, it was the mathematical heterogeneity of their *zones of enactment* and of their own activity – and thus their multiple but inter-related identities – that enabled reflection and change. These two teachers were certainly active agents within their own change, but crucial were the opportunities afforded by these different perspectives to recognise and reconcile tensions in their beliefs about mathematics. This research suggests that teacher change then is not so much a matter of telling teachers to reflect nor simply of providing access to a wide variety of mathematical experiences, but rather one of nurturing teachers' rich participation in a variety of settings: as teachers, learners of mathematics, curriculum-makers, tutors and researchers.

We note that the professional development opportunities for the teacher-researchers within Primary CAME were very different from those available to most primary teachers. The Phase 1 programme was a deliberately intensive approach: central research team meetings were fortnightly over the first year, and Thinking Maths lessons were trialled on a weekly basis, usually in collaboration with other research team members. However, even with this extensive opportunity, only two of the six teachers changed considerably. The two teachers described here both had mathematically diverse and heterogeneous *zones of enactment*. In contrast, the remaining four teachers had less developed identities as tutors and lesson-developers. Whilst these four were present during rich deliberations of the kind described in this chapter, they had fewer resources with which to participate in such rich deliberations. This would suggest that it is not sufficient to be present in rich deliberations; rather teachers need to have resources to engage with these rich deliberations. We have noted, for example, how Alexandra and Ursula were able to draw on an existing way of working, their collaborative relationship, in order to engage with the process of academic writing. Hence, although Alexandra's and Ursula's *zones of enactment* were broad and heterogeneous in a general sense, it was more important, that viewed in terms of the *specific mathematical* practices of Primary CAME, their *zones of enactment* were broad and heterogeneous. Their *zones of enactment* afforded many opportunities for the development of a variety of experiences and perspectives. Moreover, their participation was in the context of communicating with and convincing other teachers about these mathematical practices.

To replicate such intense and extended experiences for the majority of primary teachers would be an extremely difficult and expensive task. Our analysis suggests that the crucial factor in these two teachers' professional change was the richness of their experiences. The problem, then, is how to offer less intensive experiences, which nevertheless provide an imperative, rather than simply an opportunity, to reflect. Our analysis would suggest a model of teacher education in which teachers not only engage critically with the mathematics curriculum as 'curriculum-makers' (Clarke, Clarke, & Sullivan, 1996), but which also places them in situations where they encourage other teachers to engage critically in similar ways.

8. AFFILIATIONS

Jeremy Hodgen is a Lecturer in Mathematics Education at the Department of Education and Professional Studies, King's College London.
David C. Johnson is an emeritus Professor at the Department of Education and Professional Studies, King's College London.

9. NOTES

1 We refer to this second group of teachers as Phase 2 teachers to distinguish them from the Phase 1 teachers whom we refer to as teachers or teacher-researchers.

2 These are pseudonyms.

3 Note that important findings for the research with the full group of the six teachers, in particular aspects of similarities and differences in their engagement with the innovation did emerge (see Hodgen, 2002). Discussion of these have not been included as this work goes beyond the aim of the chapter.

4 An example of an algebraic solution is as follows: If the glasses originally contain X whisky and Y water, the final mixtures in each glass are (1/2 + 1/2 × 1/2) or 3/4 X whisky + 1/2 Y water, and (1/2 - 1/2 × 1/2) or 1/4 X whisky + 1/2 Y water, respectively.

5 However, an algebraic solution is more general in that it covers cases where the original amounts of whisky and water are different.

6 We note that as part of the wider study, Alexandra's mathematical content knowledge in the area of multiplicative reasoning was investigated. It appeared that the significant changes to her beliefs about mathematics were not accompanied by similarly significant changes in her knowledge about specific concepts. In particular, her mathematical knowledge lacked connections. This issue is discussed further elsewhere (Hodgen, 2003).

10. REFERENCES

Adey, P. S., & Shayer, M. (2002). Cognitive Acceleration comes of age. In M. Shayer & P. S. Adey (Eds.), *Learning intelligence: Cognitive Acceleration across the curriculum*. Buckingham: Open University Press.

Adhami, M., Johnson, D., & Shayer, M. (1998). *Thinking Maths: The Programme for Accelerated Learning in Mathematics*. Oxford: Heinemann Educational Books.

Askew, M., Brown, M., Rhodes, V., Johnson, D. C., & Wiliam, D. (1997). *Effective teachers of numeracy* (Final report). London: King's College.

Belenky, M. F., Clinchy, B. M., Goldberger, N. R., & Tarule, J. M. (1986). *Women's ways of knowing: The development of self, voice and mind*. New York, NY: Basic Books.

Clarke, B., Clarke, D. M., & Sullivan, P. (1996). The mathematics teacher and curriculum development. In A. J. Bishop & K. Clements & C. Keitel & J. Kilpatrick & C. Laborde (Eds.), *International Handbook of Mathematics Education* (pp. 1207-1233). Dordrecht, Netherlands: Kluwer.

Clarke, D. M. (1994). Ten key principles from research for the professional development of mathematics teachers. In D. B. Aichele & A. F. Coxford (Eds.), *Professional development for teachers of mathematics: The 1994 Yearbook of the National Council of Teachers of Mathematics* (pp. 37-48). Reston, VA: National Council of Teachers of Mathematics.

Cobb, P., Boufi, A., McClain, K., & Whitenack, J. (1997). Reflective discourse and collective reflection. *Journal for Research in Mathematics Education, 28*(3), 258-277.

Cooney, T. J. (1994). Teacher education as an exercise in adaptation. In D. B. Aichele & A. F. Coxford (Eds.), *Professional development for teachers of mathematics: 1994 yearbook of the National Council of Teachers of Mathematics* (pp. 9-22). Reston, VA: National Council of Teachers of Mathematics.

Cooney, T. J., & Shealey, B. E. (1997). On understanding the structure of teachers' beliefs and their relationship to change. In E. Fennema & B. S. Nelson (Eds.), *Mathematics teachers in transition*. Mahwah, NJ: Lawrence Erlbaum Associates.

Department for Education and Employment. (1999). *The National Numeracy Strategy: Framework for teaching mathematics from Reception to Year 6*. London: Department for Education and Employment.

Goldsmith, L., & Schifter, D. (1997). Understanding teachers in transition: Characteristics of a model for developing teachers. In E. Fennema & B. S. Nelson (Eds.), *Mathematics teachers in transition*. Mahwah, NJ: Lawrence Erlbaum Associates.

Grimmett, P. (1988). The nature of reflection and Schön's conception in perspective. In P. Grimmett & G. Erickson (Eds.), *Reflection in teacher education*. New York, NY: Teachers College Press.

Grouws, D. A., & Schultz, K., A. (1996). Mathematics teacher education. In J. Sikula (Ed.), *Handbook of research on teacher education* (2nd ed., pp. 442-458). New York, NY: Macmillan.

Hodgen, J. (2002). Primary teachers and cognitive acceleration in mathematics education: Transforming teachers' mathematical knowledge through reflection. In M. Shayer & P. S. Adey (Eds.), *Learning intelligence: Cognitive acceleration across the curriculum from 5 to 15 years* (pp. 118-133). Buckingham: Open University Press.

Hodgen, J. (2003). *Primary teachers, identity and professional development in school mathematics.*

Holland, D., Lachicotte, W., Skinner, D., & Cain, C. (1998). *Identity and agency in cultural worlds.* Cambridge, MA: Harvard University Press.

Johnson, D., Adhami, M., Shayer, M., Hodgen, J., Hafeez, R., Dubben, S., Longfield, A., Harvey, L., Hindshaw, J. & Davidson M. (2003). *Primary Thinking Maths Lessons.* London: BEAM Education.

Kvale, S. (1996). *Interviews: An introduction to qualitative research interviewing.* London: Sage.

Lave, J. (1991). Situated Learning in Communities of Practice. In L. B. Resnick, J. M. Levine & S. D. Teasley (Eds.), *Perspectives on Socially Shared Cognition* (pp. 63-82). Washington, DC: American Psychological Association.

Ma, L. (1999). *Knowing and teaching elementary mathematics: Teachers' understanding of fundamental mathematics in China and the United States.* Mahwah, NJ: Lawrence Erlbaum Associates.

Polya, G. (1957). *How to solve it.* Garden City, NY: Doubleday Anchor Books.

Povey, H. (1997). Beginning mathematics teachers' ways of knowing: The link with working for emancipatory change. *Curriculum Studies, 5*(3), 329-342.

Povey, H., Burton, L., Angier, C., & Boylan, M. (1999). Learners as authors in the mathematics classroom. In L. Burton (Ed.), *Learning mathematics: From hierarchies to networks* (pp. 232-245). London: Falmer Press.

Schifter, D. (Ed.). (1996). *What's happening in math class? Volume 2: Reconstructing professional identities.* New York, NY: Teachers College Press.

Schön, D. A. (1983). *The reflective practitioner: How professionals think in action.* New York, NY: Basic Books.

Spillane, J. P. (1999). External reform initiatives and teachers' efforts to reconstruct their practice: the mediating role of teachers' zones of enactment. *Journal of Curriculum Studies, 31*(2), 143-175.

Strauss, A. L., & Corbin, J. (1998). *Basics of qualitative research: Techniques and procedures for developing grounded theory* (2nd ed.). London: Sage.

Wagner, S., & Parker, S. (1993). Advancing algebra. In P. S. Wilson (Ed.), *Research ideas for the classroom: High school mathematics* (pp. 119-139). New York, NY: Macmillan.

Waring, S. (2000). *Can you prove it? Developing concepts of proof in primary and secondary schools.* Leicester: Mathematical Association.

Wenger, E. (1998). *Communities of practice: Learning, meaning and identity.* Cambridge: Cambridge University Press.

Williams, E., & Shuard, H. (1994). *Primary Maths Today.* London: Longman.

Wood, T., & Turner-Vorbeck, T. (1999). Developing teaching of mathematics: Making connections in practice. In L. Burton (Ed.), *Learning mathematics: From hierarchies to networks.* London: Falmer Press.

Yackel, E., & Cobb, P. (1996). Sociomathematical norms, argumentation, and autonomy in mathematics. *Journal for Research in Mathematics Education, 27*(4), 458-477.

ALISON MILLETT, MARGARET BROWN AND MIKE ASKEW

CHAPTER 9

DRAWING CONCLUSIONS

Abstract. In this last chapter we reflect on our reporting of change from the different perspectives within the Leverhulme Numeracy Research Programme. We consider whether and where in the course of our research we have encountered "deep" change (Earl et al., 2000, p. 39) and how this might be characterised. We develop the notion of *zone of enactment* by identifying four key conditions necessary for realising the potential of *zones of enactment* through which professional development may be promoted. Finally we discuss the contribution of the model, developed in Chapter 1, for discussing change, at a descriptive, theoretical and predictive level, to our understanding of the complex process of professional development in primary mathematics.

1. INTRODUCTION

The timing of the Leverhulme Numeracy Research Programme from 1997 to 2002 has meant that, unintentionally and fortuitously, it spanned a major reform initiative in primary mathematics in England, the National Numeracy Strategy introduced in 1999. Thus, over at least four of the five years of the research, the major influence over changes in primary mathematics has been external to schools. Policy has been mediated both externally through training and the provision of materials, and internally through the work of the mathematics co-ordinator, amongst others, within the school *situation*. Chapters 7 and 8 reported on work that was an exception to this general situation, in that they provided an intervention of a completely different nature. However, the National Numeracy Strategy overtook even this research to some extent in its effect on the participation and involvement of teachers and teacher-researchers.

In Chapter 1 we presented a model for discussing change that, in our view, went some way towards providing a bridge between individual and organisational perspectives on change (Richardson & Placier, 2001). Accepting that characteristics of both individuals and the organisation in which they work are critical to the use

Alison Millett, Margaret Brown and Mike Askew (eds.), Primary Mathematics and the Developing Professional.

and provision of opportunities for professional development that might bring about change, we felt, however, that the interface between the two had not received sufficient attention. For this reason we adopted Spillane's notion of the *zone of enactment* (Spillane, 1999) as a helpful one in focusing our attention on this interface. We have therefore looked at the different types of professional development occurring during the span of our whole research programme in terms of the participants involved and the changes perceived and observed, with particular reference to the degree to which the *zones of enactment* of classroom teachers or teacher-researchers have been affected.

We address three main questions in this final chapter:

- firstly we look at the *nature of the change* that has been reported and observed and ask whether this can be categorised as "deep" change (Earl et al., 2000, p. 39). Drawing particularly on the work of Fullan (2001) and Spillane (1999) we look for change that has a) affected the core of teachers' classroom practice, and b) changed teachers' beliefs about mathematics and its teaching
- secondly we ask what are the *key conditions* that promote the realisation of rich *zones of enactment*
- thirdly we ask whether the discussion model we have chosen and explicated in Chapter 1 contributes to a greater understanding of the *complex process* of professional development. We consider the contribution of our research at a descriptive, theoretical and predictive level to the body of knowledge on professional development in primary mathematics.

2. IDENTIFYING DEEP CHANGE

Using national test results as an indicator of change since the introduction of the National Numeracy Strategy in September 1999, we can see that percentages of pupils attaining Level 4 at age 11 have increased from 69% in June 1999 to 73% in June 2002, a rise of 4%. Earl et al. (2001), in the second report of their evaluation of the National Literacy and Numeracy Strategies, expressed the view that a good part of the initial gains in improvement scores might be:

> ... a function of changes in teaching practice that are effective and relatively easy to implement, although they may not get at the deeper understandings about teaching and learning. (p. 81)

They exemplified such changes as spending increased time on mathematics, teaching to objectives, greater consistency in lessons and a focus on targets.

Data from the Leverhulme Numeracy Research Programme compared the test results of pupils aged 8-9 years in June 1998 with those of 8-9 year old pupils in

June 2002 and found a gain of about 3%, which is the equivalent of just over 2 months' development, as shown in Table 9.1. This difference is highly statistically significant, although perhaps disappointingly small to policy-makers committed to large rises in national levels of attainment.

Table 9.1. Mean student score on identical Year 4 tests before and after the National Numeracy Strategy (Data from the same 35 schools with n>1200 pupils on each occasion)

Year	*Mean student score in Year 4 tests*
June 1998	61.6%
June 2002	64.8%
Rise	3.2%
Equivalent	2.4 mths

The picture nationally, then, is not one of change in pupil attainment in primary mathematics of great magnitude. As we have seen in Chapters 2 and 5, change perceived by teachers and observed during the research relates primarily but not entirely to structural change – greater time spent on mathematics; three parts to the lesson; greater emphasis on mental mathematics; more direct teaching; objectives-led planning; changes in structure and content of the curriculum. Other perceived changes relate to more affective issues of enthusiasm and confidence in the approaches of both pupils and teachers, and to an increased range of approaches (identified as strategies, methods, representations) to the understanding of mathematical ideas. Within these identified changes, can we, in turn, identify deep change?

2.1. Change to the core of teachers' practice

For Spillane (1999), change to the core of instructional practice meant a shift in emphasis from procedural knowledge, centring on computational procedures, to principled knowledge involving the use of key mathematical ideas and concepts in the solving of mathematical problems.

Teachers in the Core Project, *Tracking Numeracy*, and the two case-study projects *Whole School Action on Numeracy* and *Teachers' Knowledge, Conceptions and Practices,* have made frequent mention of the increased range of strategies of which they are now aware. This relates not only to strategies that they have learnt from the Framework or from their in-service training and which they now specifically introduce in their lessons, it also relates to an increased ability to recognise and understand the importance of methods suggested by the pupils. Pupils and teachers are regarded as having different preferences about which strategies/representations to use. However, there is little evidence of a growing understanding that some methods are better than others for the specific mathematical calculations involved, which would indicate a move towards principled knowledge. In many lessons observed, all methods were accepted as being equally good.

Ball and Bass (2000) provide two main reasons supporting the argument that subject matter understanding is fundamental to teaching. Firstly, they argue that there is a close relationship between ideas and their representation: "How an idea is represented is part of the idea, not merely its conveyance" (p. 85). The example of Sam's description of her use of repeated addition and arrays (see Chapter 5, Section 3.5. and discussed at greater length in Volume 2 of this series) illustrates a lack of understanding on this point. The Five-day course discussed in Chapter 5 did not, in our opinion, provide sufficient guidance on the evaluation of the efficiency of different methods for different mathematical situations.

Detailed case-study data from observations supports our conclusion about change being limited rather than fundamental. The two teachers described in Chapter 6 were found to have made small shifts in practice, but not to have changed deeply held beliefs about the role of the teacher and the nature of pupil learning. On the other hand, the two teacher-researchers that form the focus of Chapter 8, did undergo changes in beliefs that impacted on practice.

2.2. *Change to beliefs about mathematics and its teaching*

From the work reported in this volume, we can identify two aspects of beliefs about mathematics and its teaching that might be involved in deep change – beliefs about self-efficacy and beliefs about pupils.

Teachers commenting on changes in numeracy and in literacy over the span of the Leverhulme Numeracy Research Programme have in general been more positive about numeracy reforms than literacy reforms. The overwhelming majority of teachers interviewed in our research were in favour of the National Numeracy Strategy and described increased confidence in teaching mathematics. There was a feeling that the National Numeracy Strategy had stabilised practice, whereas the national literacy initiative had destabilised practice. Teachers felt that their past good practice in language and literacy was being disparaged, whereas in mathematics they were more willing to admit to failures in their own practice that the National Numeracy Strategy went a long way towards addressing. This may in part be explained by teachers' qualifications.

Primary teachers' qualifications at degree level are more likely to be in the arts or humanities than in mathematics or science (Wragg & Carré, 1989), and our own recent data supports this. When questioned about how competent they felt to teach national curriculum subjects with their existing subject knowledge in 1989, teachers expressed greater competence with English than with mathematics (Wragg & Carre, 1989). A recent survey of Year 6 teachers (of pupils aged 10-11 years) (Ward, 2002) indicates that, for the first time, confidence in teaching mathematics was higher than confidence in teaching language and literacy, with 85% saying that they were at ease with teaching the subject, compared with 80% for English.

This may in part be due to perceptions of increased confidence in subject knowledge. Jodie (see Chapter 2, Section 3.2.) was one of several teachers who described using more and different mental methods in her own life, feeling more confident in her mental mathematics than she had before. The Year 3 teacher quoted in Chapter 2, Section 3.3., described how explaining new ways of working to pupils was helping her own understanding of aspects of mathematics she had never understood in the past.

Teachers not only expressed increased feelings of confidence about their own mathematics teaching, they also attributed increased confidence to their pupils, mentioning occasions on which pupils had shown greater willingness to try new things and had not been afraid to make mistakes. Teachers claimed a raised awareness of the need to listen carefully to children's ideas. Ball and Bass (2000) suggest that if pupils' methods are to be valued, discussed and built upon, then subject understanding "is essential in listening flexibly to others and hearing what they are saying or where they might be heading" (p. 88). However, our observations indicated that listening carefully could be little more than letting pupils say their piece but not making links to the effectiveness of the methods they were describing, as we saw in Chapter 6.

Whilst not identifying these changes in beliefs about self-efficacy and pupil confidence as indicators of deep change, we nevertheless feel that they are of importance in themselves as providing a stronger foundation upon which to engage with more fundamental change.

2.3. Examples of deep change

We would suggest that only those teachers involved in P-CAME (see Chapters 7 and 8) can be said to exemplify deep change, and then not all of these. In Chapter 8, qualitatively significant change is reported in two teacher-researchers' beliefs about school mathematics. In other areas of the Leverhulme Numeracy Research

Programme's research, although teachers were making changes in some aspects of their teaching, our observations over five years have identified changes that are relatively superficial, with teachers emphasising different skills, using different apparatus and curriculum materials and using more whole-class teaching. There is little evidence of the quality of teachers' mediation of ideas through interactions with pupils being at a deeper level.

3. REALISING RICH ZONES OF ENACTMENT

Looking back over the different constituent projects of the Leverhulme Numeracy Research Programme reported on in this volume, we now identify here four key conditions necessary for the realisation of rich *zones of enactment* through which professional development may be promoted. We indicate where these resonate with the experience of other researchers.

- time
- talk
- expertise
- motivation.

3.1. Time

Time to engage in discussion and reflection and to permit follow-up and support for further learning has been noted by many writers as an essential part of successful professional development (eg. Clarke, 1994; Hawley & Valli, 1999).

We note two specific ways in which time has been seen to critically affect teachers' ability to make changes in their practice. The first of these relates to time as a resource to enable a professional to fulfil the expectations of her role. In Chapter 2 we saw how time resourcing by the school to enable the mathematics co-ordinator to carry out her role (generally as prioritised by the headteacher) was a key construct in her ability to act as an agent of change. Lack of time out of her own classroom (non-contact time) was associated with lack of knowledge of other teachers' practices and reduced opportunities for subject consultancy and peer coaching of an ongoing nature. As we saw in the case of *Wolverton* school, this time resource was critical in the development of a learning community around mathematics. 'Personal' time (Campbell 1985) was also a factor in our examples of teachers learning alone through self-initiated study of National Numeracy Strategy materials (Chapter 4).

The second view of time as a key constituent of professional development relates to sustained, iterative provision. Not only was ongoing resourcing necessary for the co-ordinator to provide opportunities for professional development for a group of colleagues, it was also critical for the individual teacher-researchers involved in P-CAME. The time resourcing provided by P-CAME enabled the participants to work within an iterative framework of trial, reflection, discussion, modification and retrial that proved successful for Alexandra and Ursula (Chapters 7/8). Ongoing provision of time was conspicuously lacking for three schools in the cascade model of training discussed in Chapter 5.

3.2. Talk

In Chapters 2 and 3 we have given examples of co-ordinators using in-service training sessions as opportunities to encourage talk between teachers, and creating their own informal opportunities for talk with one or more of their colleagues.

In the P-CAME research (Chapters 7 and 8), we have examples of the detail of talk that formed part of the professional development aspect of that intervention, with a focus similar to that suggested by Lampert and Ball (1999):

> ... on the idea of a group of teachers using a common set of materials drawn directly from practice – the same classroom and the same set of students – to pursue different questions important to learning about teaching and learning. (p. 41)

This was facilitated in P-CAME by teachers observing each others' lessons based round the same materials and using these observations as a focus for reflection and discussion. Other examples from the literature include Japanese teachers' discussion and observation of lessons as part of their planning of new activities (Stigler & Stevenson, 1991).

In Chapter 4, we saw that teachers in a small set of schools were using opportunities centred round planning to discuss the strengths and weaknesses of curriculum materials. Ball and Cohen (1996) draw attention to the value of talking about new curriculum materials, regarding them as underused as a source of professional development.

> Even when the professional development that accompanies new texts is thoughtful, it is seen as an auxiliary support needed to ensure quality implementation, not as a site for professional development. (p. 8)

Curriculum materials, they feel, have "reach" (p. 6) in the system, being already well positioned to influence teachers' work.

Other research has focused on practice-related talk about pupils' understanding (e.g. Franke, Carpenter, Levi, & Fennema, 2001; Rowley, Gervasconi, Clarke,

Horne, & McDonough, 2001) as a source of professional development, in both cases pointing to the need to go beyond the individual teacher to involvement with the wider *professional community* and externally provided support.

3.3. Expertise

We are not alone in realising the importance of having expertise readily available, both from inside and outside the school:

> ... all successful schools and districts are proactively plugged into an external network of resources, professional development, and other forms of assistance. (Fullan, 2001, p. 195)

Some headteachers in our research facilitated both the use of external support and opportunities for internal peer coaching and collaborative working (Chapter 3); classroom teachers commented on the value of the subject consultancy they experienced from co-ordinators (Chapters 2 and 3); mathematics co-ordinators valued the support and expertise they received from numeracy consultants external to the school (Chapters 2 and 5). For the teachers and teacher-researchers in P-CAME, expertise from academic researchers in mathematics education was available as an ongoing resource, enabling reflection around theory as well as practice, and, as we have seen, the extended nature of this professional development enabled strong personal relationships to be built up that facilitated the giving and sharing of expertise (Chapters 7 and 8).

3.4. Motivation

The motivation to engage with changes in practice was a key factor in Spillane's research (1999) although this area was less well developed than others in his paper. We have seen that motivation to improve practice drove some classroom teachers to seek out subject consultancy from co-ordinators (Chapter 2); co-ordinators were motivated in some cases to request support from external numeracy consultants; motivation to succeed in a new career opportunity led one teacher to engage with a course of in-service training and derive benefits from it for her own teaching as well as for advising colleagues (Chapters 5 and 6); and motivation stemming from poor self-concept as a teacher and learner of mathematics led some teachers to devote personal time to the study of mathematics curriculum materials (Chapter 4). Motivation derived from internal feelings of interest in mathematics, from fear of mathematics, from a desire to improve the teaching of mathematics, was only part of the picture. The other side of the picture was efforts to promote motivation arising from sources external to the individual, such as pressure or encouragement from colleagues, changes in responsibilities and reforms emanating from external professionals or policy-makers. Differences in sources of motivation were found to be a critical factor in whether the P-CAME teacher-researchers underwent qualitatively significant change – in the case of two of them, mathematical concerns played a key role; other teachers' motivation was more closely focused on management issues to do with career development and did not result in deep change.

We conclude that sources of motivation may determine whether deep or superficial change occurs; thus working at the level of improving the nature of mathematical interactions in the classroom (P-CAME) may lead to more teacher motivation (and hence deeper change) than arises from working at the level of delivering the implementation of a reform through a co-ordinator. However, a well-supported and resourced co-ordinator may be able to move beyond the implementation of reform to provide a source of motivation closer to the improvement of the mathematical interactions.

3.5. The zone of enactment – fresh insights

We feel that we can most productively expand on the notion of *zone of enactment* by providing insights in two key areas – relating to the individual and to the organisation.

The first insight that informs the notion of *zone of enactment* is that of teachers' identities. Those teachers who underwent substantial change drew on multiple but inter-related identities, fostered through their participation in a variety of settings – as teachers, learners of mathematics, curriculum-makers, tutors and researchers. It was the heterogeneity of their *zones of enactment* that enabled reflection and change. The co-ordinators who reported on changes in their own classroom practice (Chapter 2) may well have been benefiting from their dual identities as classroom teachers and as subject consultants; those who intuitively encouraged others to participate in tutoring activities may have made this heterogeneity available to a wider group of teachers.

The second key insight lies within the organisation, in the *situation*, and the importance of the construct of *balance* in a school (see Chapters 2 and 3) as an essential facilitator of professional development. Those attempting to act as agents of change in mathematics may have their efforts thwarted by school situations where there is a failure to recognise the conditions necessary for the creation of learning communities that make provision for, and expect, ongoing learning for all their members.

4. A MODEL FOR PROFESSIONAL DEVELOPMENT

Our model for discussing change focuses on the interface between individual teachers and their schools, identified by Richardson & Placier (2001) as one of three areas of research that "would provide important knowledge in our quest for a better understanding of teacher change" (p. 939). We have used our model in a descriptive way to illustrate the difficulties faced by primary teachers in England over the past five years in coming to terms with a nationally imposed reform, in conditions not conducive to the realisation of rich *zones of enactment*.

Our model also serves as a theoretical structure for identifying the essential constituents of effective professional development. A holistic view of the individual situated within a *professional community* and influenced by a range of factors external to this community should dictate that professional development opportunities are designed with this framework in mind, providing a congruence of effort from all components.

In predictive terms, we can use our model to identify situations where professional development will be slow and uncertain, unless changes are made to its design and provision, particularly in a situation where there is increased pressure on co-ordinators to spend what time they have on setting targets and analysing test results, rather than engaging in peer coaching or subject consultancy. We have seen how difficult the promotion of deep change has been, even when more superficial change has been established. How much more so, then, if ongoing opportunities for teachers, co-ordinators, consultants, headteachers to talk, reflect, try out new ideas and talk again are not provided. Another example relates to future attempts to use the cascade model of training to bring about change; neither time, nor expertise are adequately provided in this model.

We can also use our insights relating to the *zone of enactment* to predict that the most effective form of professional development will come about through the provision of opportunities for teachers to take on different roles, as the recipients of encouragement and tutoring from others in the *professional community*, and also as curriculum-makers, researchers and tutors of others. The spreading of the co-ordination responsibility to teams rather than resting it with individuals might thus be a course of action with great potential benefits. Interaction with other groups outside the *professional community*, such as university researchers or local working groups of interested colleagues involved, perhaps, in the writing of curriculum materials, might also be effective in providing a breadth of such roles through which to engage with change.

5. REFERENCES

Ball, D. L., & Bass, H. (2000). Interweaving content and pedagogy in teaching and learning to teach: knowing and using mathematics. In J. Boaler (Ed.), *Multiple perspectives on mathematics teaching and learning*. Westport, CT: Ablex Publishing.

Ball, D. L., & Cohen, D. K. (1996). Reform by the Book: What is – or might be – the Role of Curriculum Materials in Teacher Learning and Instructional Reform? *Educational Researcher, 25*(9), 6-8, 14.

Campbell, R. J. (1985). *Developing the primary school curriculum*. London: Holt, Rinehart & Winston.

Clarke, D. (1994). Ten Key Principles from Research for the Professional Development of Mathematics Teachers. In D. B. Aichele & A. F. Coxford (Eds.), *Professional Development for Teachers of Mathematics 1994 Yearbook* . Reston, VA: National Council of Teachers of Mathematics.

Earl, L., Fullan, M., Leithwood, K., Watson, N., with Jantzi, D., Levin, B., & Torrance, N. (2000). *Watching and Learning. OISE/UT Evaluation of the implementation of the National Literacy and Numeracy Strategies. First annual report.* Toronto: Ontario Institute for Studies in Education, University of Toronto.

Earl, L., Levin, B., Leithwood, K., Fullan, M., & Watson, N. (2001). *Watching & Learning 2: OISE/UT Evaluation of the Implementation of the National Literacy and Numeracy Strategies. Second Annual Report.* Toronto: Ontario Institute for Studies in Education, University of Toronto.

Franke, M. L., Carpenter, T. P., Levi, L., & Fennema, E. (2001). Capturing Teachers' Generative Change: A Follow-up Study of Professional Development in Mathematics. *American Educational Research Journal, 38*(3), 653-689.

Fullan, M. (2001). *The new meaning of educational change. 3rd Edition.* New York, NY: Teachers College Press.

Hawley, W. D., & Valli, L. (1999). The Essentials of Effective Professional Development: a new consensus. In L. Darling-Hammond & G. Sykes (Eds.), *Teaching as the Learning Profession. Handbook of policy and practice* (pp. 127-150). San Francisco, CA: Jossey-Bass.

Joyce, B., & Showers, B. (1995). *Student achievement through staff development.* New York, NY: Longmans.

Lampert, M., & Ball, D. L. (1999). Aligning Teacher Education with Contemporary K-12 Reform Visions. In L. Darling-Hammond & G. Sykes (Eds.), *Teaching as the Learning Profession. Handbook of Policy and Practice* (pp. 33-53). San Francisco, CA: Jossey-Bass.

Richardson, V., & Placier, P. (2001). Teacher Change. In V. Richardson (Ed.), *Handbook of Research on Teaching. Fourth Edition* (pp. 905-947). Washington DC: American Educational Research Association.

Rowley, G., Gervasconi, A., Clarke, D., Horne, M., & McDonough, A. (2001, 13-15 September 2001). *The Early Numeracy Research Project: Using interviews to monitor growth in mathematics.* Paper presented at the British Educational Research Association, Leeds, UK.

Spillane, J. P. (1999). External reform initiatives and teachers' efforts to reconstruct their practice: the mediating role of teachers' zones of enactment. *Journal of Curriculum Studies, 31*(2), 143-175.

Stigler, J. W., & Stevenson, H. W. (1991). How Asian teachers polish each lesson to perfection. *American Educator, 15*, 12-47.

Ward, H. (2002, 1 November). TES Primary Poll. *Times Educational Supplement*, pp. 4-5.

Wragg, E., Bennett, N., & Carre, C. (1989). Primary Teachers and the National Curriculum. *Research Papers in Education. 4* (4), 17-37.

ANNEX 1

CORE PROJECT: TRACKING NUMERACY

The aim of the core project of the Leverhulme Numeracy Research Programme was to obtain large-scale longitudinal value-added data on numeracy to:

- inform knowledge about the progression in pupils' learning of numeracy throughout the primary years, and
- assess relative contributions to gains in numeracy of the different factors to be investigated in the programme.

Our objectives were:

- to assess longitudinally the numeracy attainment of two overlapping cohorts of primary pupils so that a picture of year-on-year achievement in a variety of schools was obtained from Year 1 (pupils aged 5-6 years) up to Year 6 (pupils aged 10-11 years), with some limited extension both into Reception (pupils aged 4-5 years) and into Year 7 (pupils aged 11-12 years)
- to match the year-on-year value-added attainment data against data relating to *classroom practice*, including, but not limited to, teaching method, teaching organisation, and curriculum in order to investigate the influence of these factors on attainment
- to match the year-on-year value-added attainment data against data relating to each *teacher*, in particular to teachers' subject knowledge and expectations, as well as other factors, in order to investigate the influence of these factors on attainment
- to match the year-on-year value-added attainment data against data relating to each *school,* in particular to data on the existence of clear policies and agreed practices, as well as other factors (such as the experience of the headteacher and the mathematics co-ordinator), in order to investigate the effect of these factors on attainment
- to match the year-on-year value-added attainment data against data relating to individual *pupils* (in particular social class), in order to investigate the effects of these factors on attainment at different stages of schooling

- to generate hypotheses from large-scale quantitative analyses which can be further explored in the Focus Projects, in particular in Focus Project: *Case Studies of Pupil Progress*, and in addition to provide data which will allow hypotheses which arise from case study samples in the focused projects to be validated on a larger scale.

No longitudinal data is available in the United Kingdom to indicate the ways, or the rate, at which primary pupils develop over time the understanding and skills which together constitute competence in numeracy, nor of how this is related to a broader range of school and other factors.

The long-term nature of the Leverhulme Numeracy Research Programme gave an opportunity to track the progress of pupils in numeracy over five years. By selecting two overlapping cohorts, the first starting with Reception (pupils aged 4-5 years) and the second with Year 4 (pupils aged 8-9 years), this covered the full primary age range and allowed one group to be followed through to Year 7 in secondary school as shown in Table A.1.1. This provided for the first time a unique set of longitudinal year-on-year data on a large primary sample.

Table A.1.1. The two cohorts

	1997-1998	*1998-1999*	*1999-2000*	*2000-2001*	*2001-2002*
Cohort 1	Reception	Y1	Y2	Y3	Y4
Cohort 2	Y4	Y5	Y6	Y7	

The fact that Year 4 data was available for both the second cohort in 1997/98 and from the first in 2001/02 has also made it possible to evaluate the effect of the National Numeracy Strategy which was implemented across all years in all primary schools in the UK during 1999/2000.

By selecting a sample which was relatively large and covered schools drawing pupils from a variety of different social backgrounds, with differences in teaching style and organisation, it was possible to determine the effects of the different factors listed below (and the interactions between them), together with others which were later suggested.

Classroom practice factors

(a) teaching methods

(b) teaching organisation

(c) curriculum

Teacher factors

(d) teacher subject knowledge

(e) low teacher expectations

School factors

(f) school leadership

Social context factors

(g) home contexts

One important feature of the relatively long time-span of the project was that it enabled hypotheses which arose from the analysis of early rounds of data to be investigated further.

The 40 schools that took part in the longitudinal study were chosen from four Local Education Authorities, and the 10 schools in each of them included inner city schools in deprived areas, racially mixed schools and schools in pleasant suburbs with expensive housing. Two authorities were from the London area; the other two authorities were both large counties, one in the South East of England and the second in the North of England. In the North of England authority, some of the schools were in an urban area with a large population of South Asian origin. Some schools in one of the Local Education Authorities in the sample had been involved in the National Numeracy Project (See Introduction).

School sample

Within each of these Local Education Authorities the selection of 10 schools was made with the assistance of the professional advisory staff and the available performance and intake data. In this programme the focus was on the effect of particular factors and therefore a quota rather than a representative or random sample was appropriate. The aim within each Local Education Authority was to choose 10 primary schools so that they included:

- relative to the socio-economic circumstances of the population in each Local Education Authority, at least two schools from relatively advantaged, two from intermediate and two from less advantaged catchment areas
- at least two church schools
- relative to the balance within the Local Education Authority, at least two large and two small schools
- at least three schools which were identified (according to available value-added data) to be effective in teaching numeracy, together with at least two which were identified as average and two weak
- in addition to primary schools (ages 4-11 years), some linked infant (ages 4-7 years) and junior (ages 7-11 years) schools where these were a common form of school organisation within a Local Education Authority.

At the point at which the older cohort of pupils in the study transferred into secondary schools at age 11, there was no attempt to trace the progress of all the pupils. However, at least one secondary school in each Local Education Authority which received a substantial number of the pupils in the cohort, including some from different primary schools, was selected and agreed to collaborate in the study, providing some information on the achievements of the pupils at the end of the first year of secondary school. In one of the two Local Education Authorities in London, two further secondary schools were also included, and in the other one additional school was selected, making a total of seven secondary schools in the study, with over 180 pupils. It was believed that these seven schools constituted a reasonable range of types of secondary school.

37 out of the original 40 primary schools (seven of which were linked infant and junior schools) remained as participants in the project over this five year period. There was less attrition than expected, especially given the pressures on primary schools and teachers over the years 1997-2002 which included the introduction of both the National Literacy and National Numeracy Strategies (see Introduction). This meant that with students joining and leaving schools over the five years, there were more than 2000 pupils on the database for each of the two cohorts. However, in any one year, at least 1300 pupils in over 70 classes had taken part for each of the two cohorts.

Data Sources and Instruments

Pupil Data: Numeracy assessment. To enable progress in each year to be measured, pupils in the two cohorts were tested at the beginning and end of each year between Year 1 and Year 6, using a class test of numeracy. There was no formal testing in the Reception year, although results of baseline and other tests were collected.

Children were tested towards the beginning and end of each school year, within a designated two weeks towards the end of October and the beginning of June. A sequence of tests, one for each year group, was used which were derived from instruments developed from earlier research by members of the team (Hart (Ed.), 1981; Denvir & Brown, 1986; Askew et al., 1997). The items had in almost all cases been designed for one-on-one diagnostic interviews and based on reviews of related research; Denvir and Bibby (2002) have updated in a format usable by teachers and teaching assistants a diagnostic interview for low attaining primary pupils from which many of the items were drawn. These items were later adapted for whole class settings, and were thus extensively trialled in both formats. The reliability (using Cronbach's alpha) was found to be very high (of the order of 0.94). Denvir and Brown (1987) had earlier compared pupils performance on interviews and class tests using many of the items. Items were designed to assess conceptual understanding and cognitively based skills. They include contextual as well as purely numerical items. Most items required short open responses but a small number were in multiple choice format. Many items were linked with others assessing similar concepts/skills but often of varying facility. The same test was used at the start and end of the year, and was orally administered by teachers from a provided script with pupils answering in specially designed booklets. The emphasis was on mental rather than written processes. For some cases teachers were asked to display a poster for a fixed number of seconds. The number of items in the test varied from 41 in Year 1 to over 80 in older age groups.

The tests were designed both to contain a large number of common items from one year to the next (including three items which were assessed in each year from Year 1 to Year 6), and to have the same uniform distribution of facility within each test. This means that equal numerical gains were made by children at different attainment levels.

The inclusion of common items has allowed the facilities across several years of the primary school to be plotted for each item and compared for the linked sets of items. An index of difficulty has been calculated for each item which indicates the estimated age at which 50% of the cohort can succeed on it. The Rasch procedure allows children to then be assigned a 'numeracy age' for each sitting of the test.

The test was given orally by the teacher to avoid reading problems and to enable a time limit on some questions to focus on mental numeracy skills and prevent pupils from using ineffective methods. The test had been successful in differentiating within year groups and was clearly appropriate in the level of attainment it tested.

A problem solving task was developed and trialled and was administered to Year 4 pupils in the first year. However as it was found in the assessment that pupils' strategies were heavily influenced by their teachers, it was decided that the data was not sufficiently valid or reliable to justify the considerable marking costs in later years.

The Year 6 test was repeated at the end of Year 7 in the seven secondary schools included in the study.

Pupil Data: Other sources. In addition to numeracy assessment, we collected additional data on pupils in the sample. This included:

- national test data on mathematics and English for Year 2 pupils (aged 6-7 years) and Year 6 pupils (aged 10-11 years); in some cases results of nationally set tests were also available in Year 4
- reading age data where available
- baseline data where available (for pupils aged 4-5 years at the start of Reception class
- social class data (using post-code analysis as a proxy)
- gender and ethnicity data
- any relevant data from the seven secondary schools e.g. mathematics sets allocated.

These data assisted especially with the exploration of factors relating to pupil social background.

School data: interviews and school statistics. We visited each school in each year of the project, for a minimum of one day, and more than this in the case of larger schools. In the first year we interviewed the headteacher and the mathematics co-ordinator, collected relevant school data on the size and characteristics on the school population and relevant documents including curriculum policies for mathematics. This gave some information on factor (f) school leadership, in particular, clear policies and agreed practices for numeracy teaching. It also provided information on factor (e) of low teacher expectation. In later years brief interviews were held with the head teacher and co-ordinator to update information. In the final year there were again longer interviews with the headteacher and co-ordinator. Only one year-group was involved in primary schools for the fourth and fifth year of the study (Cohort 2 had by that time moved into secondary school). In the fourth year, visits were made to each of the three selected secondary schools in each Local Education Authority, to interview the head of the mathematics department.

Classroom data: observations. Lessons were observed in the classrooms of the pupils in each year of the two cohorts, starting with Reception and Year 4 classes in 1997/98. Aspects of classroom organisation, resources and teaching methods, and also brief conversations with pupils were recorded in fieldnotes. In the fourth year, visits were made to each of the seven secondary schools to observe one or more Year 7 lessons.

Teacher data: questionnaires. Over the five years, each teacher of a class in either cohort was also asked to provide brief data relating to several other factors under investigation, and where possible, this was triangulated with data from field observations. These data included:

- range of teaching methods
- classroom organisation

- curriculum materials
- assessment and recording methods
- own mathematical experience, qualifications and training (initial and in-service).

As well as information on the above factors this also included brief items on teachers' beliefs and priorities in teaching numeracy. There was about an 80% return each year on teacher questionnaires.

Teacher data: interviews. Teachers of the classes in both cohorts, starting with Reception and Year 4 in 1997/98, were interviewed each year. Interviews were semi-structured and were tape-recorded and transcribed. Protocols for teacher interviews were modified each year to take account of national developments, like the National Numeracy Strategy and targetting.

Data analysis

Tests were marked centrally by students onto optical mark reading forms which were scanned into the computer. All questions were marked simply as correct, wrong or omitted, using a marking schedule. Various checks were made on the reliability of this process. Data analyses were undertaken using Excel and Datadesk.

The responses to the closed questionnaire items were also coded for optical mark reading, and joined with manually keyed in open questionnaire items and the other data, in order to provide the most comprehensive possible dataset.

Transcripts of interviews and other qualitative data were also stored in a database. Classroom observations were in the form of fieldnotes taken either longhand or entered into an electronic notebook.

Several methods of analysing both quantitative and qualitative data were developed. Where relevant these are described in the main text.

Askew, M., Brown, M., Rhodes, V., Johnson, D., & Wiliam, D. (1997). *Effective Teachers of Numeracy. Final Report.* London: King's College.

Denvir, B. ,& Brown, M. (1986). Understanding of number concepts in low attaining 7-9 year olds: parts 1 & 2. *Educational Studies in Mathematics. 17*, 15-36 and 143-164.

Denvir, B., & Brown, M. (1987). The feasibility of class-administered diagnostic assessment in primary mathematics. *Educational Research. 29(2)*, 95-107.

Denvir, H., & Bibby, T. (2002). *Diagnostic Interviews in Number Sense.* London: BEAM Publications.

Hart, K. (Ed.) (1981). *Children's Understanding of Mathematics: 11-16.* London: John Murray.

ANNEX 2

FOCUS PROJECT: TEACHERS' KNOWLEDGE, CONCEPTIONS AND PRACTICES

This project was part of the Leverhulme Numeracy Research Programme funded by The Leverhulme Trust at the School of Education, King's College London. The aim of this project was to investigate the relationship between teachers' beliefs about, knowledge of and practices in teaching numeracy and whether changes in beliefs, knowledge and/or practices raise standards. Our objectives were:

- To understand and document the effect of the National Numeracy Strategy's programme of five day training in terms of changes in teachers' beliefs, knowledge and practices in teaching numeracy
- To examine the impact of any changes in beliefs, knowledge and practice upon pupil attainment
- To further develop understanding of which aspects of teachers' beliefs, knowledge and practices are most salient in promoting effective teaching of numeracy and raising standards.

The research tracked a group of 12 teachers and their pupils over a two year period (spanning three school years) in order to identify changes over time in teacher beliefs and practices, pupil attainment and possible reasons for changes occurring.

The schools were selected from the cohort of schools identified by the Local Education Authorities as taking part in the National Numeracy Strategy Five-day training that took place in the second year of the implementation of the Numeracy Strategy (2000/01). Hence the schools fell outside the set of schools identified as requiring intensive support within the first year of implementation of the National Numeracy Strategy but nevertheless had been identified as being capable of improving their standards (as measured by national test results) in mathematics.

Within that overall cohort of schools, the four schools, two in the north of England and two in the south, were selected to represent a range in terms of pupil intake (see Table A.2.1). In each of the four schools, we opted to work with the two teachers who would be undergoing the National Numeracy Strategy Five-day training in 2000-2001, and a third teacher within the school who would not be directly engaged in the training. Three of this latter group of four teachers subsequently undertook the training the following year (see Table A.2.2).

Table A.2.1. Details of the schools involved in the research 1999-2002

School	*Characteristics of school*
School 1	One form entry, outer urban, high level unemployment and social deprivation, 10% pupil mobility, FSM 45%, EAL 0%
School 2	One and a half form entry, outer urban, varied socio-economic conditions, many parents on temporary contracts or from army base, 33% pupils have experience of several schools, FSM 8%, EAL 14%
School 3	One and a half form entry, outer urban, mainly social housing, below average socio-economic background, FSM 41%, EAL 22%
School 4	One form entry, inner urban, high level social deprivation, 25% pupil mobility at Key Stage 2 (ages 7-11), FSM 63%, EAL 40%

Note. FSM denotes free school meals; EAL denotes English as an additional language

Table A.2.2 Details of the teachers involved in the research 1999-2002

Teacher	*Teachers' mathematics qualification and teaching experience*
Sam	GCSE mathematics. Experience: 2 years, pupils aged 7-11 years
Chris	GCE 'O' Level mathematics. Experience: 12 years, pupils aged 4-7 years
Jules	GCSE mathematics. Experience: 3 years, pupils aged 7-11 years
Jo	GCE 'O' Level mathematics. Experience: more than 10 years, pupils aged 3-7 and 11-16 years
Andy	GCE 'O' Level mathematics. Experience: over 20 years, pupils aged 7-11, 11-16 years
Pat	GCE 'O' Level mathematics, studied physics to 'A' Level. Experience: 20 years, pupils aged 7-13 years
Jess	GCE 'O' Level mathematics. Experience: 7 years, pupils aged 4-7 years
Frankie	GCSE mathematics. Studied mathematics for an additional year post 16. Experience: 3 years, pupils aged 7-11 years. Mathematics Co-ordinator
Charlie	GCE 'O' Level mathematics. Teaching experience: 9 years, pupils aged 7-11 years
Clare	GCSE mathematics. Experience: 4 years, pupils aged 7-11 years. Mathematics Co-ordinator
Toni	Access mathematics course to higher education as a mature student. Experience: 2 years, pupils aged 5-7 and 7-11 years
Jenny	No mathematics qualification. Experience: 23 years, mainly pupils aged 4-7 years; two terms with pupils aged 8-9 years

Note. The post-16 qualification was known as General Certificate of Education (GCE) 'O' Level until 1985, then as the General Certificate of Secondary Education (GCSE). The post 18 qualification is known as Advanced ('A') Level.

(dark shading)	Denotes teachers who attended the Five-day course in 2000/01
(light shading)	Denotes teachers who attended the Five-day course in 2001/02

The teachers were selected for the training by their headteachers. One teacher not initially engaged in the training was replaced early on in the project by the teacher who took over her class. One of the eight teachers engaged in the training in 2000-2001 did not take part in the final interview as she had left the school.

Table A.2.3. Details of the data sources

Interviews	*Focus of interview*
1. June/July 2000 (for the majority of teachers)	Teaching experience; experience of mathematics; description of own practice. Changes in practice since the introduction of the National Numeracy Strategy. Understanding of aspects of the National Numeracy Strategy. Knowledge of whole-school approach to mathematics
2. June/July 2000 (for the majority of teachers)	Understanding of selected aspects of mathematics through working through examples. Responses to pupils' misconceptions. Conceptions and beliefs about the teaching and learning of mathematics
3. September/ October 2000	Pre-course interview. Expectations of the course (omitted for the four teachers not attending the course)
4. November 2000	Post-course interview. Impressions and responses immediately following the course
5. June/July 2001	Responses to the course over time. Details of current practice and any changes noted
6. November 2001	Views of mathematics as a subject, both as a learner and as a teacher. Contrasting mathematics with other subjects in the curriculum
7. March 2002	Overview of changes in practice, beliefs and understanding over the course of two years. Return to selected mathematics questions from Interview 2. Return to conceptions of teaching and learning mathematics. This interview was missed for the teacher who left towards the end of the research
Observations	*Details of observations*
June 2000; March 2001; June 2001; November 2001; March 2002.	Lesson observations were recorded on video camera and supported by fieldnotes: The first observation was missed for the replacement teacher. The last observation missed for the teacher who left towards the end of the research
Tests	*Details of test administrations*
October 2000, June 2001; October 2001, June 2002	Administration by the class teacher of the Leverhulme Numeracy Research Programme assessments (see Introduction) for the appropriate year group at the beginning and end of the school year

In June or September 2000, baseline data was gathered on the 12 teachers in terms of profiles of their beliefs, knowledge and practices, prior to the training. Using methods developed in previous research at Kings' College (Askew et al., 1997) extended interviews and classroom observations probed teachers' understandings and beliefs. Each of the 12 teachers was interviewed twice (Interviews 1 and 2): once to explore their beliefs and practices, and once to elicit their understanding of aspects of mathematics. (This data was collected one term later for the replacement teacher.) The teachers were also observed teaching mathematics to establish teaching methods, styles of teaching organisation and curriculum emphasises prior to the National Numeracy Strategy training. Given the increased emphasis within the National Numeracy Strategy of aspects of mathematics that are based around understanding of multiplicative reasoning – ratio and proportion, rational numbers, models of multiplication and division – for the current study we chose to present to teachers specific mathematical problems related to these aspects. Sources for these problems were from previous research (for example, Ma, 1999) taken in conjunction with an analysis of key aspects of the National Numeracy Strategy Framework for Teaching Mathematics from Reception to Year 6 (Department for Education and Employment, 1999).

Each mathematical problem was presented to the teachers on a separate piece of paper and the teachers were asked for their initial reaction to it. They were then encouraged to try and work out the solution and talk through what they were doing. Calculators were available and the teachers were free to record whatever they wished on the paper. The extent to which the interviewer probed a teacher on their methods, particularly where these were incorrect, depended partly upon the judgement of the interviewer of the extent to which the teacher perceived the questions as stressful. Although the main emphasis in the questions was on the teachers' understanding of the mathematics, in some of the questions the teachers were also asked to comment on the ways in which they might introduce the ideas to the pupils. The interviews were recorded and later transcribed.

Seven interviews were conducted with the teachers over the course of two school years, and video recordings were made of their practice on five occasions over that time. Details of the data sources are given in Table A.2.3. All interviews were recorded and transcribed. They were analysed in conjunction with the video-recordings of lessons around several themes:

- current classroom practice
- subject matter knowledge
- pedagogic content knowledge
- responses to the Five-day course of training
- conceptions and beliefs about mathematics as a subject
- conceptions and beliefs about the teaching of mathematics
- changes in classroom practice.

Pupils in the classes of nine teachers (Reception age pupils, 4-5 years, were not tested) completed the appropriate numeracy assessments developed for the Core longitudinal project of the Leverhulme Numeracy Research Programme (see Introduction), at the beginning and end of the school years 2000/01, 2001/02.

Askew, M., Brown, M., Rhodes, V., Johnson, D., & Wiliam, D. (1997). *Effective teachers of numeracy: Final report*. London: King's College.

Department for Education and Employment. (1999). *The National Numeracy Strategy: Framework for Teaching Mathematics from Reception to Year 6*. London: Department for Education and Employment.

Ma, L. (1999). *Knowing and teaching mathematics: teachers' understanding of fundamental mathematics in China and the United States*. Mahwah, NJ: Lawrence Erlbaum Associates.

ANNEX 3

FOCUS PROJECT: WHOLE SCHOOL ACTION ON NUMERACY

Whole School Action on Numeracy (1997-2001) was one of six projects in the major research programme carried out at King's College London - the Leverhulme Numeracy Research Programme (1997-2002). The overall aim of the project was to identify whole-school and individual teacher factors, which appeared to facilitate or inhibit the development of strategies for raising attainment in numeracy.

Whole School Action on Numeracy focused on six schools as they prepared for, experienced and followed up an Office for Standards in Education (Ofsted) inspection, and continued for a total period of four years (See Table A.3.1).

Table A.3.1. Details of the six schools involved in the research 1997-2001

School	*Size*	*Characteristics*
1. Woodbury	600 pupils 3-form entry 21 classes	Suburban, mixed socio-economic, average special needs, above average free school meals, ethnic minorities
2. The Grove	70 pupils 0.5-form entry 3 classes	Rural, Low special needs, very low eligibility for free school meals, very low pupils from ethnic minorities
3. Maple	200 pupils 1 form entry 7 classes	Suburban, mixed socio-economic, average free school meals, above average pupils from ethnic minorities
4. Pennington	340 pupils 1.5-form entry 10 classes, Nursery	New town, high unemployment. About average special needs, free school meals. Few pupils from ethnic minorities
5. Sandmere	340 pupils 1.5- form entry 10 classes, Nursery	Outer urban, high special needs, high free school meals, substantial Asian and African-Caribbean minorities
6. Wolverton	200 pupils 1 form entry 7 classes, Nursery	Inner urban. High levels of pupil mobility, well above average free school meals, above average special needs and pupils from ethnic minorities

The schools (Schools 1-6, given the names Woodbury, The Grove, Maple, Pennington, Sandmere, Wolverton) were chosen to provide a range of contexts. Two schools experiencing inspection or re-inspection were added to the project each term, so that at the end of the first year work had begun in all six schools.

The schools varied in size; they were situated in inner urban, outer urban, suburban and rural environments; their populations had varied levels of economic status and spoke a range of languages other than English; their recent histories exhibited turbulence, moderate disturbance and stability; they were at different stages in their experience of development planning and self-evaluation. However they shared a concern that they had themselves established - the need to develop their mathematics and, in particular, certain aspects of numeracy. In five out of the six schools, mathematics was on the school development plan before the inspection and in the sixth school it was due for priority action during the term following inspection. Interviews with key informants in the schools revealed that all were concerned about raising attainment in mathematics. Some of this concern stemmed specifically from recent poor national test results at ages 7 and 11.

Table A.3.2. The data set 1997-2001

Year	*School visits*	*Interviews*	*Observations*
1997-98	46	6 headteacher 10 co-ordinator 13 class teacher 1 governor	23 classrooms 12 meetings
1998-99	49	6 headteacher 9 co-ordinator 16 class teacher 1 governor	25 classrooms 19 meetings
1999-2000	29	7 headteacher 11 co-ordinator 11 class teacher	9 classrooms 10 meetings
2000-2001	13	6 headteacher 10 co-ordinator 3 class teacher	1 classroom 2 meetings

Data for the research included interviews with teachers, mathematics co-ordinators or subject leaders, headteachers and school governors (school board members), observations of the teaching of mathematics in selected classrooms and notes taken at whole-school and group meetings and in-service training (Inset), both in school and out, related to mathematics/numeracy (See Table A.3.2). School documents were also collected.

Data was collected on:

- Views about, and practice of, mathematics/numeracy prior to the inspection
- Intended development as identified in the School Development Plan
- Interpretations of the requirements of Ofsted
- Preparations made by the school prior to the inspection
- Reactions to the inspection report translated into preparations for the action plan
- Strategies identified for the development of numeracy
- Ways in which these strategies were implemented
- Changes in practice or beliefs (perceived and observed)
- Pupil levels of achievement (at ages 7 and 11 and non-statutory assessments)
- Interaction with the pressures of statutory assessment and the impact of new government emphases, in particular the National Numeracy Strategy.

During the course of 1998, each school experienced an Ofsted inspection and a national initiative on literacy. In September 1999 the National Numeracy Strategy was introduced (See Introduction). One school received intensive numeracy support during this year, the remaining five received this help the following year (2000/01).

Interviews were transcribed, and the transcripts returned to interviewees for validation. Observations were written up from fieldnotes and tape recordings (not transcribed) and also returned to classroom teachers; meetings were recorded in fieldnotes. Interview transcripts and observation notes were coded to identify key categories. These categories were subject to continuous interrogation and revision using the constant comparative method (Strauss, 1987). Interviews were analysed to compare and contrast perceptions within and across schools. Data collection and analysis were contiguous and on-going to enable the feedback of analysis into data collection. Data reduction techniques and memo-ing (Miles & Huberman, 1994) were used in the building up of constructs.

Miles, M. B., & Huberman, A. M. (1994). *Qualitative data analysis: an expanded sourcebook* (2nd ed.). Thousand Oaks, CA: Sage.

Strauss, A. L. (1987). *Qualitative analysis for social scientists*. Cambridge, UK: Cambridge University Press.

ANNEX 4

FOCUS PROJECT: COGNITIVE ACCELERATION IN MATHEMATICS EDUCATION IN THE PRIMARY SCHOOL (P-CAME)

The aim of this project was to investigate the effectiveness of an intervention programme with children aged 9-10 and 10-11 years (Years 5 and 6 of primary school). The programme consists of a series of mathematics lessons conducted over two consecutive years to the same classes by their own teachers. The lessons were to be designed around key cognitive challenges across the main conceptual strands of the mathematics curriculum. The classroom conduct by the teacher was to be structured to encourage verbal interactions and metacognitive activity in whole-class and various small group arrangements of children.

The main goals of the project were to:

- provide evidence on the effect of the programme on children's cognitive development and mathematical achievement
- create and describe a model of intervention-style teaching in primary school mathematics to serve as a basis for teachers' continuous professional development.

The implementation was carried out in two overlapping phases, each with specified personnel and tasks (see Table A.4.1). Minor pragmatic modifications were needed, mainly in enlarging the role of the teacher researchers and the elaboration of the professional development methodology.

Phase 1 continued throughout the three years by the full team comprised of teacher-researchers, the Local Education Authority maths adviser, three university researchers and an attached research student. The intensity of contact within the research team was at its greatest in the first year – 20 full day whole group formal meetings plus a similar number of school visits by researchers in various combinations. In the following two years this was nearly halved to 12 days a year, including the time allotted to the main study professional development sessions.

Table A.4.1. P-CAME research implementation

Tasks	*Year 1*	*Year 2*	*Year 3*
Phase 1 Development of lessons Support material Lesson observations Assessment instruments Revising materials Quantitative data	Full research team working with 2 Y5 and 2 Y6 classes in 2 lab schools) • Pre-tests in lab schools	Full research team working with 2 Y5 and 2 Y6 classes in 2 lab schools Post tests in lab schools Pre-tests in main study schools	Full research team working in main study schools and two additional lab schools Post tests in main study schools KS2 tests
Phase 2 Main research: lesson and Professional Development observations [Development of the Professional development methodology]		19 teachers in 9 main study schools Y5 classes only King's researchers and LEA adviser Teacher-researchers as peer tutors	19 teachers in 9 schools Y6 classes only King's researchers and LEA adviser Teacher-researchers as peer tutors

One teacher-researcher went on maternity-leave at the end of the first year, did not return to teaching, and was replaced by two teachers from different main study schools at the end of Year 2 of the project. The two teacher researchers in the other laboratory school became Local Education Authority numeracy consultants, one at the end of Year 1, the other during the second year, but both continued their involvement in the project voluntarily up to the present. It was felt that, despite the personnel and position changes, the research team was the strongest component of the project. That helped to compensate for large-scale staff turnover in the main study (Phase 2) cohort of teachers, and also helped to generate important theoretical and practical innovations in the approach.

Phase 2 started in the summer of the first year, with the introduction of main study teachers to the approach. Over the following six terms there were 12 formal half-day professional development sessions, and three times that number of in-class observations and tutorial support in various formal and informal arrangements, including team teaching and peer tutoring.

In total 24 lessons (out of the 34 considered) were fully developed and offered to the main study teachers, at a regular rate of four lessons a term. They addressed concepts and reasoning patterns in number and algebra, shape and space, and handling data, but with emphasis on number relations. On average 17 lessons were conducted in the main study classes.

PROFESSIONAL DEVELOPMENT IN PRIMARY MATHEMATICS

Additional work funded by Kings' College related to Primary CAME: Research Student Jeremy Hodgen

This additional research was funded as a research studentship by King's College London in order to investigate more fully the professional development aspects of the Primary CAME intervention. The initial aim of this attached project was to investigate the professional change of classroom teachers as they participated in the Primary CAME Professional Development programme.

As the project developed, the emphasis of the research shifted to focus more specifically on the teacher-researchers in the research and development team as practitioner teacher educators. The research explored the teacher-researchers' own knowledge and practice in primary mathematics and the tutoring relationship between the teacher-researchers and the classroom teachers. An additional, but secondary, aspect to the research was the teacher-researchers' involvement in the National Numeracy Strategy. Two teacher-researchers became numeracy consultants, whilst the others had led both Local Education Authority and in-school numeracy training sessions.

Early work emphasised the importance of collaboration and reflection with teacher change. A further aspect was an identification of some philosophical challenges that primary teachers faced in relation to school mathematics. The research explored ways in which these teacher-researchers' beliefs and understandings of big mathematical ideas had evolved. A major focus was on the impact of the teacher-researchers' engagement with the research and development activities of Primary CAME and subsequently through a consideration of their roles as consultants/tutors in the National Numeracy Strategy.

INDEX

100-squares xxv
Abbott, D. 43
ability groups 70, 121, 170, 171
academic self-esteem 5
accountability 10, 20, 28, 47, 59, 66
action plan 22, 273
active consumers 132
Adajian, L.B. 1
addition 129, 140, 142, 147, 178, 196, 230, 248
Adey, P. 188, 223, 224
Adhami, M. xxix, 185, 186, 188, 189, 226
Advanced level 41
advisers 8, 48, 58, 64, 68, 74, 112, 116, 187, 276
see also local authority advisers
advisory service 31
agent of change 50, 51, 90, 250
algebra xxii, 129, 136, 175, 189, 197, 238, 239, 276
Angier, C. 225
Anthony, H.M. 53
anxiety(ies) 28, 33, 37, 41, 79, 99
artefacts 4, 29, 31, 32, 39, 53, 220, 240
Askew, J.M. xix
Askew, M. xxvi-xxviii, 6, 99, 127, 130, 133, 155-157, 161, 164, 173, 179, 225, 245, 260, 267
assessment xx, xxi, xxiii, xxviii, xxix, 21, 42, 73, 76, 98, 99, 101, 141, 151, 161, 167, 171, 188, 213, 260, 261, 263, 267, 268, 273, 276
attitudes xxviii, 5, 19, 34, 50, 63, 76, 85, 88, 135, 143, 145, 150, 183, 212
Australia xxi, 10, 13
author 224, 225, 239
authority 90, 131, 146, 225, 233, 259

back to basics xxiii
background variables 75
balance 4, 44, 48, 49, 50, 59, 62-65, 67, 68, 75, 88-90, 253, 259
Ball, D. 135
Ball, D.L. 2, 52, 122, 123, 132, 248, 249, 251
Ball, S. 6
baseline data 130, 262, 267
basic ideas 226
basic skills xxiii, xxvi
Bass, H. 133, 248, 249
Bauersfeld, H. xx
Beacon status 10
behaviour 70, 71, 175
Belenky, M.F. 225
beliefs xx, xxviii, 1, 2, 4-6, 12, 13, 24, 41-43, 92, 98, 123, 127, 130, 155-157, 159, 166-168, 176, 178-180, 182, 183, 214, 219, 220, 225, 226, 228, 233, 234, 238-241, 246, 248, 249, 263, 265, 267, 268, 273, 277
Bell, D. 64
Bennett, N. 249
Beresford, J. 7, 64
Bibby, T. xxii, 1, 5, 9, 41, 112, 260
Biggs, E. xx
Black, E. 20, 44, 51
Blair, T. xxiii
Boaler, J. 73
Booster Classes 73
Booth, L. 189
Borko, H. 135, 151
Boufi, A. 188
Boylan, M. 225
Britt, M.S. 133
Broadfoot, P. 43
Broekman, H. 215
Brown, C. 51, 52, 90
Brown, J. 188
Brown, M. xix, xxvi, xxvii, 9, 112, 128, 189, 245, 260, 261
Burton, L. 225
Bush, T. 67

Cain, C. 227
calculation xix, xxi, xxiv, 30, 33, 100, 128, 137-139, 141, 142, 147, 148, 159, 166, 168, 170, 175, 181, 248
Calculator Aware Number (CAN) xx
calculator use 102
calculators xx, xxiv, 29, 129, 268
CAME (Cognitive Acceleration in Mathematics Education) xxix, 186, 188-190, 193, 195, 198, 201-204, 209, 211-215, 221, 222, 225-227, 229, 233, 236, 237, 240-242

Campbell, P. 70
Campbell, R.J. 6, 7, 22, 25, 43-45, 47, 250
capacity xix, 5, 7, 23, 50, 51, 57, 87, 89-92, 158, 165
capacity beliefs 5, 41 *see also* beliefs
career 6, 24, 74, 132, 134, 150, 252, 253
Carpenter, T.P. xx, 2, 215, 251
Carre, C. 249
Carter, R. 145
Cartesian co-ordinates 194, 236, 237
cascade xxv, 128, 129, 144, 146, 148, 152, 153, 251, 254
Case studies of Pupil Progress xxvii, 258
catalysts 50, 105, 209, 234, 239
chains of assistance 90
characteristics 3, 4, 12, 19, 23, 40, 41, 52, 57-59, 61, 62, 75, 145, 221, 245, 262, 266, 271
- professional 4, 43
- socio-economic 75
- whole school 3
charts 129
child-centred xx
children's learning xx, 2, 118, 141, 156, 161, 176, 178, 181, 183, 226, 233
- and progression xxx
China xxii, 10
clarity of vision 23, 24, 30, 40, 48-51, 59, 68
Clarke, B. 242
Clarke, D. 52, 146, 152, 250, 251
Clarke, D.M. 15, 132, 223, 219, 224, 242
classroom experiences xxvii, 43, 147, 213
classroom practice xxvii-xxix, 12, 19, 26, 27, 30, 35, 51, 89, 123, 127, 130, 135, 147, 150, 152, 155, 156, 182, 210, 246, 253, 257, 258, 268
classroom teachers xxviii, 132, 20, 21, 23, 27, 30, 33-36, 40, 43, 49, 50, 53, 57, 76, 90, 98, 102, 123, 141, 185, 191, 202, 228, 246, 252, 253, 273, 277
Clinchy, B.M. 225
clustering 60, 61
coaching 5, 36, 41, 45, 51, 52, 66, 72, 117, 145, 146, 250, 252, 254
Cobb, P. xx, 188, 189, 203, 225, 239
Cockcroft Committee (Department of Education and Science/Welsh Office) xx, xxi
Cockcroft report 10, 94
Cognitive Acceleration in Science Education (CASE) 188
cognitive agenda 188-191, 194
cognitive challenge/conflict xxix
cognitive demand 188-192, 195, 200-202, 207, 211-213
cognitive development xxix, 186-189, 191, 193, 275
Cognitively Guided Instruction 2, 215
Cohen, D.K. 122, 123, 251
coherence of views 6, 48, 49, 59, 93
collaboration(s) xxi, 6, 53, 57, 89, 190, 204-206, 241, 277
collective capacity 7, 57, 89, 90
collective reflection 189, 203, 205, 206, 208, 209, 214
Collins, A. 1, 52, 188
colonising 92
commercial mathematics schemes 10, 98, 99, 103, 104, 141
commitment 64, 97, 178
communities of practice 201, 226, 227, 241
competition xxvi, 10
computers xx, 25, 263
confidence 25, 35, 36, 41, 43, 63, 64, 69, 75, 100, 108, 115, 116, 123, 130, 133, 139, 141, 143, 148-152, 167, 177, 181, 182, 247-249
connectedness 226
connectionist 157, 173, 176, 179, 181, 182, 225, 238
consistency of views 6, 48, 49, 59, 75, 93
constraints 2, 3, 8, 11, 20, 22, 57, 59, 69, 111, 169
construction 4, 146, 189, 192, 195, 196, 201, 202, 204, 206, 207, 210, 223, 225
constructivism 188, 223
constructivist xx, 220, 223
constructs 2, 12, 48-50, 57, 59-63, 73, 75, 86-89, 91, 93, 203, 213, 273
consultants xxiv, xxv, 8-11, 27, 32, 45-48, 62, 64, 83-85, 100, 111-113, 127, 128, 138, 144, 145, 147, 152, 252-254, 276, 277
consumers 98
- active 132
- passive 132
- reticent 132
content xx, 20, 22, 99, 108, 109, 112, 115, 127-129, 134, 135, 140, 147, 148, 150, 151, 166, 189, 194, 233, 243, 247, 268
contributions xxvii, 6, 11, 19, 39, 68, 88, 89, 122, 206, 209, 257
co-ordinates 192, 194-196, 198, 199, 204, 205, 207, 210, 236, 237
co-ordinating teams 45
Corbin, B. 26, 51, 52, 146
Corbin, J. 220
Core project xxvi-xxviii, 76, 87, 90, 91, 102, 104, 149, 247, 257
core scheme 105
core subject 65-73, 120
counting stick xxvi, 29, 32, 39, 138-140, 150, 175, 181

creative teaching 74
creativity xxii
critical friend 28, 44, 51, 66, 68
Croll, P. 43
culture of collaboration 6, 89
culture(s) xxii, xxix, xxx, 1, 2, 6, 7, 28, 52, 71, 88, 89, 91, 92, 189, 212
culture of learning 212
curriculum(a) xix-xxiii, xxvii, xxx, 4-13, 20, 21, 34, 35, 37, 43, 47, 53, 65, 66, 70, 72, 74, 91, 99-101, 103, 104, 106, 108, 109, 112, 115, 120, 122, 123, 128, 130, 135, 138, 151, 160, 168, 182, 186, 189, 191-195, 198, 200, 209, 210, 212, 213, 215, 219, 226, 233, 241, 242, 247-254, 257, 258, 262, 263
Curriculum and Evaluation Standards for School Mathematics 10
curriculum documents 20, 99, 103, 106
curriculum objectives xxx
cycles of practice 185, 214

daily mathematics lessons xxiv, 9, 32, 97, 100, 101
Darling-Hammond, L. 129
Davidson, M. 156
Davis, R.B. xx, 188
Day, C. 7, 64, 65, 88
decentering 224
decimals 129, 136, 138, 174, 175
decision-making 7, 67, 113, 117, 124, 155, 157, 161
degree xxi, xxii, 20, 26, 41, 42, 53, 70, 72, 85, 90, 98, 113, 124, 127, 133, 156, 181, 215, 246, 249
delegation 61, 63, 64
demonstration lessons 27, 28
Denvir, B. 261
Denvir, H. xxvi, xxvii, 260
Department for Education 100
Department for Education and Science xx, xxi, 99, 100
Department for Education and Employment xxiii, xxiv, 9, 31-33, 45, 73, 91, 100, 102, 110, 128, 129, 137, 139, 150, 151, 156, 159, 232, 268
Department of Education and Professional Studies, King's College London xxvi
Department of Education, Training and Youth Affairs xxi, 10
deputy head 22
dialogue 7, 24, 29, 31, 41, 57, 65, 68, 89, 146, 147, 163, 175, 181
differential effectiveness 87
differentiation 32, 34, 136, 140, 143, 151, 159, 161, 165, 166, 170, 180, 181, 211
differentiation according to complexity 170, 181
differentiation as extension 161, 180
digit cards xxv, 32, 39, 139, 171, 172, 176
diploma course 83-85
diplomas in mathematics education 41
direct interactive teaching xxiv, 30
discovery 157, 163, 164, 179, 180, 225
discussion xix, xxii, xxix, 1, 2,7, 8, 25-30, 38, 40, 51, 52, 57, 66, 70, 74, 77, 89, 92, 114, 117, 120, 122, 124, 130, 139, 140, 145, 147, 152, 155, 162-164, 168, 170, 180, 185, 188, 190, 191, 193, 194, 200-204, 209, 211, 215, 219-222, 228, 231-234, 236-238, 240, 246, 250, 251
disequilibrium 5, 92
display 31
disruption 85
division 129, 137, 138, 141, 147, 163, 171, 172, 175, 268
Dubben, S. xxix
Duguid, P. 188

Earl, L. xxvi, xxx, 13, 53, 89, 215, 245, 246
educationalist 22, 25, 43, 45, 47, 73
Effective Teachers of Numeracy project xxvii, 157, 179
Elmore, R. 156
emotions 4, 6, 48, 132
Empson, S.B. 215
enabling 45, 63, 64, 87, 115, 118, 192, 219, 224, 229, 234, 241, 252
English xxii, 24, 62, 70, 98, 169, 249, 262, 266, 272
enthusiasm 24, 35, 42, 48, 49, 59, 61, 63, 65, 75, 99, 137, 141, 150-152, 247
- for the role 40, 42, 49
Eraut, M. 2, 144
errors 128, 158, 172, 176, 205, 206, 231
estimation xxiv, 189
ethnographic methods xxix
ethos 7, 74
evaluating 20, 51, 165
Evaluation of the Implementation of National Curriculum Mathematics 99, 104
evaluators xxvi, 21, 89
exemplary role 27
expectations 7, 20, 31, 35, 43, 49, 63, 65, 71, 80, 89, 93, 116, 118, 121, 132, 134, 143, 144, 166, 182, 256-258, 262, 267
experience xxvii, 5-7, 10, 13, 24, 26, 28, 41, 43, 73, 74, 79, 91, 109, 114, 116-120, 122, 127, 132-134, 143, 144, 146, 147, 151, 157, 159, 164, 174-176, 182, 193, 194, 196, 201-203,

205, 208-214, 222, 223, 226-231, 236-238, 240-242, 250, 257, 263, 266, 267, 271-273
expertise 19, 20, 25, 26, 43-45, 51, 57, 61, 63, 64, 68, 69, 75, 89, 90, 117, 118, 121, 122, 209, 214, 215, 250, 252, 254
explanations xxv, 38, 39, 119, 160, 164, 167, 177, 180, 206, 208, 211
external authority 225
external factors 2, 3, 8, 11-13, 50, 87, 88, 98, 127
external professionals 1, 8, 10, 12, 13, 19, 45, 48, 113, 127, 144, 201, 253

Farah-Sarkis, F. 133
feedback 24, 26, 68, 127, 131, 144-148, 166, 175, 199, 201, 273
Fennema, E. 2, 129, 215, 251
Fielding, M. 144
Five-day course xxv, 46, 83-85, 102, 127-132, 136, 140, 142-144, 146-150, 152, 158, 159, 161, 165, 171, 175, 181, 182, 248, 266, 268
focus projects xxvi-xxix, 2, 5, 21, 48, 102, 155, 258, 265, 271, 275
follow-me cards 32
formal methods 139, 193
foundation subjects 91
Foxman, D. 98
fractions 129, 136, 138, 174, 175, 222, 223, 228, 229, 231-233, 235, 236, 238
Framework xxiv, xxv, 26, 31, 33-35, 45, 69, 100-104, 108-111, 116, 121, 123, 128, 142, 143, 148, 149, 155-160, 164, 165, 169, 180, 186, 190, 191, 200, 203-205, 208, 209, 212, 247, 251, 254 *see also* Framework for Teaching Mathematics from Reception to Year 6
Framework for Teaching Mathematics from Reception to Year 6 xxiv, 32, 100, 128, 155, 156, 268
Franke, M.L. 2, 215, 251
free school meals 62, 78, 79, 87, 266, 271
Freudenthal Institute xxi
friendship 6, 221
full participation 90
Fullan, M. xxvi, 2, 9, 89, 122, 123, 246, 252

gains xxvii, 40, 49, 65, 76-85, 86, 87, 91, 150, 157, 159, 188, 246, 247, 257, 261
Gale, J. xx
Gallimore, R. 1, 52, 90
Garden, R.A. 10, 98
generalisation 193-197, 207, 209
generalised number 189, 194, 196, 208
geometrical properties xxii
geometry xx, xxii, 239
Gervasconi, A. 52, 251
Givens 75, 76, 92
Goals 5, 38, 42, 43, 49, 166, 275
Goldberger, N.R. 225
Goldsmith, L. 224
gourmet omnivors 132
government control xx-xxii
government pressure xxi
governors xxv, xxvii, 22, 46, 128, 272
graphs xxiii, 129
Gravemeijer, K. xxi, 215
Gray, J. 7, 91
Grimmett, P. 223
Grossman, P. 135
Grouws, D.A. 223
growth states 88, 92
Guskey, T.R. 2, 146

Hadfield, M. 7, 64
Hafeez, R. xxix
halving and thirding 222, 223, 229, 232-234
Hargreaves, A. 6, 28, 132
Harris, A. 7, 64
Harris, D.L. 53
Hart, K. 189, 260
Hawley, W.D. 52, 250
headteachers xxiv, xxv, xxvii, xxviii, 6, 22, 23, 26, 30-32, 40, 44, 46-50, 57, 59, 61-72, 75, 82, 85, 86, 90, 92, 93, 102, 103, 106-109, 112, 113, 117, 128, 140, 144, 145, 250, 252, 254, 257, 262, 267, 272
Her Majesty's Inspectorate 9, 11, 99, 124
high attainment xix
Hodgen, J. xxix, 185, 219, 222, 228, 242, 243
Holland xxi
Holland, D. 227, 240
home xxii, xxviii-xxxi, 33, 62, 234, 259
home cultures xxix
Hopkins, D. 2, 10, 75, 87, 88, 92, 150
Horne, M. 52, 252
Horton, A. 144
Huberman, A.M. 273
Huberman, M. 2, 132
Hyde, A. 137
Hyde, P. 137

identity 6, 43, 219, 220, 226-230, 237, 240
implementation xxv, xxviii, xxx, 1, 8, 11-13, 21, 30-33, 37, 38, 50, 58, 61, 65, 66, 69, 77, 88-90, 99, 101, 103, 104, 109, 111, 113, 122, 130, 140, 143, 145, 156, 164, 189, 201, 213, 251, 253, 265, 275, 276
in-class support 21, 149
individual pupil targets 70
informants xxviii, 272

Information and Communications Technology 91
initiation 21, 88, 206
innovation 6, 11, 47, 66, 88, 141, 152, 242, 276
in-school support 13, 19, 20, 50
in-service training 2, 8, 13, 22, 24, 52, 67, 84, 85, 91, 127, 130, 143-146, 150, 155, 156, 176, 183, 247, 251, 252, 372
Inset 24-26, 35, 37, 45, 47, 66, 69, 143-145, 147-149, 152, 176, 272 *see also* in-service training
inspection reports 9, 12, 82, 92, 273
inspections xxi, xxviii, 9-12, 20-22, 47, 48, 58, 63, 65, 69, 72, 74, 79-82, 91, 271-273
inspectors xxv, 8, 9, 22, 28, 45, 47, 48, 63, 69, 72, 74, 82, 99, 102
intellectual development xxix, 189
intensive support xxv, 46, 128, 265
internal evaluation 9
international context xix, 57, 98
interpersonal skills 27
intervention xxvi, xxix, xxx, 2, 11-13, 19, 52, 58, 100, 127, 185, 186, 189, 245, 251, 275, 277
interviews xxvii-xxix, 21, 23, 30, 35, 36, 39, 42, 48, 49, 51, 58, 60, 66, 69, 72-74, 82, 102, 123, 130, 131, 134, 141-143, 146, 151, 155, 156, 159, 161, 164, 166, 190, 220, 230, 234, 238, 60-263, 267, 268, 272, 273
investigatory learning xx
Irwin, K.C. 133
isolation 7, 89, 145, 165, 180, 241

Jacobs, V.R. 215
Jantzi, D. 1, 2, 5, 23, 41, 64, 88, 92, 158
Japan xxii, 10
Jaworski, B. 137
job specification 20, 44, 48, 65
Johnson, D.C. xxvii-xxxi, 7, 9, 19, 20, 22, 48, 53, 57, 73, 92, 93, 99, 100, 104, 112, 185-189, 222
Joyce, B. 2, 6, 52, 88, 131, 132, 144-146, 150, 152, 165
justification 47, 205-208

key issues 9, 22, 67, 92, 213, 227
key stage 22, 45, 99, 103, 117, 118, 266
King, B. 1, 89
King's College London xxvi, 99, 130, 189, 222, 231, 235, 265, 271, 276, 277
knowledge xxvi, xxviii, xxx, 1, 2, 5, 12, 13, 25, 44, 51, 64, 86, 90, 100, 102, 113, 115, 118, 120, 123, 127-130, 133-138, 140, 144-146, 148, 150-152, 155-163, 165, 166, 174, 175, 181, 182, 189, 197, 209, 213, 223, 225, 226, 228, 232-234, 238, 243, 246-250, 254, 257, 258, 265, 267, 268, 277
knowledge as connected 170, 181
knowledge as hierarchical and sequential 180
Korthagen, F.A. 215
Kruse, S. 1, 9
Kvale, S. 220

laboratory schools xxix, 276
Labour Party xxiii, xxiv
Lachicotte, W. 227
lack of closure 193
Lampert, M. 52, 188, 251
Lapointe, A.E. xix
Lave, J. 1, 52, 90, 229
leaders xxv, 6, 7, 13, 19, 20, 51, 64, 88, 128, 129, 203, 272
leadership xxiii, xviii, 6, 21, 45, 57, 64, 88, 91, 92, 259, 262
leading learners 51
leading mathematics teachers xxv, 9, 27, 64, 83, 84, 90
league table xix, xxi, 9, 10, 74
learner 5, 26, 51, 123, 178, 181, 234, 237, 240, 241, 252, 253, 267
Learner, S. 48
learning as grasping 180
learning as understanding 170, 181
learning communities 1, 52, 90, 250, 253
learning cultures 1, 88, 89, 189
legitimate peripherial participation 90
Leithwood, K. xxvi, 1, 2, 5, 7, 23, 41, 42, 64, 88, 89, 92, 158
lesson development 191, 193, 219, 222, 223, 228, 229, 232, 239
lesson observationsxxvii, 28, 33, 38, 140, 178, 267, 276
lesson plans xxv, 97, 101,102, 104, 108, 110-112, 123, 213
lesson simulation 190, 202-204, 208, 209, 213, 221, 233
lesson developers 219, 227-229, 240
level 4 xxii, xxv, 40, 60, 63, 70, 246
Leverhulme Numeracy Research programme xix, xxvi, xxx,1, 2, 5, 12, 13, 57, 58, 76, 87, 102, 130, 156, 186, 245, 246, 248-250, 257, 258, 265, 267, 269, 271
Levi, L. 2, 215, 251
Levin, B. xxvi
linguistic practices xxix
linked constructs 48, 57, 59, 62, 93
- construct 1: *Enthusiasm* for the co-ordination role 42, 48-50, 59

- construct 2: *Clarity of vision* about priorities for action and ways of working 48, 50, 59, 68
- construct 3: *Balance* between headteacher and co-ordinator 48, 50, 59,62-65, 67, 68, 75, 88-90, 253
- construct 4: *Coherence and consistency* of views within the school community 6, 48, 50, 59, 62, 70, 89, 93
- construct 5: *High priority given to recoursing* the co-ordination role 49, 50, 59, 68, 70
- construct 6: *Availability and use of external support* 49, 50, 59

literacy practices xxix
local authority advisers 8
Local Education Authority xxiii, xxiv, xxvii, 8, 9, 11, 12, 27, 32, 45-48, 64, 67-69, 73, 74, 76, 82, 84, 89, 91, 100, 103, 106, 111, 113, 128, 129, 131, 144, 150, 151, 159, 185, 186, 191, 220, 259, 260, 262, 265, 275-277
logical reasoning xxii, 196
Longfield, A. xxix
longitudinal coherence 226, 232, 233, 239
loop game 32, 36, 39
Louis, K.S. 1, 9
low attainment xix, xx, xxvi, 58, 65,82

Ma, L. 226, 232, 239, 268
Maden, M. 7, 91, 92
Maher, C. xx, 188
main subject 41, 119, 169
management 6, 7, 64, 66, 67, 71, 152, 200, 213, 253
Mascall, B. 1, 2, 5, 23, 41, 88, 92, 158
Masters course module 85
materials xxii, xxiv, xxv, 4, 7, 8, 10, 13, 20, 22, 29-32, 34, 44, 53, 66, 85, 97-117, 121-124, 127-129, 135, 137, 138, 145, 147, 151, 171, 181, 187, 191, 200, 213, 214, 220-222, 229, 237, 239, 240, 245, 250-252, 254, 263, 276
math wars xx
mathematical communication xx
mathematical heterogeneity 219, 241
mathematical literacy xxii
mathematician xx,118, 119, 188, 225
mathematics as a connected discipline 225
mathematics co-ordinators xxiv-xxviii,6, 13, 19, 21-23, 25,26, 30, 32, 34, 36, 42, 43, 50, 52, 57-59, 61, 63-66, 69, 70, 72, 73, 82, 86, 88, 90, 92, 93, 102, 103, 106-110, 112-114, 117, 121, 122, 127-129, 133, 134, 139, 140, 143-147, 150, 152, 169, 175, 203, 245, 250, 252, 257, 262, 266, 272
mathematics education 9, 220, 221, 228, 252
mathematics education, diplomas in 41
mathematics topics 34, 35, 104
mathematics without closure 225, 226, 230
mathematizing orientation 225, 239
Matthews, G. xx
McClain, K. 188
McDonough, A. 52, 252
McLaughlin, M. 122
McNamara, O. 26, 51, 52, 146
Mead, N.A. xix
Measor, L. 6, 132
measure(s) xxii, 79-84,129, 156, 187, 189
media xxiii, 10, 11
mediating function 4
mediating role 23, 97
mediation 30, 50, 122, 186, 191, 250
mental agility 34
mental mathematics 20, 31-36, 38-40, 42, 44, 63, 108, 141, 247, 249
mental methods 249
mental strategies xx, xxiv, 34, 140, 142, 166
mental/oral (lessons) 38, 46, 104, 147
Mercer, N. 161, 168
merit(s) 5, 37, 104
message(s) 23, 47, 61, 87, 111,123, 129, 130, 138-140, 143, 145, 146, 148, 151, 155, 166, 167, 176, 182
metacognition 223
metacognitive activity xxix, 275
methods repertoire 141, 149
metric geometry xxii
Miles, M.B. 273
Millett, A. xxviii, 1, 7, 9, 11, 19, 20, 22, 24, 28, 73, 92, 97, 99, 100, 104, 112, 127, 133, 155, 245
Ministerial Council on Education, Employment, Training and Youth Affairs xxi
Ministry of Education xxi, 10
misconceptions 33, 128, 140, 158, 161, 165, 166, 188, 202, 231, 267
Mitra, D. 122
Miwa, T. 10, 98
model(s) xxi-xxii, 1-6, 8, 12, 20, 23, 45, 46, 50, 52, 57, 66, 73, 87, 88, 92, 97, 98, 103, 104, 112, 114, 127, 129, 131, 137, 144, 146, 148, 150-153, 156, 157, 176, 179, 187, 189, 190, 193, 199, 201, 202, 213,214, 230, 235, 236, 242, 245, 246, 251, 254, 268, 275
modelling 139, 175, 178, 185
Mok, I. 188
monitoring 20-22, 24, 27-30, 44, 47, 51, 61, 65, 66, 68, 82
morale 48
motivation 5, 89, 122, 132, 189, 190, 213, 219, 241, 250, 252, 253

Mullis, I.V.S. xix
multiple identities 219, 226, 239
multiple perspectives 226, 239
multiplication 38, 129, 137, 138, 141, 142, 222, 232, 235, 238, 268
multiplicative relations 189
Murphy, P. 156, 157

National Commission for Excellence in Education xix
National Council of Teachers of Mathematics xx, 10, 90
national director xxiv, 69
National Literacy and National Numeracy Projects xxiii
National Numeracy Strategy xix, xxi, xxii, xxiv, xxviii, xxx, 8, 9, 11, 20-25, 27-33, 35, 37, 39, 40, 43-46, 50, 58, 60, 61, 64, 65, 69, 73, 76, 77, 83-85, 88, 90, 93, 97, 98, 100, 101, 103-105, 107, 110, 111, 115, 117, 121,123, 127-130, 136, 138, 140, 141, 144-146, 148, 150, 151, 155, 156, 158, 159, 164, 165, 174, 179, 182, 232, 233, 245-248, 250, 258, 260, 263, 265, 267, 268, 273, 277
national testing xxi, 9
national training programme xxiv
Nelson, B.S.90, 129
neo-Piagetian 188, 212
New Zealand xxi, 10
newcomers 90
Newmann, F. 2, 89
Nias, J. 6, 43, 44, 70, 89
Noddings, N. 188
non-contact time 44, 61, 66, 250
norm of privacy 28
Noss, R. xxii
Nuffield project xx
number fans xxv, 34
number operations xx
number properties 189
number sense xx
number skills xx-xxiii
number system 129, 237
number-line xxvi, 29, 32, 34, 36, 39, 139, 147, 160, 162, 174, 176, 177, 195, 196, 236-238
numbers xx-xxii, xxiv, xxvii, xxxi, 30, 40, 60, 61, 71, 99, 101, 102, 129, 138-140, 163, 172, 176, 178, 189, 194, 197, 199, 205, 207-210, 229, 230, 236, 241, 268, 276
numeracy xix, xxii, xxiii, xxvi-xxxi, 9-11, 20, 21, 23, 35, 58, 66, 74, 76, 87, 91, 110-113, 118-120, 139, 142, 143, 147, 152, 157, 175, 182, 225, 248, 252, 257-263, 265, 268, 271-273, 276, 277
numeracy lesson 27, 32, 35
numeracy practices xxix
- at home and at school xxxi
Numeracy Strategy 22, 30, 34, 37, 45, 46, 49, 51, 61, 67, 91, 101, 103, 104, 106-109, 112, 113, 116, 117, 119, 124, 167, 265 *see also* National Numeracy Strategy
nurses xxii

objective(s) xxii, xxiv, xxx, 30-32, 34, 36, 63, 69, 92, 93, 101-04, 107, 108, 112, 128, 136, 141, 152, 160, 169, 171, 174, 182, 189, 193, 211, 226, 246, 257, 265
Office for Standards in Education (Ofsted) xxi, 9, 10, 20-22, 48, 58, 62, 63, 65, 69, 72-74, 79-82, 91-93, 99, 104, 271
old-timers 90
oral/mental skills xxiv
Ordinary Level/General Certificate of Secondary Education 41, 133
orientations 127, 156, 157, 161, 164, 169, 170, 174, 176, 179-182, 225, 239
Ormiston, M. 137
Osborn, M. 20, 43, 44, 51
overhead projector calculators 29, 32
overhead transparancies xxiv, 26, 32

pace 1, 23, 33, 35, 99, 141, 160, 165, 171, 174, 181, 211
Pacific Rim 98
paired work(ing) 160, 167, 170, 199
parental support 91
parents xxviii, xxix, 10-12, 37, 79, 147, 266
Parker, S. 239
participant observation xxix
partitioning 140
passive consumers 132
pedagogical content knowledge 135, 140, 150, 151
pedagogy xxix, 5, 112, 127, 146, 168, 180, 189, 193, 201, 215
peer coaching 5, 36, 51, 52, 66, 117, 145, 250, 252, 254
peer discussions 161
peer learning 161
peer-group 131, 145, 150, 152, 201
Pegboard Symmetry 186, 191-199, 203, 209, 210, 212, 236
pencil-and-paper algorithms xx
percentages 129, 136, 175
person 5, 8, 12, 32, 38, 42, 72, 97, 119, 120, 127, 131, 132, 146, 155, 160, 168, 169, 224
personal agency beliefs 5
personal goals 5, 42

personal resources 19, 41, 50
Peterson, P.L. xx
Piaget 223
Piagetian 193, 212
Piagetian levels 187, 188
Piagetian paradigms xxix
Piagetian test 187
place-value cards xxvi, 136, 176
Placier, P. 2, 3, 245, 254
planning xxiv, 7, 20, 29-34, 36, 37, 44, 46, 47, 53, 63, 66, 72, 97, 99, 101-111, 115, 117-124, 129, 141, 160, 161, 165, 167-169, 171, 186, 191, 200, 201, 221, 227, 247, 251, 272
planting seeds 189
plenary xxiv, 30, 33, 35, 38, 39, 104, 164, 169, 171, 178, 210, 211
policy xxiii, 2, 6, 8, 9, 11-13, 19, 20, 23, 45, 51, 57, 70, 71, 73, 91, 97, 98, 103, 106, 109-111, 115, 123, 127, 155, 157, 219, 220, 245
policy makers xxiii, 1, 11, 37, 247, 253
Pollard, A. 9, 43
Pollard, P. 156, 157
Polya, G. 235
population(s) xix, xxvi, 75, 259, 262, 272
postholders 47
preparation xxv, 45, 73, 189, 195, 198, 201, 202, 230, 231, 237, 273
pressure xxi, 6, 8, 9, 22, 48, 57, 66, 72-76, 79, 82, 88, 90, 111, 112, 114, 131, 191, 253, 254, 260, 273
Prestage, S. 124, 153
Primary CAME (Cognitive Acceleration in Mathematics Education), xxix, 13, 185-190, 203, 214, 219-221, 227, 241, 242, 249, 251, 253, 275-277 *see also* CAME
primary curriculum xx, 91, 226
primary mathematics xx-xxii, 5, 11-13, 19, 98-101, 157, 221, 240, 245-247, 277
- and the developing professional xxxxi
primary school xxiii, xxiv, xxvii, 1, 6, 9, 12, 13, 19, 20, 21, 42, 57, 62, 70, 75, 79, 91, 99, 100, 103, 104, 127, 134, 159, 160, 186, 215, 258, 259-262, 275
principled knowledge 247, 248
priority(ies) 9, 22, 27, 30, 43-45, 48, 49, 59, 63, 65, 68, 70, 89, 91, 92, 105, 145, 57, 263, 272
private consultants 10
private sector 1, 8, 10-13, 84, 85, 98, 114
problem solving xx, xxiii, 129, 139, 160, 166, 170, 182, 223, 235, 261
- skills xxii
procedural knowledge 163, 247
professional community(ies) 1
professional development xxviii-xxx, 1, 2, 4,-8, 12, 13, 19, 21, 41, 50-53, 57, 65, 76, 82-85, 88, 91, 97-99, 110, 111, 115, 120-122, 124, 127, 129-132, 135, 137, 144, 152, 183, 185-188, 190, 192, 200-206, 208-210, 212-215, 219-221, 224, 227, 230, 241, 245, 246, 250-254, 275-277
professional judgement 69, 106, 115
profiles xxiii, xxviii, 29, 33, 61, 64, 66, 79, 130, 267
progress xxviii, 9, 33, 40, 71, 73, 80-82, 91, 92, 129, 156, 160, 161, 169, 258, 260
progression xxvi, xxvii, xxx, xxxi, 136, 143, 182, 193, 202, 203, 257
proof 194, 235
proportion 129, 136, 232, 233, 268
public 1, 2, 8-12
public domain 9
public opinion 10
published materials 98, 104, 105, 110, 112, 171
pupil mobility 62, 75, 91, 266, 271
pupils 1, 3, 6, 7, 88, 97, 185, 201, 206, 257
Putnam, R.T. 135, 151

quadratic equations 237-239
qualifications 41, 133, 134, 248, 249, 263, 266
quality of teaching 82
Qualter, A. 156
questioning 31, 37, 47, 68, 182

range of attainment 37, 73
rankings 76-79
ratio 129, 136, 175, 232, 233, 235, 268
real world xxi
Realistic Maths xxi, 215
reasoning xx, xxii, 182, 183, 187, 189, 190, 193, 194, 196, 210-213, 235, 243, 268, 276
Reasoning about Numbers 102
recall 34, 166
records of achievement 65
reflection 2, 45, 147, 150, 173, 185, 187, 189, 191-196, 198, 199, 201-206, 208-214, 219, 220, 223, 224, 228-234, 236-241, 250-253, 277
reflection-in-action 224
reflection-on-action 224
reflective discourse 189, 203, 205, 206, 208, 209
regional directors xxiv, 9
representations 133, 135, 140, 150, 152, 173, 195, 200, 222, 231, 232, 236, 238, 247, 248
research design xxvi
resistance 47
resourcing 6, 9, 20, 31, 44, 45, 48, 49, 59, 61, 64, 68, 75, 76, 91, 93, 106, 250, 251

response to reform initiaves 21
reticent consumers 132
revisiting 34, 35, 104
Rhodes, V. xxvi, xxvii, 11, 97
rich deliberations 4, 5, 23, 30, 88, 117, 220, 241
Richards, J 145
Richardson, V. 2, 3, 245, 254
Robitaille, D.F. 10, 98
Rowley, G. 52, 251

Sample Medium Term Plans 102, 110
scheme-assisted planners 99, 105, 106
scheme-dependent planners 105, 106
scheme-driven planners 99, 105, 106
schemes xxiv, xxv, 10, 11, 31, 35, 47, 98-104, 106, 109-117, 121, 138, 141, 164, 192
schemes-of-work xxv, 65, 99, 103, 104, 110-112, 128
Schifter, D. 224, 226, 227
Schön, D.A. 223, 224
school development adviser 47
School and Community Numeracies project xxix
school districts 8, 9
school factors xxviii, 13, 75, 131, 144, 150, 259
school policies xxviii, 57, 115
schools
- Birchcroft 77, 78, 81, 84, 86, 113
- Bournside 77, 78, 81, 82, 84, 86
- Clearwater 77, 78, 81, 84, 86, 107, 117
- Elmtree 77, 78, 80, 83, 86
- Firsdown 77, 78-80, 83, 86
- Greenacres 77, 78, 80, 83, 85, 86
- Hawesmead 106
- Hawesmere 77, 78, 80, 83, 85, 86
- Juniper Street 77, 78, 81, 82, 84, 86
- Kestrel 120
- Kirkend 77, 78,81, 84, 86
- Kirkshaw 77, 78, 80, 83, 86, 121
- Larkhall 106, 107, 112, 114
- Maple 40, 60, 61, 271, 272
- Mountain Ash 77, 78, 80, 85, 86
- Pennington 40, 60-62, 271, 272
- Redshore 77-80, 83, 86
- Rowan 77, 78, 81, 84-86
- Sandmere 40, 60-62, 76-78, 81, 84,86, 91, 271, 272
- St Luke's 109, 110, 117
- St Saviour's 114, 117
- Talltrees 77-80, 82, 83, 86
- The Grove 40, 60, 61, 271, 272
- Windsmoor Infants and Juniors 77, 78, 80, 83, 86
- Wolverton 40, 60, 61-63, 65, 66, 68, 71-75, 91-93, 117, 250, 271, 272
- Woodbury 40, 60, 61, 75, 76, 91, 120, 271, 272
Schultz, K.A. 223
science co-ordinator 66
Secada, W.G. 1
self-concept 41, 252
self-confidence 5, 41
self-efficacy 5, 41, 248, 249
self-review 9
senior management team 67
senior primary adviser 58, 68
setting 1, 52, 70, 71, 73, 75, 90, 139, 214, 220, 239-241, 253, 254, 260
shape and space 35, 104, 129, 276
share an apple 222, 223, 229, 230, 232, 233, 237
shared reflection 185
sharing 45, 117, 119-122, 166, 177, 187, 189, 196, 199, 201, 202, 205, 209, 213, 235, 252
Shayer, M. xxix, 186, 188, 223, 224
Shealey, B.E. 224
shift in the object of attention 189, 207
Showers, B. 2, 6, 52, 88, 131, 132, 144-146, 150, 152, 165
Shuard, H. xx, 232
Shulman, L.S. 5, 135
Silver, E.A. 1
Simon, M.A. 215
Simon, S. xxviii, 127, 155, 156
Singapore xxii
situation(s) 1-3, 5-8, 12, 19, 42-45, 51, 57, 87-89, 91, 112, 185, 214, 245, 253
Skinner, D. 227
Smith, M.S. 1
social constructivist xx, 220
social construct 4
social interaction 1, 30, 52, 211, 228
socio-cultural perspective 90
socio-economic characteristics 75
socio-economic factors 76, 78
socio-mathematical norms 188
Sofer, A. 92
South Africa xxii, 10
South Korea xix
special measures 79-84
special needs 37, 121, 142, 167, 271
Spillane, J.P. 1, 2-4, 8, 19, 23, 28-30, 41, 50, 52, 53, 88, 122, 147, 152, 156, 158, 165, 201, 214, 219, 221, 246, 247, 252
staff mobility 85
standard written procedures xxiv
standards xix-xxiv, xxvi, xxviii, 9, 10, 20, 21, 58, 62, 66, 68, 71, 73, 74, 79-81, 90, 99, 109, 111, 128, 265, 271
starting scores 76-78, 87

states of growth 132
statistics xx, xxii, 262
Steadman, S. 144
Steffe, L.P. xx
Stein, M.K. 1, 51, 52, 90
Steinbach, R. 64, 88
Stevenson, H.W. 251
Stigler, J.W. 251
strategy(ies) xx, xxiv, xxvi, xxviii, 7, 23, 24, 33, 34, 36, 38, 58, 60, 62, 70, 73-75, 87, 135, 140, 142, 149, 158, 161-171, 173, 177, 180, 181, 183, 188, 202, 231, 247, 248, 261, 271, 273
Strategy xxiv-xxvi, xxx, 20, 22, 25, 31, 33, 36, 43, 50, 69, 85, 97, 101-103, 105-108, 111, 113, 114, 116, 124, 128, 130, 140-143, 145, 156, 157, 164, 164-269, 174, 175, 179, 181
see also National Numeracy Strategy
Strauss, A.L. 220, 273
Stray, C. 98
Streefland, L. xxi
structure xxx, 2, 7, 11, 23, 33, 34, 35, 53, 89, 98, 109, 114, 122, 141, 158, 164, 165, 167, 171, 174, 182, 189, 190, 192, 247, 254
subject knowledge xxviii, 64, 100, 127, 129, 134-137, 146, 148, 150, 151, 165, 166, 175, 249, 257, 258
subject leader xxv, 6, 7, 19-21, 64, 128, 129, 203, 272
subject matter knowledge 133-135, 140, 151, 268
subtraction 129, 141, 147, 178
Sullivan, P. 242
superintendents 8
support xxi, xxiv, xxviii, 4, 6-9, 12, 13, 19-23, 28, 29, 31, 32, 38, 44-46, 48-50, 52, 53, 57, 61-63, 66-69, 75, 76, 79, 82-84, 87-91, 97, 102, 106, 113, 119, 123, 127-129, 131, 145-147, 149, 153, 158, 165, 185, 200, 201, 205, 213, 214, 220, 223, 248-252, 265, 273, 276
Sykes, G. 129
symmetry 192-194, 198, 205
systemic reform xix, xxx, 158

targets xxiii, xxv, 62, 70, 71, 246, 254
Tarule, J.M. 225
Task Force xxiv
teacher factors xxviii, 258, 271
teacher questionnaires xxvii, 263Tolley, H. 7, 64
teacher shortages xxi
Teacher Training Agency 64
teachers and teaching xxx
Teachers' Knowledge, Conceptions and Practices and Pupils' Learning project xxviii, xxx, 102, 115, 123, 130, 155, 247, 265
teacher-researchers xxix, 13, 186, 187, 190, 191, 194, 195, 200-202, 214, 215, 219, 220, 223, 234, 239, 240, 245, 246, 248, 249, 251-253, 275-277
teaching as demonstrating 169, 170, 176, 181
teaching as explaining 160, 180
teaching methods xxi, xxii, xxx, 130, 257, 258, 262, 268
Ten (10)-day course 85
Twenty(20)-day course 85
teaching sequence xxx
teaching, learning and progression at home and at school xxxi
team-teaching 202, 221, 228-230, 276
ten (10)-day course 85
textbooks xxiv, xxv, 10, 11, 98, 99, 101, 109-110, 225, 232
Tharp, R. 1, 52, 90
Thinking Maths lessons 185-187, 189-193, 209-212, 214, 220-222, 226, 229, 231, 236, 241
Three-day course xxv, 22, 102
three-part mathematics lesson xxiv, 30
time 35, 43, 161, 214, 234, 250, 251, 254
timetables xxiv, 222
Tolley, H. 7, 64
Townsend Index of deprivation 78
tracking numeracy xxvi, 58, 76, 82, 85-87, 90, 91, 102, 104, 121, 247, 257
traditional teaching methods xxi
training materials xxiv, xxv, 111, 128
transformation 194, 195, 228, 236, 240
transformational leadership 88
transmission 25, 26, 157, 161, 164, 167, 169, 170, 174, 179-182, 225
Treffers, A. xxi
trust 63-65
Turner-Vorbeck, T. 223, 224, 240
Tutors xxix, 8, 201, 202, 204, 210, 213, 214, 219, 221, 227, 228, 230, 236, 237, 239-241, 253, 254, 276, 277
twenty(20)-day course 85

United Kingdom xix-xxiii, 6, 9, 10, 258
United States xix-xxii, 9
use of resources 31, 33, 38, 39, 139, 155, 176

Valli, L. 52, 250
value-added data xxvi, 257, 259
value-added gains 76
- less successful in providing 76
- more successful in providing 76
values-led contingency leadership 64, 88
video recording xxviii, 268
videos xxiv, xxv, 29, 138, 166

vignettes 105, 11, 112, 203-205, 208
Vulliamy, G. 64
Vygotskian paradigms xxix

Wagner, S. 239
Walsh, A. 124, 153
Ward, H. 249
Waring, S. 235
Watson, N. xxvi
Watt, D. 156
ways of working 7, 19, 22-24, 30, 36, 48-52, 61, 68, 69, 75, 104, 146, 149, 200, 210, 234, 249
Webb, R. 64
Wenger, E. 1, 52, 90, 226, 227, 229, 230, 240
West-Burnham, J. 64
whisky and water 22, 234, 235, 237, 238, 243
whiteboards xxv, 29, 32, 39, 139, 167, 177, 180
Whitenack, J. 188
whole class xxiv, xxix, 28, 33, 39, 128, 139, 160, 161, 164, 169-172, 174, 177, 178, 181, 182, 189, 198, 200-202, 209, 260, 275
Whole School Action on Numeracy project xxviii, 21, 22, 48, 58, 59, 75, 87, 102, 247, 271
whole-class teaching 26, 37, 38, 112, 141, 149, 163, 167, 170, 171, 173-175, 178, 181, 183, 250
will 5, 158, 165
Wiliam, D. xxvi, xxvii
Williams, E. 232
Wood, T. 137, 223, 224, 240
word-problems xxiii, 129, 167
workload 43, 44, 106, 111, 115, 119, 122, 123
worth 5
Wragg, E. 249
written methods 33
Wubbels, T. 215

Yackel, E. 203, 239
Yeomans, R. 44, 64

Zhang, D. 10, 98
zone of enactment 1, 3-5, 12, 19, 23, 45, 122, 131, 145, 152, 158, 164, 165, 175, 186, 219-221, 226, 227, 245, 246, 253, 254
zones of proximal development 4

Printed in the United Kingdom
by Lightning Source UK Ltd.
119196UK00002B/73-78